MOTOR VEHICLE ACCIDENT RECONSTRUCTION AND CAUSE ANALYSIS

By
RUDOLF LIMPERT

THE MICHIE COMPANY
Law Publishers
CHARLOTTESVILLE, VIRGINIA

Library of Congress Catalog Card No. 78-59080
ISBN 0-87215-212-X

PREFACE

This book is written for lawyers, claims adjusters, highway safety engineers, and investigating officers, who are interested in motor vehicle accident reconstruction.

The problems of accident reconstruction and the accurate determination of causes of collisions and injuries become evident when the trial lawyer must present or defend his case, when the adjuster must make a recommendation to the insurance carrier, when the safety engineer must evaluate high frequency accident locations, or when the investigating officer must give a citation.

An equally important problem is associated with the specific nature of motor vehicle accident reconstruction, and the generally non-engineering background of lawyers and claims adjusters. For example, a law suit might rest entirely upon the determination of trailer braking accident causation. Although a well-qualified expert can easily establish the facts, the trial lawyer may not be sufficiently prepared to accurately formulate his case.

In my activities involving the investigation and reconstruction of hundreds of collisions, and testifying in court, I have learned that the capability of combining physical understanding and the description of physical concepts in simple engineering equations is essential for a successful court room demonstration.

In following this philosophy, I have written this book. The book presents a description of physical factors such as the functioning of various vehicle components and their safety-critical contribution, and a mathematical description of a variety of different aspects of accident reconstruction. Only when these equations are available can the trial lawyer ask penetrating questions in court.

The book is divided into eight parts. Part 1, concerned with motor vehicle factors, presents the functions and different design concepts of all essential vehicle components. Their critical performance in accidents is discussed. Part 2 deals with vehicle motion analysis. Presented are motion fundamentals, tire forces, braking, vibrations, and directional control including rollover and handling of vehicles. Part 3 treats accident avoidance analysis. Included in the discussions are if and how a collision can be avoided, passing maneuver and driver view field analysis. Part 4 deals with the fundamentals of collision analysis. Both nonrotating and rotating collision vehicles are considered. Impact analyses including rotation are essential for accident reconstructions involving primary and secondary collisions. Post crash motion, occupant dynamics, human tolerances to impact loading, and computer based collision reconstruction are discussed. Part 5, concerned with safety standards, presents a brief summary of existing Federal Safety Standards and ongoing defects investigations. Part 6 treats accident investigation factors and a discussion of their relative importance to accident reconstruction. Part 7 deals with the application of reconstruction fundamentals to actual collisions. The reader will find several cases covering all major aspects of reconstruction. Part 8 is concerned with special studies. Included are special accident studies and findings about accident statistics. A brief description of a desirable profile of an expert witness and court room hints are included.

I want to express many thanks to Paul Cook and the Michie Company for their professional work that made the publication of this book possible.

Last but not least, I must thank my wife and children, whose unwavering faith in their Dad made a twenty-hour day an enjoyable task.

Salt Lake City, Utah R. L.

TABLE OF CONTENTS

CHAPTER 7. THE BRAKING SYSTEM

CHAPTER 8. THE ENGINE

Part 2: Vehicle Motion Analysis

Part 7: Accident Reconstruction

CHAPTER 40. RECONSTRUCTION OF ACTUAL ACCIDENTS

Part 8: Special Topics

CHAPTER 41. MULTIDISCIPLINARY ACCIDENT INVESTIGATION PROGRAM (MDAI)

CHAPTER 42. SPECIAL ACCIDENT STUDIES

CHAPTER 1
INTRODUCTION

In this chapter some basic considerations are presented that show how different engineering and human factors are related to motor vehicle accident reconstruction. The importance of a clear understanding of all factors contributing to accident and injury causation is stressed. An overview of accident reconstruction is presented.

1-1. OBJECTIVE OF ACCIDENT RECONSTRUCTION

The objectives are:

1. Collision Analysis: Determination of all physical factors that clearly define the collision. Included in physical factors are: impact speeds and directions, impact point(s), vehicle positions, occupant dynamics.

2. Injury Analysis: Determination of all physical factors that clearly define the production of injuries. Included are occupant vehicle contact, vehicle interior design, vehicle safety devices, human impact tolerances.

3. Accident Avoidance Analysis: Determination of all physical factors involved in possible accident avoidance. Included are vehicle accident avoidance potential, driver viewfield analysis, vehicle mechanical condition.

The details concerning the three objectives of accident reconstruction may vary from case to case. However, a complete analysis requires reasonable solutions to all three elements.

1-2. FACTORS INFLUENCING ACCIDENT RECONSTRUCTION

The vehicle is connected to the roadway by the traction forces of the tires. During normal driving maneuvers these traction forces are controlled by the driver by the use of steering wheel rotation, brake pedal or accelerator lever application. The driver may cause the tires to operate below, near or at the limit of traction. For example, during a braking maneuver the pedal force may be sufficiently large to produce wheel lockup. A locked wheel represents a limited condition in form of brake force production, and total loss of steering ability. Limit of brake force production means that an increase of pedal force does not yield any further increase of braking traction. A vehicle sliding with its wheels locked is entirely out of the control of the driver, and consequently, only vehicle, roadway and environmental factors influence the further motion of the vehicle. Vehicle factors that affect traction forces are associated with the tire and suspension design, vehicle design and vehicle loading. Roadway factors are determined by road geometry, road surface characteristics, and surface contamination such as water or mud. Environmental factors are associated with wind forces.

An evaluation of factors influencing vehicle motion in the case when the driver does control the vehicle motion is a difficult task. The task is made difficult only due to a lack of an accurate description of driver inputs to the controls. When these inputs are available, then a reasonably accurate determination of vehicle motion can be made. Many times data obtained at the accident scene or accident site may be used to determine a range of control inputs, for example, pedal force range within which the driver's pedal force must have been to produce the particular tire markings or lack of certain tire markings.

A different group of factors influencing accident reconstruction exists in the case of an automobile-pedestrian collision. Many such collisions involve young children or elderly people in connection with a partial obstruction of the view of the driver of the collision vehicle. Human factors are associated with the walking or running speed of pedestrians, and body size.

Although the brief introduction of several factors influencing accident reconstruction is by no means complete, it demonstrates the complex nature of an accurate reconstruction, the interdependence of factors, and the necessity for a clear understanding of the problem of accident reconstruction.

1-3. ACCIDENT RECONSTRUCTION OVERVIEW

The results of the reconstruction are statements that indicate how the collision occurred, why it happened, and if it could have been avoided. The data used in the reconstruction are derived from police report, vehicle damage examination, accident scene and/or site investigation, witness statement, and application of engineering fundamentals including analysis and testing. A successful reconstruction requires that certain data such as road markings, vehicle positions and conditions and witness statements are secured as quickly as possible after the accident to ensure greater data reliability.

A general formulation of the accident reconstruction involves the most complete description of each phase of the collision in terms of engineering equations, human factors consideration, and environmental factors. After the general formulation is accomplished, all possible factors bearing upon the collision are considered. The accident reconstruction process yields a collection of critical factors that must be studied for valid conclusions to be reached. The final result is a set of conclusions and supportive data that clearly define the collision, injury causation, and accident avoidance potential.

During the reconstruction process a preliminary analysis involving simplified equations may be employed to verify certain preliminary conclusions. A more complete analysis may be carried out to refine the first set of results. A complete analysis may require such tasks as skid testing using the actual tires of the accident vehicle, a simulation test using full size vehicles, a computer analysis of certain accident data files, or a fatigue fracture analysis of a vehicle component.

Plaintiff and defense lawyer will benefit from the use of the engineering equations. Many equations are simple and can be employed effectively for cross-examination or trial preparation. Engineering equations relating to vehicle handling (e.g. Eq. 22–43) are lengthy but are useful for the determination of different factors influencing the dynamic response of a vehicle.

PART 1

MOTOR VEHICLE FACTORS

Part 1 presents a discussion of vehicle components and their functions as related to the performance of the vehicle during noncollision driving maneuvers and during the crash itself. The technical concepts are described in a manner to be useful to the reader with little or no engineering background. Emphasis is placed on a language that may be understood by typical jury members.

CHAPTER 2
THE CHASSIS

2–1. THE FUNCTIONS OF THE CHASSIS

The chassis of a motor vehicle includes all those components of a vehicle that are necessary to drive, brake, steer, and suspend the wheels as well as attach them to the body or frame. The chassis consists of a frame or similar structure containing the engine, the frame (if any), the power train, which includes transmission, drive shaft and differential, the wheels, the steering and braking system (Fig. 2–1).

The functions of a chassis are to produce the forces between tire and road, to carry the vehicle weight, to drive, accelerate or brake the vehicle, and to direct the vehicle in turns. The chassis provides the basic unit carrying the road loads.

2–2. DIFFERENT CONCEPTS USED IN CHASSIS DESIGN

2–2.1. Engine Location. The location of the engine is a significant factor of the automobile design. The placement of the engine affects the space available for occupants and luggage, the basic crashworthiness, and the handling qualities due to the difference in center-of-gravity location. Three basic engine locations can be identified: front, middle and rear.

In the front-engine vehicle, efficient use of the space between the axles and behind the rear axle for occupants and luggage is provided. The frontal crashworthiness is generally greater than that of mid- or rear-engine vehicles. Recent research developments on safety vehicles have shown, however, that front-engine location in high speed frontal impacts does not yield the maximum safe crashworthiness design. Difficulties exist in preventing intrusion of the engine into the occupant compartment. The increased length of the exhaust system in front-engine vehicles provides better exhaust gas noise and emission control. The forward placement of the center-of-gravity makes front-engine vehicles nearly insensitive to sidewinds.

Two-seater sports cars frequently use the mid-engine design. Mid-engine vehicles exhibit a balanced distribution of forces between front and rear axle and thus provide a neutral turning response. Main-

Figure 2–1. Passenger Car Chassis (Mercedes Benz)

tenance and repair efforts are difficult to carry out and in connection with the inefficient use of space are the major reason for the infrequent use of the mid-engine in mass production vehicles.

The rear-engine location provides a cost and space efficient design in the case of smaller vehicles. The traction forces on the rear wheels are improved due to the increased weight on the rear axle. The steering wheel forces are small due to the lower normal forces on the front wheels. Disadvantages are associated with side wind sensitivity, possible changes in directional steering characteristics at higher speeds, and insufficient trunk space.

2–2.2. Drive Axle Location. The location of the drive axle in connection with the engine placement is the most important design factor affecting vehicle dynamics. The drive wheels can be located in the front, rear, or on both axles in the case of a four-wheel drive vehicle.

Front wheel drive which is only used in connection with front engine location, provides good drive traction on slippery road surfaces. If not compensated for by the suspension design, the directional steering characteristics of the vehicle may be excessively understeering.

Rear wheel drive in connection with front engine location is common on larger vehicles. It provides good directional stability and requires only average driving skills for most maneuvers. The drive traction on slippery roads is reduced due to the low drive axle load.

In the case of the four-wheel drive the engine power is distributed between front and rear axle. Four-wheel drive designs are most commonly used to provide sufficient traction for vehicles maneuvering in off-road conditions. In general, the four-wheel drive design provides a desirable force balance between front and rear wheels, and consequently, should yield excellent vehicle handling characteristics. Too frequently, however, the contributions of the four-wheel drive concept are negated by off-road design features such as high center-of-gravity, stiff suspensions and solid axles.

2–2.3. Transmission Location. In some modern vehicles (for example, Alfa Romeo and Porsche) the conventional front engine-rear wheel drive is altered by locating the transmission at the rear axle. The engine and transmission are connected by a tube which stiffens the chassis. Location of the transmission at the rear provides a more even weight distribution.

A comparison of the effects of different chassis design concepts on various vehicle performance measures is presented in Table 2–1.

Table 2-1. Comparison of Chassis Concepts

	CHASSIS				
Performance Measure	Standard (Impala)	Front Drive (Toronado)	Rear Engine (VW Beetle)	Mid Engine (Porsche 914)	Front Engine/Rear Drive & Transmission (Alfa Romeo/Porsche)
Handling	Low side force on RA	Low side force on RA	Low side force on FA - - - - - - - - Sensitive directional stability	Even side force on FA & RA - - - - - - - - Sensitive directional stability	Even side forces on FA & RA
Traction of Drive Wheels	Poor	Good	Good	Good	Good (–)
Braking Potential	Most on FA Not balanced	FA large, RA small, not balanced	Good	Good	Good (–)
Payload	Changes handling (–) improves traction and braking	Changes handling (–) improved braking but not traction	Changes handling (–) improves traction, no change in braking	Changes handling, improved traction, no change in braking	Little change in handling, improved traction and braking

RA = Rear Axle; FA = Front Axle

The information presented in Table 2–1 indicates general trends in performance changes for different chassis designs. Exceptions may exist when elaborate component designs are used to overcome inherent weaknesses.

2–2.4. Engine Type. The oldest power plant in motor vehicles uses steam as working medium. The operating characteristics of the steam engine are close to ideal for the motor vehicle. Factors related to weight, responsiveness and involved operation have led to different power plants.

Today nearly all motor vehicles use the internal combustion engine. It transforms the chemical energy of the fuel into mechanical work. Internal combustion engines are divided into several categories such as two- and four-cycle engines, piston or rotor type engines.

The rotary engine, commonly called Wankel engine, is smaller in size than the equivalent piston engine. The use of the Wankel engine provides the vehicle designer more freedom to improve the crashworthiness of the automobile. At present, however, the increased fuel consumption associated with the Wankel engines makes their future use difficult to predict.

The gas turbine for motor vehicle use has been in the research stage for a long period of time. It is a rotary combustion engine consisting of a compressor, a combustion chamber and a turbine. The advantages of a gas turbine for automotive use include desirable torque characteristics, clean exhaust gases, no vibrations, and low fuel quality requirements. Disadvantages are increased fuel consumption, decreased responsiveness, increased manufacturing cost, and lack of engine braking. Difficulties exist in reducing the high frequency air intake noise and the gear reduction from approximately 40,000 rpm to about 5000 rpm.

Recent developments associated with environmentally clean automobile power plants have concerned themselves with the Stirling engine, a heat engine invented in 1816. The Stirling engine is an external combustion engine in which the working medium Helium stays inside the piston-heat exchanger engine system. The Helium is heated externally. The combustion process produces little pollution, the torque characteristics are desirable for automotive use, i.e., a high torque is provided at low speeds, and no great requirements are placed upon the quality of the fuel. The manufacturing costs due to elaborate heat exchangers, involved operation and problematic control functions may push mass production of the Stirling engine in the distant future.

The electric motor is frequently used in vehicles operating in industrial environments. These vehicles include fork lifts, cranes and carts. In some areas public transportation vehicles use electric motors. The start-up power is greater than the continued power performance. This increased power can be utilized only over a limited period of time due to the increased temperature build-up. Electrically driven vehicles generally exhibit a large acceleration and great hill climbing capability. The control of the motor is accomplished by changing the voltage, the circuitry of the motor, or the field characteristics.

More details of engine design are presented in Chapter 8.

2–2.5. Chassis Maintenance. Chassis maintenance includes all maintenance operations associated with the various subunits, such as power train, steering system, and brakes. The lack of proper maintenance of certain units is more safety critical than that of others. Tires, brakes and steering are generally considered to be more safety critical than, e.g., transmission or engine. However, accidents have occurred where vehicle fires originated at the engine, where degraded shock absorbers caused a loss of vehicle traction forces, or where inadvertant engine start-up due to electrical problems crushed a person between the vehicle and loading dock.

Maintenance schedules are prescribed by the manufacturer and generally provide for a safe operation of the chassis components.

2–2.6. Safety Considerations. Safety aspects of the chassis divide into pre-crash or accident avoidance safety, and crash safety. Pre-crash safety involves vehicle dynamics and the responsiveness of a vehicle to driver control inputs such as steering or braking. No accident statistics exist at present that permit pre-crash safety related conclusions to be drawn based on different chassis design concepts. Researchers have attempted to correlate accident rate with certain dynamic or design properties of the vehicle (Refs. 1 and 2). The statistics of Ref. 1 are based on accidents that occurred in England and show accident rates as a function of various design concepts, such as wheel base, weight, and power to weight ratio. Accident statistics developed in the U.S. indicate that larger cars are more involved in multi-car collisions than small cars, large cars are involved more often in pedestrian accidents; and when large and small cars collide, the driver of the large car is more often at fault (Ref. 3, Chapter 42).

German accident statistics reveal that vehicles exhibiting high horsepower engines are over-involved in accidents (Ref. 4). For example, the Porsche 914 shows an accident frequency that is five times as high as that of the VW Beetle. Similar trends are observed for other manufacturers. The data seem to indicate that high powered sports cars are more accident prone that their "tamer" counterparts.

Accident claim frequencies in the United States involving vehicles with a longer wheel base but otherwise identical design features are lower than those associated with the shorter wheel base model.

The pre-crash safety contribution of different chassis components must be analyzed in detail as required by the particular reconstruction. For example, a low inflation pressure on the rear wheels may easily offset the effects of a forward location of the center-of-gravity on directional control.

Safety aspects of the chassis during the crash are somewhat easier assessed. An examination of the damaged vehicle generally reveals which component failed prematurely or caused excessive injuries to the occupants. Crashworthiness factors are largely influenced by the frame or floor unit of the chassis and will be discussed in Chapter 3. In general, accident statistics indicate that front engine vehicles provide better protection for their occupants when colliding with a smaller vehicle or fixed object. For impact speeds exceeding 30 to 35 mph, the rearward displacement of the engine into the occupant compartment presents a limiting condition. Special design measures are required to push the engine–transmission assembly under the vehicle floor to prevent entry into the occupant compartment.

CHAPTER 3
THE FRAME AND BODY

3-1. THE FUNCTIONS OF THE FRAME

The frame is the load carrying member of the chassis combining all other chassis components to one unit. The frame carries the body or special upper structures in the case of trucks or buses.

3-2. DIFFERENT CONCEPTS USED IN FRAME DESIGN

The frame is a structure generally consisting of box, tubular, and channel members welded or rivited together. The frame curves upward at the end to provide space for the rear suspension, and narrows in front to permit the front wheels to steer.

A perimeter frame found on most mid- or full-sized American passenger cars is illustrated in Fig. 3-1. It provides attachment points for suspension, engine, transmission, and body. The side frame rails provide occupant protection against side impact. Older frames used an X-structure as illustrated in Fig. 2-1. This frame design generally made the sides of the vehicle more vulnerable to side impacts.

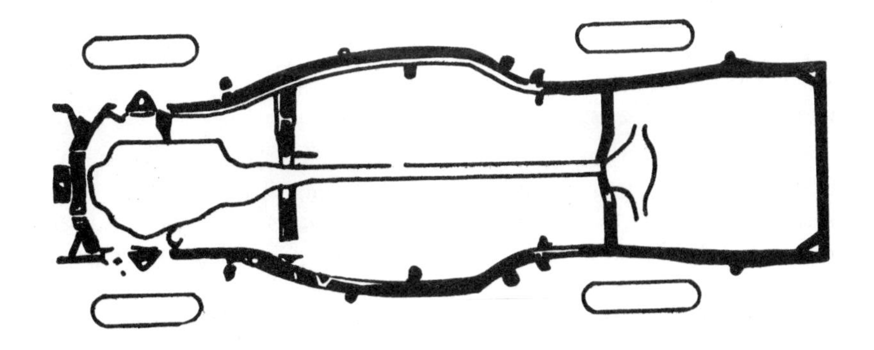

Figure 3-1. Perimeter Frame

The central backbone frame as shown in Fig. 3–2 uses a rigid tubular member and is found in some European low production volume vehicles.

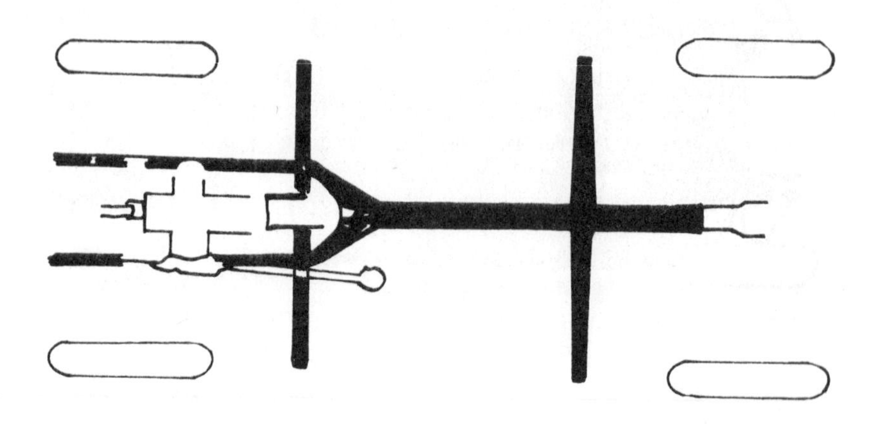

Figure 3–2. Central Backbone Frame

An extension of the central backbone frame is the platform frame as illustrated in Fig. 3–3. A central tubular member provides the required stiffness while the space between the front and rear axle is closed by welded-on sheet metal. Front and rear forks are provided for attachment of suspension and engine.

A further variation of the frame structure is the frame-floor unit as shown in Fig. 3–4. It combines the function of the frame with those of the floor panels by using sheet metal structures and cross members to form a relatively rigid and torsion resistant unit. It weighs less than the pure frame design. When connected to the body structure by welding or bolting the frame-floor unit receives its full rigidity. The VW Beetle platform frame is rigid enough to carry road loads, however, its crashworthiness is increased significantly when the body is bolted to the platform (Fig. 3–3).

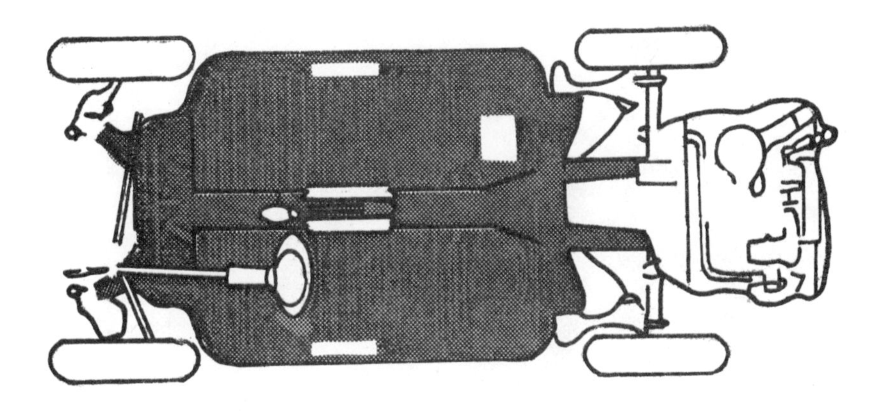

Figure 3-3. Platform Frame

Both the platform frame and the frame-floor units exhibit the first steps of the integral frame-body design. Integral frame-body designs are found on all mass production small cars such as GM Vega or VW Rabbit. In the case of the Vega only the front cross member assembly, the front cross member braces (left and right), and the transmission support cross member can be removed. All other parts are permanent parts of the integral body.

An example of a modern small car integral body is illustrated in Fig. 3-5 (VW Rabbit). In most cases only doors, lids and front fenders can be detached. The design of integral bodies is the result of computer aided analysis in which the crash performance of many body components is optimized to obtain minimum weight with maximum crashworthiness. The manufacturing costs of integral bodies are high, and consequently are found only in mass production vehicles. Sports cars and other specialty vehicles most frequently use light-weight tubular frame structures.

Another example of an integral body is illustrated in Fig. 3-6 (VW Dasher). It shows the longitudinal and cross members before the roof

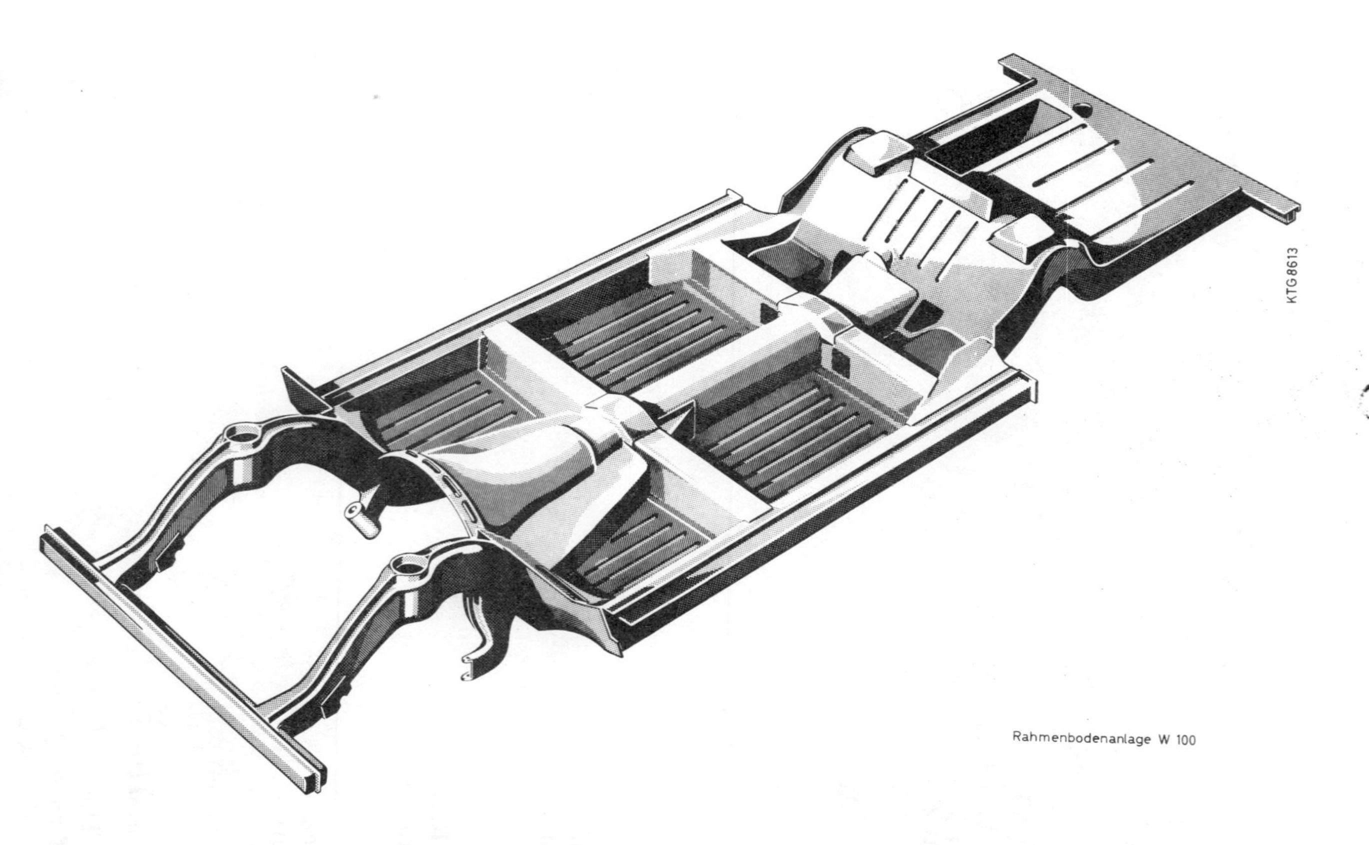

Figure 3–4. Frame-Floor Unit (Mercedes Benz)

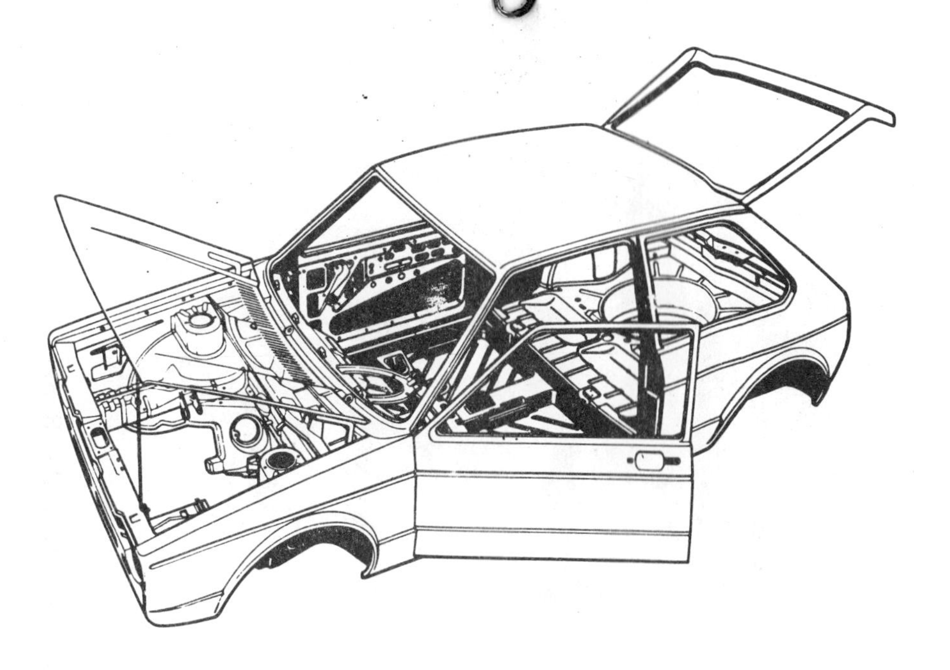

Figure 3–5. Integral Body (VW Rabbit)

sheet metal is welded into place. Also shown in Fig. 3–6 are the power train, and rear suspension, and fuel tank. The fuel tank is located directly behind the rear axle to provide protection against rear end impacts.

Recent research developments sponsored by the U.S. Department of Transportation have led to new designs in integral vehicle bodies (Ref. 5). Hollow sheet metal structures, filled with foam and located at critical areas, provide an extremely crashworthy, however lightweight integral body. Fixed barrier impact speeds up to 50 mph are survivable. Earlier safety vehicle designs were plagued with extremely heavy body structures to provide sufficient stiffness for the occupant compartment.

3–3. THE FUNCTIONS OF THE BODY

The body is the shell comprising the occupant compartment in cases of passenger cars or buses and includes the shell carrying payload in the case of trucks. The body provides support for many other functions, such as lighting, signals and mirrors.

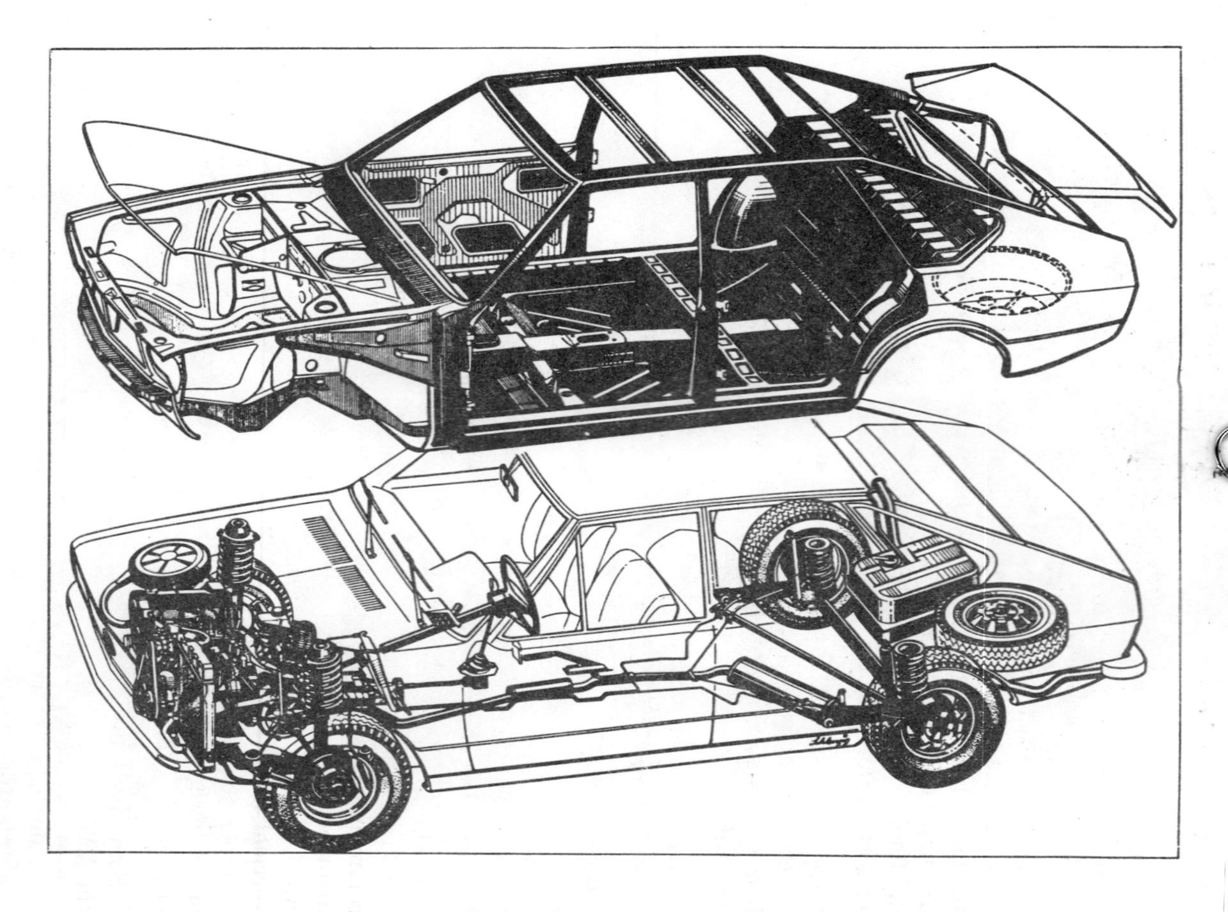

Figure 3–6. Integral Body (VW Dasher)

3-4. DIFFERENT CONCEPTS USED IN BODY DESIGN

Today the design of a vehicle body, besides its intended function, is affected by many factors. These factors include fuel economy, i.e., aerodynamic efficient shape, weight, compactness; traffic safety, i.e., crashworthiness, bumper damage, visibility, manufacturing cost; maintainability and serviceability.

Domestic vehicles using self supporting frames have complete body units mounted to the frame. Frame vibrations are minimized by cushions and proper torquing of the fasteners. Separately attached are major body elements such as hood, lid, doors, and wheel housing and fenders. Nearly all domestic mid- and full-size sedans utilize this separate frame and body design.

The assembly of the frame-floor unit (Fig. 3-4) with the body structure (Mercedes-Benz Type 180) is shown in Fig. 3-7. Body and floor unit are welded together to form a crashworthy-efficient body structure.

Modern small cars use the integral body design where body and frame form a unitized structure.

Buses generally use a steel frame supporting a light-weight-box or channel member structure comprising the occupant space.

3-5. BODY TERMINOLOGY

In the investigation of vehicle damage it has become convenient to use certain notations for specific body regions or areas. The most common descriptions are illustrated in Fig. 3-8. The major structural members of the body are divided into left and right, upper and lower A,B,C, or D pillars or posts. For example, the lower A pillar is the vertical member carrying the door hinges, the upper A pillar is the member connecting the front corner of the roof with the upper end of the lower A pillar. Inspection of Fig. 3-8 allows a clear identification of pillars A through D.

Some body designs do not clearly show D pillars as in the case of the VW Beetle.

To describe interior damage areas similar divisions are used. For example, the instrument panel is divided, e.g. into upper-, mid-, and lower-panel. More information on the present damage coding format is found in the Collision Performance and Injury Report (Ref. 6).

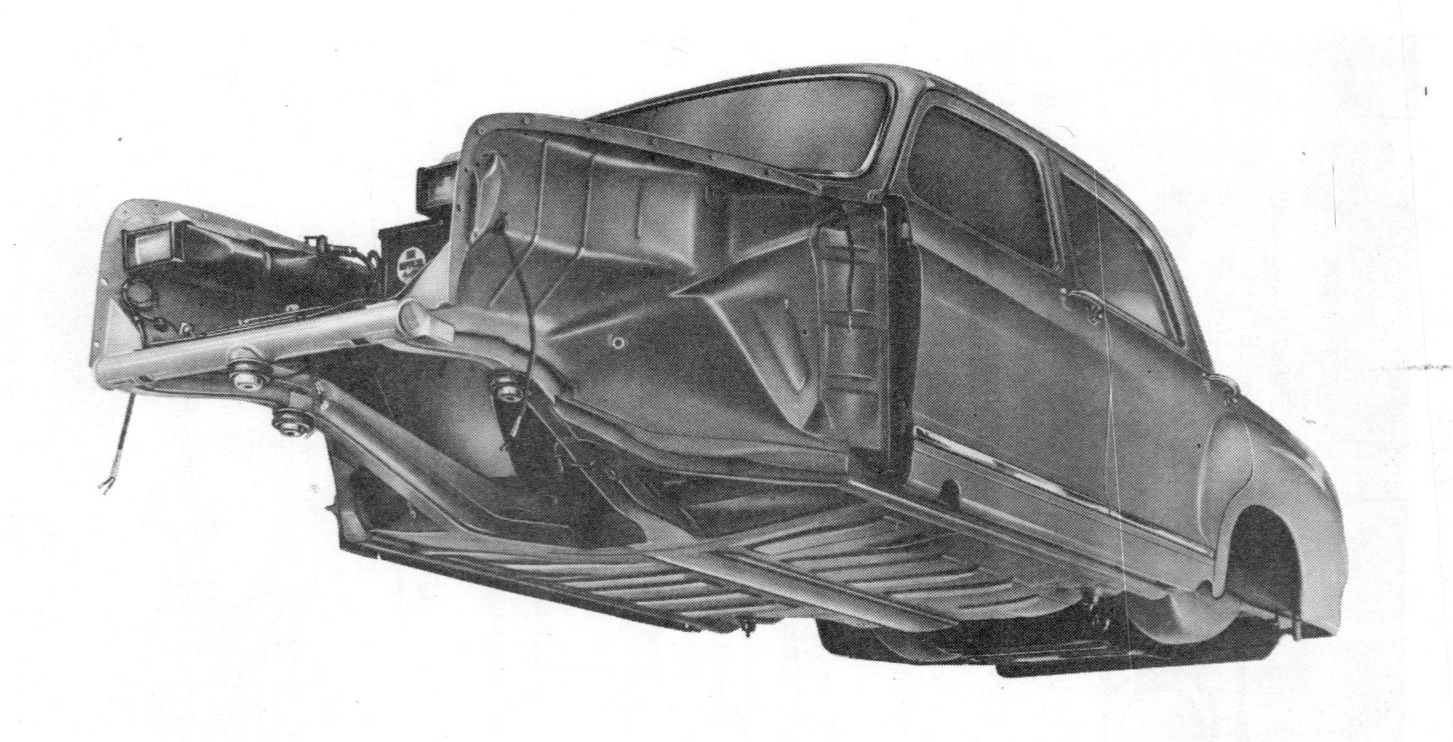

Figure 3–7. Assembly Frame-Floor Unit with Body (Mercedes-Benz)

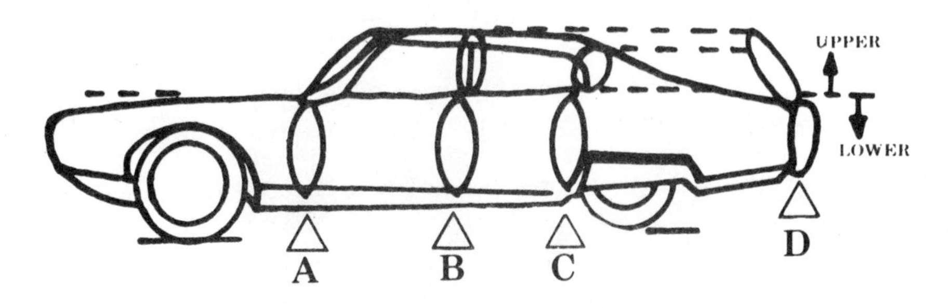

Figure 3-8. Body Pillar Notation

3-6. SAFETY CONSIDERATIONS

The design of the frame-body assembly or the integral body significantly affects the crashworthiness of the vehicle. The earlier belief that frame vehicles provide increase passive safety is not correct anymore in every case. Important design factors are the provision of soft crush zones at the front and rear of the vehicle to yield desirable force levels sustained by the occupants and little or no reduction of the occupant compartment (Fig. 3-9). The integral body designs are developed by both computer analysis and crash test evaluation. New integral body designs which must meet Federal Safety Collision Standards require large dollar investments before the design is finalized. Crash test results obtained with the VW 1200 (Beetle) and the new VW Polo which uses many of the design features of the Rabbit,

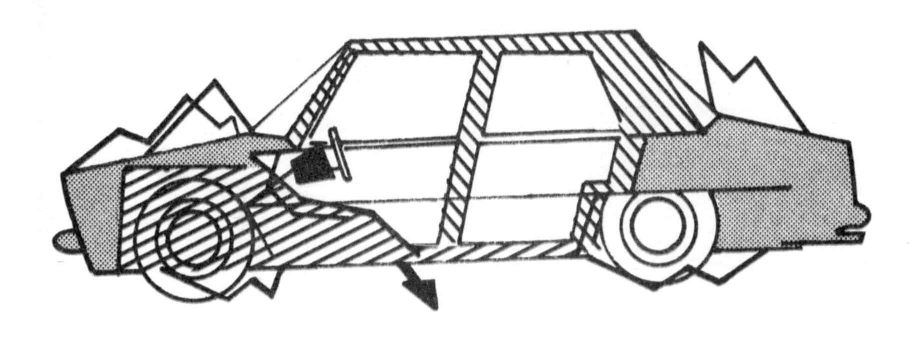

Figure 3-9. Front and Rear Crush Zones

are used in the following paragraphs to illustrate the progress made in vehicle crashworthiness (Ref. 7).

In comparison crash tests against a solid wall at 25 mph the Beetle exhibited a maximum deceleration of 49 g as compared to 37 g for the VW Polo. The total crash deformations were 15 in. for the Beetle and 11 in. for the Polo. The forces experienced by the restrained test dummy were significantly less in the case of the Polo.

Reasons for this difference in crash performance are varied. The relatively long crush distance of the Beetle is not used efficiently for the reduction of vehicle energy. The large vehicle deceleration developed near the end of the crush is caused by rigid front portions of the platform frame. The Polo front end is designed to crush in a manner that yields low force levels to the restraint occupants.

Other safety factors associated with body design involve unnecessary injuries to pedestrians, motorcyclists, and other road users due to designed-in hazardous protrusions. In a particular accident case involving a 1968 Mercury station wagon and a motorcyclist, the rider sustained very serious injuries due in large part by contacting a sharply pointed triangular metal projection in the Mercury's turning signal and parking light assembly.

CHAPTER 4
THE SUSPENSION SYSTEM

4-1. THE FUNCTION OF THE SUSPENSION SYSTEM

The wheel suspension system includes all components required for the positioning of the wheels and their displacement relative to the body. The wheel suspensions must transmit drive, braking, and side forces produced by the tires and must also transmit spring and shock absorber forces. An additional function is the isolation of road induced vibrations and tire noise from the vehicle. Safety considerations such as road holding on rough road surfaces require minimum weight for wheel suspensions.

4-2. DIFFERENT CONCEPTS USED IN SUSPENSION DESIGNS

Design concepts differ due to factors such as cost, wheel positioning while turning, vehicular function (truck, passenger car, off-road vehicle), axle steering, and tire wear. The production of traction forces between tire and ground is the result of the capability of the pneumatic tire to produce shear forces under a variety of conditions. However, only one set of conditions produces a maximum brake, side, or drive force. Ideally, the tire should be positioned vertically under all driving conditions including cornering. An upright tire contacts the road surface with a large rubber area, a requirement for maximum force production in nearly all cases. A detailed discussion of tire force production is presented in Chapter 18.

4-2.1. Solid Axle. The solid, beam or live axle ("live" axle because it transmits power) is used on most trucks and buses on both front and rear axle. Most of today's larger domestic sedans have a solid rear axle.

In a solid axle both wheels are connected rigidly by a solid beam and thus remain parallel to each other. Both wheels will be positioned vertically to the road when the vehicle is operating on a smooth road. When one wheel is deflected by road roughness, then the other wheel will be oriented under an angle to the road resulting in a disturbance of tire force production. In its simplest form the solid axle is located by leaf springs mounted longitudinally to the chassis at their ends as illustrated in Fig. 4–1. Leaf springs are elastic components and consequently permit the axle to move under certain loads. The drive torque of the axle shafts to the wheels produces a reaction which causes the solid axle to wind and unwind. The windup may be reduced sufficiently by installation of a pair of trailing arms. Another disadvantage of the simple solid axle is the steering effect produced by a rotation of the axle about a vertical center line going through the differential. This rotation is caused by an unequal lengthening of the leaf spring on the left and right side of the vehicle during severe cornering. The same effect can be achieved when a vehicle travels over rough road surfaces causing severe body roll. The axle steering effect can cause the vehicle to alter its usual steering characteristics.

Figure 4–1. Solid Axle, Front and Rear

The large weight of the solid axle including the differential and a portion of the propeller shaft may cause severe changes of the tire-to-ground normal force when driving on rough roadways. If this force approaches zero, i.e., the tire bounces off the ground no drive, braking, or vehicle guiding forces can be transmitted. Particularly critical are excitations of opposite polarity at the left and right wheel. Opposite polarity exists when, e.g., the left wheel is displaced upward by a bump while the right wheel is displaced downward into a pothole. These tramping oscillations are a direct result of the solid connection between left and right wheel and may assume values that are one and a half times greater than those exhibited by independent suspensions.

Significant improvements of the dynamic performance of a solid axle can be achieved by firmly locating the axle in both longitudinal and lateral direction by installation of two pairs of linkages positioning the axle in the longitudinal direction, and a Panhard rod, locating the axle in lateral direction (Fig. 4–2).

For American passenger cars mostly operating on smooth road

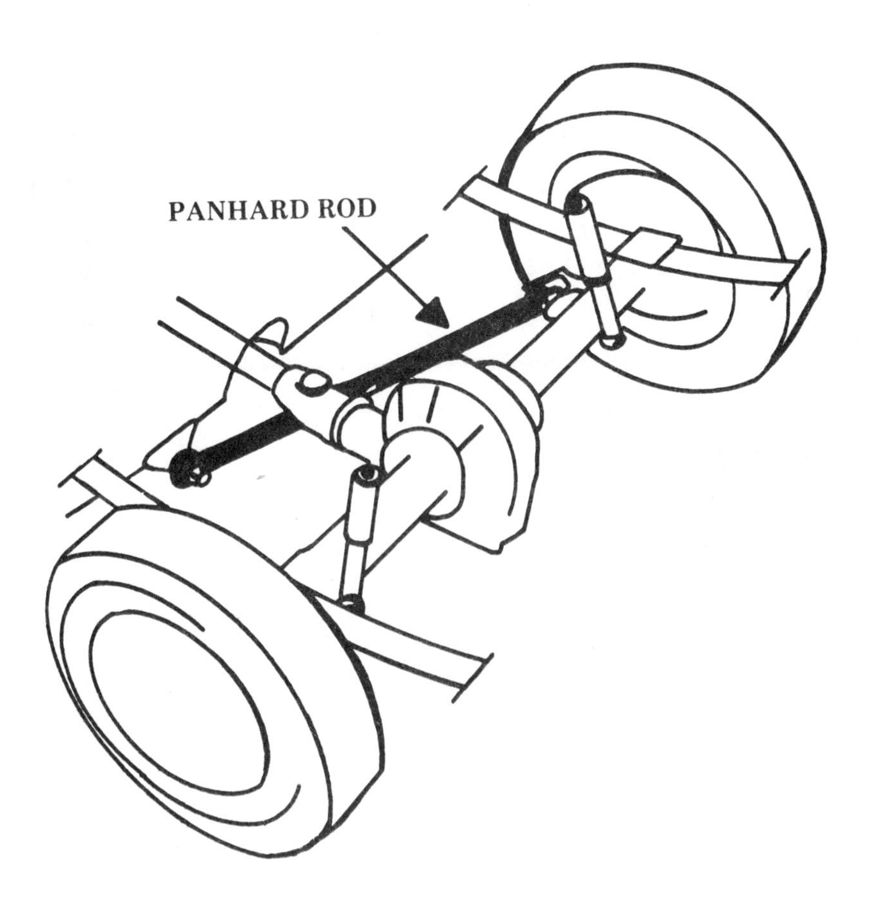

Figure 4–2. Panhard Rod

surfaces the solid axle is widely used. Large payload changes of full-size sedans and body roll during cornering result in no chamber change, i.e., the wheels remain vertical to the road surface, and thus render the vehicle directionally predictable for the average driver. The lack of side displacement of the wheel during up and down motion of the wheel reduces tire wear. The inexpensive and simple construction make the solid axle an attractive design solution. Improvements in tire performance and careful tuning of springing and damping (by the shock absorbers) has resulted in a refinement of the solid axle which makes it competitive with many more elaborate independent suspension systems. Today the solid axle is used as inexpensive rear drive axle on most large American sedans and station wagons and as rear axle for many front wheel driven vehicles.

4–2.2. De Dion Rear Suspension. The De Dion suspension, named after the French inventor, combines the advantages of constant wheel position associated with the solid rear axles with the decreased unsprung weight associated with the independent suspension. Both rear driven wheels are connected firmly by a light weight tubular or similar axle structure, while the differential is attached to the chassis or another frame member (Fig. 4–3). The axle structure is located by longitudinal and cross links with coil or cross leaf springs providing the springing functions of the suspension. Due to space availability near the differential, the brakes are often located close to the differential thus further reducing the unsprung weight of the suspension. De Dion rear suspensions exhibit very good dynamic performance but involve elaborate designs and consequently are only found on expensive vehicles.

4–2.3. Swing Axle. Swing axles are generally only used for the independent suspension of driven rear wheels. Due to the larger camber and track width changes during wheel deflections, the swing axle cannot be used for steerable front wheels. The swing axle is an independent suspension, i.e., the motion of one wheel is not influenced by that of the other. In the swing axle the axle shafts are connected to the differential output shafts by U-joints, which determine the arc of suspension and wheel travel. The swing axle of earlier VW Beetle vehicles is illustrated in Fig. 4–4. The wheel is located by the axle shaft and the longitudinal trailing arm, connected to the torsion bar. Consequently, the wheel travels about a line determined by the location of the U-joint and the attachment of the trailing arm to the chassis.

An alteration of the double pivot swing axle, the single pivot swing

Figure 4–3. De Dion Suspension

axle, had been developed by Mercedes-Benz. In the past Mercedes vehicles used the single pivot swing axle illustrated in Fig. 4–5. It provides a greater swing radius for the wheels and thus produces smaller camber and track width changes than the double pivot swing axle. Although the single pivot swing axle has a low roll center and consequently somewhat improved cornering performance, both the single and double pivot swing axle are plagued with increased tire wear and reduced road holding on icy surfaces. Advancements in independent suspension designs have led to their replacement by different suspension design except for their use in a variety of European military vehicles primarily intended for off-road operation.

Figure 4–4. Double Pivot Swing Axle (VW Beetle)

4–2.4. Trailing Arm Suspension. The pure trailing arm is an arm holding the wheel on one end and pivoting at a right angle to the car. The effective and simple trailing arm design of the VW Rabbit is illustrated in Fig. 4–6. The wheels always retain their upright position relative to the car, except as changed by small elastic deflections at the attachment points, the wheels also lean as the body rolls while cornering. A "leaning" tire generally means reduced tire side force production and consequently may affect the steering characteristics of the vehicle. Trailing arm rear suspensions are frequently used in vehicles having front wheel drive.

The twin trailing arm front suspension was used in earlier VW Beetle vehicles. Two parallel trailing arms were connected to the hub carrier and two torsion bars. The design is expensive and requires valuable space between the front wheels. Trailing arms are also used to locate driven or non-driven solid axles in the longitudinal direction. Panhard rods are installed to fix the lateral position of the axle. An example is the rear axle of the VW Dasher (Fig. 3–6).

4–2.5. Semi-Trailing Arm Suspension. The semi-trailing arm suspension may be used for driven and non-driven wheels. It combines

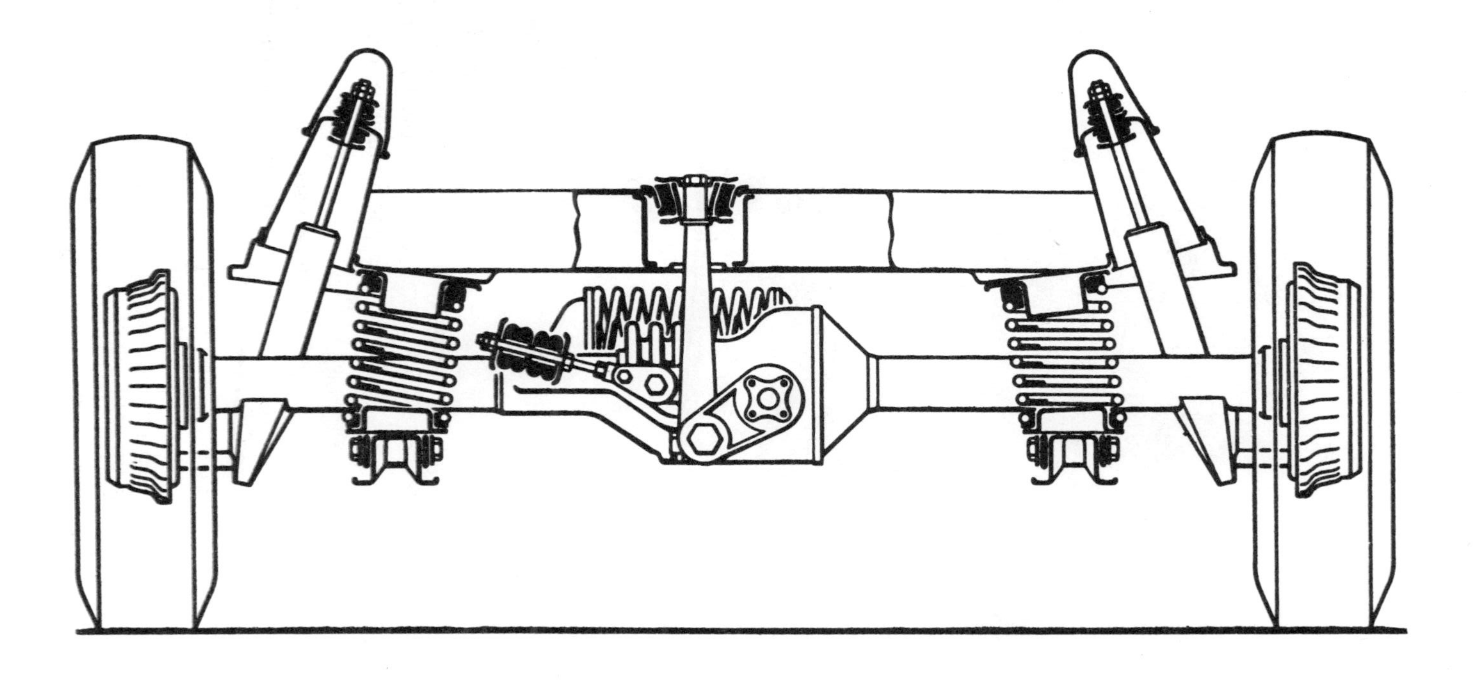

Figure 4–5. Single Pivot Swing Axle (Mercedes Benz)

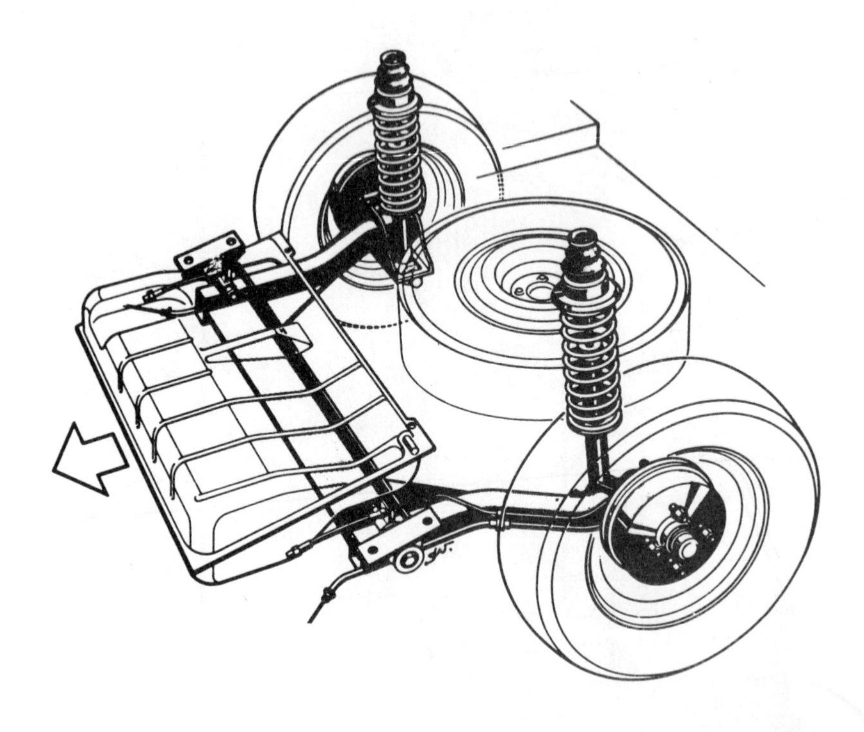

Figure 4–6. Simple Trailing Arm (VW Rabbit)

elements of the double pivot swing axle with those of the trailing arm suspension. It consists of a light weight trailing arm whose pivot axis is usually at approximately 25 deg. to a line perpendicular to the longitudinal axis of the car as illustrated in Fig. 4–7. The word semi is used to indicate that the wheel travel is somewhere between that of a pure trailing arm without camber change and that of the double pivot swing axle with a larger camber change. The motion of the wheel relative to the body during cornering introduces steering effects which generally increase the understeering tendency of the vehicle.

4–2.6. Unequal-Arm Front Suspension. The disadvantages associated with solid front axles found in passenger cars before 1940

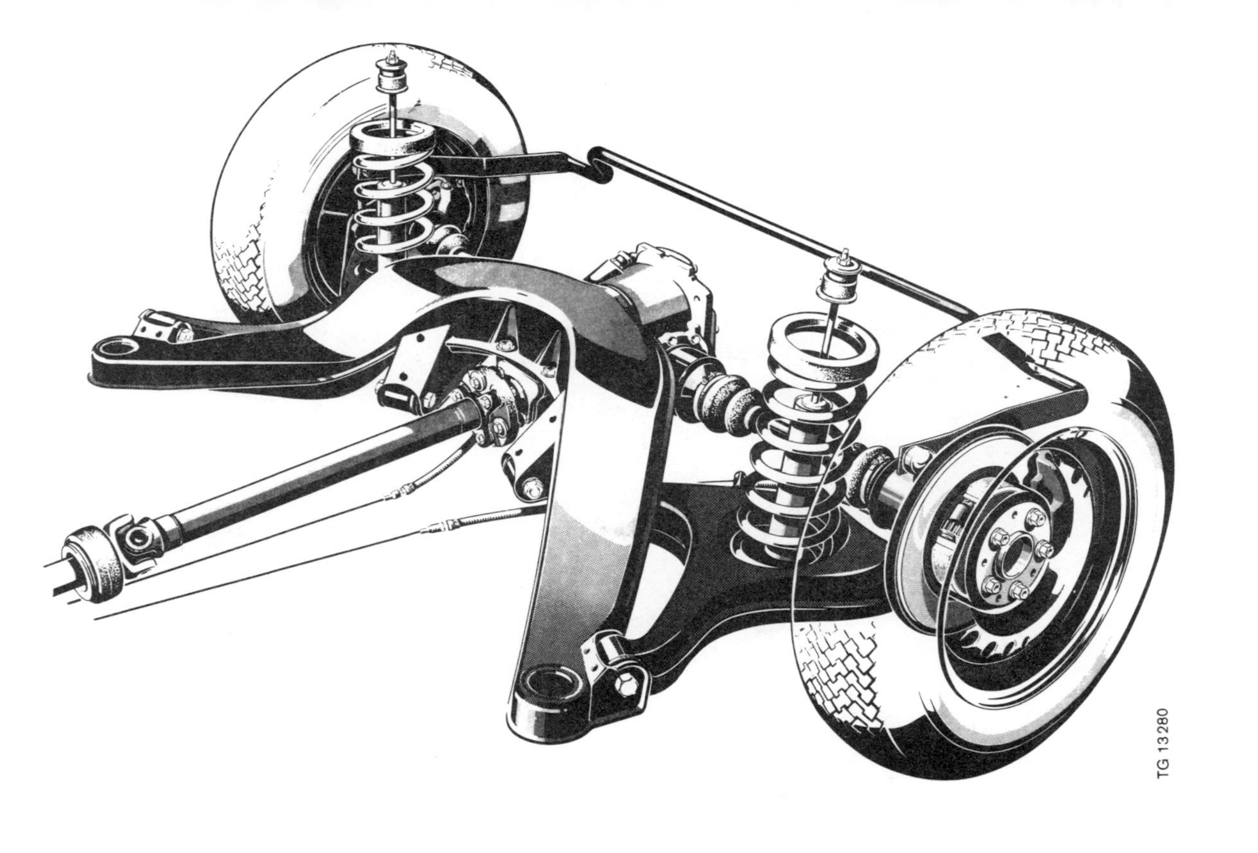

Figure 4-7. Semi-Trailing Arm (Mercedes Benz)

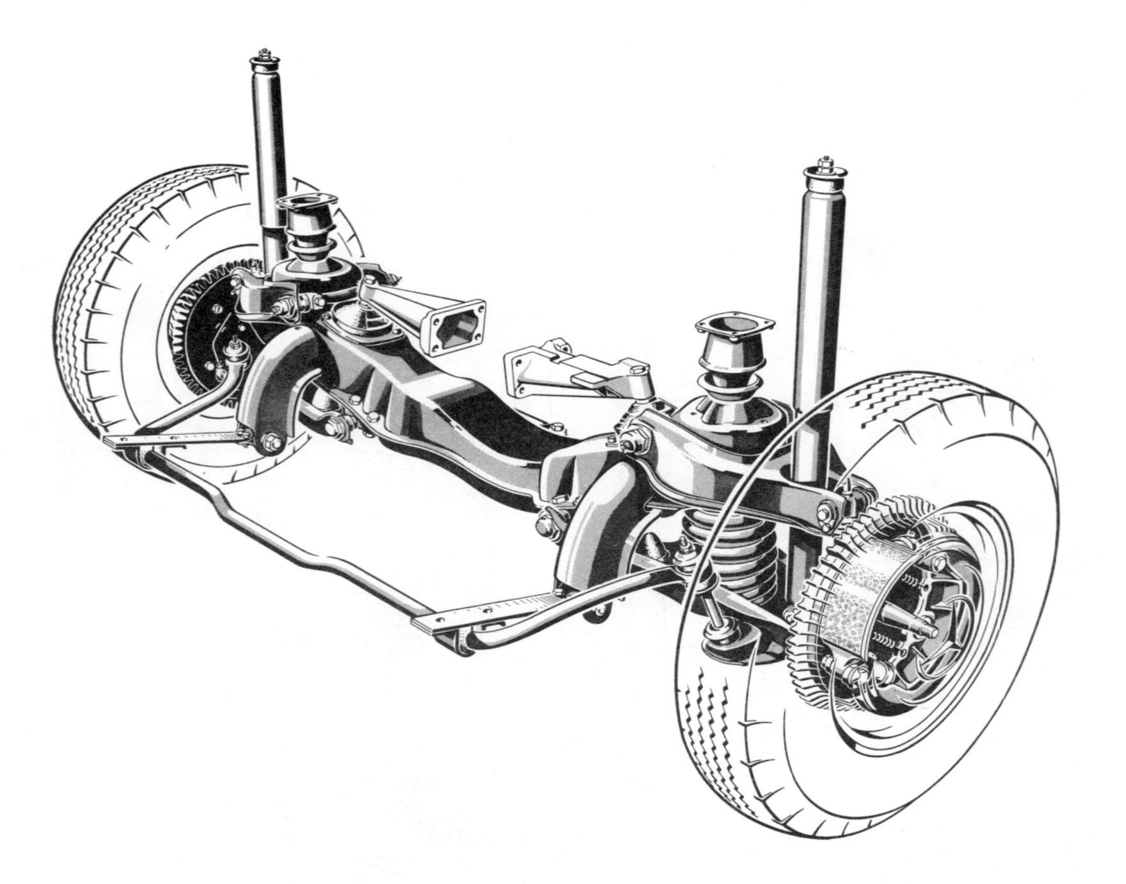

Figure 4–8. Upper and Lower Control Arm, Front Suspension (Mercedes Benz)

soon became apparent as speeds and operating requirements increased. The most common front suspension today is the unequal arm independent suspension. It consists of two A-shaped cross members per front wheel, located above each other as illustrated in Fig. 4-8. The base of the A is connected to the body or a frame attached to the body, the tip of the A is connected to the hub carrier. The location of the pivot axis of the upper and lower control arms determines the wheel travel during cornering or when operating on irregular road surface. The lower arm is always longer than the upper to provide desirable camber angle changes. Race cars usually use a lightweight tabular upper and lower control arm suspension on both front and rear wheels.

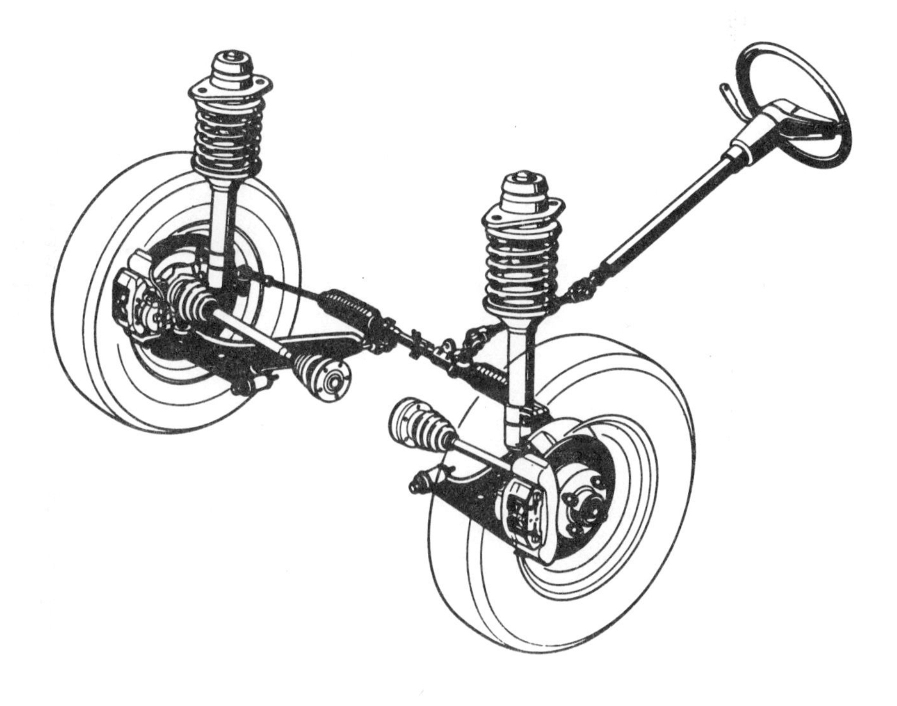

Figure 4-9. McPherson Strut Front Suspension (VW Rabbit)

4–2.7. McPherson Strut Suspension. The McPherson strut suspension shown in Fig. 4–9 uses the lower control arm of the unequal arm suspension together with a long strut containing coil spring and shock absorber, attached to the wheel housing of the integral body. The McPherson strut exhibits little changes of camber angle or track width during wheel deflections and provides increased space between the wheels for transverse engine installation. The design provides large suspension travel. The outer tube of the shock absorber is rigidly connected with the hub carrier and the steering linkage. During rotation of the steering wheel the entire strut rotates with the front wheel about a bearing at the bottom and the piston rod of the shock absorbers. The friction in the strut may cause some sticking between sliding components, and consequently, a hard initial suspension response may result. Advanced designs (e.g., BMW) use excentric installation of the spring to reduce the bearing forces between the sliding components to improve responsiveness of the suspension.

In the Chapman strut suspension the basic McPherson design is adapted to rear suspensions as for example in the Fiat X1/9 mid-engine car.

4–2.8. Tandem Axle Suspension. Tandem axle suspensions are used on heavy trucks to increase the load carrying capacity of the vehicle and to improve the tire-to-ground normal force for operation on rough road surfaces. The most common layout today consists of solid axles connected by various rods and leaf springs to the frame of the truck or trailer. Their advantage is improved braking performance due to a better utilization of available friction.

4–3. TYPES OF SPRINGS

Road safety and ride comfort require that an elastic suspension system, i.e., springs are installed between the wheels and the body. The springs reduce road impacts caused by bumps and potholes to an allowable level. The decreased dynamic forces between tire and road increase road life, i.e., road damage is decreased and increase the life of vehicle suspension components. The proper selection of springs is one of the critical factors affecting vehicle handling. It is a somewhat easier task for heavy vehicles than for light-weight small cars. Details of vehicle vibrations and what affects them is discussed in Chapter 21.

4–3.1. Leaf Springs. Leaf springs are single or multiple steel plates. Their elastic deflection during wheel motion is accomplished in a bending mode. Leaf springs can transmit longitudinal and lateral force, and consequently, can locate the axle. Multiple leaf springs suffer from friction between individual leaves and, consequently, may produce a harsh ride. Single leaf springs cannot be made very soft without obtaining fatigue failure problems. In some cases leaf springs are installed as transverse springs, serving the function of both the spring and the A-arms. An example of a semi-elliptical multiple leaf spring is shown in Fig. 4-10.

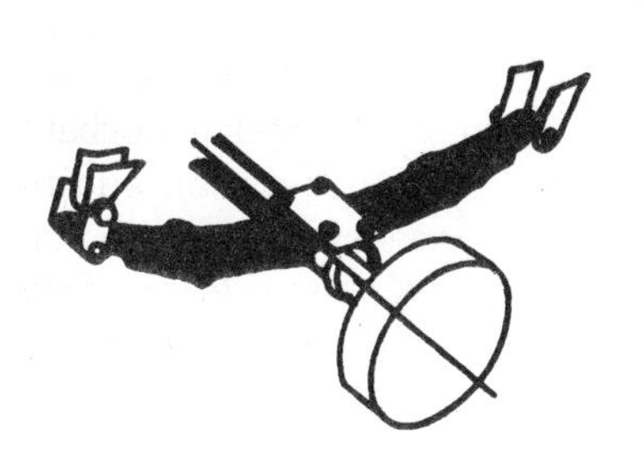

Figure 4-10. Leaf Spring

Figure 4-11. Coil Spring

4-3.2. Coil Springs. Coil springs consist of a long rod wound in a cylinder as illustrated in Fig. 4-11. The elastic action of the coil spring is produced by torsion. Coil springs are simple and inexpensive, exhibit low weight and require no maintenance. Coil springs respond quickly to road bumps and permit a progressive spring force by means of a change in the number of turns. Coil springs have no internal friction and thus provide for a more consistent ride. They cannot transmit any longitudinal or lateral forces for axle location.

4-3.3. Torsion Bar. The torsional spring is a rod whose spring action consists of the twisting of a bar. In most cases the bar has a circular cross section, but may have differently shaped forms or even multiple leaves. The torsion bar can be located longitudinally or laterally across the vehicle. The suspension spring force can be adjusted easily by rotation of the bar, and thus provides a simple means of compensating for a fatigued and sagging spring. Both torsion bars and coil springs use the twisting of a rod as elastic spring action, and consequently no basic differences exist between the two spring types. An example of a torsion bar is shown in Fig. 4-12.

4-3.4. Rubber Springs. Rubber springs use the elastic properties of rubber to provide the spring function of the suspension. In some cases truck suspensions use the torsional or shear properties of rubber to absorb wheel deflections.

Figure 4–12. Torsion Bar Suspension

Rubber elements are common on all modern suspensions to mount suspension components to frame, chassis or body. Although the rubber does not serve the function of the spring, its elasticity eliminates vibration as for example associated with radial tires on cobbled pavement. Rubber bushings also influence the vehicle steering characteristic under severe cornering.

Rubber elements are used as stops to limit the maximum wheel travel.

For small vehicles with short wheel base rubber springs are sometimes used in connection with an integral hydraulic suspension system (see Section 4–3.6). British vehicles with hydroelastic suspensions frequently use rubber springs.

4–3.5. Air or Gas Spring. Air or gas springs use the elastic compressibility of air (or a different gas) to provide the elastic function of the suspension. Air springs are bellows mounted between a movable suspension component and the frame or body as shown in Fig. 4–13. Air suspensions provide constant wheel travels independent of vehicle loading. Air suspensions require an air pressuring system and the control system for automatic adjustment of the air pressure in the bellows. Due to high cost, air suspensions are only found on expensive cars. Air springs exhibit a good response to small road irregularities and desirable progressivity or a high spring force production at large bumps, caused by an increase in spring stiffness due to a decrease in air compressibility at higher wheel travels. Air springs are frequently used on furniture-carrying vans to improve ride and to provide an adjust-

Figure 4–13. Air Suspension (Mercedes Benz)

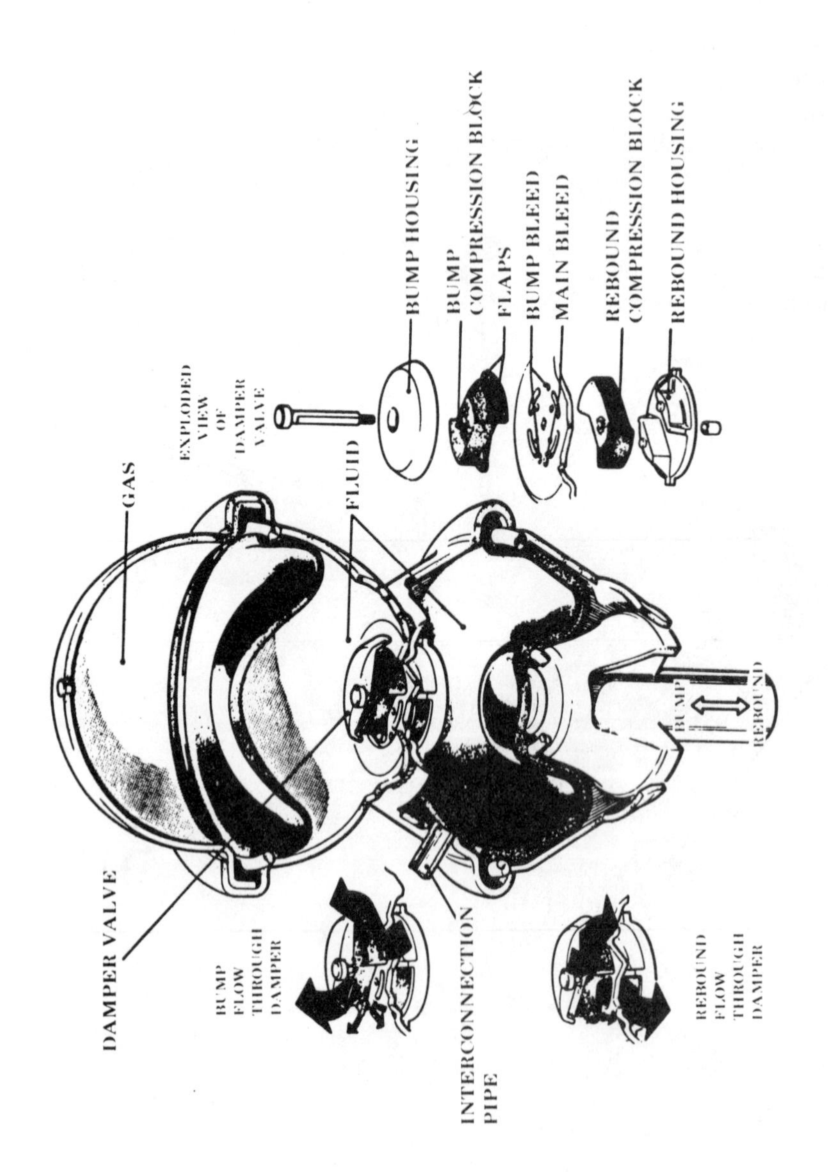

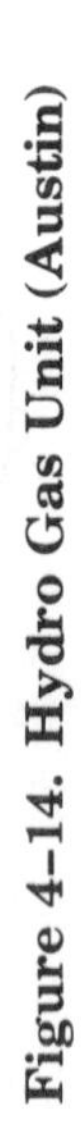

Figure 4–14. Hydro Gas Unit (Austin)

able spring rate. The automatic adjustment is accomplished by load sensitive valves that control air pressure to the bellows or air bags.

4–3.6. Hydro-Gas Springs. Hydro-gas suspensions use a gas or air spring to provide the elastic function of the suspension. Incompressible fluid such as oil, separated by a bladder from the air or gas, acts upon a piston which moves as determined by the wheel displacement (Fig. 4–14). The central oil hydraulic can be arranged such that the displacement of one wheel affects the spring stiffness or wheel position of other wheels (Fig. 4–15). If, for example, the left front wheel is pushed up by a bump, then the displaced oil at the left front wheel flows to the left rear suspension where the oil pressure raises the body

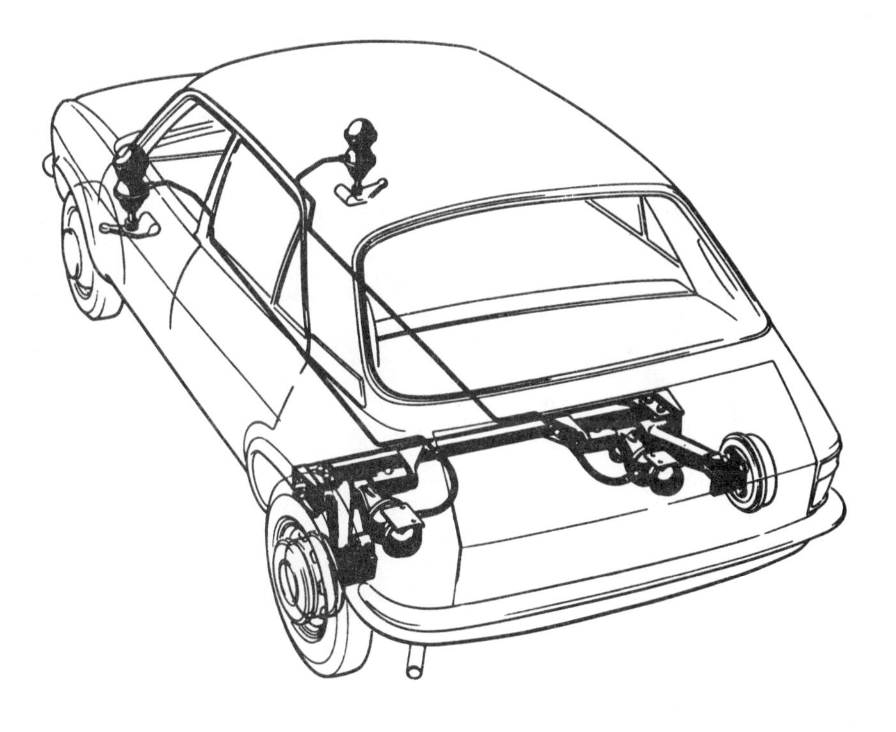

Figure 4–15. Hydro Gas Suspension (Austin)

and thus provides for a smoother ride on rough roadways and reduced pitching vibrations of the vehicle. Hydro-gas suspensions do not require additional shock absorbers or roll bars since the damping function is provided by special valves within the hydraulic circuit.

Hydro-gas suspensions provide a smoother ride since the "spring stiffness" is automatically adjusted to vehicle weight, a problem especially present in connection with steel spring equipped small cars. Road holding, i.e., the normal force between tire and ground does not benefit from air or gas springs, however, a complicated hydrocircuit may provide certain suspension features which improve handling.

4–4. TYPES OF DAMPERS

The functions of dampers are to reduce undesirable vibrations of vehicle body (sprung mass) and to keep the tire in contact with the road surface when operating on rough roads at higher speeds (Fig. 4–16). During compression or shortening of the damper the damper force is small thus permitting the suspension springs to absorb the impact from the road bump. During lengthening of the damper, i.e., when the wheel moves away from the body, the damper produces the damping force which prevents wheel hop. The common name of shock absorber is misleading since the damper does not absorb road forces, a function of the springs. The damper (or shock absorber) is a critical element of the suspension system, and if degraded, i.e., not properly reducing vibrations, causes excessive body vibrations and tire wear and even more critically, increases wheel hop with a significant loss of tire traction. Details are discussed in Chapter 21.

4–4.1. Frictional Damper. Frictional dampers use the friction force developed between elements sliding on each other. Since friction is a function of the properties of the contact surfaces, the damping performance varies greatly with environmental factors. The damping force is acting during up and down travel of the wheel and consequently, a harsh ride results.

4–4.2. Hydraulic Lever Damper. The lever damper uses the displacement and subsequent pressure buildup on a fluid for the damping action. Lever dampers require little space, exhibited however high operating pressures and, in the case of inadequate cooling, excessive wear.

4–4.3. Hydraulic Shock Absorbers. Nearly all automotive "shock absorbers" or dampers are of the single or double tube design. Both types are available as singly or doubly acting dampers. The compression or shortening stroke is soft, i.e., no large force is developed across

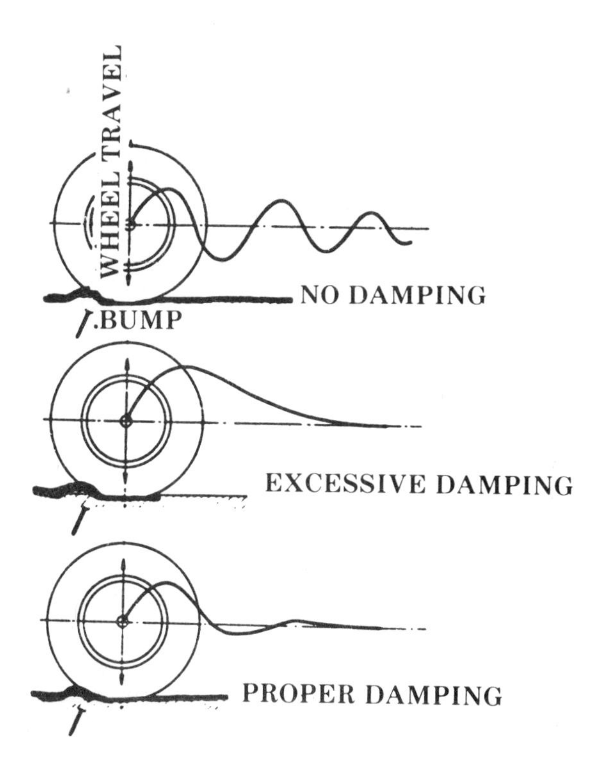

Figure 4–16. Wheel Vibrations for Different Damping Effects

the dampers. The extension or lengthening stroke is harder, i.e., a larger force is developed across the damper. A defective damper shows little or no difference between the forces produced during shortening or lengthening stroke. All hydraulic dampers transfer the kinetic or vibration energy into thermal energy by forcing the damper fluid through small holes. A piston pushes the fluid through a spring loaded valve system. In the single tube damper the fluid volume changes caused by the entrance of the pushrod of the piston into the fluid chamber is balanced by an elastic gas volume at the bottom as illustrated in Fig. 4–17. In the double acting damper the inner working cylinder is surrounded by a partially filled outer shell serving as fluid reservoir. During the compression stroke the fluid displaced in the working cylinder can flow past a foot valve into the outer shell or reservoir as illustrated in Fig. 4–18. Since the foot valve has a higher flow resistance than the valve in the piston, only an amount of fluid equivalent to the fluid volume displaced by the pushrod is pushed into the reservoir. During lengthening of the damper, the fluid flows back from the reservoir past a different valve into the working cylinder. The orifices of the different valves are designed to produce the desired damping force. Mass production dampers are built with only one performance characteristic, while special dampers with variable damping force for use in race cars are adjusted or tuned for optimum per-

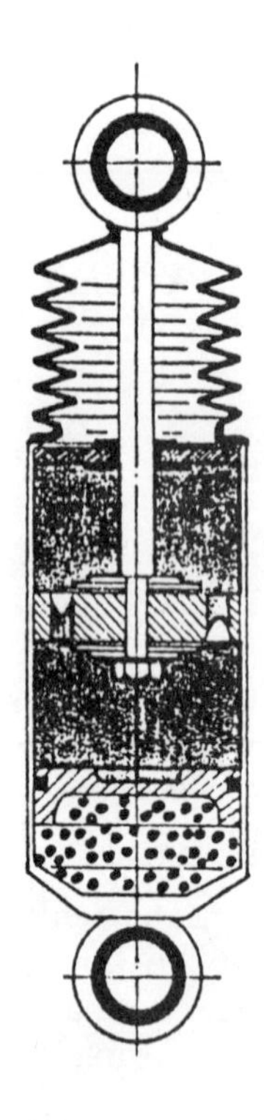

Figure 4–17. Single Tube Shock Absorber

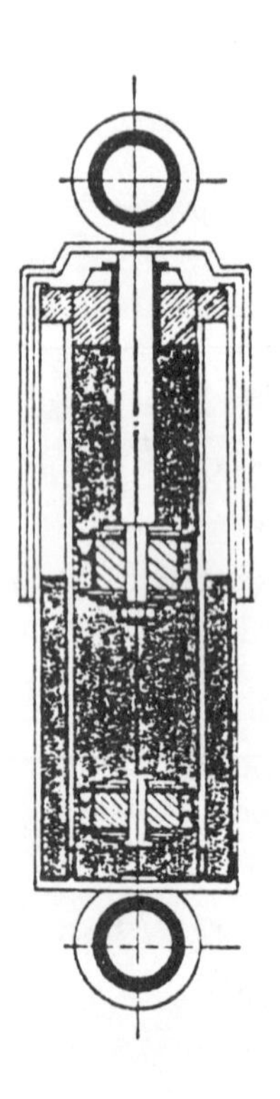

Figure 4–18. Double Tube Shock Absorber

formance for the particular race track under consideration. Hydraulic damper degrade and wear and must be safety inspected for leakage and performance.

4-5. AUXILIARY SUSPENSION SYSTEMS

Auxiliary suspension systems are springs that assist the primary suspension springs in their elastic function during increased vehicle weight or while cornering.

Expensive cars often use an auxiliary spring which increases the stiffness of the suspension when the vehicle is heavily loaded. The spring is activated automatically and may consist of a torsion bar (Fig. 2-1) or a coil spring. A similar effect is achieved by means of overload springs on trucks using leaf spring suspensions.

A completely different auxiliary suspension system is the anti-roll bar. The anti-roll bar is a torsion bar mounted across the vehicle (Fig. 4-7). The center portion of the bar is attached to the body by means of rubber bushings which permit free rotation of the bar. The ends of the bar are angled and firmly attached to the upper or lower A-arm (see Fig. 4-8), or the hub carrier. The anti-roll bar transmits a torque only when one wheel of the suspension moves up or down relative to the other as in cornering, or when one wheel is deflected by road roughness. When both wheels are deflected simultaneously, the anti-roll bar has no effect upon suspension stiffness. Anti-roll bars produce increased vehicle roll stiffness while keeping the regular suspension springs, i.e., ride comfort is not affected. Anti-roll bars are used to improve the steering characteristics of motor vehicles by affecting the tire slip angle production during cornering.

4-6. SUSPENSION MAINTENANCE

Maintenance and adjustment procedures associated solely with suspension components are minor and generally involve only lubrication (if any). The appropriate shop manual should be reviewed for details.

4-7. SAFETY CONSIDERATIONS

If vehicle suspension factors are involved in accident causation, then only either as a design or manufacturing defect, or as degradation defect due to a lack of proper maintenance. Design defects cause an unsafe functioning of the suspension system and may be the result of inadequate material, insufficient fatigue life, or inadequate size. Vehicle defects investigations are routinely carried out by the U.S. Department of Transportation (NHTSA), and involve a variety of suspension components (Chapter 36).

CHAPTER 5
THE TIRE AND RIM

5-1. THE FUNCTIONS OF TIRE AND RIM

The tire-rim assembly is commonly called wheel. The rim is the connecting component between vehicle and tire and is subjected to high forces and moments. The tire is the connecting element between vehicle (rim) and road surface. Tires support the vehicle with its payload and produce driving, braking, and vehicle guiding forces. Tires also serve as a spring and damper (shock absorber) between vehicle and road.

5-2. DIFFERENT CONCEPTS USED IN RIM DESIGN

The rim is part of the unsprung weight of the vehicle, and consequently should be as light as possible. Mass production rims consist of the actual rim and the center portion, welded together to form the entire rim (sometimes called wheel). The steel rim production costs are lower than those associated with aluminum or magnesium alloy wheels. Light alloy wheels are cast or forged and are often used in connection with wide tires installed by the aftermarket. Spoke wheels are used in some cases on sports cars. The spokes provide an increased air flow to the brakes for improved cooling.

In the case of heavy trucks and race cars the rim can be disassembled to mount the tire on the rim. Tubeless belted tires use so-called hump rims to prevent a separation of tire and rim during severe cornering and low inflation pressure. The hump can be located on the outside (valve side) of the rim or on both sides. The humps make it difficult to mount the tires, and consequently, proper installation requires tire mounting devices or machines.

The rim size is given in inches, where the first number designates the rim width, the second the rim diameter. Rim dimensions are standardized by the Tire and Rim Association for size and contour (Ref. 8). Rims may be identified, i.e., stamped with maximum load and maximum cold inflation rating. Letters are often used to define the rim contour.

5-3. DIFFERENT CONCEPTS USED IN TIRE DESIGN

Different tire construction, in general, influences the tire mechanical characteristics, and it is not possible to rate one type of tire superior to another in all respects. The carcass, an inflated enclosure of rubber fiber composite, is the basic tire structure. It is reinforced with the fibrous cord following a set path pattern, bias ply (the conventional tire) and radial ply, and consists of different numbers of layers embedded in rubber or other commonly used polymer matrix. The cord structure provides the necessary structural rigidity to the otherwise soft and highly elastic rubber or polymer mix to withstand the static and dynamic stresses of inflation and other forces without excessive creep. Some tires are built with a belt under the tread to provide structural integrity. The belt is influential in controlling the wear characteristics of the tire.

There are two ways to apply the plies: bias and radial. For many years most tires were of the bias type. These had the plies crisscrossed with one layer running one way and the other running so that they were more or less perpendicular. This pattern gave a carcass that was strong in all directions because of the overlapping plies. The difficulty was that the plies tended to move against each other, generating heat, particularly at high speed. Also, the tread tended to squirm as it met the road and this caused tread wear. Bias ply tires are less expensive due to simpler manufacturing procedures than radial ply tires.

To remedy this problem, tires with radial plies were introduced. On these the plies all run parallel to each other and perpendicular to the tire rim. To provide strength in the direction parallel to the tire rim, belts are applied all the way around the tire. The tread is then vulcanized on top of the belts. The belts are made of rayon, glass fiber, or steel. All perform in a similar manner and provide additional strength to the circumference of the tire. In addition, the belted tire has a larger contact area. It is less stiff because of the radial plies and thinner sidewalls, and thus flexes more to apply a greater part of the tread to the road. Because the sidewalls can be thinner and more flexible, the tread has less tendency to heel up when cornering and provides increased traction in turns.

Bias-ply tires may also be belted. The belted-bias tire generally will have performance properties midway between the other tire types.

Tread design has little effect on a dry road traction. However, on wet road surfaces the tread must maintain effective tire-road contact by removing water coming under the tire. This removal becomes more difficult at high speeds because of the hydrodynamic forces generated due to the water between the tire and the road. The importance of tread design on wet road performance is well recognized with individual design features such as sipes in the form of narrow slots, grooves, tread width, and crown radius influencing performance. An obvious improvement in the wet road performance is obtained with grooved tires compared to smooth surfaces with fine texture or at high speeds on wet surfaces since the grooves provide escape channels for the interface water. The effectiveness of grooves increases with the number and width of grooves up to some limit with the sideway skidding resistance also increasing. Although straight circumferential grooves are very effective, some advantage may be gained using zig-zag circumferential grooves of some optimum dimension. The use of narrow slots or sipes also provides an improvement in the wet skidding performance, and this effect is more pronounced on polished smooth wet surfaces. The blades or sipes not only provide a wiping action through the exposed sharp cut edge at right angles to the tread sliding, but also act as reservoirs for water. The belt of radial tires serves a contact patch "stabilizing" function which causes the grooves to be open under nearly all driving conditions, and consequently a better drainage of the water between tire and road is provided. Wet traction properties and hydroplaning characteristics of radial tires are better than those associated with bias ply tires. Radial tires exhibit longer life due to less relative sliding motion of the individual tread elements between rubber and road surface. This decreased relative sliding generally results in improved traction on icy roadways.

Tread pattern is not as influential on rough and harsh textured surfaces. It normally is said that it is the smooth road surfaces which discriminate between tread designs while rough surfaces discriminate between tread materials.

It has long been known that rubber sliding friction is dependent on velocity and load, and that this behavior is a function of the viscoelastic property of the rubber or rubber-like materials. Since the different rubbers are composed of different molecular structures with different mechanical properties, it is not strange to find that rubber may possess a wide range of frictional characteristics (Ref. 9).

Besides natural rubber a large number of rubber materials are used in tires. Laboratory and road skid tests indicate that polybutadiene is a longer wearing tread material than others with improved wet skid resistance. It also reduces tread groove cracking, and cutting and chipping of tire treads during service.

Truck tires generally have a larger amount of natural rubber content than passenger car tires, resulting in lower rolling resistance at the cost of a decreased longitudinal tire friction coefficient. Tire force production and friction coefficients are discussed in Chapter 18.

5-4. TIRE NOTATION

Tire notations have been changed over the years and are often confusing. They differ for domestic and foreign manufacturers. Generally, however, letters and numbers are used to designate dimensions and application. The first number (in the older notation system) designates tire section width in inches (or millimetres in the metric system), the second number defines the rim diameter in inches (also used in the metric system). Letters following the last number identified tire application such as LT (light truck) indicating the tire to be permitted for trucks, buses, trailers, or multipurpose vehicles using a certain rim, or ML designating tire for use in mining or logging operations. Common notations on European and Japanese tires include the letter R for radial ply construction immediately following the section width. For example, a tire size 165 R-13 indicates a section width of 165 mm, radial ply construction and a 13 in. rim diameter. European tires also use suffix letters S, H, or V indicating maximum allowable speeds of 112 mph, 131 mph and greater than 131 mph, respectively.

Load ranges are indicated by letters A through N identifying increasing load carrying capacity. Formerly ply ratings were used to indicate load capacity.

The size designation giving section width and rim diameter does not provide size information on tire cross section. New tire size notation includes the ratio of section height to section width. For example, a 70 series tire has a tire section height to width ratio of 0.70. The first letter in the new notation denotes load rating but may also be used to designate approximate section width. European tire sizes use a number to give the actual width in mm. Radial ply construction is indicated by the letter R. For example, the tire size GR 70–14 indicates a tire section width of approximately 8.85 in. (letter G), a radial ply construction (letter R), section height to width ratio of 0.70, and a 14 in. rim diameter. A European tire size of 205/50 VR 15 indicates a tire section width of 205 mm (8.1 in.), a section height to width ratio of 0.50, a maximum speed of more than 131 mph (letter V), a radial ply construction (letter R), and a 15 in. rim diameter.

In the past tire height to width ratios were close to unity. Modern tires have ratios less than unity. The reasons for this development are related to the improved tire characteristics exhibited by low aspect ratio tires. These advantages include high cornering force, improved driving and braking traction, smaller rolling resistance and increased load carrying capacity. The most common ratio is 0.8 or 0.78 with radial tires going as low as 0.70 and even 0.60 in special cases. Disadvantages of low aspect ratio tires are increased tendency of hydroplaning, i.e., loss of traction on wet road surfaces, decreased straight-ahead running ability, especially on roads having longitudinal grooves, and reduction in ride qualities. Racing tires may have aspect ratios as small as 0.25.

Details on tire and rim dimensions selection and permissible practices are published by the Tire and Rim Association, Inc.
Year Book (Ref. 8).

5-5. SPECIAL SAFETY TIRE DESIGNS

Several safety tires have been designed that permit vehicle operation with a defective tire.

The captive-air tire prevents air escape by means of a special sealing coating inside the tubeless tire.

The puncture-proof tire has a special concave design that prevents puncture of the tire.

The run flat tire permits vehicle operation with a deflated tire. A second inner "tire" supports the outer failed tire. Speeds up to 50 mph are possible. A similar concept is a thin steel ring for emergency operation.

5-6. TIRE RETREADS

Retreading and regrooving are the common techniques for improving the traction of a worn tire without having to replace it. The advantages gained by these methods are substantial and economical but only when the tire carcass still has enough structural integrity. Regrooving will add extra skid resistance only where the undertread has sufficient regrooving allowance which is commonly built in most of the truck and bus tires.

Standards for retread processing were formulated by the Tire Retreading Institute in Washington, D.C. and have upgraded the product to ensure the motoring public that quality retreads are safe and dependable.

Tires retreaded for use on passenger cars must meet Federal Government standards effective June 1, 1973. The performance requirements of retreads are similar to those for new tires. Both bias and radial ply tires can be retreaded.

5-7. WHEEL BALANCE

Wheel balance involves the equalization of forces on a rotating wheel by means of attaching lead weights on the rim of the wheel.

An imbalance exists due to a non-uniform distribution of mass (or weight) of the wheel and associated rotating components such as the brake rotor. Static imbalance is commonly referred to as the imbalance causing a vertical bounce of the wheel assembly. The imbalance increases with the square of the velocity, i.e., doubling the speed increases the imbalance four fold. Dynamic imbalance results in a wobble or shimmying, i.e., horizontal oscillation of the wheel assembly. Dynamic imbalance also increases rapidly with vehicle speed. Wide tires and rims require a careful dynamic balancing.

The use of the word static imbalance is a poor choice since wheel rotation, i.e., a dynamic process, is required for the production of the imbalancing forces. Both the static and dynamic imbalance are the result of dynamic processes with the latter imbalance representing the more general case of the imbalancing mass (or weight) being located outside the mass symmetry axis of the wheel.

A balanced wheel assembly causes no dynamic force production, and consequently does not subject an adjacent vehicle component to unnecessary stresses. Immediate benefits of a balanced wheel are:

1. Longer tire life
2. Improved steering and vehicle directional stability
3. Reduced driver fatigue
4. Increased vehicle component life
5. Increased safety

More details on the effect of the wheel balance on vehicle performance are presented in Chapter 21.

5-8. TIRE WEAR

A certain amount of tire wear is natural for any tire. The production of drive, braking or side forces, particularly when operating near the limit of tire traction, requires a certain amount of relative motion between tire and road, a prerequisite for wear.

5-8.1. Causes of Tire Wear. Under-inflation causes excessive tire wear at the edges of the tire tread. The tire-to-road pressure is much greater at the edges than in the center since the tire side walls must carry a greater load in the under-inflated tire.

Over-inflation causes excessive tire wear at the center of the tread due to a high tire-to-road pressure concentration at the tread center.

Wear on one side of the tire tread may have three reasons:

1. Wheel camber causes the tire to run at an angle from a vertical line, resulting in uneven or side wear.

2. Turning maneuvers produce side forces which distort the tires such that side wear occurs. In a left turn the outside shoulder of the right tire and the inside shoulder of the left tire exhibit most of the wear. Cornering wear shows wear and skuff marks on the worn edge.

3. Crowned roads produce an uneven pressure distribution between tire and road, resulting in side wear.

Toe-in (or toe-out) misalignment wear causes a side sliding motion to be developed as the tire rotates which scrapes the tread rubber off, leaving the tread edges feathered. Front tires will show wear on the outside with a toe-in condition and on the inside with a toe-out condition. This wear pattern is reversed when considering toe for rear tires.

Uneven tire wear such as a single spot or a series of cuppings around the tire circumference may also be noted on tires. Such uneven wear is generally the result of excessive toe-in or toe-out in connection with under-inflation, uneven camber, unbalanced wheels or worn suspension components.

The operating temperature of the tire has a significant effect on tire wear. An increase of 40° F in tire temperature may reduce tread mileage by one-third. In some vehicles differences in steady-state tire operating temperatures may develop due to radiator cooling air vented into the wheel housing. This problem may be more pronounced with small front engine front wheel driven cars.

5–8.2. Effects of Tire Wear. Uneven and regular tread wear influences the skid resistance or traction of a tire. Even or regular wear reduces the flow capacity of drainage channels and reservoirs, and considerably impairs the advantages gained with tread pattern. Uneven wear reduces wet traction of the tire at the worn side and makes vehicle steering control extremely difficult since the loss of tire traction may occur suddenly in a steering maneuver when the load carrying tire-to-road area is shifted from the treaded (normal friction) to the worn (low friction) side of the tire.

Worn tires when operating on a smooth clean roadway generally do not exhibit an appreciable decrease in sliding friction from that observed with a grooved tire.

Uneven wear of tires causes wheel imbalance to develop, and consequently represents a safety hazard both in terms of tire blow-out and steering control of the vehicle.

5-9. TIRE MAINTENANCE

Tire maintenance schedules are specified in appropriate shop manuals. Schedules include proper inflation pressure, tire rotation for balanced wear, and proper tire repair in case of a flat. Tire repairs include rubber plug method, and cold and hot patch methods. In most cases these repairs are carried out by skilled service personnel.

5-10. SAFETY CONSIDERATIONS

Tire defects investigations by the U.S. Department of Transportation occur on a regular basis. More details on tire safety standards and performance requirements are presented in Chapter 33.

rotated less than the inner front wheel to meet the requirement of common intersection. The front-end steering system must provide this difference in outer to inner wheel rotation, and must move with the up and down travel of the suspension and wheels.

The basic steering parallelogram as shown in Fig. 6–2 consists of five major elements: two adjustable tie rods (which tie the steering knuckles together), one relay rod (which connects to the tie rods), one pitman arm (which connects to the steering gear and the relay rod), and one idler arm (which connects to the relay rod and the frame).

The basic parallelogram with connecting rod frequently used on trucks with solid front axles consists of seven major components: two short tie rods, one frame crank, one connecting rod (or center link), one bell crank, one drag link, and one pitman arm. Also shown in Fig. 6–2 is a steering damper or shock absorber, located most frequently in a horizontal direction. One end of the shock absorber is attached to the frame or body, the other connects to the relay rod. Steering dampers absorb impacts transmitted from the road and reduce possible front wheel vibrations.

Independent front suspensions require two (or more) tie rods to properly position the front wheels while turning while solid front axles used on trucks use only a single connecting rod.

6–2.2. Wheel Position. The steering force produced by a tire depends on its position relative to the straight-ahead position of the vehicle. Both steering and suspension systems must be designed to provide optimum traction with minimum tire wear. The position of the wheel is defined by several angles in space.

Camber is the tilting of the wheel from the vertical axis as shown in Fig. 6–3. The camber angle is the angle between the wheel axis and the vertical axis. Positive camber is defined by a tilting that brings the wheels closer together on the bottom than on the top (Fig. 6–3). Negative camber involves tilting that brings the wheels closer together on the top than on the bottom. Positive camber causes the tire to side-slip more than a vertical tire to produce the same cornering force. Details on tire force production are discussed in Chapter 18.

In some cases the camber angle of the right wheel is different from the left wheel to provide longer tire life for heavy-duty vehicles operating on crowned highways.

The steering axis, i.e., the axis about which the wheel rotates for steering is inclined from the vertical toward the vehicle as illustrated

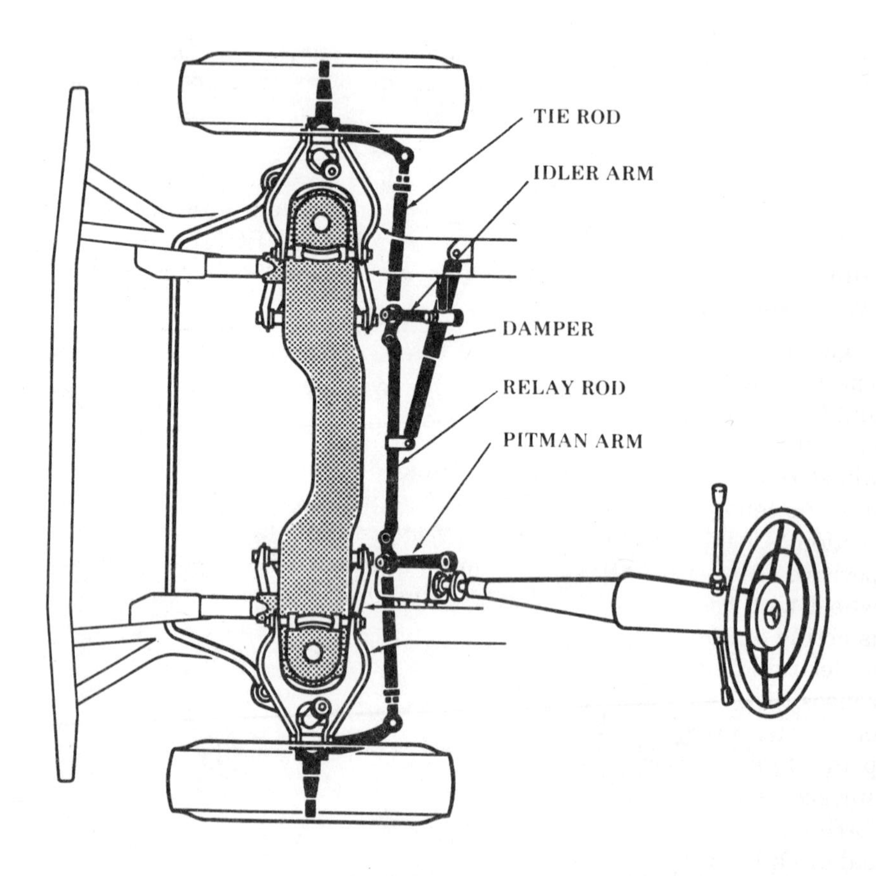

Figure 6-2. Steering Geometry (Mercedes Benz)

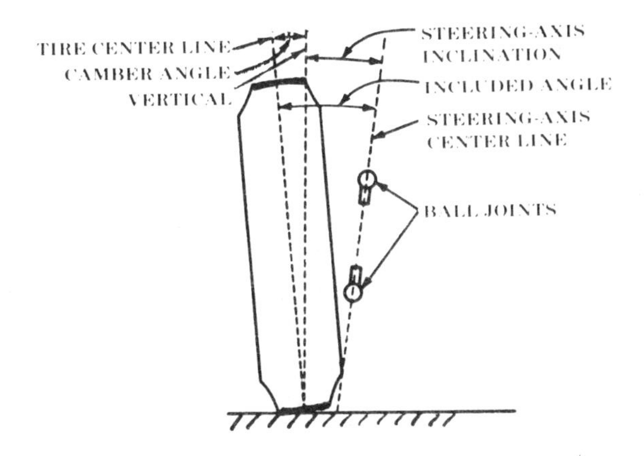

Figure 6-3. Wheel Position

in Fig. 6-3. Steering axis inclination provides steering stability by automatically returning the wheels to the straight-ahead position after turning and reduces steering wheel effort and tire wear.

The included angle is the camber angle plus the steering axis angle. The included angle determines the point of intersection of the wheel and the steering (Figs. 6-4 and 20-6). When the point of intersection is at the road surface, then the lever arm between tire and axis of wheel rotation is zero. Driving (front wheel drive) or braking forces have no tendency to turn the wheel in or out. When the point of intersection is below the road, the lever arm, also called scrub radius, is positive. A positive lever arm results in an outward turning of the wheel with the larger brake force when an unbalanced braking force is acting on the front wheels. Outward turning of the wheel causes an undesirable steering motion of the vehicle. A positive scrub radius causes the front wheel to be pushed against the inside bearing which eliminates excessive play. A negative scrub radius exists when the point of intersection between wheel and steering axis is above the road surface. A negative scrub radius automatically provides a stabilizing force on the vehicle by inward turning of the wheel in case of an imbalanced braking force on the front wheels. The wheel exhibiting the larger brake force will turn inward resulting in a stabilizing side force. Passenger cars manufactured in the United States generally have a positive scrub radius, Mercedes Benz vehicles exhibit a zero scrub radius, Volkswagen and Audi a negative scrub radius.

Toe-in of the front wheels refers to a geometry determined by a smaller distance between two points on the front of the left and right

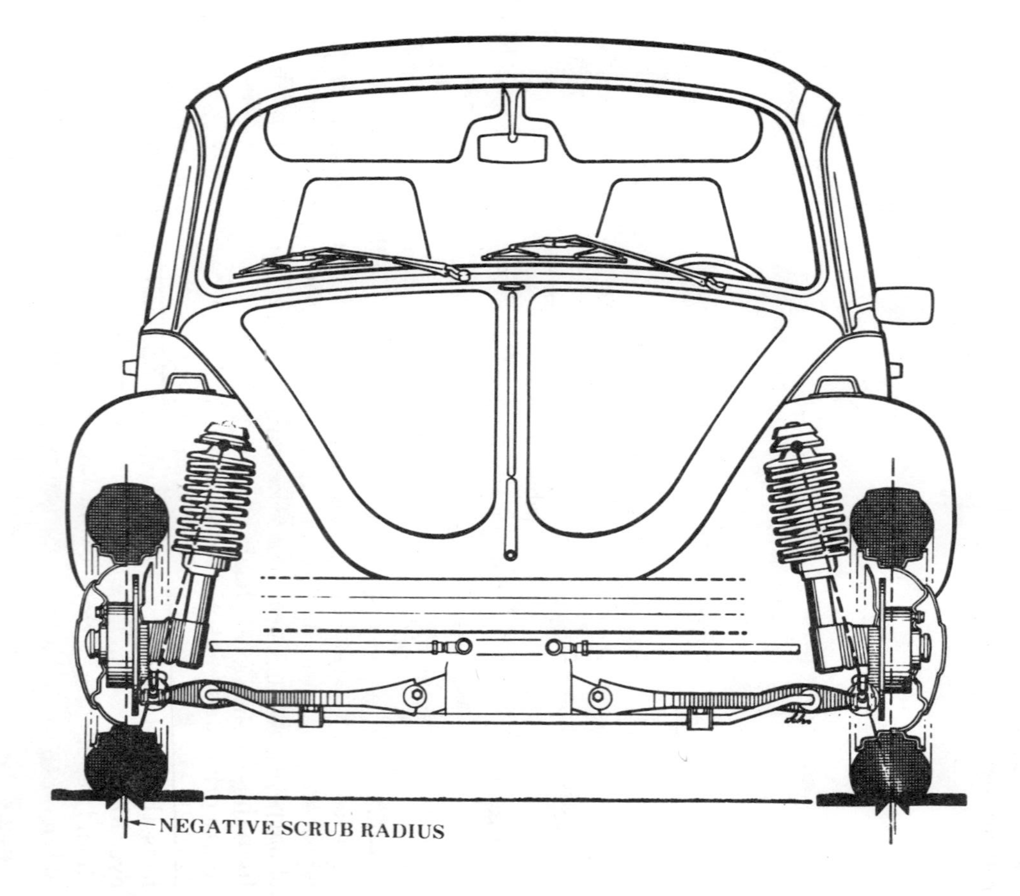

Figure 6–4. Front Suspension with Negative Scrub Radius (VW)

wheel as compared to two points located at the rear of the wheels (Fig. 6–5). Toe-in is measured on a horizontal line through the center of the wheel. It is generally less than 1/8 in. and reduces front wheel vibrations. Forces between tire and road at higher speeds cause the toe-in to decrease. Excessive toe-in reduces tire life and generates rolling resistance.

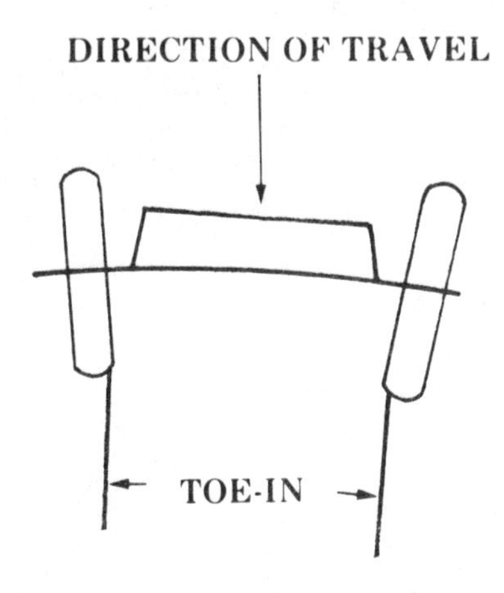

Figure 6–5. Front Wheel Toe-In

6–2.3. Rear Wheel Steering. Motor vehicles except for specialty vehicles do not permit steering of the rear wheels by the driver. Four-wheel steering experimental vehicles have demonstrated that driving of such vehicles required special driving skills significantly different from that of the typical driver. A related problem exists when attempting to drive a regular vehicle backwards at higher speed (see Section 22–3.2). The suspension travel occurring during severe cornering affects the position of the wheels and consequently contributes to the overall steering of the vehicle. These automatic steering contributions should render the cornering maneuver more stable (Porsche 928 rear axle).

6–2.4. Steering Gear System. The steering gear converts the steering wheel rotation provided by the driver into the rotation of the pitman arm attached to the output shaft of the steering gear. The steering gear also provides the necessary steering ratio between steering wheel and pitman shaft, and pitman arm. The steering ratio determines effort and angle required at the steering wheel. Common steering systems require 2.5 to 4 steering wheel rotations from complete left to complete right position. When a small steering wheel rotation is required for a specific maneuver, the steering is said to be direct, otherwise indirect.

Several different steering gear systems are in use. Most motor vehicles except small cars use a worm shaft (at the end of the steering column or shaft) and a toothed pitman shaft sector. The toothed sector meshes with the worm. When the worm is turned by rotation of the steering wheel, the pitman arm sector rotates providing the rotation of the pitman arm. The sliding friction between worm and sector has been reduced by the recirculating-ball-nut type as shown in Fig. 6-6. Steel balls running in the worm grooves lower the friction. The steel balls are held in place by the ball nut. The system is called recirculating because the balls can continuously recirculate from one end of the ball nut to the other through a pair of ball guides.

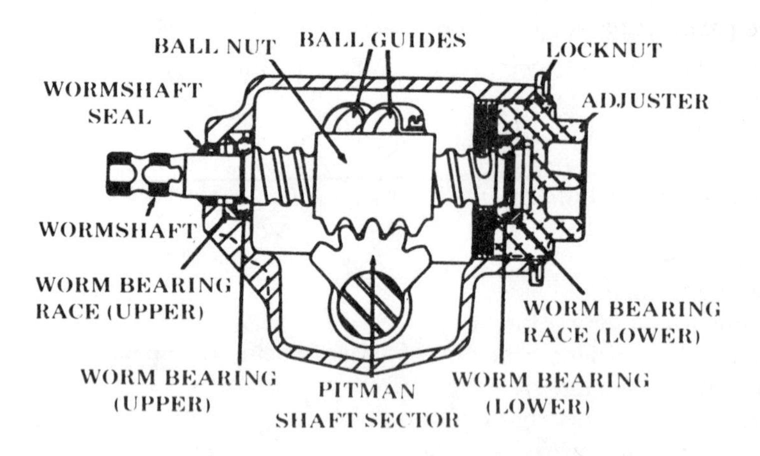

Figure 6-6. Steering Gear Schematic

Smaller cars not requiring large steering gear ratios often use the rack-and-pinion steering gear illustrated in Fig. 4-9. The steering has a pinion or small toothed wheel at the end of the steering shaft which meshes with a toothed rack. The rack is a major component of the steering linkage and often replaces the relay rod. Rack-and-pinion systems are simple and less expensive than the worm-and-nut type steering gears.

The steering ratio (in connection with other dynamic properties of the vehicle) is an important factor of vehicle handling, and consequently is critical for safe vehicle operation. The steering ratio indicates how many degrees the steering wheel has to be turned for one degree turning of the front wheels. Part of the ratio is developed by the steering linkage system but the greatest part is produced by the steering gear itself. The steering ratio of heavy-duty vehicles and vehicles using manual steering systems, i.e., no steering assist, is greater to reduce the steering effort. Power steering systems use smaller steering ratios. The steering ratio is not constant over the entire steering wheel rotation. The steering ratio may vary, as e.g., in the case of the GM Vega from 16 to 1 for straight ahead driving to 13.1 to 1 in full turns. From the straight-ahead position the steering ratio stays constant for the first 40 deg. of left or right steering wheel rotation, then decreases very gradually at first. Since highway driving rarely requires steering wheel inputs in excess of 40 deg., the steering ratio close to 16 provides good steering sensitivity and control. The steering ratio decreases to a value at or slightly above 13.1 to 1 when turning at intersections, while parking, or in similar maneuvers.

The difference between manual and power steering systems is that hydraulic pressure is used to assist the driver in the production of the rotary motion of the pitman shaft or the linear motion of a tie rod. Power steering systems have two major advantages: they relieve the driver and contribute to active safety when increases in front axle loads, front wheel drives, and increased traffic density and smaller parking spaces require higher steering wheel efforts. Many drivers including women and older people cannot always produce the required steering wheel effort. In the past, these problems were solved by increasing the steering ratio which resulted in larger steering wheel angle, and consequently, a reduction in steering responsiveness. Power steering systems are designed to use a more direct steering response, i.e., the steering ratios are lower, and to reduce steering effort.

Two basic power steering gears of the integral type, where all components are contained in one housing, have been in use.

The in-line power steering consists of a recirculating-ball steering gear, a control valve and an actuating booster piston. The assisting action comes into effect when the turning effort exceeds a certain torque at the steering wheel. For common steering wheel diameters this effort is generally less than 1 lb. This slight resistance causes the worm shaft to displace slightly and to operate the control or spool valve. The displacement of the spool valve admits oil at high pressure from the pump to one side or the other of the assist piston. The motion of the assist piston is transmitted directly onto the pitman shaft sector. Since the assist piston meshes with the pitman sector, it is commonly called rack piston.

The effort to displace the spool valve is provided by the driver. The more resistance to turning the driver encounters, the more he turns the steering wheel and the more the spool valve is displaced. This design feature permits the driver to sense the steering effort.

The rotary-valve (torsion bar) power steering of the integral type uses a small torsion bar to actuate the rotary control valve. When no turning effort is applied at the steering wheel, the slots in the valve are positioned so that oil can circulate from the pump through the return passage to the reservoir. The chambers at both ends of the rack piston are filled with oil, which serves as a cushion to absorb or dampen road shocks, and lubricates all steering gear components.

When steering effort is applied, the rotary spool valve is positioned to permit application of oil pressure to one side of the piston and oil return from the other. At the instant the driver stops applying turning effort to the wheel, the spool valve is forced back into its neutral position by the torsion bar. Oil pressure on the applied end of the rack piston decreases so that equal pressures exist on both sides of the piston and the front wheels return to the straight-ahead position when the car is moving.

Particular designs may vary for different manufacturers and then mostly in terms of the spool valve actuation (Ref. 10).

The linkage-type non-integral power-steering system uses a regular manual steering gear with the assist components added to the steering linkage. The assist force most commonly is applied directly to the relay rod by a double acting booster cylinder. The control of oil flow to and from the booster cylinder is accomplished by a control valve activated by the pitman arm. Linkage-type power systems are more subject to environmental factors since piston and piston rod and connecting hoses are located between the front wheels and can be damaged more easily.

6-3. STEERING SYSTEM MAINTENANCE

The steering gear is factory-filled with steering gear oil and no lubrication is required for the life of the steering gear. The gear should be inspected for leakage.

Adjustments to the steering gear should be made only after the front end geometry and components have been checked. Adjustments are not complicated, however, the appropriate shop manual should be reviewed.

6-4. STEERING SYSTEM FAILURE

Power steering system failures may involve two basic factors: lack of assist or self steering, i.e., inadvertant turning of the vehicle to one side without driver input.

Lack of power assist may be caused by a stalled engine, defective hydraulic pump, damaged hose, fluid leakage or damaged steering gear. An internal damage of the steering gear causing a loss of power assist is unlikely to exist.

Self steering, i.e., not driver induced steering wheel rotation to one side may be the result of a damaged spool valve or spool valve actuating mechanism. The defect will cause the spool valve to remain fixed in one position with the consequence of applying assist to the rack piston without the driver commanding this steering response by an appropriate steering wheel rotation. Although infrequent, the defect may develop after a period of trouble free vehicle operation.

A different type of steering failure may develop as a result of fatigue fracture of linkage components. These components include ball studs and joints where stress raisers in form of bolt and nut threads may initiate cracking.

The following provides a list of alleged steering defects. As of January 1, 1977 the U.S. Department of Transportation was investigating possible defects of: front wheel spindle (fatigue), steering wheel (fracture), steering arm ball (instability upon hard braking), front end suspension (overload problems), steering relay rod (lockup by foreign objects), tie rod (ball separation from socket), power steering gear (lockup and self-steering problem, leakage), rack and pinion (steering difficulties and loss of control), pitman arm (fatigue fracture), idler arm, steering gear coupling.

Although this list appears to be impressive, not all alleged defects are design or manufacturing related.

6-5. STEERING COLUMN PERFORMANCE

The steering column must comply with Federal Motor Vehicle Safety Standard 203 in terms of the rearward displacement of the steering wheel during a crash and its energy absorbing capacity (see Section 33-2.3).

Chest and head injuries are reduced significantly when the force between driver and steering wheel or column is kept below a certain value during the collision.

The energy absorbing function of the steering column is accomplished by using devices that produce a limited force as the steering wheel is pushed forward by the driver's chest. These devices include controlled metal forming, mesh deformation (Japanese lantern) or shearing of special pins. The rearward displacement of the steering column is often prevented (especially in smaller cars) by a sectioned steering shaft (Fig. 4–9) which deflects sideways during a front-end collision.

CHAPTER 7
THE BRAKING SYSTEM

7-1. THE FUNCTION OF THE BRAKING SYSTEM

The brake system of the vehicle in connection with the tires produces the forces between the tires and the ground necessary to reduce vehicle speed or to hold the vehicle stationary. The brake system must permit the control of the braking forces as demanded by the pedal force of the driver. Since friction brakes in use on motor vehicles involve the conversion of kinetic energy of the moving vehicle into thermal energy at the brakes, the brake system also serves the function of heat storage and heat dissipation.

7-2. DIFFERENT CONCEPTS USED IN BRAKING SYSTEMS

Federal standards demand certain performance and design requirements of automotive brake systems. Many aspects of modern braking systems reflect their great accident avoidance potential and contribution to highway safety.

7-2.1. Intended Braking Function. Motor vehicles are equipped with brake systems which produce vehicle retardation even if certain components of the brake system fail.

The service brake is the primary system producing the design performance with the system in an unfailed condition. Levels of braking performance in terms of stopping distance or deceleration are dictated by Federal Government Standards for both hydraulic and air brake systems. Some brake system components such as brake pedal may be shared by the service brake and the emergency brake system.

The emergency brake system is that intact portion of the service brake system which produces a braking force in the event of a failure in the brake system. Failure modes include circuit or brake line failure (fluid leakage), power assist failure, and indirectly brake fade, i.e., a loss of braking effectiveness mostly due to overheating or brake lining contamination.

The parking brake uses an independent brake application system, either foot or hand operated, but may use the friction surfaces between brake drum (or disc) and brake lining of the service brake. Foot operated parking brakes do not permit a gradual brake force modulation, and consequently are unsafe for vehicle deceleration in an emergency stop. Hand operated secondary or emergency systems permit brake force modulation. European brake standards—contrary to U.S. Standards—require a certain vehicle deceleration produced by the secondary brake system, commonly called hand brake.

7–2.2. Brake Force Production. During braking, the kinetic energy due to vehicle speed and potential energy due to down hill travel of the vehicle are converted into thermal energy at the friction surface of the brake and at the tire-road interface. When a wheel locks up and slides over the ground all energy is converted into thermal energy at the sliding tire-to-ground interface. In the braking process the brake generates a retarding torque as a function of the applied pedal force. The pedal force–braking torque characteristics are determined by the mechanical/pneumatic or mechanical/hydraulic parameters of the braking system. The actual deceleration or decrease in speed of the vehicle is determined by the brake torque, the tire size, tire-to-road friction characteristics, and the normal force between tire and road. Details of braking analysis are discussed in Chapter 20.

(*a*) *Mechanical Brakes.* Mechanical brakes use mechanical devices such as cables and linkages to transmit pedal force to the wheel brakes. In current design practice, mechanical brake systems are used for parking and hand brakes. Their mechanical efficiency is low with approximately 65%. An efficiency of 65% indicates that 35% of the pedal effort is lost in terms of friction and is not available for vehicle braking. Mechanical brakes in poor condition may exhibit efficiencies below 60%. Frequent adjustment and lubrication is required for proper operation.

(*b*) *Non-Powered Hydraulic Brakes.* Non-powered hydraulic brakes are used commonly on small light-weight vehicles. Non-powered or standard brakes do not use any assist to increase the braking performance of the vehicle. All hydraulic brake systems consist of three major elements: the pedal force actuating system, the pedal effort transmission system, and the wheel brakes. Fig. 7–1 illustrates a typical hydraulic brake system. Application of the pedal force causes the brake pedal to be displaced. The pedal linkage is designed to produce a mechanical force advantage between the pedal and the master cylinder piston resulting in a displacement of the piston which is less than the pedal displacement. The master cylinder traps the brake fluid in the brake line, thereby developing a hydraulic brake line pressure.

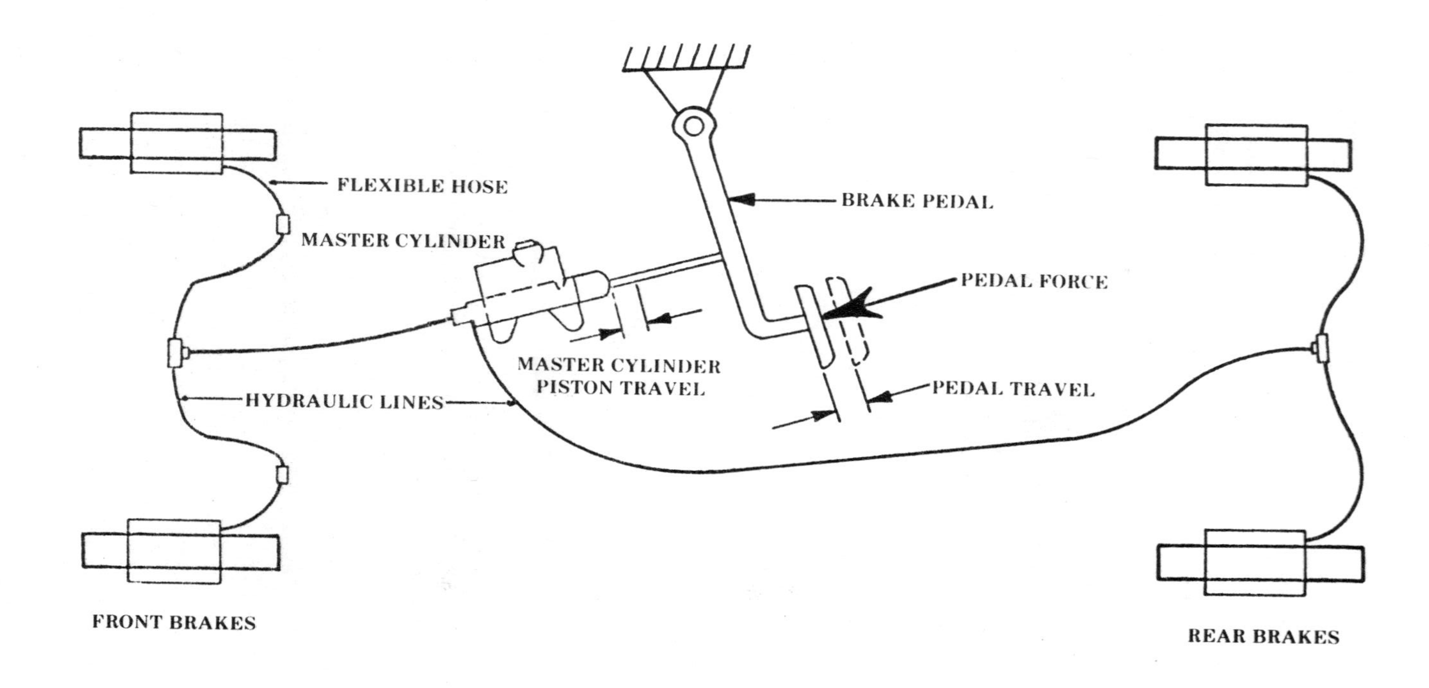

Figure 7-1. Hydraulic Brake System

Since the hydraulic pressure is transmitted equally throughout the system, all wheel cylinders experience the same brake line pressure, and consequently all brakes are evenly applied. The cross-sectional area of the master cylinder and those of the wheel cylinders are chosen to produce an increase of force transmitted between master cylinder and wheel cylinders. This force increase is accomplished by having wheel cylinder cross-sectional areas that are greater than that of the master cylinder. Since the master cylinder piston travel is limited by the pedal ratio and pedal travel, the transmission ratio between master cylinder and wheel cylinders is limited also. In order to keep the pedal force level below a certain maximum value (frequently 150 lb. is considered as the upper maximum pedal force for maximum braking performance), an assist unit (vacuum booster) is added to the standard brake system.

Advantages of hydraulic brakes are rapid response, good modulation or controllability by the driver, and equal transmission of brake line pressure to all wheel brakes. Hydraulic brakes have a high efficiency, are insensitive to environmental factors, and self lubricating.

(c) *Vacuum-Assisted Hydraulic Brakes.* Vacuum-assisted hydraulic brakes use a vacuum booster to assist the driver in his braking effort. The common system sometimes called mastervac, involves a vacuum assist unit in which the gradual control of the vacuum assist is accomplished by a reaction or control disc illustrated in Fig. 7–2. The vacuum booster is installed between the pedal and the master cylinder. The assist force, acting upon the pushrod which actuates the master cylinder piston, is produced by the difference in pressure across the booster piston with the vacuum or low pressure on the master cylinder side, and the atmospheric or high pressure on the input side. The vacuum developed in the intake manifold of gasoline engines is sufficient to actuate the booster. Diesel and Wankel engines require separate vacuum pumps due to their insufficient manifold vacuum.

Vacuum boosters increase the brake system gain by as much as 8 for most domestic passenger cars and approximately 4 for foreign cars. A gain of 8 means that the effect of the pedal force is increased eightfold. Although high gains permit maximum braking performance with small pedal forces, in the event of a booster failure the driver will most likely be unable to produce sufficient pedal force to decelerate the vehicle at an acceptable level.

The application of the assist force may be controlled hydraulically by a special valve arrangement. The hydraulic control of the vacuum application is used frequently in speciality vehicles, vans, and motor

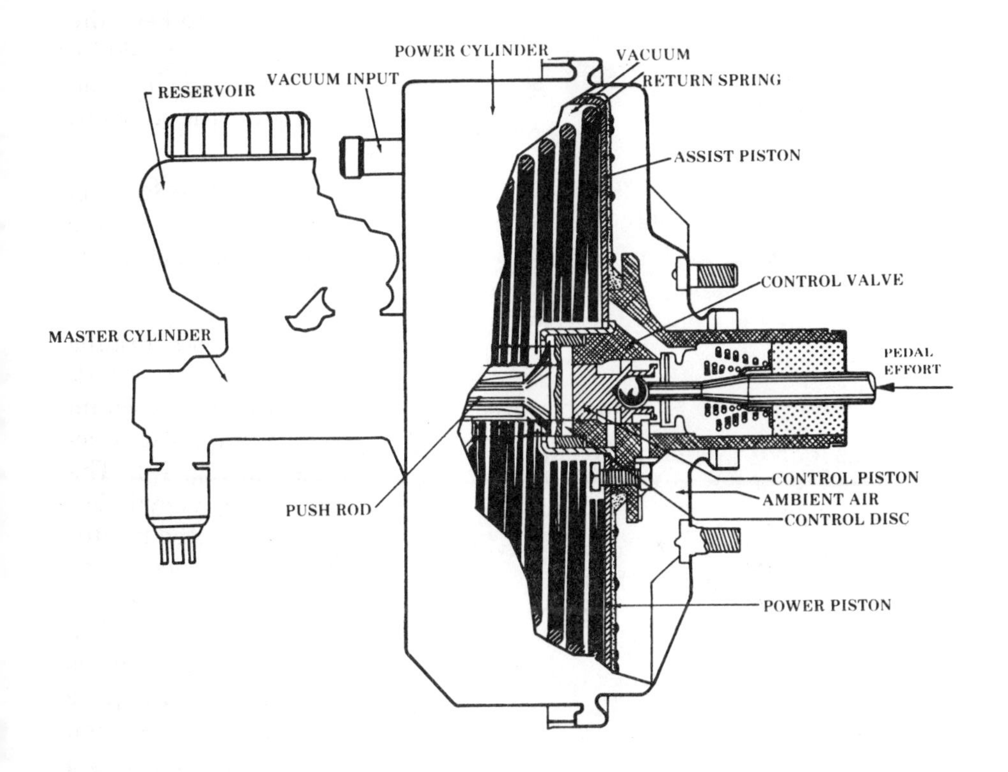

Figure 7-2. Mastervac in Applied Position

homes. The hydraulic control, sometimes called hydrovac, requires two master cylinders and a valve arrangement. One master cylinder is foot operated and produces the hydraulic line pressure required to control the vacuum application. The second master cylinder mounted directly to the vacuum booster traps the brake fluid in the brake lines and produces the hydraulic brake line pressure. The piston of the second master cylinder is actuated by the vacuum booster force and by the pressure produced by the pedal effort.

Booster saturation is defined as that point of booster operation beyond which no further assist increase is accomplished, i.e., the maximum assist pressure difference is acting across the booster piston. Further increases are only possible by means of drastic increases in pedal force. Details of brake system analysis are found in Ref. 11.

(*d*) *Full Power Hydraulic Brakes.* Full power hydraulic brakes use a pump to produce high oil pressure for the assist function.

Two different designs of full-power hydraulic brake systems can be identified: 1. The pump brake system with master cylinder and 2. The pump brake system with accumulator without master cylinder. Discussion follows:

1. Pump Brake System with Master Cylinder:

The pump system with master cylinder consists of the standard hydraulic brake system equipped with a special master cylinder. Connected to the master cylinder is the pump circuit. Both the brake and assist circuits are completely separate but use the same type of brake fluid so that in the event of leakage no fluid contamination occurs. The schematic of the system is shown in Fig. 7–3. The brake system consists of the pump (1), reservoir (2), the master cylinder (3), the assist unit or booster (4), the standard hydraulic brake lines (5), wheel cylinders (6), and wheel brakes (7). The assist characteristics, defined as the ratio of force upon the master cylinder piston to pedal force into the master cylinder, is a function of the effective area and the pushrod area of the assist unit. In the case of pump failure the pedal effort is transmitted directly upon the master cylinder piston and a reduced manual brake application is available. An important design consideration is the use of moderate assist characteristics so that no excessive pedal forces are required in the event of a power failure.

The pump is a separate pump or the pump of the steering system. It delivers a constant flow of fluid through the assist unit. In the event of brake application, the fluid flow is obstructed which results in an increase of fluid pressure. This pressure acts upon the master cylinder

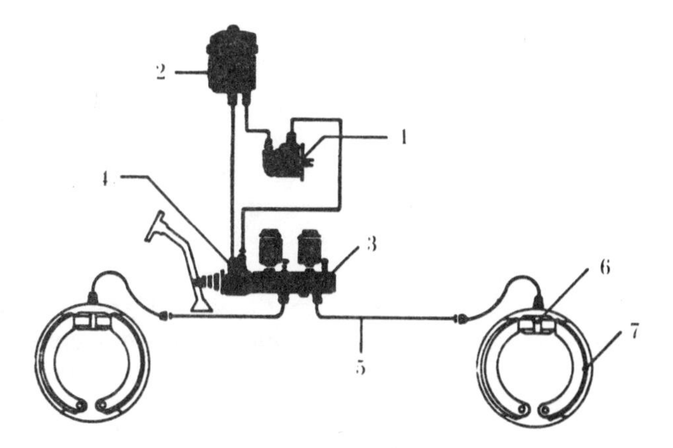

Figure 7-3. Schematic of Pump Power Hydraulic Brake System

piston and the pedal force input rod. This condition allows a very sensitive pedal force modulation by the driver. The maximum pressure level is limited by a check valve. Assist pressure has to be developed from zero to the desired level. The response time of the assist system is a direct function of the time required to build up pressure. Full power systems using an accumulator for storage of pressurized assist fluid have shorter delay times. The pump, either driven directly off the engine or by an electric motor delivers high pressure fluid only when the accumulator pressure has decreased below a certain value. If the same brake application energy had to be stored by a vacuum assist unit, a volume approximately 40–50 times larger than that associated with a medium pressure accumulator, or 100–130 times larger than that associated with a high pressure accumulator would be required.

The energy stored in the accumulator is affected by ambient temperature. The fluid volume available for braking at high pressures decreases with decreasing temperature. For example, an accumulator having a volume of 40 in.^{3} available between the pressure range of 2600 and 2100 psi when operating at 176°F, provides only 15 in.^{3} when the temperature is minus 40°F (Ref. 11).

2. Pump Brake System with Accumulator Without Master Cylinder:

The accumulator system consists of the pump, the accumulator, the foot valve, and the standard hydraulic brake system. The accumulator pressure is modulated by the foot valve and is applied directly upon the wheel cylinder of the wheel brakes. Since no master cylinder is used, no manual brake application is available in the event of a power source failure. For this reason a separate emergency brake system is provided in case the major system fails. In many cases the accumulator capacity is designed so that several brake applications are possible if the pump fails.

The pumps used in accumulator brake systems are either vane or radial piston designs. Vane pumps are generally limited to a pressure of approximately 1400 psi, extreme pressure levels may go as high as 2000 psi. Radial piston type pumps may produce pressures up to 3000 psi and volume flow rates of approximately 0.06 in.^{3} per revolution. Pumps are commonly driven directly by the vehicle engine by pulleys and belts or gears. In some applications electrically driven pumps are used.

A comparison of full power systems with vacuum-assisted brakes indicates the latter to be the most economical power source, assuming a sufficient quantity of vacuum is available. However, exhaust emission regulations and fuel injection systems have much reduced the degree of vacuum available as a power source. Consequently, more and more future designs will require a hydraulic energy source consisting of a pump, and if necessary, a gas-loaded accumulator. The latter becomes necessary for the efficient and high-performance-oriented operation of advanced antiskid brake systems. In the case of an accumulator installation, a relatively small pump, which only charges the accumulator when the charge pressure falls below a certain level is sufficient.

(*e*) *Air Brake Systems.* Air brake systems use principles similar to those of full-power accumulator brakes. The pedal force of the driver is used only to modulate the flow, and thus pressure, of the working fluid between the accumulator and the wheel brakes. As the name implies, the working fluid is air. Since air brake systems operate at maximum pressures of approximately 120 psi, the size of the components is significantly larger than those found in full power hydraulic brake systems.

Air brake systems consist of a variety of components which are used to maintain a supply of compressed air, to direct and control the flow of air, and to transform the stored energy of the air into mechanical force at the wheel brakes.

The air compressor is driven by the engine, either by belt or gears. The lubricant of the engine serves also to lubricate the compressor. Standard compressors are cooled by air from the fan assembly. Optional compressors are cooled by the coolant from the engine cooling system.

The number of air tanks used and their location on the vehicle vary. The purpose of the air tanks is to provide a place to store compressed air for several brake applications with the engine stopped. A second function of the air tanks is to extract the moisture from the compressed air. The tanks allow the air heated during the compression to cool and the water vapor to condense. Most of this condensation occurs in the wet tank. The wet tank receives the compressed air from the compressor. The condensate is drained from the brake system by special drain valves. Optional moisture ejection valves are available. The supply of air for braking action is taken from the dry tank. A check valve between the wet and dry tanks prevents loss of air in the event of leakage in the wet tank or compressor discharge line.

Safety valves, installed in the air tanks, prevent a pressure level beyond a safe maximum.

The pressure protection valve is used to close the air lines to horns, doors, and other auxiliary equipment when the pressure in the main air system falls below 65 psi. With this valve, sufficient brake power will be available to stop the vehicle in the event of a pressure loss to 65 psi.

Air brake systems are equipped with one or more quick release valves. The quick release valve is used at both front and rear brakes on most vehicles. The purpose of the valve is the quick release of the brakes by increasing the exhaust of the air from the brake chambers without requiring the return flow of the discharged air to go through the application valve.

The brake application valve is used by the driver to modulate the degree of braking effort. Often termed foot valve or treadle valve, it only controls the flow of air, and consequently, in the event of complete air pressure loss no manual braking action is available. Some brake application valves provide a gradual application of the parking brake if the foot pedal is depressed beyond its normal level.

The brake chamber is used at each wheel to convert the energy of the compressed air into the mechanical force and motion required to apply the brakes. The brake chamber serves the same function as the wheel cylinder in hydraulic brake systems.

For vehicles towing trailers equipped with air brake systems, additional components are provided in the tow vehicle.

The trailer brake hand control valve controls the air pressure delivered to the trailer brakes. The tractor protection valve controls the operation of the trailer brakes in emergency situations. It will automatically be activated when the pressure in the tractor brake system falls below 45 psi.

The tractor protection break-away valve also is used in conjunction with the tractor protection control valve to control the operation of the trailer brakes in emergency situations. Both service and emergency trailer brake lines run through this valve. Its main function is to protect the tractor air brake system from loss of pressure in the event of pressure loss in the trailer brake system.

Since the tractor-protection valve is easy to use by the driver by means of the control lever in the cab, it is frequently used to apply the trailer brakes for parking the tractor-semitrailer. However, this should not be done. If a leak develops, no more air can be supplied to the trailer reservoir from the tractor since the tractor protection valve has vented the supply or emergency line between the tractor protection valve and relay-emergency valve.

When a trailer is added to the tractor, special provisions are made on the trailer to apply the trailer brakes. A trailer reservoir is used to store the compressed air for the trailer brakes. A relay-emergency valve installed on the trailer is used to supply the trailer reservoir with compressed air from the tractor reservoir and to control the brake line pressure and hence the brake force of the trailer—as demanded by the driver. The control line comes from the brake application valve and, when the driver depresses the foot pedal, pressure equal to the tractor brake line pressure opens a port in the relay-emergency valve and allows air at the same pressure level to leave the trailer reservoir and go through the relay-emergency valve to the trailer brake chambers. In case of a trailer breakaway the trailer brakes will be applied automatically because the emergency section of the relay-emergency valve will use full trailer reservoir pressure to apply the trailer brakes. If a severe trailer brake leak, or trailer breakaway occurs, the tractor brake system is protected by the tractor protection valve. It is designed to control the service and supply lines to the trailer. It is both automatic and manual. In an emergency the driver can activate it by use of the manual control located in the cab. If the driver does not operate the control, the tractor protection valve automatically will apply the trailer brakes—when the trailer brake line pressure has decreased to between 20 and 45 psi—by venting the supply or emergency line and thereby triggering the emergency section of the relay-emergency valve. The relay-emergency valve is combined with a quick-release valve to allow a quick release of the air from the trailer brake chambers when the brakes are released.

In the case of heavy trucks and trailers various secondary systems have been designed. If air brakes are used, the entire system can be duplicated and multi-diaphragm chambers can be used. More commonly, spring brakes are used which use a compressed spring as actuator of the wheel brakes in the event of a malfunctioning of the service brake. Recently, spring brakes have been installed on both tractor and semi-trailers to provide increased parking brake performance. Light to medium weight trucks frequently use a band brake—mounted behind the transmission—as secondary brake system.

Special valves are used to proportion the brake force among axles. The front brake limiting valve in combination with the quick release valve permits delivery of full brake pressure to the front brakes when on dry roads, or at the option of the driver, limits pressure to the front brakes to 50% of the brake application valve delivery pressure when on slippery roads.

The proportioning valve is used to modulate the brake line pressure to the rear axle(s) according to the loading condition of the vehicle. When manually operated, the driver adjusts the valve position according to the load, when automatic, the static suspension deflection is used as input for valve adjustment. Manually operated proportioning valves can greatly advance safety during braking for short wheel base vehicles such as tractors operating in bobtail condition or mobile home tow tractors without load. Although domestic manufacturers do not commonly use these valves, foreign trucks frequently use valves that can be adjusted to four different brake force levels at the rear wheels: full, half, quarter and no brake force.

(*f*) *Compressed Air-Over-Hydraulic Brakes.* The air-over-hydraulic brake uses compressed air as assist medium to actuate a standard master cylinder in the hydraulic brake circuit. The major advantage of the air-over-hydraulic brake is the availability of compressed air for braking trailers equipped with air brakes when connected to a hydraulically braked tractor.

Air-over-hydraulic brakes can be designed as dual circuits by either using two assist units or a tandem master cylinder connected to a single assist unit.

A single circuit air-over-hydraulic brake system is illustrated in Fig. 7–4 with all essential components identified. The air compressor (1) charges the air tank (2). The air pressure is adjusted by the pressure regulator (3). The application valve (4) controls the air flow to the assist unit (5) and force application to the master cylinder (6). Hydraulic brake line pressure is transmitted to the wheel brakes

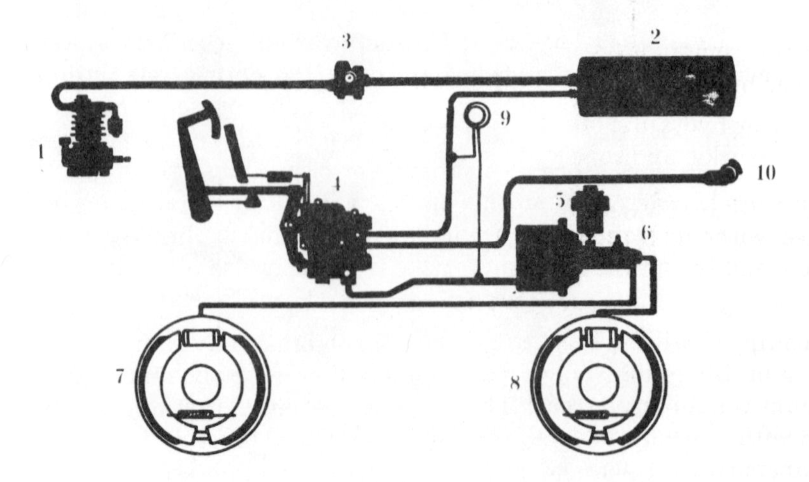

Figure 7-4. Air-Over-Hydraulic Brake System (Single Circuit)

at the front (7) and rear axle (8). Air pressure is measured by the gauge (9). Trailer brake supply line connections are indicated (10).

A more efficient design is provided by combining the air application valve with the master cylinder into one unit. This system allows hydraulically braked trucks to tow pneumatically braked trailers, allows the combination of hydraulic and air brakes on the same vehicle, and provides for the efficient design of dual circuit brakes for heavy vehicles. An example of the application of the combination brake valve to the brakes of a tandem axle truck is illustrated in Fig. 7-5. The components are: compressor (1), air tank (2), pressure regu-

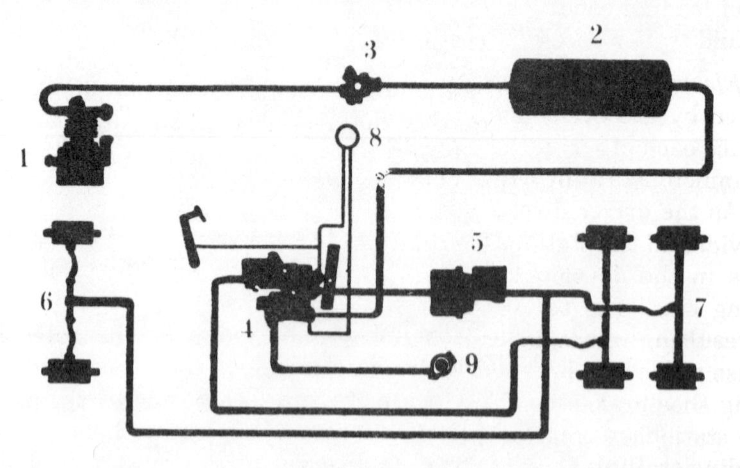

Figure 7-5. Air-Over-Hydraulic Brakes for Tandem Axle Truck

lator (3), combination brake valve (4), assist unit (5), front brakes (6), rear brakes (7), pressure gauge (8) and trailer brake line (9).

Air-over-hydraulic brakes are frequently used on military vehicles, foreign trucks, and construction equipment.

(*g*) *Surge Brakes.* Surge brakes are designed to apply the trailer brakes without requiring a hydraulic connection between the tow vehicle and the trailer.

The trailer is connected to the truck by the tongue. If the trailer is not equipped with a braking system, the inertia force of the trailer during braking must be absorbed by the brakes of the truck. Light to medium weight trailers and particularly rental trailers are equipped often with a surge brake. During braking the inertia force of the trailer is transmitted through the tongue to the truck. The surge brake uses this tongue force to actuate either a mechanical system of linkages or a hydraulic master cylinder. The deceleration of the trailer is a function of the trailer weight. For trailers with varying loading conditions the surge brake offers significant advantages.

Surge brakes are generally not used on heavy trailers. Since the surge brake requires that a tongue force exist between truck and trailer, the vehicle combination may become unstable when braking in a turn. The tongue force may be sufficiently large to cause the truck rear axle to slide sideways. Heavy trailers are therefore equipped with brakes that are actuated by a signal from the driver and not by the tongue force. Stability requirement on braking of heavy truck-trailer combinations is to reduce the tongue force to zero for all braking and loading conditions. This requirement is achieved when both truck and trailer decelerations are equal.

(*h*) *Electric Brakes.* Electric brakes are used in trailers and are actuated by the driver by a special lever. A rotating and stationary ring face each other in the wheel brake. The stationary ring replaces the common hydraulic wheel cylinder and is used to actuate the brake shoe. As the driver displaces the trailer brake lever, electric current is provided to the stationary ring resulting in magnetizing of it which results in the development of a torque between the stationary and rotating ring. The torque causes a slight rotation of the stationary ring resulting in an application of the brake shoes against the drum. The use of electric brakes is generally limited to duo-servo and two-leading shoe brakes. Reasons for this limitation are that the rotation of the stationary ring can actuate brake shoes in one direction only. A leading-trailing shoe brake, e.g., requires actuation of the leading shoe in the counter-clockwise direction and of the trailing shoe in the clockwise direction. Gradual control is generally difficult to accomplish due to little or no feedback to the control lever.

(*i*) *Continuous Brakes.* Continuous brakes are auxiliary retarding systems that provide low but continuous brake force particularly in long downhill vehicle travel.

Auxiliary brakes may be divided into two classes: engine brakes (engine speed dependent) and transmission or drive shaft brakes (drive shaft speed dependent). In the case of the engine brake, the retarding torque transmission can be interrupted by disengaging the clutch or selecting a neutral gear position. The drive shaft brake, once applied can be disconnected from the retarded wheels only through release of the control lever.

The engine of a vehicle in motion will, if the throttle is closed, exert a retarding force on the vehicle as a portion of the kinetic energy is absorbed by the frictional, compressive, and other mechanical losses in the engine. This retarding force is, however, very limited, and various methods have been devised for increasing the effectiveness of the engine as a brake. One such improvement consists of increasing the compressor action of the engine by closing off the exhaust. Retarders of this type are generally termed exhaust brakes (Chapter 19). This type of retarder consists of a throttle in the exhaust system which can be closed either by mechanical, electrical, or pneumatic means. The brake torque generated depends on the gearing and engine speed. In general, at moderate and high velocities the primary braking system also must be applied since the generated brake torque is limited to about 70% of the motor drive torque. The major limiting design factor of an exhaust brake is associated with the exit valve spring. Increased pressure in the exhaust system tends to overcome the valve spring, forcing the valve to stay open and consequently limiting the compressor action.

Further improvement in engine brake torque can be achieved by altering the camshaft timing such that the compressor action of the engine is increased. The engine brake torque may be over 100% of the maximum drive torque of the engine. Large retarding torques, however, can only be achieved by using a low gear, which in turn results in undesirably low cruising speeds and thus increased per mile operating costs. No adverse effects on engine wear have been observed with this type of brake. It is claimed that shoe and drum wear can be reduced from 25–50% with the use of exhaust brakes, depending on conditions. Reference throughout has been to diesel-engine equipped vehicles for which the brake specifically is intended, but an exhaust brake also can be fitted to a gasoline engine. Its performance may be slightly lower since the gasoline engine, operating on a lower compression ratio, necessarily has a larger clearance volume and is thus less effective when used as a compressor.

The hydrodynamic retarder is a device that uses viscous damping as the mechanism for producing a retarding torque. The viscous damping or internal fluid friction is transformed into thermal energy and dissipated by a heat exchanger, commonly the engine radiator. In its design the hydrodynamic retarder is similar to that of a hydrodynamic clutch (Chapter 9); however, its turbine or drive rotor is stationary. The retarding torque is produced by the rotor that pumps a fluid against the stator. The stator reflects the fluid back against the rotor, and a continuous internal pumping cycle is developed. The reaction forces, and hence the retarding torque, are absorbed by the rotor which is connected to the drive wheels of the vehicle. The magnitude of the retarding torque depends upon the amount of fluid in the retarder and the pressure level at which it is introduced into the retarder.

One important advantage of this type of retarder is that the retarding force is greater at higher vehicle speeds. Hydrodynamic retarders operate independently of engine, clutch, transmission, or electrical power supply. They are connected to the drive axle and represent an almost indestructible no-wear braking element when properly designed. When used on a trailer, a separate cooler becomes necessary. Skidding at the wheels is impossible since the retarding torque approaches zero with decreasing retarder drive shaft speed. When the retarder is installed in a powered unit, i.e., a tractor or truck, it prevents undercooling of the engine below normal operating temperature on long mountain grades by transferring the thermal energy generated through viscous damping in the retarder to the engine cooling system.

The principle of the electric retarder is based on the production of eddy currents within a metal disc rotating between two electromagnets which develop a retarding torque on the rotating disc. When the electromagnets are partially energized, the retarding torque is reduced. When the energization is zero, the retarding torque is zero also. The eddy current results in heating of the disc. The cooling of the disc is accomplished by means of convection heat transfer with ventilated rotors. Initially, all retarding energy is absorbed by and stored in the rotor material. Only at elevated temperatures does convective cooling occur. The major problem of the eddy current retarder is associated with the necessity of high brake temperatures for efficient convective cooling capacity—similar to that experienced with friction-type wheel brakes. The high temperatures cause a decrease in retarding effectiveness due to the demagnetizing of the rotor. Depending on the particular material composition involved, this limiting temperature lies near 1350° F.

7-3. BRAKE SYSTEM COMPONENTS

7-3.1. Standard Master Cylinder. The master cylinder governs the braking operation. It is controlled by foot application. A single circuit brake system consists of one brake line for pressure transmission between master cylinder and all wheel cylinders. If a brake fluid leak develops at any point of the brake line, the entire service brake fails. A master cylinder used for a single circuit brake system is illustrated in Fig. 7-6. The essential elements of any master cylinder are

1. Reservoir
2. Piston
3. Secondary seal
4. Feed port
5. Compensation port
6. Breather hole
7. Stop-light switch (optional)
8. Primary seal
9. Seal protector
10. Residual-pressure check valve
11. Pressure chamber

The functions of a master cylinder are as follows: The master cylinder has a self regulating fluid supply which ensures that the brake system is always full of brake fluid and that for drum brakes a slight residual pressure remains in the brake lines. The fluid enclosed in the master cylinder, brake lines, and wheel cylinders is constantly subjected to pressure and volume variations. When the brakes are released, the brake system fluid is directly connected to the reservoir by the compensating port. The check valve is used in connection with all drum brake systems and provides for a slight pressure (7-20 psi) to remain in the brake system after the brakes are released. The residual pressure keeps the pedal free-travel to a minimum, forces the wheel cylinder seal lips lightly against the cylinders bore to avoid entry of air, and to enable bleeding of the brake systems by the use of the brake pedal. Disc brake systems do not have residual brake line pressure; otherwise brake pads constantly drag on the brake rotors

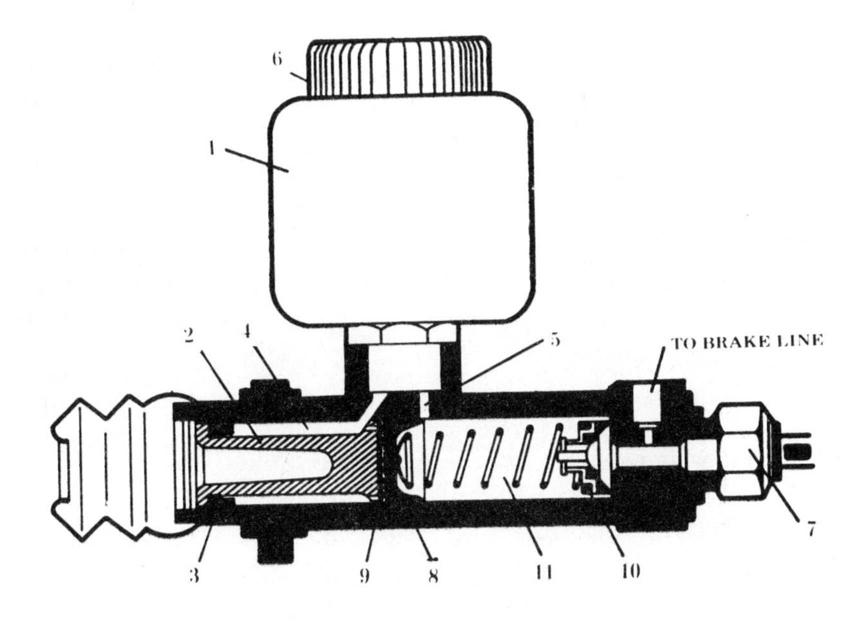

Figure 7-6. Master Cylinder (Single Circuit)

resulting in hot brakes, possibly brake fluid vaporization, and excessive pad wear. The primary seal serves three functions. It seals off the pressure chamber; closes off the compensation port, and allows reverse flow of fluid upon releasing the brakes. Behind the primary seal a space is provided which is always full of brake fluid and sealed off by the secondary seal. When the brake pedal is released after a brake application, the fluid in the space behind the primary seal is forced through the holes in the forward flange of the piston and the depressed primary seal into the pressure chamber. Consequently, no air can be drawn into the system due to the return flow of brake fluid past the primary seal and from the reservoir through the feed port. The reservoir is connected to the master cylinder pressure chamber by the compensation port. The reservoir may be an integral part of the master cylinder or connected by a pipe or hose.

7-3.2. Tandem Master Cylinder. A dual brake system consists of two brake circuits that are hydraulically separated. The individual brake systems may be designed to divide the system front to rear, diagonally, or in various other fashions (Section 20-9.2). If a brake fluid leak develops in one circuit, the other circuit still provides emergency stopping capability. A dual brake system uses a tandem master cylinder for pressure build up. A tandem master cylinder basically consists of two master cylinders behind one another in a common housing. The operation is in principle the same as that of a single circuit master cylinder. When the push rod piston is moved toward the floating piston, the compensation port is closed and the resulting pressure build up in the chamber in front of the push rod piston is transmitted by means of the floating piston to the floating piston chamber. The floating piston moves forward and closes off the compensation port and the brake line pressure production begins.

7-3.3. Stepped Bore Master Cylinder. A stepped bore master cylinder functions similar to a tandem master cylinder. The smaller diameter bore pressure chamber produces higher operating pressures than the larger diameter bore chamber. Frequently, the smaller diameter chamber is connected to the front disc brakes which require a higher brake line pressure than the rear drum brakes.

7-3.4. Special Stepped Bore Tandem Master Cylinder. The special stepped bore tandem master cylinder basically functions like a normal tandem master cylinder. In the event of a brake circuit failure it provides better pedal force/deceleration characteristics closer to the unfailed performance than those of the normal tandem master cylinder (Ref. 11).

7-3.5. Wheel Cylinder. The wheel cylinders transmit the hydraulic brake line pressure to the brake shoes. The wheel cylinders are bolted to the backing plate and consists of housing, seals, piston or pistons, and tappets which link the pistons with the brake shoe. A retainer spring between seal and housing is used to preload the seal by means of a spreader. Wheel cylinders may be single- or double-acting. Wheel cylinders may be designed to have stepped bore cylinders to produce different brake shoe actuating forces for the same brake line pressure input. Long stroke wheel cylinders are used for applications requiring long strokes that cannot be produced by wheel cylinders mounted inside the brake.

7-3.6. Brake Chamber. An air brake chamber is used at each braked wheel to convert the energy of compressed air into mechanical force and motion to apply the brake shoes. Brake chambers commonly use diaphragms that cause a reduction in actuating force as push rod travel exceeds 1.75 to 2 in. (Ref. 11). For emergency braking or parking air brake chambers are combined with a spring brake. During normal operation the spring is pressed together by compressed air. Only during an emergency situation when the system pressure falls below a certain level, or when the brake system is exhausted as in a parking application, does the spring force actuate the pushrod and the brake shoes.

7-3.7. Brake Shoe Configuration. Basic drum brakes are illustrated in Fig. 7-7. Drum brakes are identified by the leading or trailing shoe effect. A leading shoe increases the effectiveness of the brake by the self actuating force due to lining-to-drum friction (servo effect). A trailing shoe has no servo action. Shown in Fig. 7-7 are the leading-trailing shoe brake, the two-leading shoe brake, and the duo-servo brake. In the case of the duo-servo brake the support force at the end of the first or primary shoe becomes the actuating force of the second or secondary shoe. The duo-servo brake exhibits the highest self ener-

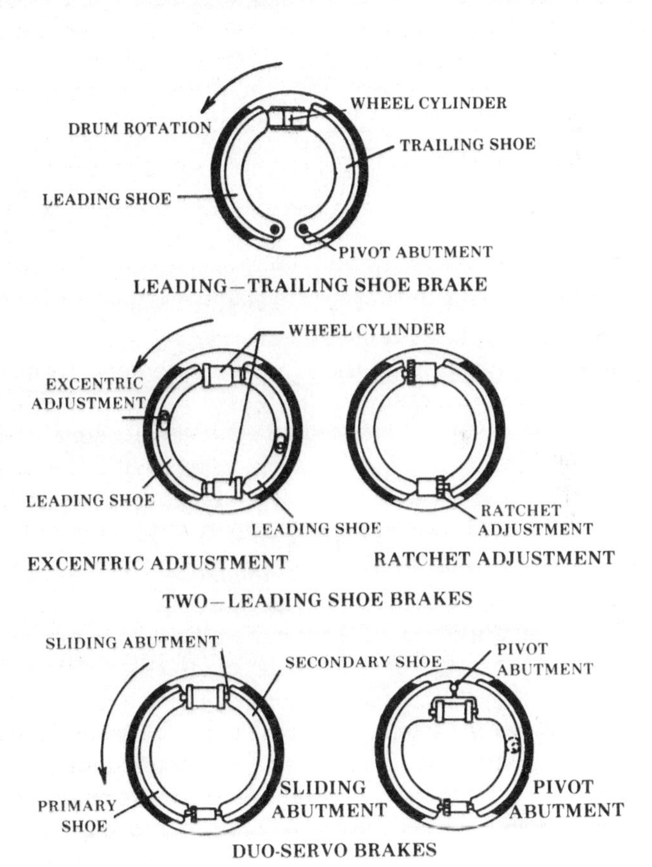

Figure 7-7. Basic Drum Brakes

gizing or servo effect. Although the brakes shown in Fig. 7-7 are of hydraulic brake systems, each of the shoe configurations shown can be used in connection with mechanical or air brake systems.

7-3.8. "S" Cam Brake. "S" cam brakes are used in heavy trucks and trailers equipped with air brakes. The brake shoe configuration most frequently is of the leading-trailing shoe type. A cam—commonly referred to as "S" cam due to its letter "S" shape—is located between the movable ends of the brake shoes. Rollers are installed at each movable end of each brake shoe to reduce friction between cam and shoe. The rotation of the cam is accomplished by a lever arm—commonly referred to as slack adjuster—connected between cam and brake chamber. Although less frequently, different cam geometries are used.

7-3.9. Wedge Brake. Wedge brakes are used mostly in heavy trucks and trailers in connection with air brake systems. The brake shoe configuration can be either of the leading-trailing or two-leading shoe type. However, the two-leading shoe wedge brake is used most frequently. In a wedge brake the shoe actuation is accomplished by a wedge which is forced between the ends of the brake shoes. The wedge is actuated by an air brake chamber—in the case of an air brake system—or an externally mounted wheel cylinder—in the case of a hydraulic brake system. The entire assembly consists of the air chamber push rod, rollers, and plungers. Rollers are used to reduce friction between wedge surfaces. The air chamber may strictly be operated by air pressure or in a different design by a preloaded spring in the event the air pressure is reduced below a certain level.

7-3.10. Brake Shoe Adjustment. Brake shoe adjustment is required to compensate for lining wear. Manual adjusters should only be adjusted when the brakes are cold and the parking brake is in the fully released position. Frequently, adjusting mechanisms consist of a screw which is turned in or out to move the position of the tappet relative to the brake shoe. Adjusters may be located at the wheel cylinder or at the abutment. Automatic adjusters most frequently use a mechanism consisting of a threaded eye bolt and a split sleeve with corresponding thread fixed to the brake shoe. After initial installation a basic play is provided. If the play increases due to lining wear to a level of basic play plus one thread, the split sleeve will snap into the next thread and thereby reestablishing the basic play. Split sleeve type adjusters may be designed to fit in a wheel cylinder.

Adjustment of "S" cam brakes can be accomplished manually by rotating the slack adjuster on the camshaft to compensate for lining wear. In some cases automatic slack adjusters are provided. Wedge brakes generally are equipped with automatic adjusters.

7-3.11. Disc Brake. Disc brakes use calipers which press the brake pads against the brake rotor. Common disc brakes are of the fixed caliper or floating caliper design. The floating caliper disc brake is used when space limitations between caliper and rim do not permit the installation of a fixed caliper disc brake. Floating calipers tend to operate at lower temperatures during severe braking with reduced danger of brake fluid vaporization due to a greater exposure of the wheel cylinder to the cooling air stream. In some design applications the brake pad is extended to form a complete circular ring. The pad application and pressing action between rotor and pad ring may be accomplished by means of a ball and ramp mechanism. A disc brake of this type may exhibit a self-energizing behavior not found in common caliper disc brakes.

The adjustment of caliper disc brakes is automatic. Disc brake rotors may be solid or self-ventilated. Solid rotors are used on light weight vehicles.

Recently disc brakes for air brake systems have been designed. In most cases a screw rotated by a standard slack adjuster is used to press the pads against the rotor.

7-3.12. Parking Brake. Parking or secondary brake systems have been designed for disc brakes. The actuation is accomplished by forcing the brake pad against the rotor by means of wedges or cams. In designing the system care must be taken that the entire parking brake assembly is as rigid as possible to avoid elastic distortions which reduce the design application force below levels generally required for acceptable parking brake performance. Since hand application force and displacement are limited by human factors, parking disc brakes are generally not found on heavy vehicles due to their low brake factor.

7-3.13. Hydraulic Brake Line. Brake lines transmit the brake line pressure from the master cylinder to the wheel brakes. Brake lines are made of coated steel tubing. The pipe lines are connected by flared end sections and "T" and other special fittings. Fittings should be mounted as accessible as possible to provide for proper brake system inspection. Pipes should be installed such that protection against grit and stone impact is maximized. Loops that might trap air must be avoided. Brake lines must be installed such that heat from the exhaust system will not cause fluid overheating and possibly brake fluid vaporization.

Brake hoses are used to connect a moveable component of the brake system to the rigid chasis or body unit. Brake hoses must be as short as possible while still providing sufficient length to allow all movement, e.g., wheel vertical displacement and front wheel steering rotation. Torsional and tensile stress must be avoided in the installation. When undercoatings are applied to the bottom side of the car, extreme care must be taken to protect brake hoses from exposure to sprays and paints. Deterioration and failure of brake lines is discussed in Chapter 20.

7-3.14. Pressure Regulating Valves. Brake line pressure regulating valves are designed to modulate the pressure applied to a particular axle or wheel brakes in relationship to the supply pressure at the master cylinder or application valve. The regulating valves can be divided into three basic groups: (1) brake force limiting valve; (2) brake force proportioning valve with fixed shift point; (3) brake force proportioning valve with load or deceleration sensitive shift point adjustment.

1. Brake force limiting valve. The valve closes off the rear brake line at a certain brake line pressure and holds the brake line pressure in the rear brake line constant regardless of increases in supply pressures to the valve. Increases in brake fluid requirement in the closed off brake line due to thermal or elastic deformations of the brake drum or caliper are automatically adjusted by the valve through a brief reopening of the valve to the supply pressure. Once the pressure adjustment is completed, the valve automatically closes off the brake line with the limited pressure.

2. Brake force proportioning valves with fixed shift point. The valve permits the brake line pressure to increase in equal amounts in the supply line and brake line leading to the modulated axle. When the supply pressure has reached the shift point pressure, the valve closes and only a reduced brake line pressure reaches the modulated axle. Some valves use differential or stepped bore piston with the effective area ratio determining the proportioning between supply and exit pressure of the valve.

3. Brake force proportioning valves with load or deceleration sensitive shift point adjustment. The pressure proportioning (and pressure limiting) valve can be made more effective for different loading conditions or deceleration levels if the shift point is moved in proportion to the loading or deceleration of the vehicle. Load sensitive valves function in a fashion similar to proportioning valves with a fixed shift point. An additional mechanism is installed by which the force acting against the stepped bore piston can be varied according to the axle load. The shift point location is changed in proportion to the force acting on the stepped bore piston. Since axle load is a function

of both static and dynamic axle load changes, the shift point location is sensitive to loading and load distribution, and deceleration level. The variation of the force against the stepped bore piston of the valve is achieved by an adjustable linkage installed between vehicle body and axle, and consequently, changes the value setting as the suspension deflects.

Deceleration sensitive brake force proportioning devices use inertia valves in which a steel ball rolls up an inclined ramp at a certain deceleration. The movement of the ball causes a spring loaded valve to close which disconnects the modulated axle from the supply pressure. In some applications a pendulum controlling the brake line pressure to the modulated axle as a function of vehicle decelerations has been used.

Brake line pressure regulating valves of hydraulic brake systems are often combined with other valves into a single unit generally called a combination valve. Most combination valves serve three functions: (1) to function as brake force regulator; (2) to reduce the brake line pressure to the front disc brakes until the return spring force of the rear drum brakes is overcome, frequently called metering valve; (3) to actuate a switch in the event of a hydraulic leak in the brake system. Most combination valves are designed to bypass the proportioning function of the valve in the case of a front brake circuit failure. This feature becomes necessary to provide sufficiently large braking forces at the rear brakes when the front brakes failed.

7-4. WHEEL ANTILOCK BRAKE SYSTEM

7-4.1. Fundamental Considerations. Wheel-antilock brake systems prevent the wheels from locking during braking by adjusting the braking effort to the traction force available at the tire-roadway interface. Under normal braking conditions the driver operates the brakes as usual; however, on slippery roadways or during severe braking, as the driver causes the wheels to approach lockup, the device takes over and modulates the brake force independent of pedal force.

In general, wheel-antilock brake systems should provide the following:

1. Prevention of wheel lockup for all braking, loading, and road surface conditions
2. Minimum stopping distance
3. Vehicle stability and retention of steering and controllability.

Tests using wheel-antilock devices on dry pavement have demonstrated that, in some instances, a slight increase in stopping distance results, while in other cases a slight decrease in stopping distance is noted. However, wheel-antilock braking systems contribute considerably to the improvement of vehicle directional stability during braking. Skidding in normal cornering maneuvers is prevented by the lateral friction forces in the tire-road contact area. During braking, the capability of the tire to produce lateral friction forces is somewhat decreased, as is shown for a typical tire in Fig. 18–4. Note that this capability to produce lateral forces is a minimum when the wheel is locked. The antilock system keeps the tire slip at relatively low values during braking, which in turn allows the tire to produce lateral forces adequate to maintain vehicle directional stability.

7–4.2. Hydraulic Systems. A schematic of a typical wheel-antilock brake is illustrated in Fig. 7–8. A wheel speed sensor transmits the signal of impending wheel lockup to the logic control which in turn signals a modulator to release brake line pressure which causes the wheel rotational speed to increase again. The operation of a typical vacuum-assisted modulator is shown in Fig. 7–9. In the normal position during which no wheel-antilock braking occurs, a vacuum is maintained on both sides of the diaphragm with the displacement plunger holding the hydraulic shutoff valve open. If wheel lockup is imminent, the logic controller sends a signal to the solenoid valve, closing off the vacuum to the front side of the diaphragm. At the same time, the air valve is opened, producing a pressure differential across the diaphragm and movement of the plunger to the right. This closes the hydraulic shutoff valve which isolates that particular brake from the system. As the diaphragm and plunger move to the right, the brake line volume is increased, reducing brake line pressure. When the wheel begins to accelerate, the solenoid valve is closed, and the spring returns the diaphragm. Modulators may be a two-stage type that allow the brake line pressure to be reapplied at a slow or fast rate. Vacuum-powered modulators can be cycled between three to five times per second.

Ideally, an antiskid brake system would modulate all four wheels independently so that maximum longitudinal as well as lateral tire forces are produced. Furthermore, such a system would allow panic brake applications even while operating near or at the limit turning speed of the vehicle. Limit turning speed is defined as the maximum speed the vehicle can maintain in the absence of braking without losing front or rear wheel lateral traction. Obviously, these specifications require brake systems designed with sophisticated electronic and hydraulic hardware.

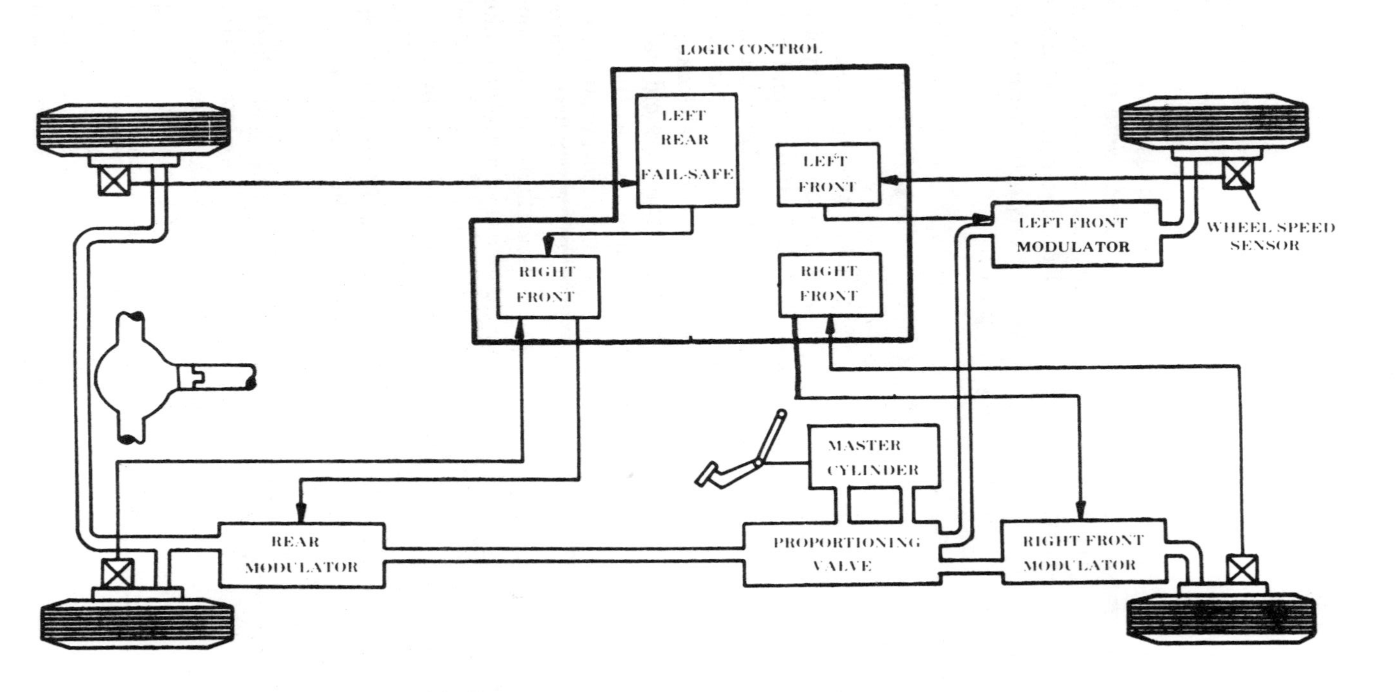

Figure 7–8. Independent Front, Select-Low Rear, Control Method Wheel-Antilock Brake System

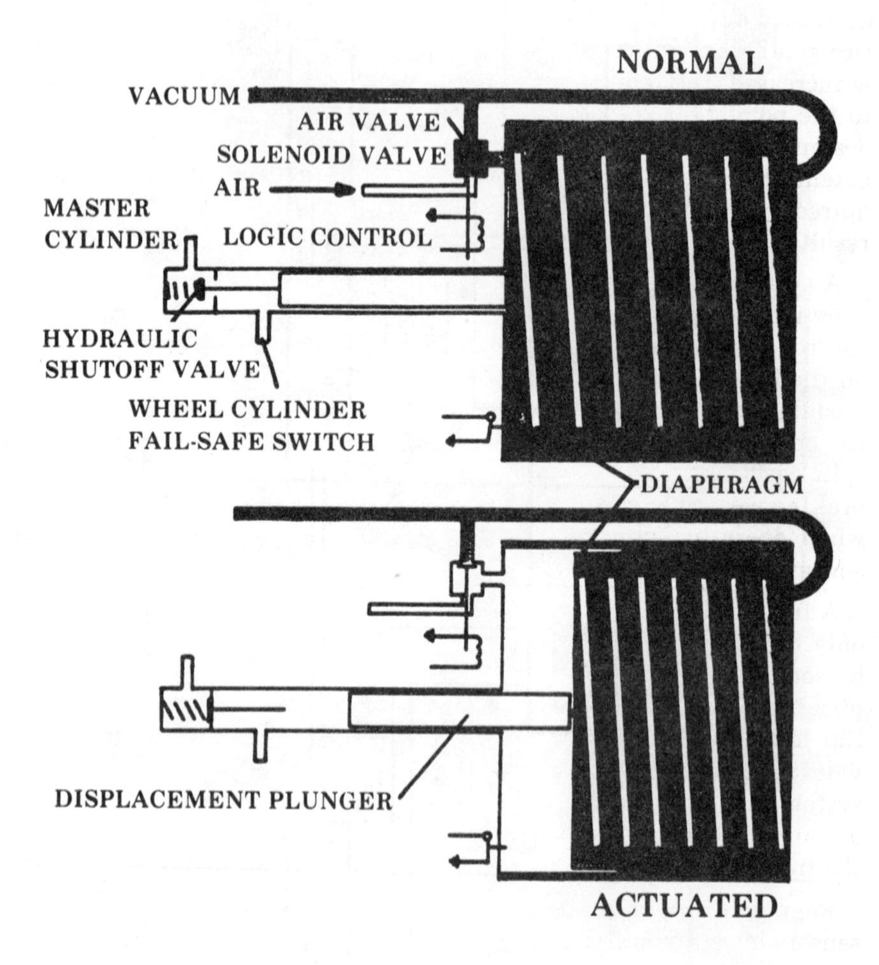

Figure 7–9. Typical One-Stage Vacuum Assisted Modulator

The performance characteristics of these systems are such that the longitudinal slip or brake force increases less rapidly—approximately 0.3 sec is required to reach maximum value; consequently, the lateral tire force is not degraded appreciably. Also, the vehicle speed has decreased during the buildup of the brake force, causing a decrease in tire side forces required to continue a stable turn. As the brake force is increased, the lateral tire force demand also continues to decrease to the point that corresponds to the controlled longitudinal tire slip design threshold. However, now the vehicle speed has decreased to the extent that the lateral tire forces available exceed the demand required by the turning vehicle, and a totally stable braking maneuver results.

A system, less expensive than the four-wheel independent system, uses independent front wheel modulation and select-low, rear axle control. Here, select-low refers to the fact that the rear wheel operating on the low coefficient surface of a split coefficient surface controls the modulation of both rear wheels. Some performance degradation from the optimum braking on the rear axle is suffered when operating on split coefficient surfaces. Braking in a turn, as well as straight-line braking performance, approximates that of four-wheel control systems when operating on typical highways including wet and dry road surfaces.

A further decrease in costs is obtained through systems modulating only the rear axle, either each wheel independently, or the rear axle by sensing the propeller shaft angular rotation. In a panic brake application or while operating on slippery road surfaces, the front wheels can lock, thus rendering the vehicle unsteerable. Although this provides a stable stop, the accident avoidance characteristics of such a system may not prove to be cost beneficial. When braking in a turn, a rear wheel or axle controlled vehicle will leave the curved path when the front wheels are locked.

Rear axle controlled antiskid systems employing propeller shaft sensors have several shortcomings, both from a theoretical as well as a practical point of view. This type of inexpensive modulation device apparently was designed to circumvent problems associated with large rear-brake-torque bias typically found on large and medium domestic passenger cars. However, when operating such vehicles in a turn without locking the front wheels, the lateral load transfer on the rear axle causes a decrease of the normal force on the inner rear wheel resulting in wheel lockup for that wheel. In this condition the propeller shaft sensor averaging the signal it receives may cause the outer wheel to lock up also, rendering the vehicle unstable. The cause of this instability lies in the operational characteristics of the differential sensor. If the brake force modulation is designed to achieve minimum stopping distances in straight-line stops, the modulation signal will be selected for that condition. For straight-line braking the propeller shaft speed changes proportionally with the changes of wheel speed, assuming uniform tire-road friction for each wheel. In a turning maneuver, however, the differential housing speed with the inner wheel locked will be half the speed of the outer wheel. The propeller shaft speed will decrease correspondingly. This information will be interpreted by the sensor as if both wheels were approaching wheel lockup. The system responds with a rapid decrease in brake line pressure and, thus, near-zero brake torques on both wheels and nearly free-rolling wheels. At this instant, the sensor may over-react, causing excessive brake line pressure buildup and subsequent lockup of both rear wheels for a time period which, although short, is sufficient to cause the rear wheels to lose lateral stability.

It is obvious that a poorly designed antilock brake system may not yield meaningful safety benefits. Properly engineered conventional or proportional brake systems will produce equal or even better results. Furthermore, rear wheel antilock brake systems still render the vehicle nonsteerable during panic brake application with the front wheels locked. Investigations of accident studies indicate that no significant safety benefits may be expected with stable yet nonsteerable rear antiskid vehicles, especially in intersection type accidents. Similar or even improved, yet less costly, braking performance is available with a properly designed brake system exhibiting sufficiently low values of rear brake bias.

Pump pressurized or full hydraulic brake systems use high fluid pressure as energy source for brake line pressure regulation rather than engine vacuum. High pressure permits the design of compact components and the operation at higher frequencies than vacuum-powered systems. If the pressure regulator possesses a sufficiently large frequency range and adaptive capability, the pressure regulating frequency may be varied with changing conditions at the tire-road interface. Some full hydraulic pressure regulators have frequencies that vary between 2 and 8 cycles per sec (Fig. 7–10) and may go as high as 12 or 15 cycles per sec. Higher frequencies will cause the wheel brakes to be applied and released near the natural frequency of vehicle suspensions. This condition, however, leads to undesirable suspension and vehicle body vibrations and may result in loss of vehicle control. Pressure regulating frequencies below 2 cycles per

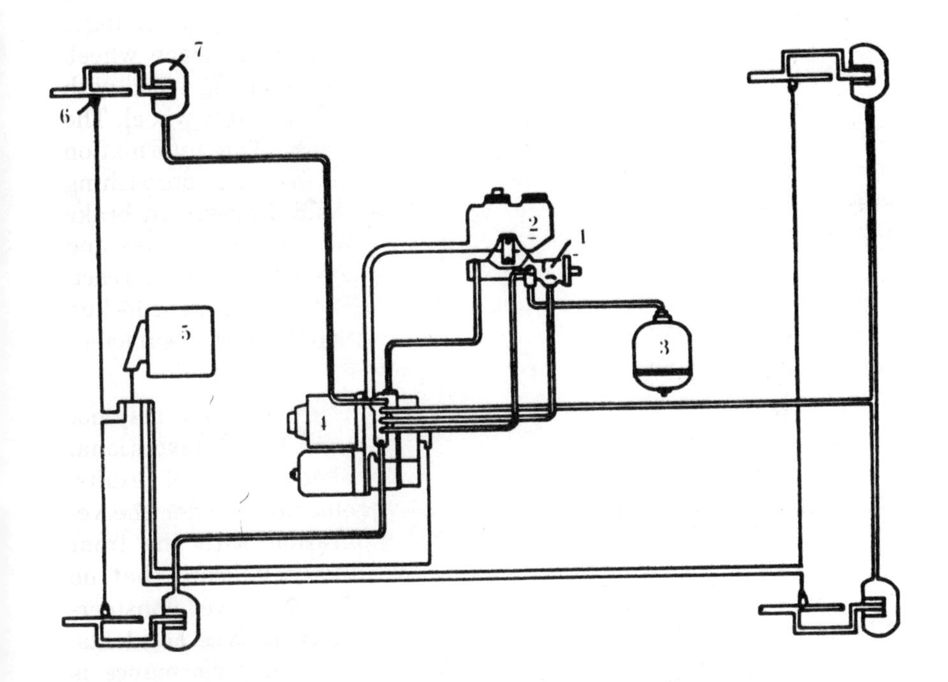

1 MASTER CYLINDER
2 RESERVOIR
3 ACCUMULATOR
4 PRESSURE MODULATOR AND ENERGY SOURCE
5 LOGIC CONTROL
6 WHEEL SPEED SENSOR
7 WHEEL BRAKE

Figure 7-10. Schematic of Pump Pressurized Wheel Antilock System

second generally are not capable of adapting sufficiently fast to changing frictional conditions at the tire-road interface.

7–4.3. Pneumatic Systems. Wheel-antilock control systems for air brakes use concepts similar to those of hydraulic brake systems. Major components are: wheel sensors, usually one for each wheel on the axle; an electronic control, which collects the sensor information, processes it, and sends control signals to the air pressure control valve; and an air pressure control valve which accomplishes the air pressure modulating function by the use of electrical solenoids. The air pressure application and release cycle may be varied between 1 to 5 cycles per second for most current systems.

In the event of malfunction of the major elements in the antiskid control system, the brake system will revert to the standard service brake operation. For tractor-trailer combinations the trailer antiskid control system generally is powered through the brake light signal going from the tractor to the trailer. This condition allows also the intermixing of antiskid equipped tractors with trailers having standard brakes and conversely.

In the case of a hydraulic brake system, the brake fluid must be conserved during the period of pressure decrease as contrasted with air brake systems where air is ventilated from the brake chamber through the control valve into the ambient. However, due consideration must be paid to the fact that the air consumption must remain within the reservoir capacity of the brake system. This is of significance when braking on slippery roadways requiring long stopping distances and continued brake force modulation.

The wheel-antilock system is designed to prevent any regulated axle from locking up during braking for speeds above approximately 5 to 10 mph. The system consists of the modulator assembly, the wheel speed sensor assembly, the rotor assembly, and the failsafe monitor unit. A tractor wheel-antilock control system includes a modulator consisting of an antilock control/relay valve and electronic controller for each braked axle, a wheel speed sensor and rotor assembly at each braked wheel, and a fail safe monitor assembly.

1. Modulator Assembly. The modulator assembly consists of the wheel-antilock control/relay valve and an electronic controller. The modulator assembly is connected to the brake system plumbing system through the supply, service and delivery ports. In normal operation the modulator valve supplies air pressure to the brake chambers at a pressure equal to that demanded by the driver with the application valve. When wheel-antilock action is required by signals from

the controller, pressure to the brake is reduced, either partially or completely, by two solenoids which actuate a small valve. The solenoids operate either independently as in the case of individual wheel control or simultaneously as in the case of an axle control to regulate the air pressure to the brake chambers. This pressure reduction to the brakes generally occurs in steps of 33%, 67%, or 100%.

2. Controller. The controller is a small computer which contains the circuits necessary to control the vehicle wheel rotational speed. The electronic unit is totally enclosed and protected from the ambient effects. The controller circuitry is fully solid state and receives electrical signals from the wheel speed sensors, interprets the signals in terms of existing conditions, and sends corresponding signals to the wheel-antilock control relay valve to regulate brake pressure. Recent accident investigations have shown that moisture had entered the controller box (and fuse box) causing the antiskid control system to malfunction.

3. Fail-Safe Monitor Unit. The fail-safe monitory is an electronic warning unit which processes signals from the controller and energizes an indicator light, mounted on the instrument panel, if an electrical or electronic malfunction occurs. The fail-safe indicator light will come on and remain on if any of the following occurs on any axle with wheel-antilock control:

a. An open or short in a wheel sensor or wiring harness

b. An open or shorted power lead

c. An open or shorted fail-safe lead

d. A shorted fail-safe monitor unit

e. A blown fail-safe unit fuse

f. A continuous solenoid signal

g. An open or shorted solenoid lead

h. A malfunctioning controller

i. On a very slippery road with patches of ice, the indicator light may come on due to one drive wheel accelerating at a very high rate when starting to move the vehicle. Reset fail-safe light by turning key off and back on.

4. Wheel Speed Sensor Assembly. The wheel speed sensor is a self-generating electromagnetic device which generates a signal whose frequency is directly proportional to wheel rotational speed. The sensor generates a pulse each time a gear tooth travels past it. The speed sensor consists of a stationary permanent magnet assembly, a coil, and an output cable assembly. The speed sensor is attached to a

mounting bracket and the speed sensor assembly is mounted to the brake backing plate. The rotor assembly is attached to the hub and drum and rotates with the wheel. Federal Braking Standard 121 necessitates the installation of antiskid brake systems on trucks and trailers equipped with air brakes. Initial field experience indicates the wheel speed sensor to be the critical component of the system.

7-5. BRAKE FLUIDS

The development and production of brake fluids is based on scientific research. Brake fluids must comply with performance requirements of the U.S. Federal Government (FMVSS 571.116/DOT or DOT 4) and generally meet the requirements of SAE J 1703 d.

Generally, all brake fluids can be used in brake systems designed for brake fluids meeting the above requirements.

Brake fluids should exhibit the following properties to guarantee safe functioning of the brake system:

1. High boiling point temperatures up to 550° F to prevent vaporization of brake fluid during severe braking.
2. Viscosity stability to provide a quick responding brake system at extremely low ambient temperatures.
3. Neutral behavior relative to metal and rubber components of the brake system.
4. Chemical and physical properties of the brake fluid should not be affected by aging, and heating or cooling cycles of the brake system.
5. Lubrication should not be affected at high temperatures.
6. A desirable property is that brake fluids of different manufacturers can be mixed without degrading the performance.
7. Brake fluids meeting requirement DOT 3 and DOT 4 are hygroscopic, i.e., they absorb water from the ambient air. The water in the brake fluid will increase the tendency to produce vapor at lower temperatures, i.e., the boiling point temperature will be decreased. Water absorption should be as low as possible.

7-6. BRAKE SYSTEM MAINTENANCE

Proper brake system maintenance is important for the safe operation of the vehicle. Maintenance and adjustment procedures vary as a function of system and difference of components. The appropriate shop manual should be reviewed for details.

Maintenance and repair schedules include brake system bleeding, i.e., removal of air trapped in hydraulic brake lines, brake lining or pad changes, wheel and master cylinder repairs, and servicing of the parking brake. It is important to note that the infrequent use of the parking brake often results in a partial or complete loss of its braking effectiveness due to cable corrosion.

7-7. SAFETY CONSIDERATIONS

A detailed discussion of brake system failure analysis and its consequences is presented in Chapter 20. Accident statistics indicate that only about 2% of all collisions are caused by the brakes, and that more than 75% of these are caused by the after market or owner factors.

The defects investigations of the U.S. Department of Transportation as of 1/1/1977 included the following braking elements: master cylinder (failed due to corrosion), brake proportioning valve (rear wheel lockup), brake drum (failure of drum), brake lining (erratic performance), power brake vacuum (no assist with failure), front caliper (leakage), tandem power brake booster (diaphragm), hydraulic brake line, master cylinder check valve, brake hose and foot brake lever.

CHAPTER 8
THE ENGINE

8-1. THE FUNCTION OF THE ENGINE

The engine or motor produces the motive power that propels the vehicle. The controls of the engine are designed so that the operator can modulate vehicle speed within certain boundaries. Since the engine represents the single largest concentrated mass of the motor vehicle, it significantly affects the collision performance, injury production in certain accident modes, and vehicle handling.

8-2. DIFFERENT CONCEPTS USED IN ENGINE DESIGNS

Engine designs can be divided into several groups. Engine designers generally attempt to optimize the relationship between such factors as engine weight and space requirements, material selection, production cost, fuel economy, emission pollutants, and the useable power output at the crankshaft.

8-2.1. Power Development. Combustion engines in use today develop insufficient torque and power at low crankshaft speeds. This problem is overcome by the clutch and transmission.

The intermittent reciprocative (up and down motion of the piston) engine uses one (or more) cylinder heads on one side and a movable piston on the other. Fuel is burned in the cylinder(s) resulting in an increase of temperature and pressure of the combustion gases. The increased pressure displaces the piston, causing the connecting rod between piston and crankshaft to convert the straight line motion of the piston into rotary motion of the crankshaft. The effective force upon the piston is intermittent, i.e., it varies between a low and high value. Intermittent reciprocative engines are used in nearly all motor vehicles today.

The intermittent rotary engine (commonly called Wankel engine) uses one or more excentric-triangularly shaped rotors which serve the function of the piston of the reciprocative engine. Control of gas flow is relatively simple without a complicated valve arrangement. Advantages of the intermittent rotary engine include small size, low weight, decreased vibrations. The major disadvantage is the approximately 15% higher fuel consumption when compared to standard piston engines.

The continuous rotary engine (commonly called gas turbine) uses one or more rotors as compressors, one or more combustion chambers, and one or more rotors as turbine. Ambient air is compressed by the radial compressor, and burned with the fuel injected into the combustion chamber. The gas-air mixture expands in the turbine and drives the turbine motors. The turbine drives the compressor and the surplus power is available for propulsion of the vehicle. Automotive use requires a variety of different measures to increase the thermal efficiency of the gas turbine. High fuel consumption and production costs thus far have prevented a regular use of the gas turbine in motor vehicles.

8–2.2. Engine Cycle. A cycle includes all processes occurring in the cylinder from one state to the repetition of the same state.

The *two-stroke system* uses a cycle that involves one crankshaft rotation or two piston strokes. The piston strokes are identified as expansion (power producing) and compression strokes. Near the end of the expansion stroke the piston edge slides over the exhaust port and hence opens the exhaust port and a sudden pressure drop results. Further travel of the piston opens the inlet ports and fresh air-fuel mixture enters the cylinder and flushes the exhaust gases out through the exhaust port. Although special designs have been developed to improve the flow characteristics to more efficiently control the exhaust and inlet of the air-fuel mixture, the high fuel consumption, the rough running qualities of the engine, and the undesirable smoke and odor associated with the exhaust gases due to lubrication oil added to the fuel have prevented the successful use of two-stroke engines in motor vehicles. In some cases Diesel engines utilize the two-stroke principle in connection with special exhaust valves and air compressors. The main advantages of two-stroke engines are their simple and inexpensive construction.

The *four-stroke system* uses a cycle that involves two crankshaft rotations or four piston strokes. The piston strokes are identified as intake, compression, expansion (power producing), and exhaust stroke. Although more power is required to compensate for the three powerless strokes and thus decreases the mechanical efficiency, the clear separation of the individual strokes yields a higher fuel economy than is obtained with two-stroke engines. Flexibility in valve timing yields improved idling and engine torque characteristics, and permits better adjustment to road driving requirements.

The four-stroke system is used for gasoline, Diesel, and rotary engines. Their advantages include good fuel economy and smoke free exhaust gases due to a separate lubrication system for engine components. Disadvantages include expensive manufacturing cost, maintenance of valve train, limited maximum number of rotations, and lower mechanical efficiency when compared to a two-stroke engine.

8–2.3. Valve Design and Control. Mushroom shaped valves are generally used in combustion engines. The mushroom geometry is insensitive to thermal deformation, wear, and can be easily machined. The opening of the valves is accomplished by rocker arms, the closing by springs. Special designs for high crankshaft speeds are used to close the valves.

Hanging valves located in the cylinder head above the piston are used in all modern piston engines. The design permits efficient combustion chamber geometry and good thermal efficiency. The valves may be actuated by an overhead camshaft (OHC) as shown in Fig. 8–1 or by a camshaft located in the engine block requiring lifters, pushrods and rocker arms for valve operation.

Standing valves located beside the cylinder require a special cylinder head (commonly called L-head) to account for the side location of the valves resulting in generally poor gas flow geometry and lower thermal efficiency. Advantages are simple construction of valve train.

The *camshaft* has cams for exhaust and inlet valve actuation and is driven at one-half crankshaft speed by gear or toothed belt chain (Fig. 8–1). The cam geometry is important for valve timing and hence efficient engine operation.

8–2.4. Fuel-Air Mixing. In the *external* fuel-air mixing process the fuel-air mixture is produced outside the combustion cylinder in the intake manifold. Either liquid fuel is mixed with air in the carburetor or liquid fuel is injected into the air in the manifold. Engines using external fuel air mixing are commonly called Otto or gasoline engines. Fuel injection accurately metered for reasons of fuel economy and emission pollutants is becoming more frequent. Problems may exist due to the larger numbers of fuel lines not requiring the mechanical rigidity of Diesel engines (high pressure) and consequently leakage and fire hazards may develop.

In the *internal* fuel-air mixing process (Diesel engine) the fuel-air mixture is produced inside the combustion cylinder. The fuel (Diesel oil) is injected into the compressed, hot air at the end of the compression stroke and self-ignites. Due to its good fuel economy and low

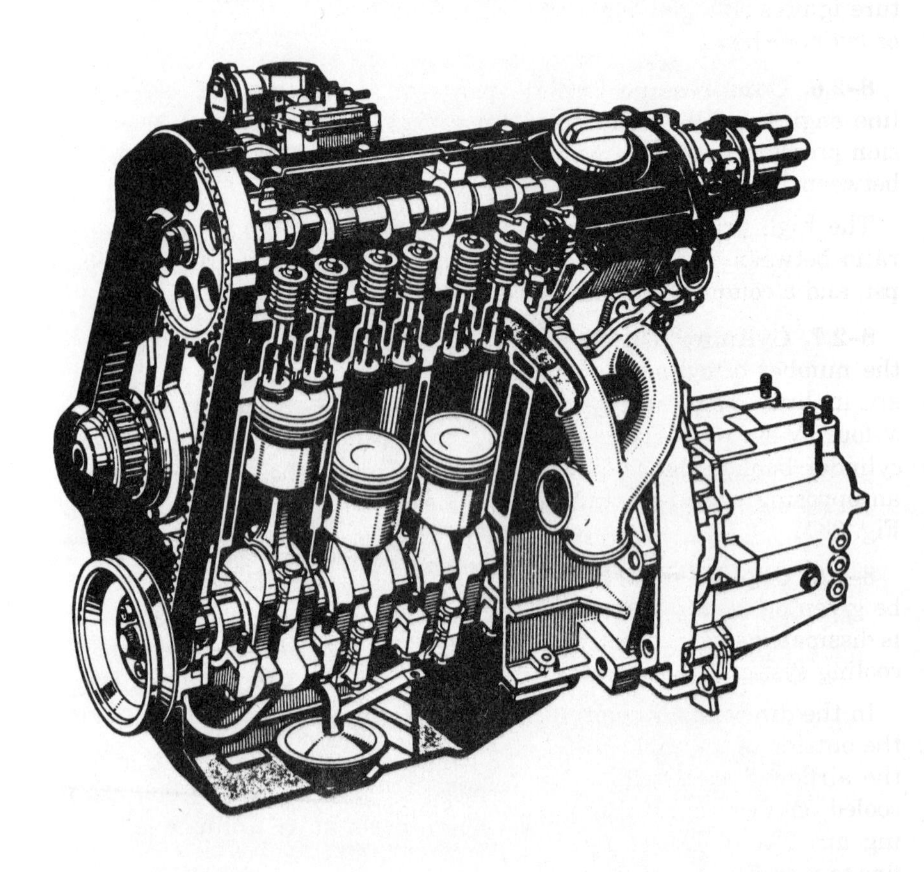

Figure 8-1. Four-Cylinder Gasoline Engine (VW)

emission pollutant, the Diesel engine experiences an increased use in smaller passenger cars. Heavy trucks generally use Diesel engines.

8-2.5. Type of Ignition. The *indirect ignition* system ignites the externally mixed fuel-air mixture by means of a high voltage spark produced by a spark plug. Indirect ignition is used on Otto or gasoline engines. Electrical elements of indirect ignition systems are discussed in Chapter 15.

In the *direct* or *self ignition* system the internally mixed fuel-air mixture ignites by means of the highly compressed and hot air (Diesel engine).

In the *glow head* ignition system the internally mixed fuel-air mixture ignites on a glowing, uncooled section of the combustion chamber or cylinder head.

8–2.6. Compression Level. The low pressure engine (Otto or gasoline engine) exhibits a compression ratio between 6 to 10, a compression pressure between 120 to 250 psi, and a compression temperature between 750 to 1150° F.

The high pressure engine (Diesel engine) exhibits a compression ratio between 14 to 24, a compression pressure between 450 to 900 psi, and a compression temperature between 1150 to 1700° F.

8–2.7. Cylinder Arrangement. Piston engines are identified by the number of cylinders and cylinder locations such as two, four or six in line, indicating straight-line orientation of the cylinders, or V-four, V-six or V-eight, indicating a V-shaped arrangement of the cylinder banks. Flat two, four, or six designation is used to describe an opposing cylinder location. A four in line engine is illustrated in Fig. 8–1.

8–2.8. Cooling System. A certain amount of thermal energy must be given off by the engine for proper operation. This thermal energy is dissipated either directly to the air or indirectly by means of a water cooling system to the ambient air.

In the direct or air cooling system the cooling air is in contact with the outside of the combustion and cylinder. In the case of motorcycles, the airflow due to vehicle speed is sufficient for engine cooling. Air cooled engines in automobiles use a blower to provide sufficient cooling air. The cylinders and combustion chambers are equipped with fins to increase the surface area and thus transfers heat to the ambient air.

Advantages of air cooling systems are simple construction, little maintenance, no leakage potential, no winter or summer problems. Disadvantages include high noise level and increased oil temperature often requiring a special oil cooler.

In watercooled engines the thermal energy is transferred to the water surrounding the cylinder and combustion chamber walls. Subsequently, the hot water is pumped through a heat exchanger or radiator which is cooled by ambient air. The water is pumped by a water pump which usually carries the fan. In some cases the fan is driven by an electromotor. The fan pulling air through the radiator together with the forward motion of the vehicle produces the cooling effect in the radiator. Automatic cooling fans either electromagnetic or by a fluid coupling are only operating when the engine temperatures are high enough to require cooling. Advantages of automatic fans are improved horsepower and better fuel economy. Most water cooling systems operate at a pressure slightly above ambient to increase the operating temperature of the engine. Some systems use an expansion tank to provide a sealed cooling system. Advantages of water cooling systems include low noise level, lower oil temperatures and better thermal balancing of the engine due to a more uniform cooling.

Special provisions on both cooling systems are used to improve performance. One such device is the thermostat used to disconnect the radiator from the engine cooling circuit until optimum water temperatures have been achieved by the engine after a cold start. Optimum water temperatures are important for minimizing engine wear.

8-2.9. Engine Components. Engine components include all components required for power production and transmission, engine control by the driver, and control and manipulation of exhaust gases. Electrical components are discussed in Chapter 15. Any of the components can fail and cause engine stalling, insufficient power, or a runaway engine. The appropriate shop manuals should be studied for details of defect causation.

Federal requirements on exhaust gas pollutants have forced certain changes on existing components and the development of new devices. Changes on combustion chamber geometry and ignition timing, fuel injection and others are intended to provide a more favorable combustion process. Some engines require a special treatment of the exhaust gases in the exhaust system, using catalytic converters and thermal reactors to reduce pollutants. The catalytic converter causes a chemical reaction without entering into the chemical reaction itself resulting in a reduction of exhaust pollutants. The operating temperature can be low (Ref. 12).

Thermal reactors involve a final burning of the hydrocarbons and carbon monoxide still in the exhaust gases, thus reducing exhaust gas pollutants. A high operating temperature is required.

8-2.10. Engine Maintenance. Engine maintenance schedules are provided by the manufacturers and include mechanical checks or adjustments of spark plugs, engine compression, ignition system, valve clearance, timing belt tension, fuel system, carburetor, and cooling system. A large variety of instruments are available for engine checking.

8-2.11. Engine Failure. Engine failure involved in accident causation may be divided into several areas including engine stalling, runaway engine, inadvertent startup of engine (basically an electrical problem), fuel fed fires, and fatigue fracture of critical components. Critical components are those usually possessing a high level of dynamic rotational energy without sufficient shielding.

The carburetor is connected by means of the manifold to the individual combustion chambers of each cylinder. Improper ignition timing or valve clearance adjustment, extremely lean or cold air-fuel mixture, or nonsealing or sticking valves can cause a carburetor fire. Reasons for the inadvertent ignition are the backfiring of the combustion process through the unscheduled valve opening and subsequent firing of the air-fuel mixture in the carburetor.

The formation of ice on the carburetor may sometimes be the cause of engine stalling. The ice is the result of water condensation from the air on the carburetor. Since the vaporization of the fuel involves a temperature decrease, ice may form when the ambient temperature is between 35 and 45° F, and the relative humidity exceeds 65%. Most engines use designs to prevent carburetor ice formation.

Engine runaway will always be a possibility due to carburetor controls jamming, forcing the throttle to remain in the open position. The U.S. Department of Transportation is presently (1/1/1977) investigating alleged throttle jamming in a number of vehicles.

The causation factors of engine fires are usually related to flooding of carburetors (sticky float), or loose or defectively designed fuel line connections. The latter problem may be more prevalent in engines using fuel injection. DOT is presently conducting defects investigations on several vehicles.

Rare yet potentially very hazardous conditions may develop in connection with the rupture of a component rotating at high speed. Cooling fan blade separation due to fatigue fracture may occur. The flywheel is also subjected to severe stresses due to the centrifugal force existing at high engine revolutions and due to the possibility of a temperature gradient sufficiently steep to cause thermal cracking. The temperature gradient is the result of manually engaging and disengaging of the clutch causing a heat generation at the friction surface. In one known case involving a modern passenger car the combination of mechanical and thermal stresses and/or possible weakening of the flywheel due to crack propagation caused a sudden explosion-type fracture of the flywheel while driving at highway speed.

CHAPTER 9
THE CLUTCH

9-1. THE FUNCTION OF THE CLUTCH

Engines in use on motor vehicles today can only produce sufficient torque above a certain crankshaft speed. The clutch provides a gradual connection of the rotating engine crankshaft to the initially stationary input shaft of the transmission in the case of vehicle acceleration from a stop. The clutch also disconnects the power flow from the engine to the transmission in a stationary vehicle or before gear shifting.

9-2. DIFFERENT CONCEPTS USED IN CLUTCH DESIGN

9-2.1. Torque Transmission. *Friction* clutches consist of two or more rotating ringshaped surfaces which are pressed together so that the tangential friction forces between the surfaces transmit the torque from the input to the output shaft of the clutch. The input shaft is connected to the crankshaft of the engine, the output shaft to the transmission shaft. The gradual increase in the normal force pressing the surfaces together permits a smooth engagement of the clutch. Slipping between friction surfaces occurs mostly during engagement, the power loss and heating become significant only when frequent engagement is required, or when the slipping is excessive due to improper operation or insufficient normal force between surfaces. In the friction clutch the input torque always equals the output torque.

The *fluid* or *hydraulic* clutch serves the same function as the friction clutch. The fluid clutch automatically connects or disconnects the input and output shaft as a function of input, i.e., engine crankshaft speed. The concept is identical to that of a waterwheel: a fluid pushes against the blades of a wheel causing it to rotate. As the fluid velocity increases the wheel speed increases also. When the fluid velocity approaches zero, the wheel stops. In the fluid clutch a radial pump connected to the input shaft pumps a special fluid against the blades of a rotor (turbine) connected to the output shaft. The input shaft of the clutch, i.e., the radial pump, is connected to the engine crankshaft, the output shaft, i.e., the turbine wheel to the input shaft of the transmission. When the engine runs at idling speed, the fluid flow produced by the pump is not sufficient to turn the turbine, i.e., engine power is disconnected from the drive wheels. As the engine crankshaft rotates at a higher number of revolutions, the fluid force upon the turbine wheel increases and the turbine begins to turn. At rated crankshaft speeds the fluid in the clutch provides an almost complete connection. Since the input speed is always slightly greater than the output speed, i.e., a small amount of slip exists, thermal energy is generated which heats clutch fluid and housing. The input torque always equals the output torque.

Advantages of the fluid clutch include little or no wear and maintenance, maximum torque when moving from rest, automatic disengagement when the engine is idling, smooth engagement and no dependence on driver skills. Hydraulic clutches can be used to evaluate engine horsepower. In direct gear with the vehicle held stationary by the brakes or blocks, the engine speed must achieve a certain level with open throttle if the rated horsepower is developed; otherwise the engine horsepower is below rated value due to defective parts or tuning.

9-2.2. Types of Friction Clutches. *Plate* clutches are used on motor vehicles. The clutch plate is a concentric ring whose surface is covered on both sides with friction material. The plate is free to move axially on the splines which transmit the torque to the output shaft. One surface of the plate presses against a machined surface on the flywheel, the other against the spring-loaded pressure plate. The pressure plate is bolted to the flywheel. The clutch is engaged at all times, except when the springs of the pressure plate are forced back by the release mechanism.

Heat generation between plate and flywheel under certain conditions may be sufficient to cause thermal cracking, and, in combination with high mechanical stresses in the flywheel at maximum engine speed, may result in flywheel failure.

Double- or *multiple-*plate clutches permit the transmission of higher torques required in some heavy-duty trucks and race cars.

Conical clutches using a cone-shaped friction surface are not used for torque engagement in motor vehicles. Conical clutches are used in some transmissions for improved gear shifting.

9-2.3. Type of Plate Pressuring. The normal force between the pressure plate and the flywheel determines the maximum torque of a given clutch. The normal force in many automotive clutches is produced by a number of small *coilsprings* located concentrically in the pressure plate. Difficulties may exist to obtain accurate dynamic balancing at high engine speed due to imprecise location of the spring masses.

The *diaphragm* spring is a one-piece conical spring exerting a uniformly distributed pressure against the friction plate. Diaphragm springs require less space, simplify the clutch design by providing part of the clutch release function, and are less sensitive to vibrations at higher engine speeds.

Centrifugal force clutches use centrifugal force for plate pressuring. Clutch disengagement does not require a manually operated clutch pedal, rather is accomplished automatically as engine speed is reduced. Above a certain speed the flyweights produce a centrifugal force which, when transmitted by linkages, is sufficiently large to press the pressure plate against the flywheel. This type of clutch has been used in the past in combination with semi-automatic transmissions. Today the hydraulic torque converter has replaced the centrifugal force actuated friction clutch (Chapter 10).

Electromagnetic forces may be used to produce the normal force between two friction surfaces. This clutch is rarely used in power trains. Its use is restricted as automatic clutch of certain components such as cooling fans, hydraulic pumps, or compressors of air conditioning systems.

9–2.4. Clutch Actuation. Clutch actuation is the process that disengages and engages the clutch friction surfaces.

Mechanical actuation involves a foot pedal, mechanical linkages or cables and release or throw-out bearing. The foot travel is transmitted to the release mechanism and used to displace the spring-loaded pressure plate for clutch disengagement.

Hydraulic actuation involves the hydraulic transmission of the foot travel to the release bearing. A hydraulic cylinder—similar to the master cylinder of the brake system—is actuated by the clutch foot pedal. The hydraulic line pressure is transmitted to a hydraulic cylinder—similar to the wheel cylinder of the brake system—which displaces the lever of the throw-out mechanism.

Pneumatic operation involves the actuation of the throw-out lever by means of an air cylinder.

Electromagnetic activation involves the force of a magnet to displace the clutch release lever.

The operation of the clutch release mechanism may be manually as in the case of a pedal-operated clutch or semi-automatic using pneumatic, hydraulic, or electric actuation at the instant the gear-shift lever is moved. Automatic operation may use centrifugal force clutches or pneumatic actuation with automatic control from the intake manifold vacuum. In some cases, two clutches are used. A centrifugal clutch is used for vehicle acceleration from rest, and a vacuum controlled clutch for gear shifting (Opel-Olymat).

9-3. CLUTCH FAILURE

A defective clutch results in a power loss and overheating of clutch components due to slipping. Generally, the performance of an automotive clutch is not a major factor in accident reconstruction, except in cases where maximum vehicle acceleration in the shortest possible time must be computed.

CHAPTER 10
THE TRANSMISSION

10-1. THE FUNCTION OF THE TRANSMISSION

Transmissions are torque and speed converters. They provide the maximum engine power, which is produced over only a small range of engine speed, at any driving condition, i.e., at low and high speeds. In the gasoline-piston engine the power is constant over a relatively large crankshaft speed range thus requiring only three to four transmission gears. In the Diesel engine the power is available only at one engine speed requiring five to ten or more gears.

10-2. DIFFERENT CONCEPTS USED IN TRANSMISSION DESIGN

10-2.1. Manual Transmission. The manual transmission requires driver inputs in the form of clutch release and gear shifting.

In the transmission, gears, chains or belts are used to transmit power. Gears are common in motor vehicles. Gear shifting is accomplished by disconnecting the power flow from the engine, i.e., depressing of the clutch, and engaging of the appropriate set of gears.

Most transmissions consist of the input or clutch shaft, the countershaft with the counter gears, and the mainshaft with the different speed gears. The clutch shaft and associated gear drive the countershaft. Early transmission designs required axial displacement of the speed gear to mesh with the appropriate counter gear for torque transmission. Since the counter gear is always rotating when the clutch is engaged gear shifting is made difficult by the difference in gear speeds (gear clashing). Constant-mesh transmissions overcome this problem by having counter and speed gear in constant mesh. The speed gear rotates freely on the mainshaft. Only when the gear shift lever is displaced a synchronizing clutch engages the speed gear to the mainshaft and the power flow between transmission input shaft and mainshaft is accomplished. Synchromesh transmissions improve vehicle operation since no double-clutching is required for clash free gear shifting. Details on transmission are published by the manufacturers in appropriate shop manuals.

10–2.2. Semi-Automatic Transmission. The driver only selects and operates the gear shift lever. The clutch is actuated automatically prior to shifting the gear. The clutch release may be actuated by hydraulic, pneumatic or electric means. Gears may be planetary or regular. Starting from rest is accomplished by a centrifugal clutch or a fluid clutch–torque converter. The fluid clutch–torque converter is similar to a fluid clutch (Section 9–2.1), however, has an additional rotor (stator) located between the pump and turbine rotor of the clutch. The stator funnels the oil back to the pump rotor. Initially the speed difference between pump rotor and turbine is large and the oil returning from the turbine exhibits a large amount of kinetic energy. The returning oil is redirected by the stator to impact the pump rotor under no-loss conditions. This added energy from the return oil and the energy put into the pump by the engine increases the kinetic energy of the oil leaving the pump and thus increases the torque experienced by the turbine rotor. The startup torque may be two to three times as big as the regular torque developed when both the pump rotor and turbine rotate at nearly equal speed. During engine idling the torque transmission is interrupted, at the rated speed the clutching effect is completed and only small oil pumping occurs which also determines the efficiency of the torque converter. Since torque converters provide an automatic adjustment of input to output torque between 2 to 1 and 3 to 1, the gear ratios of the mechanical transmission may be limited to three to obtain the overall gear ratio range required for smooth vehicle operation under a variety of conditions.

Transmissions using centrifugal or fluid clutches, or torque converters require special parking pawls to hold the vehicle stationary since these clutches do not provide direct connection between engine and drive wheel.

Although semi-automatic transmissions are less expensive than full automatic transmissions, their automotive use is limited.

10–2.3. Automatic Transmission. Most automatic transmissions use a hydraulic torque converter in combination with a three-speed planetary gear transmission. Gear changing occurs without interruption of the power flow. The planetary gears are in constant mesh, and are actuated automatically by conical, single or multiple plate clutches, or brakes as a function of vehicle speed and engine load. Common control modes are normal, slow and reverse driving, and parking. Automatic transmissions significantly improve traffic safety by relieving the driver of two control inputs, i.e., clutch and gear shift lever operation.

An automatic transmission involving toothed belts has been developed for small cars and recreational vehicles such as snowmobiles. The transmission ratio changes are accomplished by pulleys whose effective diameter is varied as a function of speed. In some applications engine manifold vacuum is used to control the transmission variable drive. The input and output pulleys are designed so that one pulley-half can slide axially on a splined shaft. As the pulley spreads apart as a function of shaft speed the belt is drawn closer to the center and the effective diameter is reduced. At the same time the output or driven pulley-halves are pushed together thus increasing the diameter of the pulley by an amount sufficient to take up the slack developed by the diameter decrease of the input pulley. Malfunction of the drive may occur by excessive belt slack during sudden speed changes resulting in abrupt lowering of the speed due to belt wedging. Malfunctioning may occur more frequently in off-road recreational vehicles and snowmobiles due to poor design, manufacturing, or maintenance.

10–3. GEAR SHIFT LEVER LOCATION

The gear shift lever provides the controls required for gear shifting.

10–3.1. Direct Shifting. The gear shift lever is located directly above the transmission. The lower end of the lever directly moves the engagement mechanisms. It is mostly used in combination with manual transmissions. The lever location may under certain conditions cause injuries due to occupant impact.

10–3.2. Indirect Shifting. The gear shift lever is located next to the steering column below the steering wheel. A number of linkages are used to transmit the lever displacement to the transmission. Cables are used less frequently to transmit shifting motion. Steering column location of the indirect shift lever is common with automatic transmission, but is also available with manual transmission. The preciseness of the shifting process may be lower than in direct shifting due to a large number of linkages, levers, and connections.

10–4. TRANSMISSION FAILURE

Accident causations due to transmission failure are infrequent but may be related to a sudden lack of performance due to malfunctioning. The strength of the parking pawl is tested in impact tests as required in Federal Motor Vehicle Safety Standard 105 (Section 33–1.5). Although uncommon, problems including fire may develop as a result of the additional electrical wiring required to display gear lever position information at the dashboard and to prevent ignition key removal unless the gear lever is in the parking or another specified position. Delayed fires may develop due to switch malfunctioning and excessive electrical heating of the padding material near the transmission cover. During driving the air stream may be sufficient to suppress the development of a fire. However, once the vehicle is parked the smoldering material may develop into a vehicle fire.

CHAPTER 11
THE DRIVE SHAFT

11-1. THE FUNCTION OF THE DRIVE SHAFT

The drive shaft—also called propeller shaft—transmits the power from the transmission to the rear axle. Rear- and mid-engine vehicles do not require the usual drive shaft. The drive shaft must move with the engine/transmission assembly in the front and the solid rear axle in the back. Independent rear suspensions do not cause vertical drive shaft motions due to attachment of the differential housing to the body.

11-2. DIFFERENT CONCEPTS USED IN DRIVE SHAFT DESIGN

11-2.1. Drive Shaft Arrangement. The drive shaft is a steel tube with a splined slip yoke and a universal joint located at the transmission end of the shaft. The slip yoke permits fore and aft movement of the drive shaft as the rear axle moves up and down. A second universal joint attached by U-bolts or straps is used where the drive shaft connects to the flange of the differential.

Drive shafts rotate at high speed when the transmission is in direct gear. At high rotational speeds small imbalances will cause vibrations and noise. For vehicles requiring long drive shafts a two-piece drive shaft is used. A shaft is connected between the transmission and a center bearing attached to the floor of the body. The second piece of the drive shaft runs from the center bearing to the drive axle absorbing all relative motion between rear axle and center bearing. Single-piece drive shafts are used for smaller cars when the shaft length is sufficiently short to prevent vibrations.

11-2.2. Coupling System. Drive shafts must provide a flexible connection between input and output ends to absorb relative movement between suspension and transmission.

Metal *universal joints* permit rotation with an angular deflection of the shaft. The joint consists of two forks or Y-shaped yokes—one connected to the end of the drive shaft, the other to the input of the final drive, and a four-pronged cross spider or member. Opposite prongs are held in each yoke by needle bearings.

The spider allows the two yoke shafts to rotate at an angle to each other. When torque is transmitted at an angle, the driving yoke rotates at a constant speed while the driven yoke speeds up and slows down twice per revolution. The differences in input to output speeds increases as the deflection angle increases. This variable speed effect is the major reason why single universal joints are not used for angles exceeding four degrees. At this angle the speed may fluctuate by as much as 0.5%. In a one-piece drive shaft speed fluctuations can be eliminated by locating two simple universal joints with the yokes rotated 90 degrees, thus cancelling the speed effects.

Flexible joints using elastic rubber or textile discs are used in connection with drive shafts not subject to inputs from suspension travel.

Universal joints are lubricated for life and cannot be serviced while on the car. If worn or noisy, they must be replaced as a unit.

CHAPTER 12
THE FINAL DRIVE

12–1. THE FUNCTION OF THE FINAL DRIVE

The final drive changes the longitudinal direction of the drive line to the transverse direction of the axle shafts and transmits the drive shaft power to the drive axle. The gear ratio of the final drive reduces rotational speed and increases torque.

12–2. DRIVE SYSTEM

The common layout is the pinion and ring gear system. The pinion/ring gear drive uses two toothed conical surfaces for the directional change from the drive shaft to the axle. When spiral bevel gears are used, the axis of the pinion intersects the center of the ring gear. Special hypoid gears are used in which the pinion gear is located below the center of the ring gear resulting in a lowering of the drive shaft tunnel in the floor of the vehicle for improved occupant comfort.

The worm drive is used less frequently in motor vehicles. In this system the worm shaft is driven by the drive shaft and the worm gear drives the axles. Worm drives permit a large gear reduction up to 14 to 1. The mechanical losses due to friction are generally larger for the worm drive than for the pinion and gear drive.

12–2.1. Final Drive Reduction. Final drive gear ratios vary as a function of vehicle use. Passenger cars and small trucks generally range between 3 and 8, buses and trucks between 4 and 12, and heavy-duty tractors between 5 and 18. In some cases the gear ratio of the final drive can be changed by means of a shift lever operated by the driver, thus increasing the number of gears between engine and drive wheels. The direct connection between engine and drive wheels is lost when the final drive reduction gear is in neutral or in between gears. In heavy vehicles relying upon engine braking during continued downhill driving the loss of retardation due to an out-of-gear position of the final drive reduction has contributed to accident causation.

CHAPTER 13
THE DIFFERENTIAL

13-1. THE FUNCTION OF THE DIFFERENTIAL

The differential apportions the power to the left and right wheel of a drive axle in the event that the rotational speeds of the left and right wheel differ due to vehicle turning or road surface conditions. Vehicle turning at small radii causes the outside wheel to travel a longer distance, and consequently to rotate at a higher speed.

13-2. DIFFERENT CONCEPTS USED IN DIFFERENTIAL DESIGNS

13-2.1. Standard Differential. A differential is an arrangement of gears that divides the torque coming from the drive shaft between the axle shafts and allows them to rotate at different speeds if necessary. A standard differential consists of two differential side gears each splined to an axle shaft, and two differential pinion gears mounted on a differential pinion shaft. Some differentials use four pinion gears.

The operation is as follows: The pinion gear of the final drive rotates the ring gear. The ring gear being bolted to the differential pinion shaft turns with the case, and consequently, the differential pinion gears press against the differential side gears. The axle shafts are splined and connected to the differential side gears. When both wheels have equal traction, the pinion gears do not rotate about the pinion shaft, however, their rotation with the case is transmitted directly upon the differential side gears, thus rotating the axle shafts and wheels.

When a vehicle turns a corner, the outer wheel travels a longer distance than the inner one, i.e., the inner wheel slows down. The side gear slows down also. Since the side gear now turns slower than the differential case and differential pinion shaft, the differential pinion gear begins to turn resulting in a higher speed of the outside gear and axle shaft. The balancing lever action of the pinion gears maintains an equal load and hence torque on both side gears. The power transmitted to each wheel is different since the wheels turn at different speeds. The kinematic relationships are always such that the sum of the wheel speeds equals twice the speed of the differential case.

The characteristic of the differential is that when one wheel produces no traction between tire and road (ice), no drive torque is transmitted to the other wheel. If the vehicle is stationary, the wheel on the ice may spin at twice the differential case speed, while the other rests on a grippy road without drive force. The total drive thrust always equals twice the drive thrust produced by the low traction wheel. An accident reconstruction involving vehicle acceleration on split-friction surface is presented in Section 40–2.

13–2.2. Limited Slip Differential. The limited slip differential functions as the standard one, however, provides more driving force to the wheel with traction when one wheel begins to spin. It modifies load-equalization by suppressing the standard function of the differential in adverse conditions to enhance vehicle capability and operation.

Most limited slip differentials involve friction plates or brake cones which cause a frictional connection between the side gear of the wheel with traction and the differential case, resulting in a rotation of the axle shaft connected to the wheel with road traction.

13–2.3. Locking Differential. Locking differentials have driver-actuated connectors which totally eliminate the balancing function of the differential. Care must be exercised in their operation to avoid damage to gears and shafts.

CHAPTER 14
THE DRIVE AXLE

14-1. THE FUNCTION OF THE DRIVE AXLE

The drive axle applies torque to the wheel for vehicle motion. In some suspensions the drive axle is also used to locate the wheels. In the front wheel drive vehicles the drive axle also allows front wheel steering.

14-2. DIFFERENT CONCEPTS USED IN DRIVE AXLE DESIGN

14-2.1. Solid Drive Axle. The solid drive axle consists of a tube rigidly connecting left and right wheels. The drive shafts rotate inside the tube and transmit the drive torque from the differential side gears to the wheel.

14-2.2. Divided Drive Axle. The divided drive axle allows relative motion of one wheel to the other as, e.g., in the swing axle. The torque is transmitted by an axle shaft to the wheel. In front wheel drives, DeDion rear axles and semi-trailing arm rear suspensions the wheels are driven by a pair of axle shafts using special universal joints at each end. The joints are designed to provide a constant torque and speed, to eliminate effects from steering rotation and wheel travel. The constant velocity (CV) joints are lubricated for life and protected against dust and water entry. Regular universal joints using spider and yoke are used infrequently due to their increased speed and torque fluctuation at larger inclination angles as commonly associated with front wheel drive axles.

14-2.3. Tandem Drive Axle. Tandem axles use two solid axles. They are used on heavy trucks to distribute the weight over more tires, to allow a greater drive thrust and braking utilization, and to provide better tire-to-ground contact when operating on rough surfaces. Some specially off-road vehicles frequently use independent suspensions in tandem design.

14-3. DRIVE AXLE FAILURE

Drive axle failures are not frequent. When they occur, they are mostly defective due to improper machining, material selection, manufacturing, or fatigue fracture.

CHAPTER 15
THE ELECTRICAL SYSTEM

15–1. THE FUNCTIONS OF THE ELECTRICAL SYSTEM

The electrical system provides all electrical functions required for vehicle operation. In its standard form the electrical system consists of the electricity charging subsystem, the ignition system of the engine, and the electricity user subsystem.

15–2. COMPONENTS OF THE ELECTRICAL SYSTEM

15–2.1. The Battery. The battery stores electricity to operate certain electricity users when the engine is not running. The battery is a chemical power plant normally designed for 12 volts. During the battery charging process hydrogen is produced and due to its flammability, a fire hazard may exist when an open flame comes near the battery. Whenever the battery poles are shorted out, i.e., the positive and negative poles come in direct metal connection, sparks will be produced. This is of importance in collisions where both fuel leakage and body damage at or near the battery occurs. Similar conditions may exist in vehicle roll-over collisions, or in side impacts of trucks which frequently have fuel tanks and battery exposed at the side of the vehicle.

15–2.2. The Generator. The generator charges the battery and supplies users with electricity during vehicle operation with engine speeds exceeding idling conditions. A regulator is located between the generator and the remaining electrical system. The regulator connects the generator with the battery for charging when the generator speed exceeds a certain level. The regulator is designed to provide the correct voltage level under varying operating conditions. The generator involves the electrical concept of moving an electrical conductor (wire) through a magnetic field, causing an electrical current to flow through the wire. The major disadvantage of the generator is its limited speed of approximately 5000 revolutions per minute. This constraint requires a pulley ratio which causes the generator to rotate below 5000 RPM during normal vehicle operation. The consequence is little or no production of electricity at generator speeds below 1500 RPM, i.e., when the engine is idling.

15–2.3. The Alternator. The alternator involves a design that allows shaft speeds as high as 14000 RPM since it is not hindered by sparking and excessive brush wear. The alternator system produces a current sufficiently high to commence battery charging already during engine idling.

15–2.4. The Starter Motor. Starting of the engine is accomplished by an electric motor powered by the vehicle battery. The starter motor gear automatically engages with the toothed ring of the flywheel when starting the engine. The motor is capable of producing a large starting torque to overcome initial engine drag, especially at low temperatures.

15–2.5. The Lighting System. The lighting system must provide sufficient visibility for the driver during night and must make the vehicle visible to other road users. Other functions include illumination of dashboard instruments, vehicle interior, identification plate, and others. The light intensity and location of lights on the vehicle are regulated by federal standards. Defective light bulbs, and in the case of older vehicles, oxidation or contamination of contact surfaces or the presence of water usually reduce electric power to the light bulb reducing light intensity. A discussion of factors involved in determining if lights were in use prior to a collision is presented in Section 39–2.8.

15–2.6. The Fuse. The electrical system is equipped with several fuses of different ratings. The function of the fuse is to prevent overheating of the wiring system in the event of an electrical short, thus reducing non collision fire hazard. If a particular circuit is overloaded, the fuse melts and interrupts the flow of current eliminating the fire hazards.

15–2.7. The Engine Ignition System. Automotive ignition systems produce the spark to ignite the fuel-air mixture in the combustion chamber. The standard system consists of the ignition coil, the distributor and breaker, the condensor, and the spark plugs.

Most electrical systems use 12 volts. The spark plugs require a voltage between 10,000 and 20,000 volts to produce a spark sufficiently strong to ignite the fuel-air mixture. The coil and breaker are involved in producing the high-voltage spark, the condensor prevents a weakening of the spark and enhances the life of the breaker contact points. The time at which the spark is fired must be varied between limits for optimizing engine operation. Automatic timing advance or retardation is accomplished by manifold vacuum and speed dependent centrifugal force actuation.

Conventional coil ignition systems produce a weak spark at low and very high crankshaft speeds.

Improved ignitions have been developed. Transistorized ignitions may work with or without the standard breaker component. The former system uses a transistor for interrupting the primary coil current while the breaker and distributor serve the distribution and control function. The electric current flowing through the breaker contacts is only a fraction of that of standard systems since it only serves a control function and does not carry the high voltage spark plug current. Transistorized ignition systems without standard breaker use contact-free breakers employing inductive or optical sensors.

Advantages of transistorized ignition include longer maintenance intervals, stronger spark over a wide speed range including at low speed during engine startup.

Condensor ignition systems use a special conductor for storage of a high electric energy which is discharged over the primary side of the coil. Condensor ignition systems produce a significantly higher spark voltage than the conventional coil systems improving engine operation at low and high crankshaft speeds.

15-3. ELECTRICAL SYSTEM FAILURE

Failures of the electrical system are varied and have included fire causation due to wire melting, ignition switch defect, bulkhead connectors, air conditioner blower relay (overloading of wiring), and battery cable shorting.

PART 2
VEHICLE MOTION ANALYSIS

Part 2 presents a discussion of general motion analysis, the production of forces by the tires, and the effect of forces on vehicle motion. The effects of different retarding mechanisms including braking and braking under failure conditions on stopping distance are analyzed. Vehicle vibrations, steering, and vehicle stability are analyzed in some detail. Examples are used throughout to provide the reader with a better understanding of the use of engineering equations and to demonstrate interrelationships of different factors influencing a particular performance measure.

CHAPTER 16
FUNDAMENTALS OF MOTION ANALYSIS

16–1. DEFINITION OF MOTION

Straight line motion (also called translation or rectilinear motion) exists when a point or particle, or each point of a body moves in a straight line.

Curved line motion (also called rotation or curvilinear motion) exists when a point or particle, or each point of a body moves in a circle or curved path.

Combined motion exists when a body rotates while moving in a straight line.

16–2. STRAIGHT LINE MOTION

16–2.1. Measures of Straight Line Motion. Any motion can be analyzed by means of the following four physical measures:

1. distance S
2. time t
3. velocity V
4. acceleration a

The velocity V of a body is the ratio of distance S and time t:

$$V = \frac{S}{t}, \text{ ft/sec} \tag{16–1}$$

where

$$S = \text{distance, ft}$$
$$t = \text{time, sec}$$

The term speed, often used to describe velocity, only refers to the magnitude of the velocity and does not indicate in which direction the body is moving.

The velocity of a body is *uniform* (or **constant**) when the body travels the same distances in equal time intervals.

The velocity of a body is *nonuniform* when the body travels different distances in equal time intervals.

The *average* (ficticious) velocity of a body traveling at a nonuniform velocity is obtained by dividing the total distance by the total time. Consequently, a ficticious body traveling at this average velocity would travel the same total distance in the same total time as the actual body traveling at a nonuniform velocity.

A body traveling at a nonuniform velocity is either accelerating or decelerating, i.e., its velocity is either increasing or decreasing. The nonuniformity of the motion can be expressed by the change in velocity occurring within a certain time interval, say one second.

The acceleration a (or deceleration a) of a body is the ratio of velocity change ΔV and the associated time interval Δt:

$$a = \frac{\Delta V}{\Delta t} = \frac{V_2 - V_1}{t_2 - t_1}, \frac{\text{ft}}{\text{sec}^2} \tag{16-2}$$

where

V_2 = velocity at time t_2, ft/sec
V_1 = velocity at time t_1, ft/sec
t_2 = time at beginning of velocity change, sec
t_1 = time at end of velocity change, sec

The acceleration (or deceleration) of a body is uniform, when the same velocity changes occur in equal time intervals.

The acceleration (or deceleration) of a body is nonuniform, when different velocity changes occur in equal time intervals.

The *average acceleration* (or deceleration) of a body moving at a nonuniform acceleration (deceleration) is obtained by dividing the total velocity change by the total time interval during which the velocity change occurs.

16–2.2. The Velocity-Time Diagram. The velocity-time diagram is a graphical representation of the motion of a body. Even complicated velocity changes occurring in vehicle collisions can be clearly shown in the velocity-time diagram.

The velocity-time diagram of a body traveling at constant velocity is illustrated in Fig. 16–1. Since V = constant, the velocity curve is a straight line parallel to the horizontal time axis. From Eq. 16–1 it is evident that the product of velocity and time equals the distance traveled ($V \Delta t = S$). However, the product of velocity and time interval also equals the area of the rectangle under the velocity curve (line) of Fig. 16–1. This statement is valid for any motion and may be expressed as:

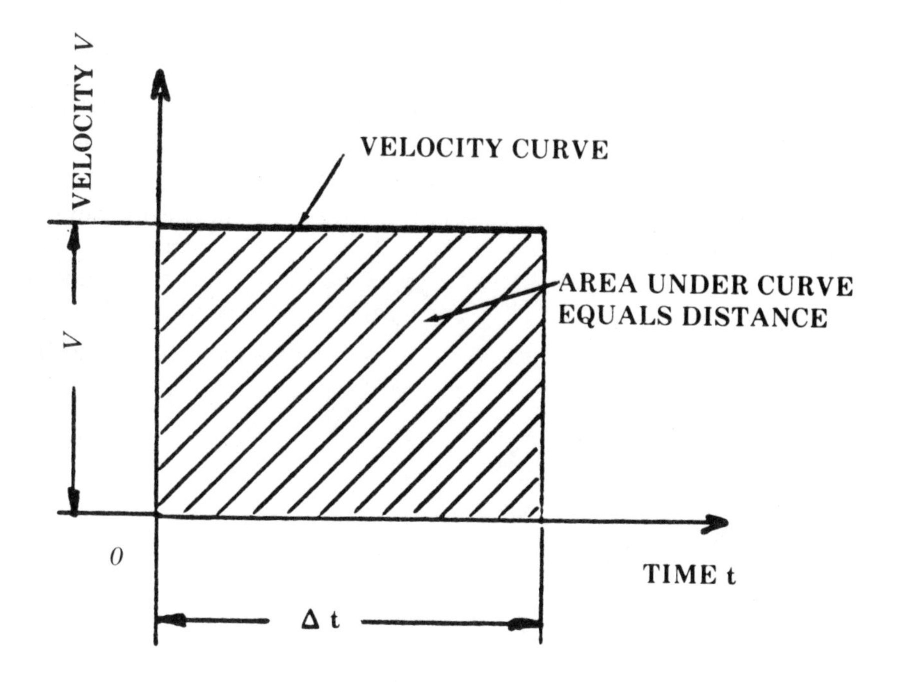

Figure 16-1. V-t Diagram, Constant Velocity

The area under the velocity curve in any velocity-time diagram is always equal to the distance traveled.

Uniform Acceleration Without Initial Velocity

The V-line is a straight line, intersecting the origin and sloping upwards as illustrated in Fig. 16-2. The area under the V-curve is the distance traveled. By use of the common triangle area relationship, the distance S is

$$S = \frac{V_1 \Delta t}{2}, \text{ ft} \tag{16-3}$$

The uniform acceleration is

$$a = \frac{\Delta V}{\Delta t}, \text{ ft/sec}^2 \tag{16-2}$$

The acceleration may be used to develop equations involving different physical measures of motion. For example, Eq. 16-2 may be solved for

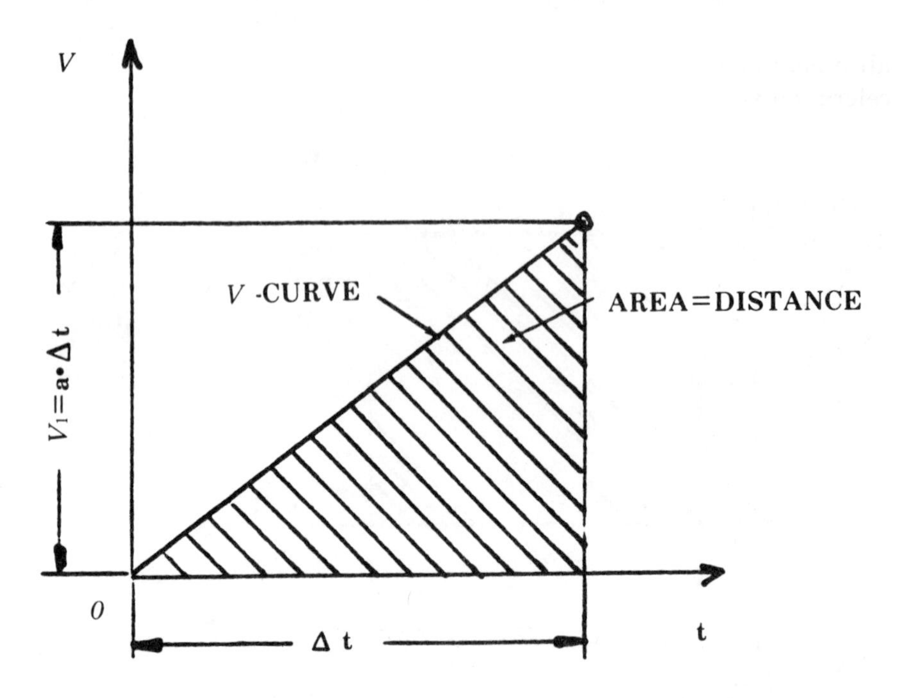

Figure 16–2. V-t Diagram, Uniform Acceleration Without Initial Velocity

Δt and substituted into Eq. 16–3, yielding the distance traveled ($\Delta V = V_1$)

$$S = \frac{V_1^2}{2a}, \text{ ft} \tag{16–4}$$

or eliminating ΔV

$$S = \left(\frac{a}{2}\right)(\Delta t)^2, \text{ ft} \tag{16–5}$$

Inspection of Eqs. 16–3 to 16–5 indicates that two pieces of information, e.g., velocity and acceleration, or acceleration and time must be known before the distance traveled can be computed. An important requirement is also that the acceleration a must remain constant throughout the acceleration process when the above equations are used. If the acceleration is not constant, an average acceleration value must be used. If this procedure is not accurate, then the motion must be divided into smaller segments, the first one starting from zero velocity, all others having an initial and final velocity and the associated acceleration values must be used.

Uniform Deceleration Without Final Velocity

The V-line is a straight line sloping down as illustrated in Fig. 16–3. The area under the V-curve again yields the distance traveled

$$S = \frac{V_0\,\Delta t}{2}, \text{ ft} \tag{16–6}$$

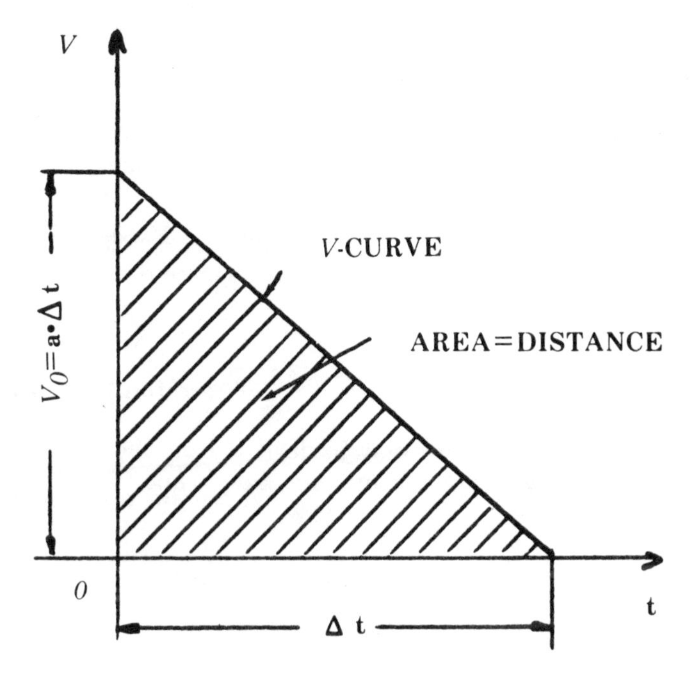

Figure 16–3. V-t Diagram, Uniform Deceleration Without Final Velocity

By the use of the deceleration

$$a = \frac{\Delta V}{\Delta t}, \text{ ft/sec}^2$$

one obtains the different expressions for distance as ($\Delta V = V_o$)

$$S = \frac{V_0^{\,2}}{2a}, \text{ ft} \tag{16–7}$$

or

$$S = \left(\frac{a}{2}\right)(\Delta t)^2, \text{ ft} \tag{16-8}$$

Eqs. 16–6 through 16–8 apply to conditions such as a vehicle sliding to rest after impact, or braking a vehicle to a stop from an initial velocity V_0. Eqs. 16–7 and 16–8 are only valid if the deceleration a remains constant throughout the motion. If the deceleration is not constant over the entire process, piece wise calculations must be carried out.

Uniform Acceleration With Initial Velocity

The V-line is a straight line sloping upward. The velocity increases from the initial velocity V_0 at time 0 sec to the final velocity V_t at time t as illustrated in Fig. 16–4. Since the same velocity changes occur in equal time intervals, the acceleration a is constant.

The distance traveled equals the area (trapezoid) under the V-line yielding

$$S = \left(\frac{V_t + V_0}{2}\right)\Delta t, \text{ ft} \tag{16-9}$$

The equations that follow may be derived from the basic equations and a division of the trapezoid into a rectangle and triangle. Distance traveled:

$$S = \frac{V_t^2 - V_0^2}{2a}, \text{ ft} \tag{16-10}$$

$$S = V_0\,\Delta t + \left(\frac{a}{2}\right)(\Delta t)^2, \text{ ft} \tag{16-11}$$

$$S = V_t\,\Delta t - \left(\frac{a}{2}\right)(\Delta t)^2, \text{ ft} \tag{16-12}$$

Acceleration

$$a = \frac{\Delta V}{\Delta t} = \frac{V_t - V_0}{\Delta t}, \text{ ft/sec}^2 \tag{16-13}$$

Uniform Deceleration With Final Velocity

The V-line is a straight line sloping downward as shown in Fig. 16–5. The velocity decreases from the initial velocity V_0 at time 0 sec to final velocity V_t at time t.

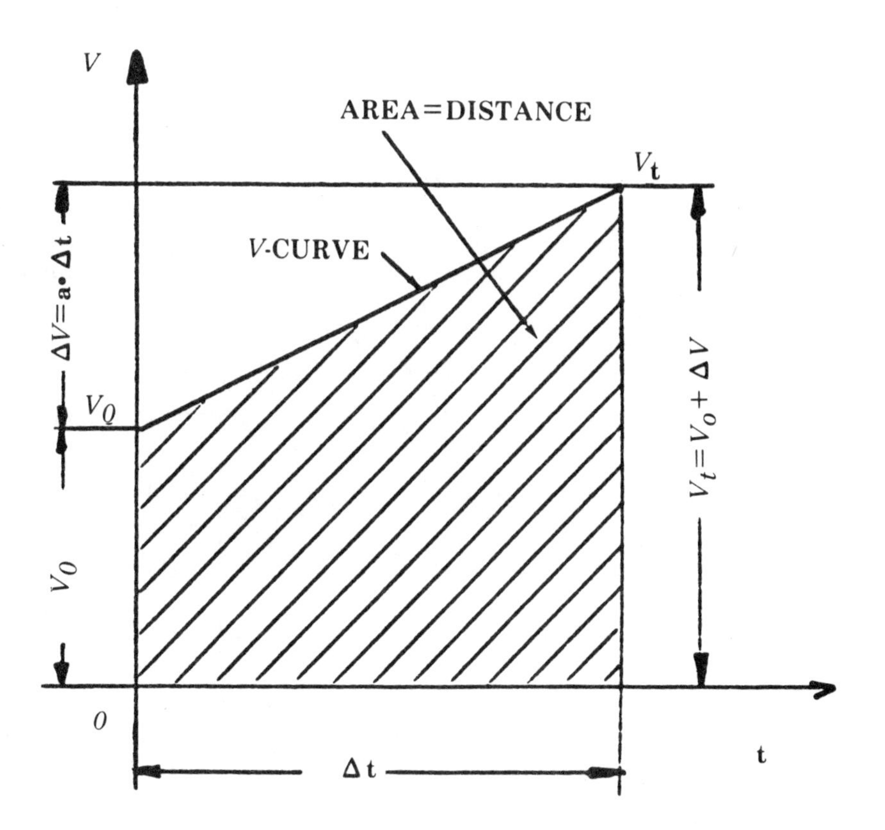

Figure 16-4. V-t Diagram, Uniform Acceleration With Initial Velocity

The equations for distance traveled are:

$$S = \left(\frac{V_0 + V_t}{2}\right) \Delta t, \text{ ft} \tag{16-14}$$

$$S = \frac{V_0^2 - V_t^2}{2a}, \text{ ft} \tag{16-15}$$

$$S = V_t \, \Delta t + \left(\frac{a}{2}\right) (\Delta t)^2, \text{ ft} \tag{16-16}$$

$$S = V_0 \, \Delta t - \left(\frac{a}{2}\right) (\Delta t)^2, \text{ ft} \tag{16-17}$$

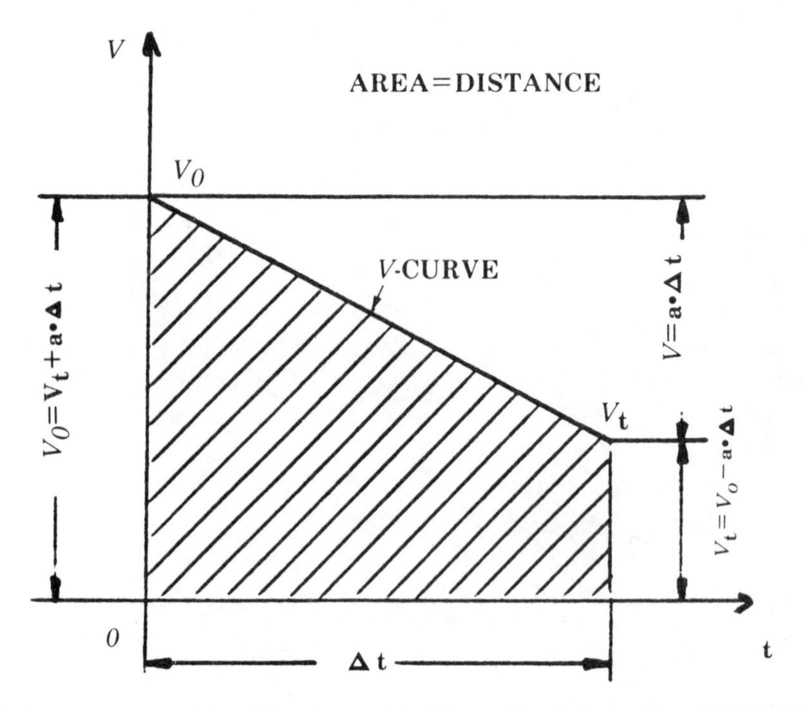

Figure 16–5. V-t Diagram, Uniform Deceleration With Final Velocity

Deceleration

$$a = \frac{\Delta V}{\Delta t} = \frac{V_0 - V_t}{\Delta t}, \text{ ft/sec}^2 \qquad (16\text{–}18)$$

A vehicle sliding with its wheels locked into a vehicle represents a case of deceleration with final velocity. In this case the final velocity is the impact speed of the vehicle. Often the tire markings on the road surface allow the determination of the distance S traveled prior to impact, and of the average deceleration a from the tire-road friction coefficient. Frequently, it becomes necessary to compute the velocity V_0 prior to braking. Eq. 16–15 may be solved for V_0, i.e., the higher initial velocity, yielding

$$V_0 = \sqrt{V_t^2 + 2aS}, \text{ ft/sec} \qquad (16\text{–}19)$$

In some cases involving accident avoidance considerations, it becomes necessary to compute the time elapsed during the deceleration process from V_0 to V_t. The deceleration time may be obtained from Eq. 16–17 by solving for Δt, yielding

$$\Delta t = \frac{V_0}{a} - \sqrt{\left(\frac{V_0}{a}\right)^2 - \frac{2S}{a}}, \text{ sec} \tag{16–20}$$

When the final velocity V_t is known, Eq. 16–16 may be used to compute Δt.

Example 16–1

A vehicle is traveling initially at a uniform velocity when at time zero the driver recognizes a hazardous situation. Three quarters of a second later the driver has braked and the wheels are locked and the vehicle slides 85 feet at which time it impacts another vehicle at 23 mph. The road surface is dry and a tire-road friction coefficient of 0.8 may be assumed.

Determine the initial speed of the vehicle.

The motion consists of three different phases as illustrated in Fig. 16–6.

1. The driver has released the accelerator pedal and is moving the foot onto the brake pedal; velocity is approximately constant.
2. The braking system begins to produce brake force; the deceleration of the vehicle increases from zero to its final value.
3. The braking system produces sufficient force to lock all wheels; the deceleration is assumed to remain constant until vehicle impact.

During the first phase the engine speed has to reduce in order to produce engine braking. Depending on speed and transmission, no significant velocity changes may occur over the small time interval considered here. A driver reaction time and pedal switch over time of 0.5 sec may be assumed for a fast responding driver (Ref. 13). Details on driver reaction times are presented in Chapters 23 and 24.

During the second phase the deceleration is not uniform, however, it is reasonable to assume a linear (straight line) increase of deceleration from a zero value to a value corresponding to locked wheel conditions (Section 20–3). The velocity curve between the points 1 and 2 identified by the beginning of braking and the beginning of sliding, respectively, is not a straight line, rather, a curve.

The initial velocity V_0 may be computed by

$$V_0 = V_1 + \left(\frac{a}{2}\right)(t_1 - t_0), \text{ ft/sec} \tag{16–21}$$

Where a = vehicle deceleration, ft/sec^2.

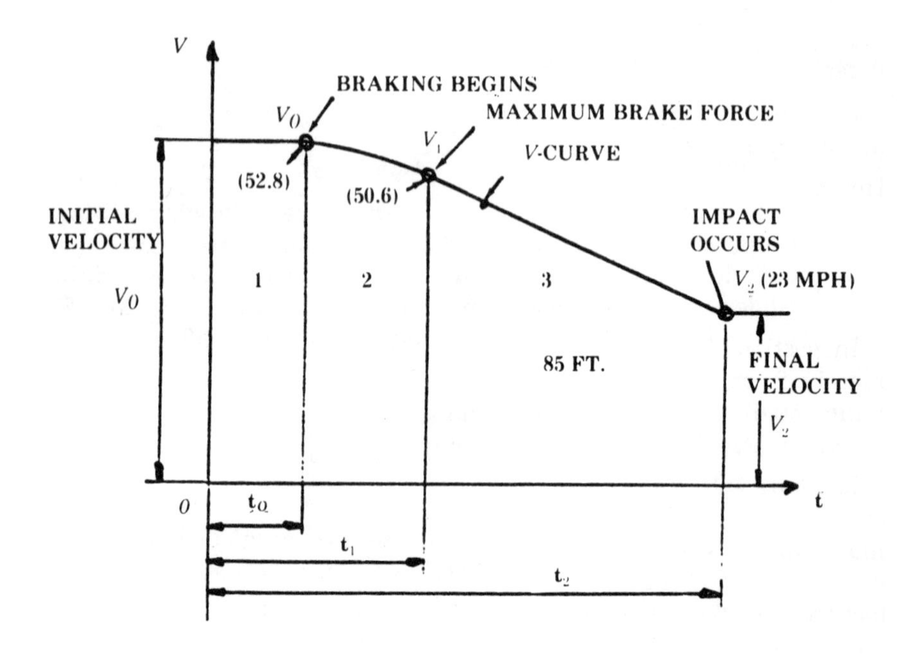

Figure 16–6. V-t Diagram, Braking Before Impact

During the third phase the deceleration is assumed to be uniform. The tire-road friction coefficient varies as a function of speed, and consequently, an average value must be used in this analysis (see Eq. 18–4). Eq. 16–19 may be used to determine the velocity at the instant the wheels are locked and constant deceleration motion exists. By the use of the notation of this example, one obtains

$$V_1 = \sqrt{V_2^{\,2} + 2aS} =$$

$$V_1 = \sqrt{[(23)(1.466)]^2 + (2)(0.8)(32.2)(85)} = 74.27 \text{ ft/sec or } 50.6 \text{ mph}$$

The velocity at the beginning of skid mark appearance is 50.6 mph.

As inspection of previous equations indicates the units of velocity are ft/sec. Consequently, prior to making any calculations all units of speed must be changed to ft/sec as indicated by the multiplication of 23 by 1.466. Also, the sliding tire-road friction coefficient must be multiplied by 32.2 ft/sec^2 to yield the actual vehicle deceleration in ft/sec^2.

Eq. 16–21 may now be used to compute the velocity of the vehicle at the instant deceleration begins.

Hence,

$$V_0 = V_1 + \left(\frac{a}{2}\right)(t_1 - t_0) = 74.27 + \frac{(0.8)(32.2)}{2}(0.75\text{–}0.50)$$

$$= 77.49 \text{ ft/sec or } 52.8 \text{ mph}$$

Inspection of the results indicates that a velocity decrease of approximately 2 mph occurred during the process of wheel locking (52.8 minus 50.6). A braking-system response time of 0.25 sec was assumed to exist (details are shown by Eq. 20–10).

It is interesting to note that the use of a tire-road friction coefficient of 0.7 (instead of 0.8) reduces the velocity V_1 to 70.48 ft/sec (or 48 mph) indicating a decrease of about 5.1% for a drop in friction of approximately 12%. The reasons for this difference in change are due to the fact that the friction coefficient is under the radical sign, reducing its mathematical effect.

16-3. CIRCULAR MOTION (ROTATION)

All previous equations are valid for both straight-line and circular motion. The circle has a certain number of mathematical laws associated with it which are incorporated in the equations of motion to provide more convenient relationships.

The following parameters are defined for a circle (see Fig. 16–7):

Angle α at one revolution $\alpha = 2\pi$, rad

Angle α at n revolutions: $\alpha = 2\pi n$, rad

Arc $\Delta S = r \cdot \alpha$, ft

where

r = radius, ft

α = angle, rad

Arc at n revolutions $\Delta S = r\,\alpha \cdot n$, ft

The arc is the distance traveled by a point located on the circumference. The unit for the angle is obtained by dividing arc ΔS by radius r. The ratio of two length units (ΔS and r) yields, e.g., ft/ft, i.e., unity. In order to know that this ratio of unity is actually an angle, the word radian (rad) is used in place of the number "1" to indicate angular displacement. The commonly used angle measured in degrees can be obtained from the angle in rad by multiplication by 57.3, i.e., one rad = 57.3 degrees.

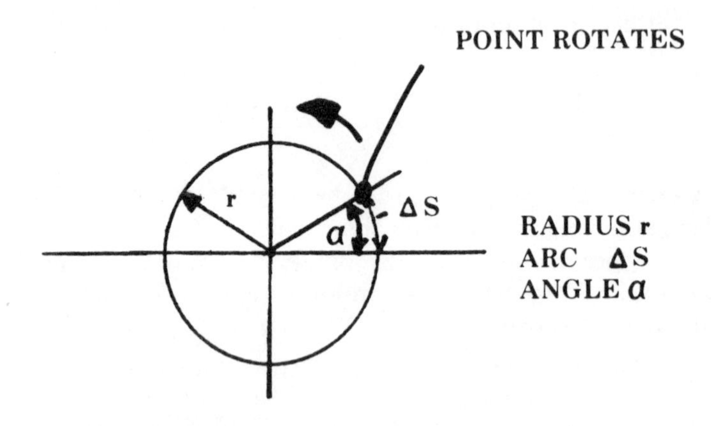

Figure 16-7. Circular Displacement

16-3.1. Angular Velocity. The angular velocity ω is the ratio of angular rotation α and time interval Δt (see Eq. 16-1):

$$\omega = \frac{\alpha}{\Delta t}, \frac{\text{rad}}{\text{sec}} \text{ or } \frac{1}{\text{sec}} \tag{16-22}$$

The average angular velocity is obtained by dividing the total angular displacement by the total time interval.

16-3.2. Angular Acceleration. Angular acceleration ϵ (or deceleration) is the ratio of the change of angular velocity $\Delta\omega$ and the associated time interval Δt (see Eq. 16-2):

$$\epsilon = \frac{\Delta\omega}{\Delta t} = \frac{\omega_2 - \omega_1}{t_2 - t_1}, \frac{\text{rad}}{\text{sec}^2} \text{ or } \frac{1}{\text{sec}^2} \tag{16-23}$$

where

ω_2 = angular velocity at time t_2, rad/sec

ω_1 = angular velocity at time t_1, rad/sec

t_2 = time at beginning of angular velocity change, sec

t_1 = time at end of angular velocity change, sec

16-3.3. Angular Velocity and Circumferential Velocity. The circumferential velocity V_c of a point on the circumference is oriented tangentially to the circle and related to the angular velocity ω by

$$V_c = \omega r, \text{ ft/sec} \tag{16–24}$$

where

r = radius of circle, ft

ω = angular velocity, rad/sec

16–3.4. Angular Acceleration and Tangential Acceleration. The tangential acceleration a_t of a point on the circumference is oriented tangentially to the circle and related to the angular acceleration ϵ by

$$a_t = \epsilon r, \text{ ft/sec}^2 \tag{16–25}$$

16–3.5. Centrifugal Acceleration. The velocity of a body traveling in a circular path experiences a constant change even if the magnitude of the velocity does not change as in the case of constant angular velocity. This velocity change is the result of a continuing change of velocity direction, requiring a force to be accomplished. In the case of a ball held by a string in a circular motion, the force is equal to the tension in the string. In a vehicle turning a corner the redirection or change of velocity is accomplished by the side forces produced by the tires induced by a steering wheel rotation.

The centrifugal acceleration a_c of a point on the circumference is oriented radially toward the center of the circle and related to the circumferential velocity V_c by

$$a_c = \frac{V_c^2}{r}, \text{ ft/sec}^2 \tag{16–26}$$

or with Eq. 16–24

$$a_c = r\omega^2, \text{ ft/sec}^2 \tag{16–27}$$

16–3.6. Angular Velocity-Time Diagram. When the straight-line velocity of the V/t-diagram is replaced by the angular velocity ω, the angular velocity-time diagram is obtained. As in the V/t-diagram, the area under the angular velocity curve is equal to the angular displacement or total angle of rotation. The different diagrams developed in connection with straight-line motion may be applied to the corresponding rotational motion.

Uniform Rotational Velocity

The angular velocity line (ω-line) is a straight line parallel to the horizontal time axis.

$$\omega = \frac{\alpha}{\Delta t}, \frac{\text{rad}}{\text{sec}} \tag{16–28}$$

Uniform Angular Acceleration Without Initial Angular Velocity

The ω-line is a straight-line sloping upward and intersecting the origin as shown in Fig. 16–8. The associated equations are:

Angular displacement

$$\alpha = \frac{\omega_1 \Delta t}{2}, \text{ rad} \tag{16–29}$$

$$\alpha = \left(\frac{\epsilon}{2}\right)(\Delta t)^2, \text{ rad} \tag{16–30}$$

Angular acceleration

$$\epsilon = \frac{\Delta\omega}{\Delta t}, \frac{\text{rad}}{\text{sec}^2} \tag{16–31}$$

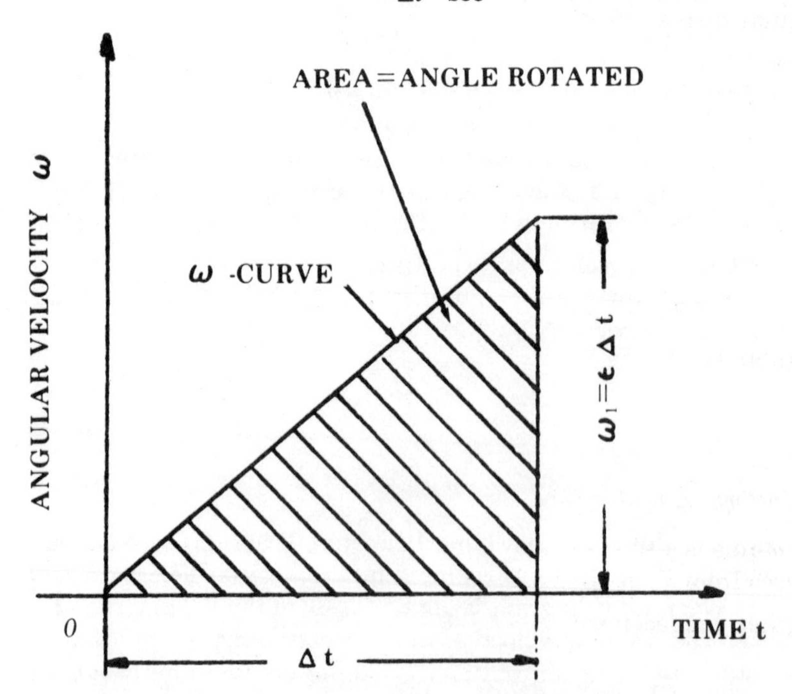

Figure 16–8. ω-t Diagram, Uniform Angular Acceleration Without Initial Velocity

Uniform Angular Deceleration Without Final Angular Velocity

The ω-line is a straight line sloping downward

Angular displacement

$$\alpha = \frac{\omega_0 \Delta t}{2}, \text{ rad} \quad (16\text{–}32)$$

$$\alpha = \left(\frac{\epsilon}{2}\right) (\Delta t)^2, \text{ rad} \quad (16\text{–}33)$$

Angular acceleration

$$\epsilon = \frac{\Delta\omega}{\Delta t}, \frac{\text{rad}}{\text{sec}^2} \quad (16\text{–}34)$$

Uniform Angular Acceleration With Initial Angular Velocity

The ω-line is a straight line sloping upward. The angular velocity increases from ω_0 at time zero to the final value ω_t at time t.

Angular displacement

$$\alpha = \left(\frac{\omega_t + \omega_0}{2}\right) \Delta t, \text{ rad} \quad (16\text{–}35)$$

$$\alpha = \frac{\omega_t^2 - \omega_0^2}{2\epsilon}, \text{ rad} \quad (16\text{–}36)$$

$$\alpha = \omega_0 \Delta t + \left(\frac{\epsilon}{2}\right) (\Delta t)^2, \text{ rad} \quad (16\text{–}37)$$

$$\alpha = \omega_t \Delta t - \left(\frac{\epsilon}{2}\right) (\Delta t)^2, \text{ rad} \quad (16\text{–}38)$$

Angular acceleration

$$\epsilon = \frac{\Delta\omega}{\Delta t} = \frac{\omega_t - \omega_0}{\Delta t}, \frac{\text{rad}}{\text{sec}^2} \quad (16\text{–}39)$$

Uniform Angular Deceleration With Final Angular Velocity

The ω-line is a straight line sloping downward. The angular velocity decreases from ω_0 at time zero to the final velocity ω_t at time t.

Angular displacement

$$\alpha = \left(\frac{\omega_0 + \omega_t}{2}\right) \Delta t, \text{ rad} \quad (16\text{–}40)$$

$$\alpha = \frac{\omega_0^2 - \omega_t^2}{2}, \text{ rad} \quad (16\text{–}41)$$

$$\alpha = \omega_t \Delta t + \left(\frac{\epsilon}{2}\right) (\Delta t)^2, \text{ rad} \quad (16\text{–}42)$$

$$\alpha = \omega_0 \Delta t - \left(\frac{\epsilon}{2}\right) (\Delta t)^2, \text{ rad} \quad (16\text{–}43)$$

Angular deceleration

$$\epsilon = \frac{\Delta\omega}{\Delta t} = \frac{\omega_0 - \omega_t}{\Delta t}, \frac{\text{rad}}{\text{sec}^2} \tag{16–44}$$

Example 16–2

Non-central two-vehicle collisions often involve post crash rotation and translation or straight-line motion. The following pertinent data exist: After impact the vehicle rotated 400 deg about its vertical axis from its initial position at impact, the time interval is 1.8 sec from beginning of rotation to rest.

The motion is assumed to be uniform angular deceleration without final angular velocity. The angular displacement α may be expressed in radians as 400/57.3 = 6.98 rad. The angular velocity immediately after impact may be determined from Eq. 16–32 by solving for ω_0.

$$\omega_0 = \frac{2\alpha}{\Delta t} = \frac{(2)(6.98)}{1.8} = 7.76\ \frac{\text{rad}}{\text{sec}}$$

The corresponding angular deceleration ϵ is determined by Eq. 16–34,

$$\epsilon = \frac{\Delta\omega}{\Delta t} = \frac{7.76}{1.8} = 4.31\ \frac{\text{rad}}{\text{sec}^2}$$

Each point of the vehicle rotates with an initial angular velocity of 7.76 rad/sec. Occupants are often ejected as a result of vehicle rotation. The centrifugal force exerted on a body within the car is a function of its distance from the center of rotation. If a distance or radius r = 2 ft is assumed, Eq. 16–27 may be used to determine a centrifugal acceleration of $(2)(7.76)^2 = 120.4$ ft/sec². The centrifugal force is given by the product of mass and acceleration, i.e., for an occupant weighing 150 lb the mass is 150/32.2 = 4.66 lb sec²/ft, yielding a force of 4.66 times 120.4 = 561 lb. The force of 561 lb is attempting to accelerate the occupant outward against the interior walls of the vehicle, or window and door openings.

CHAPTER 17
FUNDAMENTALS OF FORCE ANALYSIS

17-1. DEFINITION OF FORCE

A force is acting when a body changes its form or motion. A car crashing against a solid wall changes its motion from a certain velocity to zero, and its form. The cause of the force is the resistance of the wall. The leaf spring of a solid axle rear suspension deforms under the load. The cause of the force is the gravity force of the load.

Forces are distinguished by their cause or by the effect. For example, spring force, friction force, or pedal force are designated by their cause, whereas braking force, cornering force, or acceleration force are designated by their effects.

17-2. DEFINITION OF MASS

The mass is a fundamental physical measure. The mass of a body is determined by its makeup, i.e., the number of molecules, and is independent of location on the earth or the moon. The mass of a given body does not change. The weight of the body (having a mass m), however, is a function of the gravity effect of the earth. Consequently, care must be exercised in distinguishing between mass and weight. The unit of the mass is $\frac{\text{lb-sec}^2}{\text{ft}}$ (or kilogram (kg) in the metric system).

The mass of a body can also be considered as a measure of the body's inertia or resistance to a change of motion.

17-3. RELATIONSHIP BETWEEN MASS AND FORCE

A body remains at rest or moves with a uniform velocity, unless a resulting force (net force) causes a change of the existing conditions.

The equation relating force and mass was found by Newton. Often called Newton's second law, it is

$$F_{res} = ma, \text{ lb} \qquad (17\text{-}1)$$

where

a = acceleration of the body, ft/sec²

F_{res} = resultant force acting on the body, lb

m = mass, $\frac{\text{lb sec}^2}{\text{ft}}$

Eq. 17–1 indicates that a resultant force F_{res} causes a body of mass m to accelerate at an acceleration a. The weight of a body is acted upon by gravity. In this case acceleration a due to gravity is 32.2 ft/sec^2, commonly designated by the letter g. Consequently, the weight of a body may be expressed by

$$W = mg, \text{ lb} \qquad (17\text{–}2)$$

Eq. 17–2 may be solved for mass m and the result substituted into Eq. 17–1, yielding

$$F_{res} = \left(\frac{W}{g}\right) a, \text{ lb} \qquad (17\text{–}3)$$

Eq. 17–3 indicates that a body having a large weight yields a small acceleration (or deceleration) for a given resultant force. A motor vehicle moving at a given uniform velocity has no resultant or net force acting on it, i.e., for example both aerodynamic drag and rolling resistance are balanced by the drive thrust of the driven wheels. Upon application of the brakes an excess of force is produced, i.e., a resultant or net force is acting on the body, attempting to change the state of motion of the vehicle. In this case the motion is changed to deceleration, producing an inertia force. The deceleration a is a function of the weight and the resultant force, determined by Eq. 17–3 as

$$a = \frac{F_{res}}{W/g}, \text{ ft/sec}^2 \qquad (17\text{–}4)$$

Inspection of Eq. 17–4 indicates that the deceleration increases with increasing resultant force, e.g., braking effort, and decreases with increasing weight. The resultant force can be computed from a brake system analysis (Chapter 20).

The deceleration (or acceleration) computed by Eq. 17–4 may then be used in the appropriate equations of Chapter 16 to compute other motion parameters such as distance or time.

17-4. FORCE AND MASS IN ROTATION

The rotational acceleration of a flywheel requires a resultant force acting on a lever arm, or torque, e.g., the crank of the crankshaft. The rotational acceleration for a given torque depends upon the distribution of mass of the flywheel. For example, a slender long rod exhibits a smaller rotational mass resistance than a ring of the same weight with a large portion of the weight concentrated at a large diameter. Automobiles having a large mass (or weight) concentrated between the axles as in mid-engine vehicles have a smaller rotational mass resistance than conventional vehicles with front engine location and heavy front and rear bumpers.

The rotational mass resistance is commonly called mass moment of inertia. Equations for computing mass moment of inertia may be found in texts on basic mechanics. Values of mass moment of inertia of wheels and automobiles are found in Sections 20–3.2 and 22–3.4 respectively.

The dynamic law of rotation (similar to Newton's 2nd law, Eq. 17–1) is

$$M_{res} = I\epsilon, \text{ lb·ft} \tag{17–5}$$

where

$$I = \text{mass moment of inertia, lb·ft·sec}^2$$

$$M_{res} = \text{resultant or net moment, lb·ft}$$

$$\epsilon = \text{angular acceleration; } \frac{\text{rad}}{\text{sec}^2}$$

The resultant moment is caused by the forces acting on the body through a lever arm. When the resultant force acts through the point of rotation, no lever arm exists and no moment can be produced, and consequently, no rotational acceleration can occur. The latter observation is significant in vehicle impacts, when the impact force may or may not act through the center of the body (Chapter 28).

17–5. THE FRICTION FORCE

Friction forces are an important element in motor vehicle accident reconstruction. Friction forces are produced by a rolling or sliding tire on wet and dry roadways, by a vehicle sliding on its side, by a beam penetrating into the vehicle, and many other mechanisms. Friction exists when complete or partial sliding occurs between two surfaces.

In general friction is the result of four components: adhesion, tearing, viscous damping, and internal losses.

Adhesion is a molecular mechanism attempting to pull two surfaces together, similar to water adhering to a surface.

Tearing is the mechanism of forcefully pulling particles off the surface.

Viscous damping exists in the presence of a liquid between the two sliding surfaces, when one surface pushes the liquid away similar to a water ski.

Internal losses cause friction due to, e.g., the constant bending of the tire contact patch as it meets the road.

For a car sliding on its roof, adhesion and tearing are the major contributions to friction; for a tire sliding on a dry road, adhesion and tearing, on a wet road viscous damping and adhesion.

The force existing between two surfaces just prior to sliding is usually called static friction. The friction produced between two sliding surfaces is generally called dynamic friction.

The coefficient of friction is the ratio of friction force and the associated normal force (force pushing both surfaces together). The friction force must be measured, and consequently, the computed friction coefficient depends upon the experimental conditions. The coefficient is a function of velocity, temperature, contact pressure, and others.

More information on tire forces is presented in Chapter 18.

17-6. MECHANICAL ENERGY

The concept of energy is an important factor in accident reconstruction. During a collision kinetic energy, i.e., the motion energy of a vehicle, is transferred into thermal, noise, and deformation energy of vehicle components. Energy must be available to cause injuries, shear trees or destroy road objects.

Energy is stored within the body and is the capability to do work, once released.

A weight prior to dropping through a certain height possesses a potential energy, computed by

$$E_{pot} = Wh, \text{ lb·ft} \tag{17-6}$$

where

$$W = \text{weight, lb}$$
$$h = \text{height, ft}$$

A vehicle moving at a velocity V possesses a kinetic energy, computed by

$$E_k = \left(\frac{m}{2}\right)V^2 = \left(\frac{W}{2g}\right)V^2, \text{ lb·ft} \tag{17-7}$$

where

$$g = 32.2 \text{ ft/sec}^2$$

During a collision the velocity of a vehicle changes. The kinetic energy change ΔE_k is computed by

$$\Delta E_k = \left(\frac{W}{2g}\right)(V_1^2 - V_2^2), \text{ lb·ft} \qquad (17\text{–}8)$$

where

V_1 = velocity immediately before impact, ft/sec
V_2 = velocity immediately after impact, ft/sec

The total energy of all components involved in a collision must remain constant. The changes in kinetic energy of all vehicles involved and the deformation energy associated with the crush must balance. For example, in a rear end collision involving a stationary vehicle, the kinetic energy of the impacting vehicle is reduced due to a decrease of speed, the kinetic energy of the impacted vehicle is increased due to a speed increase, and the crush deformation of both vehicles requires energy. In this case the kinetic energy of the impacting vehicle is reduced by an amount equal to the kinetic energy increase of the impacted vehicle and the deformation energy of the crushed components. The energy balance equations cannot be used to compute velocities before and after the collision, since in general, no assessment of the deformation energy on a piece by piece evaluation is possible. The deformation energy of many materials including steel is a function of the displacement, i.e., crush distance, the deformation velocity, the material properties temperature, and design factors.

CHAPTER 18
THE TIRE FORCE

18-1. FUNDAMENTAL CONSIDERATIONS

The pneumatic tire is an integral part of the vehicle system. The tire contributes significantly to the safety of highway transportation.

The performance of a tire can be divided into mechanical and structural performance.

The mechanical tire performance relates to the driving function of the tire and consists of the shear or traction force performance, involving brake force, drive force, and side force, and the rolling performance, involving ride comfort and rolling resistance.

The structural tire performance relates to the load carrying function of the tire and consists of endurance performance, involving fatigue life, resistance to wear, bond life, material insensitivity to chemical and thermal effects, and the load and stress performance, involving static and dynamic load carrying capacity, resistance to penetration, bead unseating resistance, and vibration performance.

Both mechanical and structural tire performance are important elements of accident reconstruction. Mechanical tire performance relates directly to vehicle motion. Structural tire performance analysis is an essential element of tire defect investigations.

18-2. FORCES ACTING ON A STANDING TIRE

The standing tire transmits vehicle loads to the road. The load carrying mechanism of the tire consists of two parts.

1. The load carrying capacity of the tire material itself, i.e., its strength without any inflation pressure, and the increased tire wall stiffening caused by the inflation pressure.

2. The load carrying capacity of the compressed air in the tire, consisting of the product of inflation pressure and tire-to-road contact area, commonly called contact patch. An increase in tire inflation pressure due to compression of the air by a high tire load results in a slight increase in load carrying capacity.

The inflation pressure multiplied by the contact patch area contributes approximately 85% to the load carrying capacity of a tire, while the basic strength and stiffness of the side walls account for the rest.

The maximum load carrying capacity of a tire is limited by the strength of the material since it has to carry some of the load and must contain the inflation pressure. The material strength decreases with temperature. Since a rolling tire produces heat and thus increases tire temperature, the maximum load carrying capacity is limited by thermal factors.

The maximum safe load carrying capacity is specified by the tire manufacturers and indicated on the tire as a function of inflation pressure (Ref. 8).

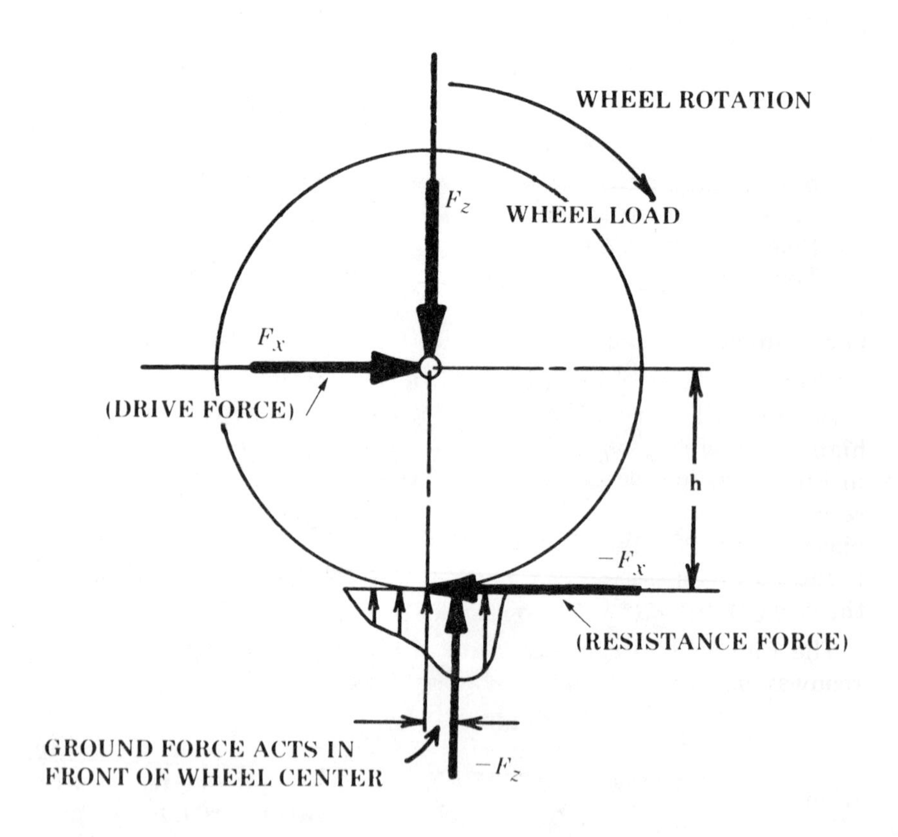

Figure 18–1. Forces Acting on a Free-Rolling Wheel

18-3. FORCES ACTING ON A ROLLING TIRE

The rolling resistance of a tire is the force required to push or pull the tire over a surface. The reasons for rolling resistance are connected to the bending and straightening of the tread and carcass when the rubber meets and leaves the road surface. A second reason is the nonuniform pressure distribution between tire and road, resulting in a forward shifting of the resultant ground force as illustrated in Fig. 18–1. On loose ground the deformation of the soil or sand, and the friction of the ground on the sides of the tire contribute to rolling resistance.

The rolling resistance coefficient is the ratio of rolling resistance force to normal load carried by the tire (F_x/F_z). Some typical values for passenger car tires are presented in Table 18–1 (Ref. 13).

Table 18–1

Roadway	Rolling Resistance Coefficient
Smooth Asphalt Surface	0.015
Smooth Concrete Surface	0.017
Smooth Dirt Road	0.045
Loose Sand	0.05 to 0.30

For example, a vehicle weighing 3000 lb has a rolling resistance of $3000 \times 0.015 = 45$ lb when traveling on smooth asphalt.

Due to construction differences, conventional bias ply tires exhibit a higher rolling resistance coefficient than radial ply tires as illustrated in Fig. 18–2. Inspection of the curves indicates an increase of rolling resistance with speed for speeds exceeding approximately 75 mph for bias ply and 100 mph for radial ply tires. The reasons for this increase is caused by increased internal losses, and a wave formation around the circumference of the tire.

The rolling resistance coefficient f_R of pneumatic tires on a paved roadway may be determined by

$$f_R = a + \frac{0.15}{p} + \left(\frac{b}{p}\right)\left(\frac{V^2}{100}\right), \text{ d'less} \qquad (18\text{–}1)$$

where

p = tire inflation pressure, psi
V = vehicle speed, mph
radial ply tire: $a = 0.005$; $b = 0.67$
bias ply tire: $a = 0.009$; $b = 1.00$

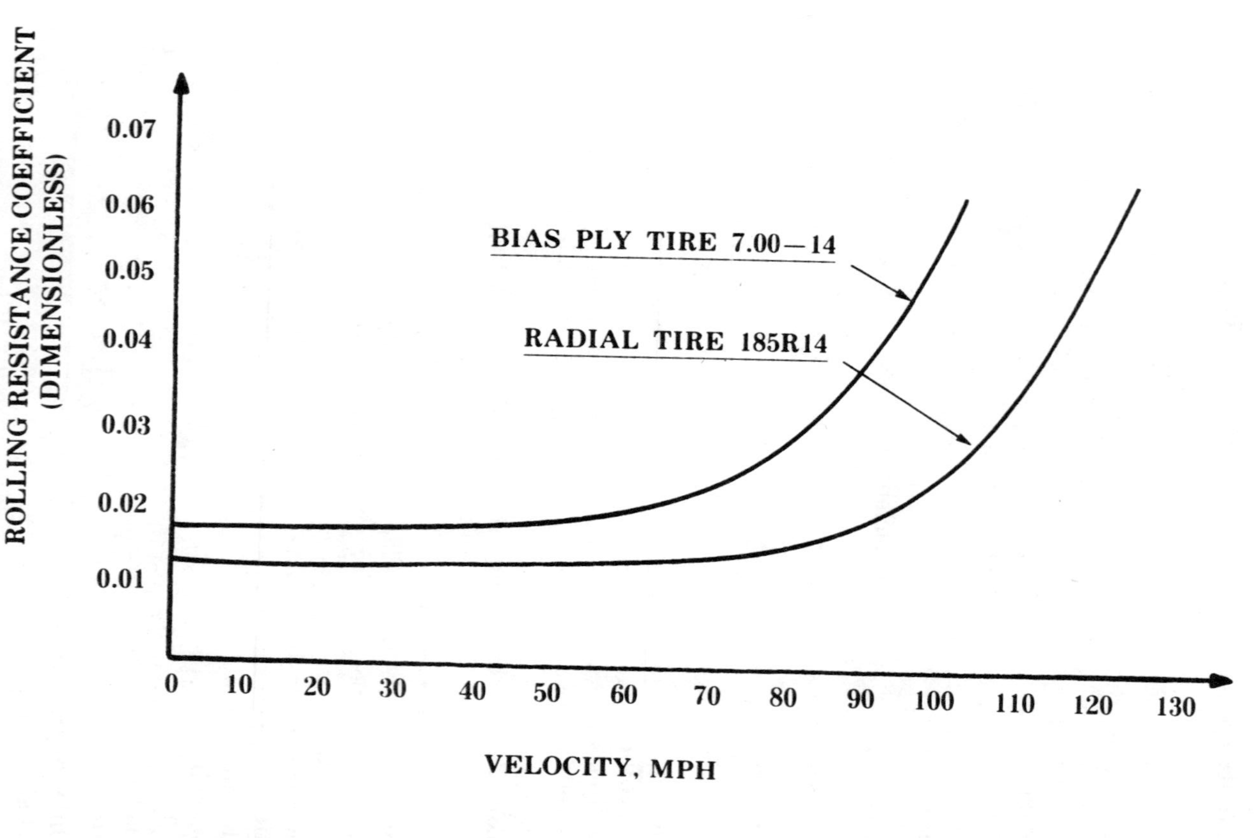

Figure 18–2. Rolling Resistance Coefficient as Function of Velocity

The rolling resistance force F_R is computed by

$$F_R = f_R F_z, \text{ lb} \tag{18-2}$$

where

F_z = normal force supported by tire, lb.

Truck tires generally exhibit rolling resistance coefficients that are approximately 25% lower than those of passenger car tires. Truck tires generally have a larger amount of natural rubber content than passenger tires, resulting in a decreased rolling resistance coefficient at the cost of a decreased longitudinal, i.e., braking friction coefficient. Radial tires also exhibit a lower rolling resistance coefficient than conventional construction.

18-4. FORCES ACTING ON A BRAKED OR DRIVEN TIRE

A braked tire develops a shear or traction force between the contact patch and the road surface. The braking torque acting between brake shoe and drum causes the tire to decelerate, i.e., the velocity of the tire circumference is less than the forward velocity of the vehicle. This difference in velocity causes the tire to slip over the road surface. A free rolling tire exhibits zero slip whereas a sliding (locked) tire exhibits 100% slip.

Tire slip s_T may be determined by

$$s_T = \frac{V_V - V_T}{V_V} \times 100, \text{ percent} \tag{18-3}$$

where

V_V = vehicle velocity, ft/sec

V_T = circumferential velocity of tire, ft/sec

The shear force is limited by the conditions associated with a sliding tire, i.e., 100% slip. Pneumatic tires produce a friction-slip curve as illustrated in Fig. 18-3. The maximum dry friction occurs at a slip between 10 and 20%, the corresponding value for wet surfaces may exceed 30 to 50% slip as illustrated in Fig. 18-4. The coefficient of friction is defined by the ratio of shear or traction force to normal force on the tire.

While the friction forces on dry pavement are affected somewhat by wheel slip values beyond 10% and vehicle speed, the results obtained on wet surfaces indicate a pronounced effect of velocity and slip on the friction force produced by the tire.

An important characteristic of tires is their almost total loss of side friction when the tire is sliding. While a sliding tire produces little

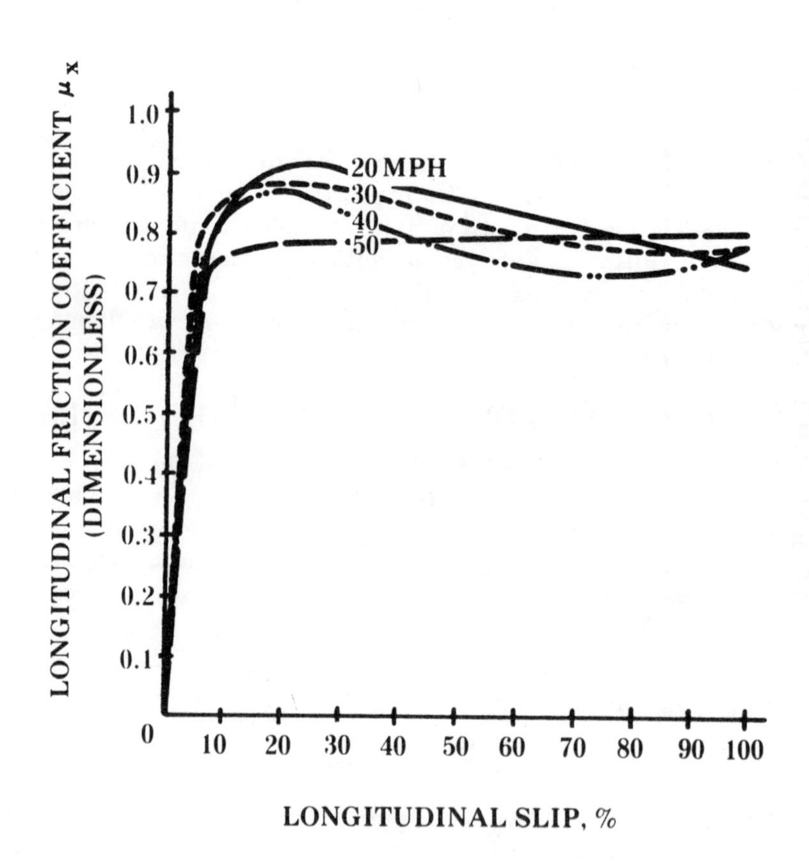

Figure 18–3. Friction-Slip Curve for Dry Concrete as Function of Speed

or no side friction, a rolling tire produces maximum friction. This behavior is the major reason for the use of antiskid brake systems. A typical side friction curve is illustrated in Fig. 18–4.

Tests with bias ply tires (sizes 6.40 × 13 to 6.00 × 15) have shown that the speed dependence of the tire-road surface friction may be expressed reasonably accurately by

$$\mu = \mu_o - kV, \text{ d'less} \qquad (18\text{–}4)$$

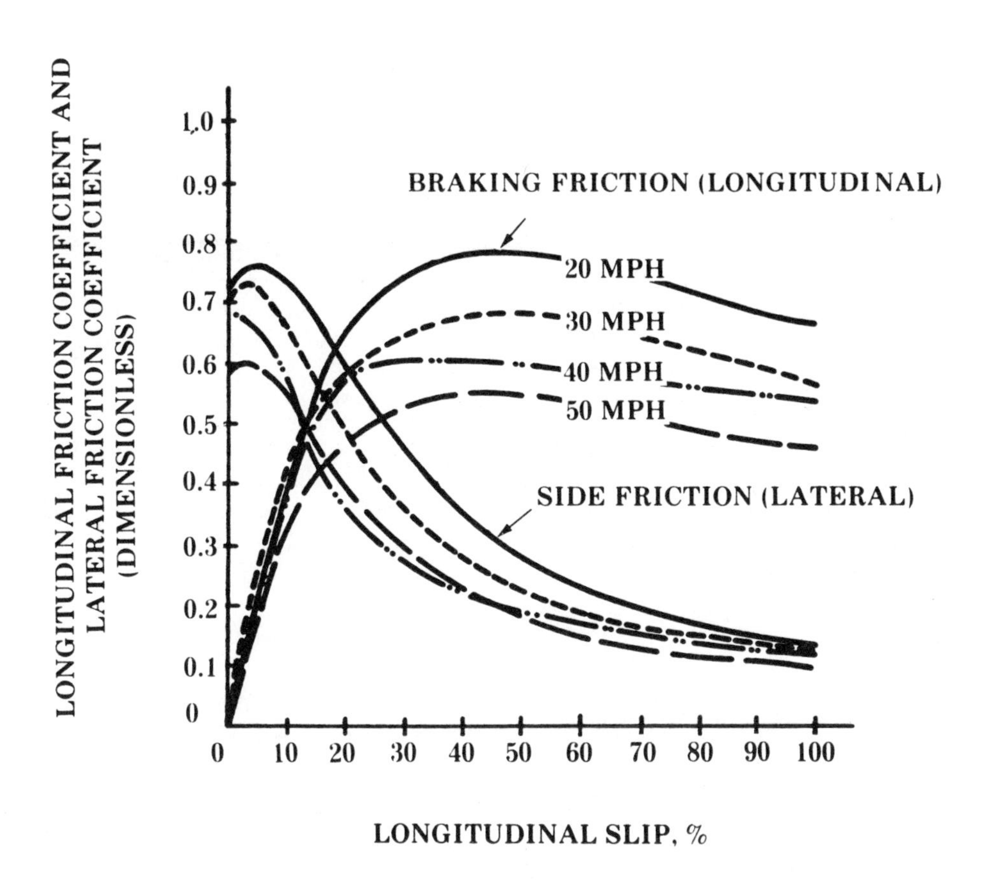

Figure 18–4. Friction-Slip Curve for Wet Concrete Road as a Function of Speed Obtained for an Automobile Tire

where

μ = tire-road friction coefficient, d'less

μ_o = tire-road friction coefficient at low speed, d'less

k = constant expressing speed effect, $\frac{1}{\text{mph}}$

V = velocity, mph

Eq. 18–4 may be used for dry or wet road surfaces, using the μ_o and k values shown in Table 18–2. The values represent average values observed on concrete and asphalt road surfaces:

Table 18–2

Parameters for Eq. 18–4				
	Dry Road		Wet Road	
	Peak	Sliding	Peak	Sliding
μ_o	0.95	0.85	0.75	0.7
k	0.0017	0.0025	0.0033	0.005

For example, a tire sliding at 40 mph on a dry road surface exhibits a friction coefficient $\mu = 0.85 - 0.0025 \times 40 = 0.75$. If the surface were wet, the coefficient of friction would reduce to 0.5. The corresponding values at 60 mph are 0.70 and 0.40, respectively.

The measured wet coefficient of friction for a public road may vary seasonably and from lane to lane on the highway. Tests under wet conditions have shown maximum road traction to occur during early spring and minimum traction during late summer. A reason for this has been found to exist in the degree to which road surfaces were polished. Road surfaces appear to be more polished in late summer than in early spring. This seasonal variation in wet-road friction is believed to be caused by second order asperities on the road surface. Basically, it is possible that the skid resistance of a roadway appears to be sufficient and within acceptable limits when obtained under favorable seasonal conditions. However, since the minimum value of skid resistance should be used for identifying hazardous road surface conditions, seasonal effects as well as for example effects of repaired road sections upon skid resistance should be clearly identified.

Skid tests taken five years after opening a highway for public use showed wet sliding friction coefficient of 0.25 to 0.30 for the truck lane and 0.40 to 0.50 for the car lanes. In other tests, measured wet road friction coefficients for different passenger car tires on the same road surface varied considerably with the design (Ref. 14). Some important findings published in Ref. 14 are discussed below.

For wet concrete roadways the lowest peak friction coefficient measured was 0.45, the highest 0.75. The majority of tires (over 50 different tires) produced peak friction coefficients between 0.6 and 0.7.

For wet asphalt surfaces the lowest peak friction coefficient measured was 0.4, the highest 0.75. The majority of tires produced peak friction between 0.5 and 0.6.

On slippery road surfaces (produced by wet Jennite) the lowest peak friction coefficient measured was 0.1, the highest 0.55. The majority of tires produced peak friction values between 0.25 and 0.4. The sliding friction coefficients measured on wet concrete are: low 0.45, high 0.65, majority of tires between 0.4 to 0.55. On other wet surfaces the sliding friction coefficients measured are: wet asphalt, low 0.3, high 0.6, majority between 0.3 and 0.45; wet Jennite: low 0.05, high 0.35, majority between 0.1 and 0.2.

Measured friction coefficients for studded and nonstudded snow tires on wet concrete surfaces showed no significant difference. For example, the peak friction coefficient for the studded tire is 0.6, for the nonstudded tire 0.61. The sliding friction coefficients are 0.50 for both tires. Friction coefficients for light truck tires are similar to those of passenger car tires.

The tire-road friction coefficient varies as a function of tire normal force. For example, a light truck tire model 7.50–16 D Highway on a Portland Cement road surface having an ASTM skid number of 75 produces a peak dry friction coefficient of 0.97 at 400 lb tire load, and 0.78 at 2400 lb. The friction coefficients were obtained for an inflation pressure of 30 psi. At an inflation pressure of 60 psi the corresponding friction values increase to 1.02 and 0.87, respectively. The above values are averaged between speeds of 50 and 60 mph.

The approximate peak friction coefficient μ as a function of tire load for typical light truck tires may be expressed by

$$\mu = 0.95 - 0.22\left(\frac{F_z}{N}\right), \text{ d'less} \tag{18–5}$$

where

F_z = actual (dynamic) tire load, lb

N = tire rated load for the particular inflation pressure, lb

The approximate load and speed sensitivity of light truck tires may be expressed as

$$\mu = 0.95 - 0.00027V - 0.22\left(\frac{F_z}{N}\right), \text{ d'less} \tag{18–6}$$

where

V = speed, mph

The sliding friction coefficients are more affected by speed than the peak friction values. The reason for this difference is due to the substantially different traction force production mechanism associated with peak and sliding friction.

Mud and snow tires produce a lower friction for a given load than highway tires. For example, a 8.00 × 16.5 highway tire produces a friction coefficient of 0.9 at 40% of its rated load and 0.74 at 130% of its rated load. A 8.00 × 16.5 mud and snow (M & S) produces corresponding friction coefficients of 0.81 and 0.63.

Heavy duty truck tires produce peak friction coefficients of approximately 0.7 with the sliding friction value near 0.55 at sliding speeds of 50 mph.

In general, the following factors apply to the friction of pneumatic tires:

1. Passenger car tires of radial construction exhibit lower peak dry traction than bias ply construction.
2. Radial ply tires exhibit superior wet friction properties.
3. Traction increases with tire size, provided other factors remain unchanged.
4. Higher inflation pressure produces higher traction.
5. Peak dry friction is substantially affected by load.

Actual friction testing is often carried out by the investigating officers to determine the sliding friction coefficient at the accident site. Although this procedure yields a friction coefficient, proper care must be taken to truly duplicate accident conditions. Details of data measurement are presented in Section 39.4.

The shear or traction force F_X induced by a sliding tire or a tire operating at peak friction may be determined by

$$F_x = \mu F_z, \text{ lb} \quad (18\text{–}7)$$

where

F_z = tire normal force, lb

μ = peak or sliding friction coefficient, d'less

The subscript x always denotes longitudinal direction, i.e., along the vehicle forward axis. The subscript z denotes vertical direction, i.e., along the upward vehicle axis. As will be used later, the subscript y denotes lateral direction, i.e., along the transverse axis of the vehicle.

The subscript x may designate a braking or driving force produced by the tire. The shear forces produced by a braking or driven tire under similar conditions are approximately equal. Differences for standard tires are less than 3 to 5%.

It is important to recognize that the tire shear or braking force level acting on the vehicle must be computed by one of two methods. If the operating conditions are such that the tire is forced to operate in a peak or sliding friction mode, then Eq. 18–7 may be used to compute the braking force produced by the tire. The total vehicle tire shear force is the summation of the individual tire shear forces. If the tire operates below peak or sliding friction conditions, then the tire force must be computed by a brake system analysis. An actual accident relating to this problem is discussed in Section 40–1. A detailed discussion of braking analysis is found in Chapter 20 and Ref. 11.

18–5. FORCES ACTING ON A CORNERING TIRE

A straight rolling tire can only produce a braking or driving force when the tire is partially or totally slipping. Similarly, a tire can only produce a side force when it is sideslipping. The process of side force production can best be explained by use of a simple experiment.

A tire free to rotate about a shaft is pressed against a rotating drum as illustrated in Fig. 18–5. Initially, the axis of the drum and tire are parallel. As the drum rotates, no axial force is produced by the tire. As the tire is steered, i.e., tire and drum axle are not parallel anymore, the tire attempts to displace the drum sideways. This force between tire and drum is the tire side force. It is obvious that the magnitude of the side force is a function of the angle through which the tire axis is rotated. The actual production of side force is the result of an elastic deformation of the pneumatic tire. As the angle of axis rotation increases to higher and higher values, larger and larger areas of the contact patch begin to slip until complete sidesliding occurs. When this occurs

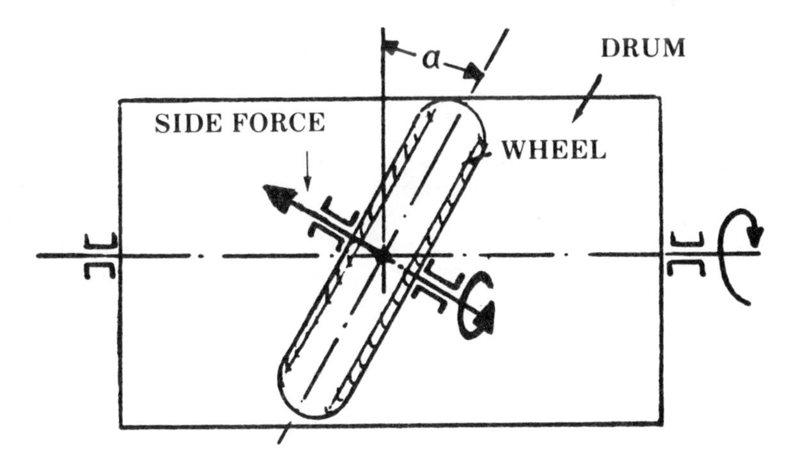

Figure 18–5. Side Force Production and Slip Angle

the tire is not capable of producing any controlled vehicle guiding forces.

The angle of tire axis rotation, i.e., the angle between the longitudinal axis of the tire-wheel assembly and the velocity vector (direction in which tire is forced to move by the drum) is commonly called the slip angle α. In the tire/drum experiment the drum circumferential velocity determines the direction in which the tire-wheel assembly would travel if it were free to move. Slip angles for normal turning maneuvers are usually less than 3 to 5 degrees, for limit turning maneuvers near tire side force saturation between 10 to 15 degrees.

The tire side force F_y as a function of slip angle α is illustrated in Fig. 18–6 for a bias ply and radial ply tire. Inspection of the curves indicates that a linear force/slip angle relationship exists only for slip angles below 4 to 5 degrees. The relationship becomes nonlinear for slip angles greater than approximately 5 degrees. This observation has been made for all pneumatic tires. Fig. 18–6 also indicates that the radial ply tire produces a higher side force for equal slip angles than the bias ply tire.

Tests have shown that the tire side force increases with the normal force to a certain value and then decreases until side force saturation is reached as illustrated in Fig. 18–7. This finding indicates that a higher slip angle is produced when a tire is subjected to increased normal forces when operating beyond the peak side force. A comparison between radial ply and bias ply tires is shown in Fig. 18–8.

Experimental results indicate that the tire side force increases with increasing inflation pressure as shown in Fig. 18–9. Since the slip angles developed by front and rear tires have a significant effect upon vehicle handling and stability, information on inflation pressure is important in certain accident reconstructions.

The side force of a tire decreases with increasing positive camber angle as illustrated in Fig. 18–10. A comparison between radial ply and bias ply tires is shown in Fig. 18–11.

A braked or driven tire also decreases the side force of a tire as shown in Fig. 18–12. Since the side force must be produced to maintain the cornering maneuver, the tire operates at a higher slip angle, causing it to reach tire saturation more quickly than an unbraked or undriven cornering tire.

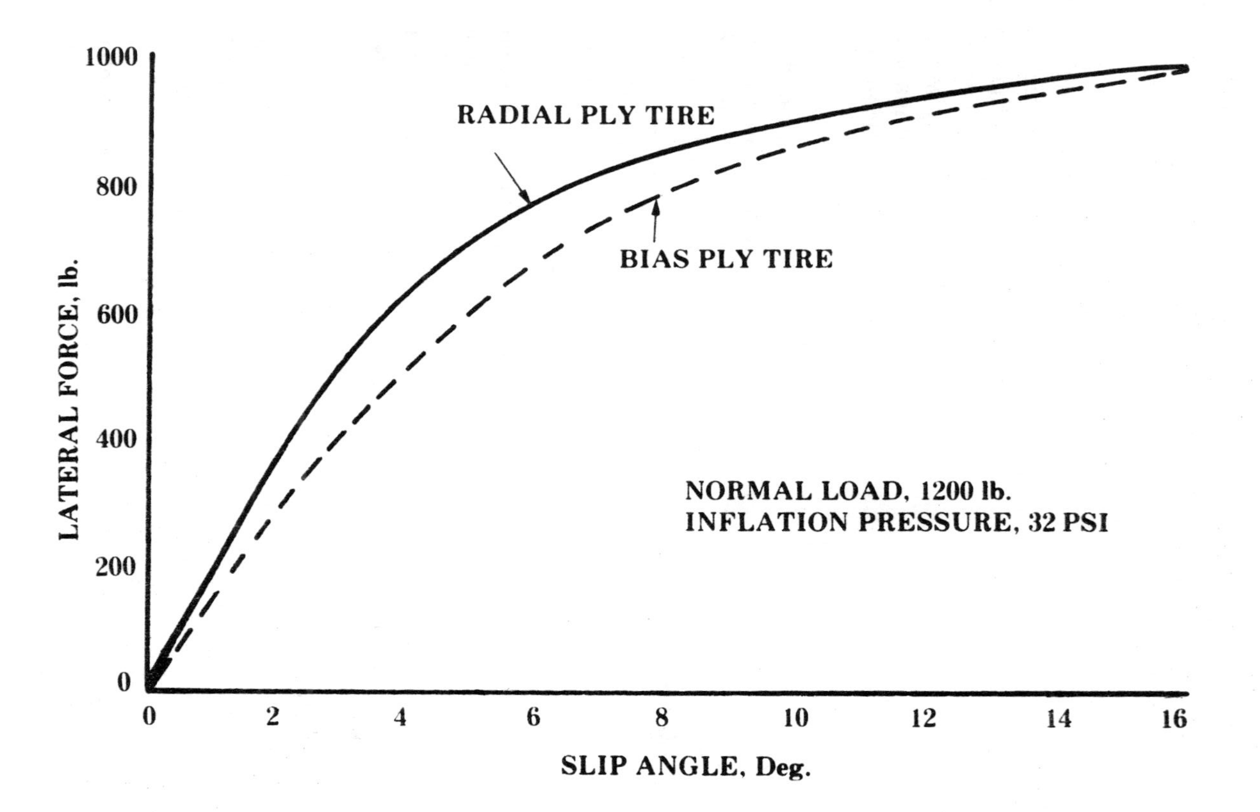

Figure 18–6. Side Force vs. Slip Angle

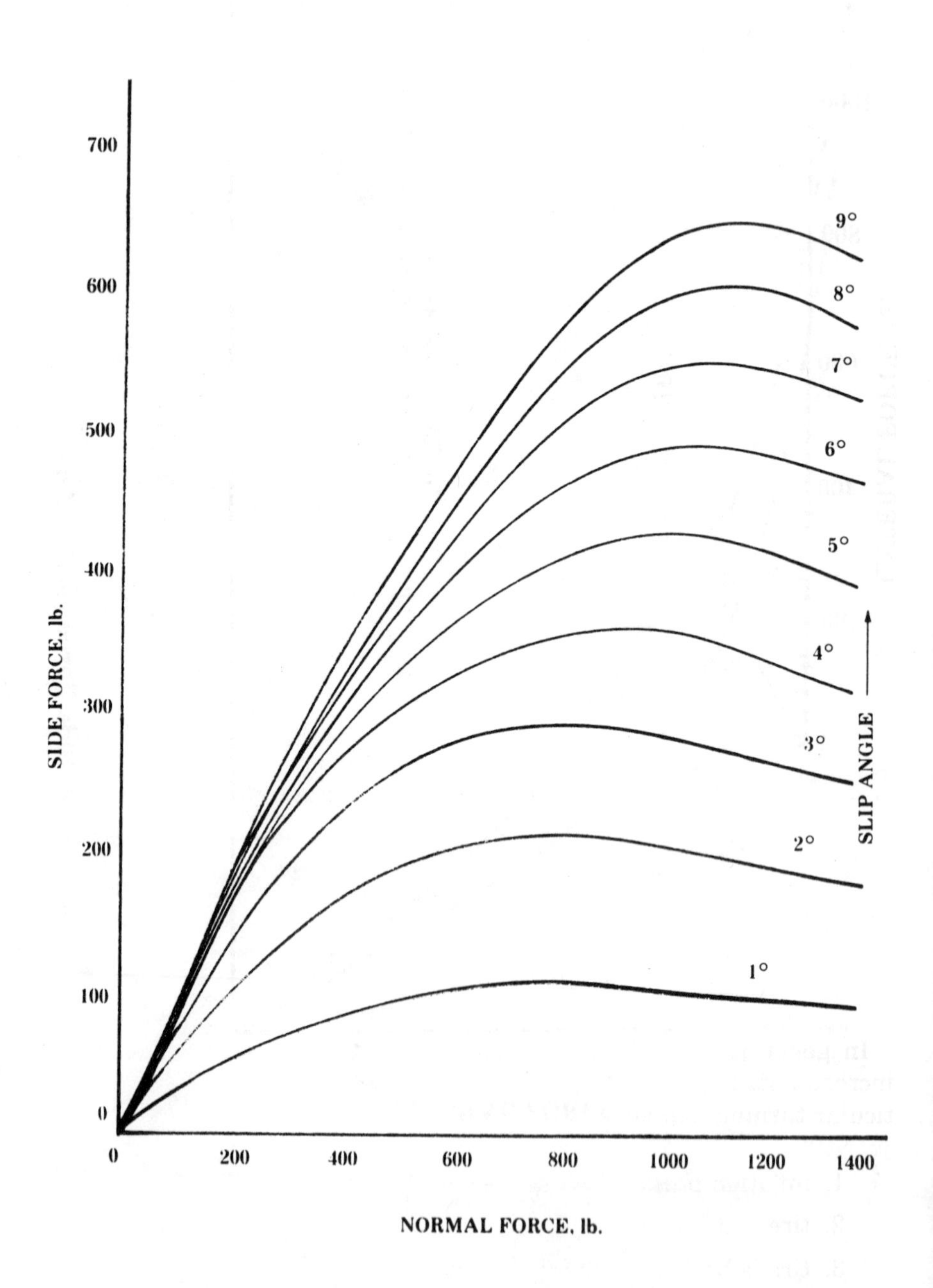

Figure 18-7. Side Force For Different Normal Force Tire 5.60-15, 26 psi, 31 mph

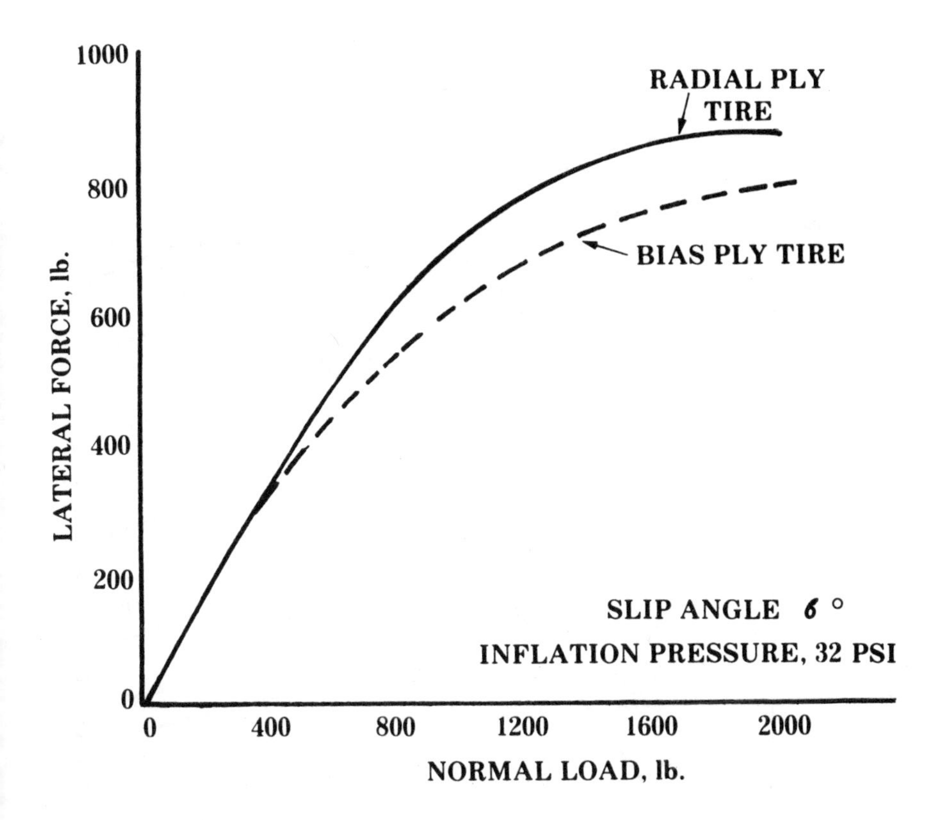

Figure 18–8. Side Force vs. Normal Load

In general, the following observations are made: a cornering tire increases its slip angle to maintain the side force required for the particular turning maneuver when:

1. inflation pressure is decreased
2. tire is driven (front or rear wheel drive)
3. tire is braked (brake force distribution)
4. tire has a positive camber angle (suspension)
5. normal force is increased for limit side force.

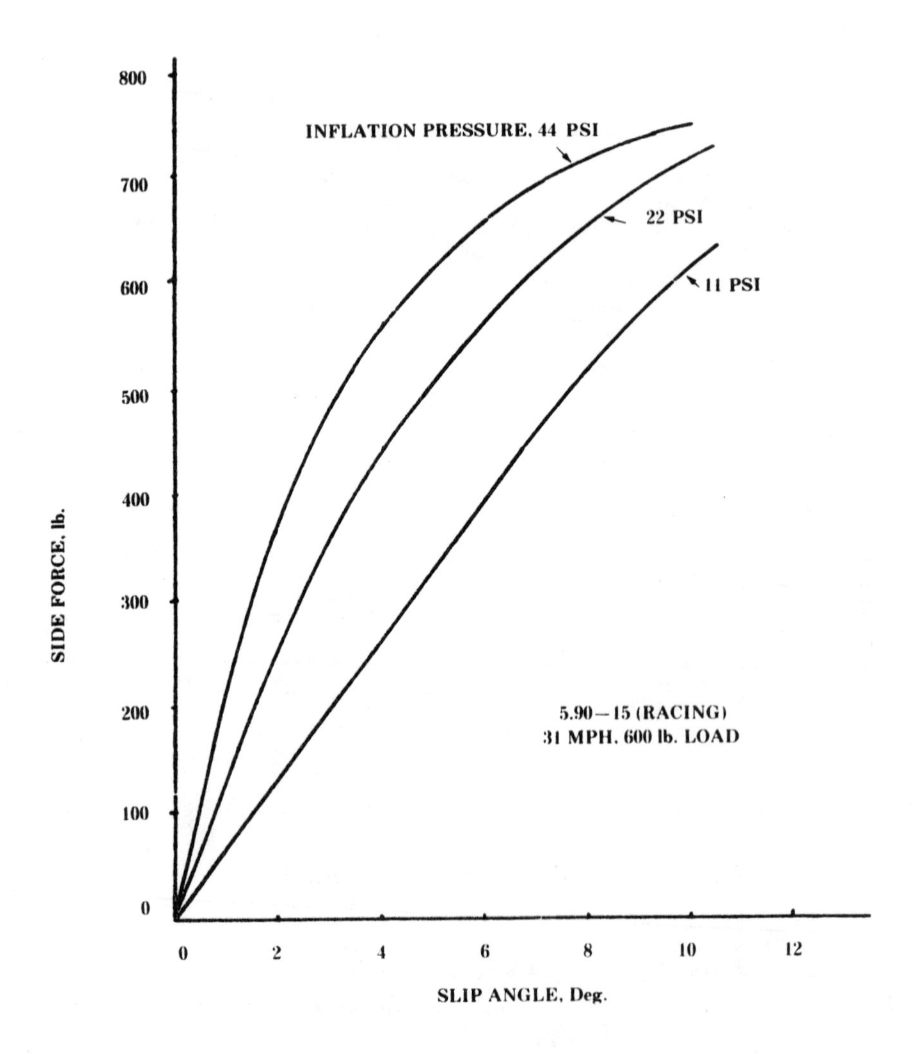

Figure 18-9. Side Force vs. Inflation Pressure

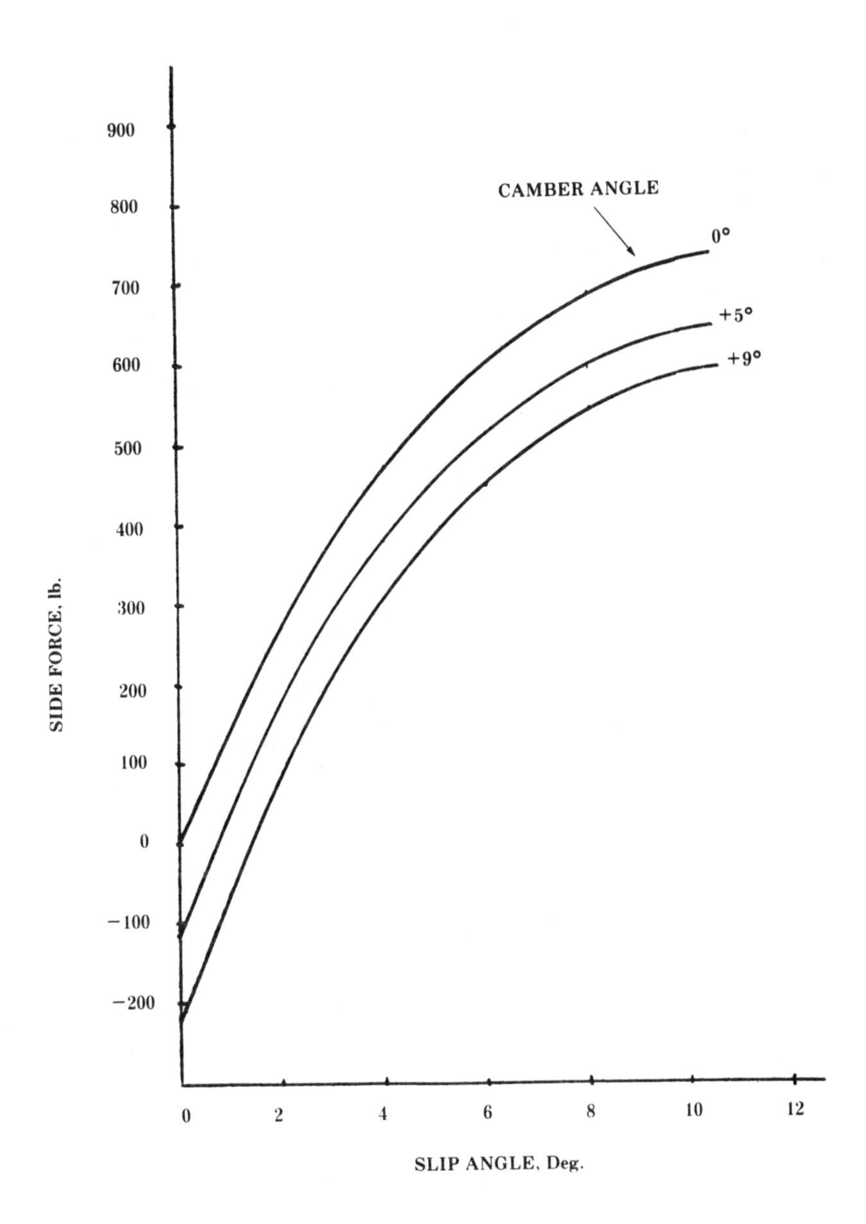

Figure 18-10. Side Force vs. Camber Angle

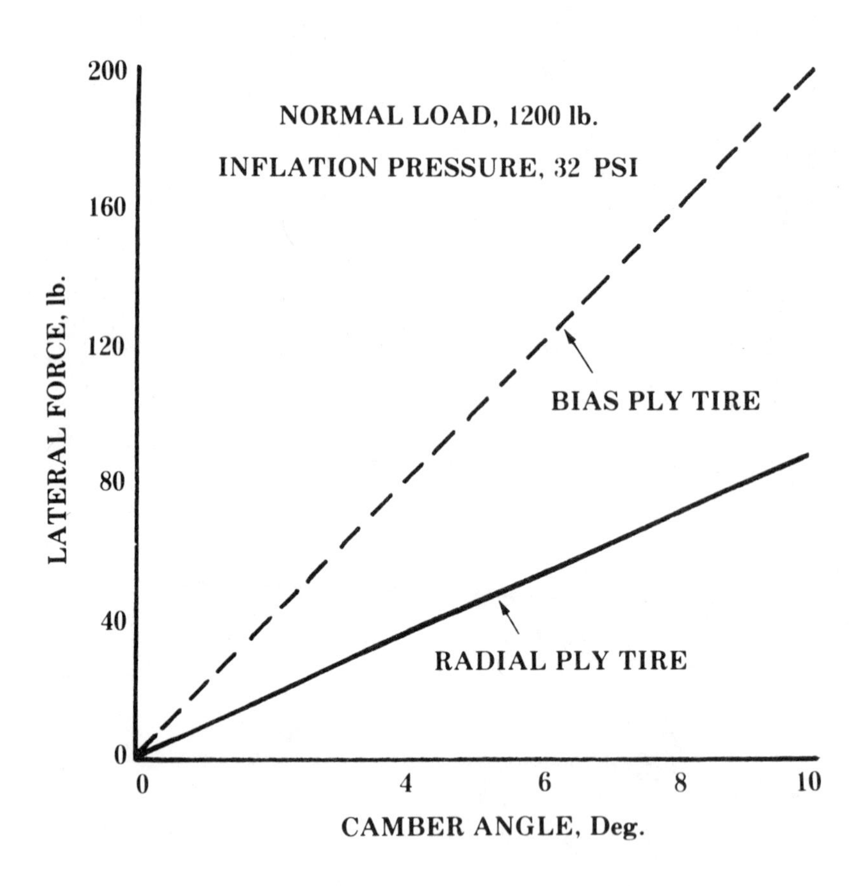

Figure 18–11. Side Force vs. Camber Angle

In the linear range of tire side force – slip angle relationship the side force may be determined by

$$F_y = C\alpha, \text{ lb} \tag{18–8}$$

where

$$C = \text{cornering stiffness, } \frac{\text{lb}}{\text{rad}} \text{ or } \frac{\text{lb}}{\text{deg}}$$

$$\alpha = \text{slip angle, rad or deg.}$$

Cornering stiffness data vary for tires and test conditions. Typical values for C for properly inflated tires range between 50 to 150 lb/deg.

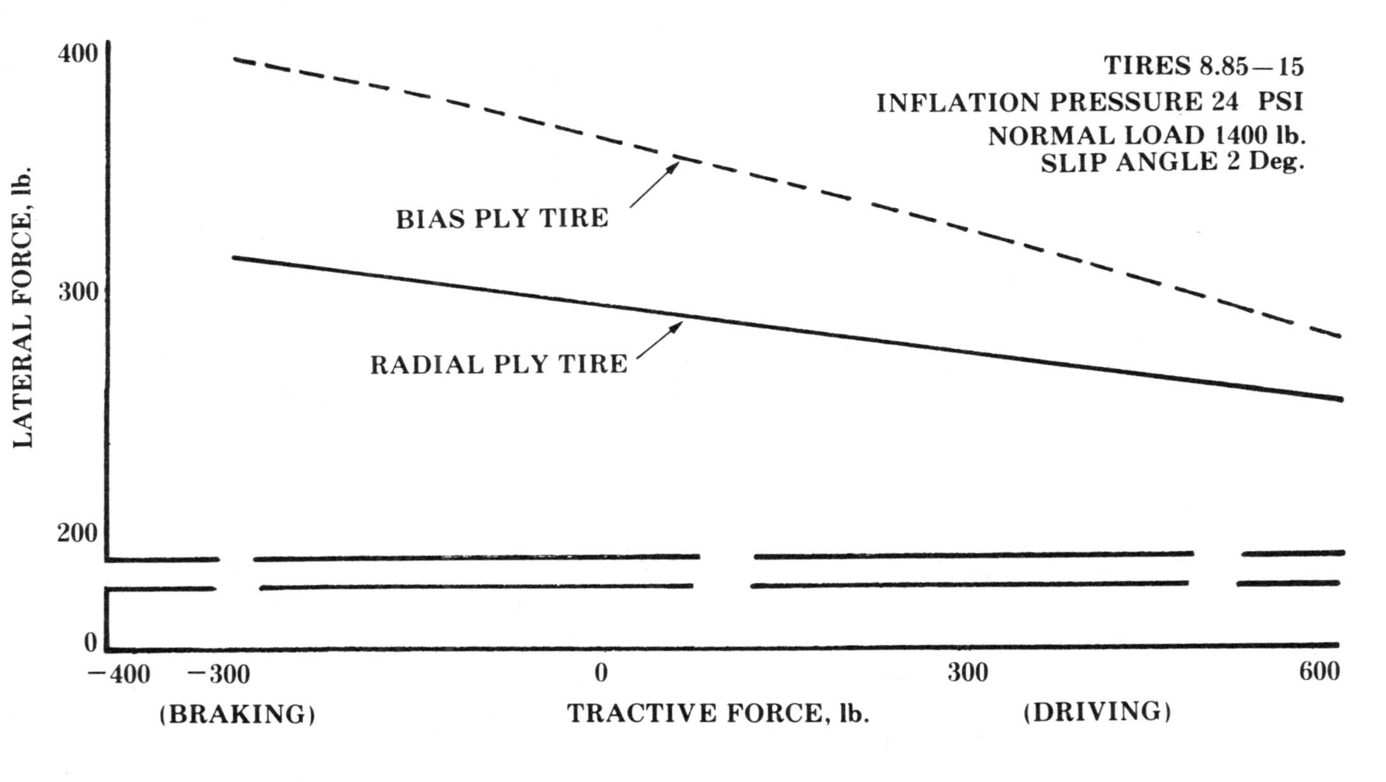

Figure 18-12. Side Force vs. Tractive Force (Braking or Drive Thrust)

Radial tires generally exhibit side forces that are 15 to 30% higher than those of bias ply tires.

Eq. 18–8 may be expanded to include tire normal force effects, and tire design parameters to approximate the non-linear tire side force region.

18–6. FACTORS INFLUENCING TIRE FRICTION

18–6.1. Dry Road Surfaces. A dry road surface may produce a significantly increased friction when altered from a medium to a high grip surface geometry. The influence of the tire tread geometry, i.e., new, partially, or badly worn tires upon dry road friction generally is only as high as 10%. Tests have shown that tread design and condition have only a minor effect upon tire traction. Rubber composition, however, affects tire traction to some extent. Truck tires, for example, have a larger amount of natural rubber content than passenger car tires, resulting in a lower braking friction coefficient. More details on tire design factors are found in Section 5–3.

18–6.2. Wet Road Surfaces. For wet road surfaces tire-road friction is a function of vehicle speed, water film thickness, and road surface and tire tread geometry. For a given tire and road surface geometry the wet friction depends upon water film thickness and speed. When road surfaces become flooded or puddles form in road surface irregularities, motor vehicles can at some critical speed encounter the phenomenon of tire hydroplaning. The effects of hydroplaning are to separate the tire either partially or in the extreme completely from the road surface and the tire rides on a water film. The results of this hydrodynamic lift (similar to the lift of a water ski) are a significant reduction or even total loss of braking traction and tire side force rendering the vehicle virtually uncontrollable. Hydroplaning is likely to occur on highways exhibiting considerable wear under the wheel path resulting in longitudinal grooves, particularly from the use of studded tires. The road surface may be rough, however, no sufficient drainage is provided in the case of heavy rain allowing a water film to develop which in connection with high vehicle speeds may lead to hydroplaning accidents. At high speeds the tire tread does not have sufficient time to penetrate the water film to make contact with the road surface. Worn tires with little or no tread will cause hydroplaning at lower speeds than new tires.

A different type of hydroplaning condition may develop if the water depth is not sufficient for the hydrodynamic lift to raise the tire off the road. The lubricating effects of the water film may be sufficient to cause a significant reduction in tire forces. When a relatively uniform pressure exists between a tire tread element and the road surface any water present may act as a lubricant. This lubricating action will be more pronounced in the case of smooth, polished road surfaces and worn tires. Accidents caused by viscous lubrication are likely to occur on sections of highways that do not exhibit sufficient surface roughness.

Experimental results have led to an empirical relationship for the critical speed of hydroplaning,

$$V_{crit} = 10.35\ \sqrt{p_i},\ \text{mph} \tag{18–9}$$

where

$$p_i = \text{tire inflation pressure, psi}$$

The constant 10.35 applies to smooth or low tread tires. New tires with good tread will develop hydroplaning at higher speeds. For example, a new tire (size 5.60–15) produces the following approximate sliding friction coefficients at the indicated speed(s) and water depth (Ref. 13):

$$\mu = 0.35\ (0.15)\ \text{at 37 (75) mph and 0.0078 in. water depth}$$

$$\mu = 0.18\ \text{at 37 mph and 0.078 in.}$$

The same tire without any tread produces the following friction coefficients:

$$\mu = 0.16\ \text{at 37 mph and 0.0078 in.}$$

$$\mu = 0.09\ \text{at 37 mph and 0.078 in.}$$

Wet road friction coefficients as a function of speed determined by Eq. 18–4 are valid for water depths insufficient to produce hydroplaning.

In general, there are two speeds to consider when discussing hydroplaning. The first is the hydroplaning-speed-in-rolling in the absence of any braking or driving forces. The tire will begin to spin down to zero speed and control will be lost if this limit speed is exceeded. The second speed is the hydroplaning-speed-in-slipping. This is the maximum speed at which a braking or driving force can be applied without wheel lockup or spinning and loss of control. This speed is also the maximum at which a cornering force can be applied without loss of control and spin-down. It is usually between 50 and 75% of the hydroplaning-speed-in-rolling. At any speed between these two values, hydroplaning can be induced by a side wind, a road irregularity or a driver input.

CHAPTER 19

CONSTANT SPEED AND ACCELERATION ANALYSIS OF VEHICLES

19–1. EQUATION OF MOTION

In Chapter 17 the basic relationships of vehicle acceleration were introduced. It stated that a body remains at rest or constant velocity motion when all external forces are in equilibrium. For a vehicle traveling on a level highway this means that aerodynamic drag and rolling resistance force are equal to the drive thrust at the drive wheels. When the driver increases the engine power by depressing the accelerator pedal, the drive thrust increases, i.e., the external forces are not in equilibrium anymore. Since this condition cannot exist, the vehicle accelerates to a higher speed until the higher aerodynamic drag and rolling resistance are once again in equilibrium with the drive thrust.

19–2. RESISTANCE FORCES TO VEHICLE MOTION

19–2.1. Rolling Resistance. The rolling resistance of a tire may be determined by Eq. 18–2. The rolling resistance of a vehicle is the summation of all individual tire rolling resistances.

19–2.2. Toe-In Resistance. The toe-in of the front wheels (Section 6–2.2) causes a small retarding force on the front wheels. For properly adjusted wheel position the toe-in-force is negligible, especially at moderate to higher speeds.

For calculations one can assume a toe-in resistance which is approximately 5% of the rolling resistance force.

19–2.3. Rough-Road Resistance. On rough roads, an additional resistance to forward motion of the vehicle is produced by the energy absorbed by the shock absorbers (Section 4–4). Similar to the internal damping of a tire contributing to rolling resistance, the damping associated with vertical motion of a wheel produces the damping drag force F_{DD}, (Ref. 13).

$$F_{DD} = n\, c_{DD}\, k/V, \text{ lb} \qquad (19\text{–}1)$$

where

n = number of damped wheels, d'less

c_{DD} = damping coefficient, lb · sec/ft

k = factor characterizing road roughness, ft²/sec²

V = vehicle speed, ft/sec

Maximum values of the factor k at 75 mph range from 0.5 ft^2/sec^2 for smooth concrete roadways to 5 ft^2/sec^2 for gravel roads. At speeds below 15 mph the factor k approaches negligible values regardless of road surface roughness.

By use of Eq. 19–1 a four-wheel vehicle with a damping coefficient of 600 lb · sec/ft yields a damping drag of only approximately 11 lb on a smooth concrete road at 75 mph. The corresponding drag on a gravel road is approximately 109 lb.

19–2.4. Turning Resistance. The resistance produced by the tires to forward motion of a vehicle in a turn is a function of the severity of the turn.

The turning resistance coefficient R_T is

$$R_T = a_y\ [(1-\psi)\sin\alpha_F + \psi\sin\alpha_R],\ \text{d'less} \qquad (19\text{–}2)$$

where

a_y = lateral acceleration, g-units

ψ = static rear axle load divided by total vehicle weight, d'less

α_F = slip angle on front wheels, deg

α_R = slip angle on rear wheels, deg

Slip angle α is defined as the angle between a line perpendicular to the axis of wheel rotation and direction of wheel motion (Section 18–5). The slip angle required for the side force production necessary to hold a vehicle in a desired turn is a function of a large number of vehicle parameters and changes in a nonlinear fashion with lateral acceleration. For purposes of estimating the turning resistance coefficient R_T equal slip angles front and rear may be assumed of the magnitude of 2 deg for $a_y = 0.2\,g$, 6 deg for $a_y = 0.6\,g$ and 10 deg for $a_y = 0.8\,g$. The turning resistance force F_{TD} is

$$F_{TD} = R_T\,W,\ \text{lb} \qquad (19\text{–}3)$$

where

W = vehicle weight, lb

By use of Eq. 19–3 a 6,000 lb vehicle with $\psi = 0.50$ turning at $0.6\,g$ lateral acceleration yields a turning resistance force of approximately

376 lb, i.e., the forward motion is resisted by 376 lb. At 0.2 g lateral acceleration the corresponding value is only 42 lb.

19-2.5. Aerodynamic Resistance. A vehicle traveling on the ground has airflow forced under, around, and over the vehicle. The streamlines separate behind the vehicle. The airflow is turbulent in the speed ranges of interest to automotive use. The aerodynamic force resisting vehicle motion is the result of a pressure difference between the front and the rear of the vehicle, and of the frictional forces between the surface area of the vehicle and the air.

The existing aerodynamic drag force F_{AD} is

$$F_{AD} = c_{AD} A(\rho/2)(V^2_{\text{rel}}), \text{ lb} \tag{19-4}$$

where

A = frontal area of vehicle, ft²
c_{AD} = aerodynamic drag coefficient, d'less
V_{rel} = relative speed between vehicle and wind, ft/sec
ρ = air density, lb sec²/ft⁴

The aerodynamic drag coefficient c_{AD} ranges from 0.3 for race cars to 1.1 for tractor/trailer combinations. For example, the aerodynamic drag coefficients are: 0.445 (VW 1200), 0.38 (Porsche 911), 0.286 (Ferrari 250 GT). The following values may be used for aerodynamic drag evaluation when no exact values are available:

Standard square box-type body with trunk: 0.41

Fast back type body: 0.38

Van type body: 0.44

Trucks: 0.85

Motorcycles: 0.55

19-2.6. Engine Drag Resistance. Engine drag is discussed in Section 7-2.2.

The retarding moment M_e of a combustion engine may be computed from the approximate relationship

$$M_e = 0.0065\, p_m V_e, \text{ ft} \cdot \text{lb} \tag{19-5}$$

where

p_m = average retarding pressure in combustion chamber, psi
V_e = engine displacement, in.³

The average retarding pressure associated with engine braking ranges from approximately 45 to 75 psi for gasoline engines and 60 to 95 psi for diesel engines. The upper values are associated with high levels of revolutions per minute of the engine crankshaft, the lower values with lower levels.

The retarding force F_x at the drive wheels of the vehicle is

$$F_x = \frac{M_{er}\,\rho}{\eta R}, \text{ lb} \quad (19\text{–}6)$$

where

R = effective tire radius, ft

η = mechanical efficiency between engine and wheels, d'less

ρ = transmission ratio between engine and wheels, d'less

Frequently it is possible to measure vehicle retardation due to engine drag directly by the use of a simple decelerometer in road tests.

19–2.7. Inclined Road Force. The motion of a vehicle traveling on an inclined road is affected by gravity. The force due to inclination F_I is

$$F_I = \pm W \sin \alpha, \text{ lb} \quad (19\text{–}7)$$

where

W = vehicle weight, lb

α = slope angle, deg

sin = sine of angle α, a known number once the angle α is given.

The plus sign in Eq. 19–7 indicates that the incline force attempts to accelerate the vehicle, i.e., the vehicle travels downhill. The minus sign indicates the opposite, i.e., uphill travel.

19–2.8. Acceleration Resistance. Acceleration of a vehicle causes an inertia force to be developed which may be determined by Eq. 17–3, i.e., $(W/g)a$ = inertia force.

Example 19–1

Compute the total resistance force of a Corvette automobile, when traveling at 120 mph on a 3 degree-downhill freeway. Use the data that follow: weight 3857 lb, drag coefficient 0.36, projected cross-sectional area 20.5 ft^2, air density 0.0023 lb · sec^2/ft^4, tire inflation pressure 25 psi, radial ply tire.

1. Rolling resistance

By the use of Eq. 18–1

$$f_R = 0.005 + \frac{0.15}{25} + \left(\frac{0.67}{25}\right)\left(\frac{120}{100}\right)^2 = 0.049$$

By the use of Eq. 18–2 rolling resistance force

$$F_R = 0.049 \times 3857 = 189 \text{ lb}$$

2. Aerodynamic drag

By the use of Eq. 19–4 the aerodynamic drag is with 120 mph = 176 ft/sec

$$F_{AD} = \frac{(0.36)(20.5)(0.0023)(176)^2}{(2)} = 263 \text{ lb}$$

3. Rough road resistance

By the use of Eq. 19–1 the rough road damping force is

$$F_{DD} = \frac{(4)(600)(0.5)}{176} = 6.8 \text{ lb}$$

A damping coefficient $c_{DD} = 600$ lb · sec/ft was used. A lower value associated with a degraded shock absorber would only have a little effect on rough road resistance of paved roads.

4. Toe-in resistance

At a speed of 120 mph the toe-in may be neglected since toe-in effects decrease with vehicle speed.

5. Inclined road force

By the use of Eq. 19–7 the downhill pushing force is

$$F_I = (3857) \sin (3) = (3857)(0.052) = 202 \text{ lb}$$

The total resistance force attempting to retard the vehicle is

$$F_{\text{retard}} = F_R + F_A + F_{DD} - F_I = 257 \text{ lb}$$

Consequently, the drive wheels have to provide a thrust of 257 lb to sustain a velocity of 120 mph under the given conditions. On a level roadway the corresponding force would be 457 lb, and on a 3 degree uphill road 661 lb. The latter may not be possible due to engine power limitations.

19–3. ENGINE AND TORQUE CONVERTER CHARACTERISTICS

In some accident cause analyses it becomes necessary to compute the maximum acceleration of a motor vehicle either from rest or in a passing maneuver.

Maximum acceleration is achieved when the maximum possible drive thrust is acting on the drive wheels for each individual gear position. The manual and automatic transmission are torque converters to better match the different torque requirements on the drive wheels with the torque characteristics provided by the engine.

The "ideal" drive thrust as a function of vehicle speed is illustrated in Fig. 19–1. Inspection of the curve indicates that at low speeds, i.e., either shortly after acceleration begins or when hill climbing, the drive thrust and hence the torque on the drive wheels is high. At higher speeds the drive thrust decreases. The product of drive thrust and velocity remains constant since it is equal to the power delivered to the drive wheels. If an automatic transmission is used the delivered drive thrust approaches the ideal curve more closely. (Fig. 19–2).

The maximum drive torque can be computed from the engine torque/engine crankshaft speed characteristics and the overall gear ratio including final drive existing for a particular gear or speed range for automatic transmissions.

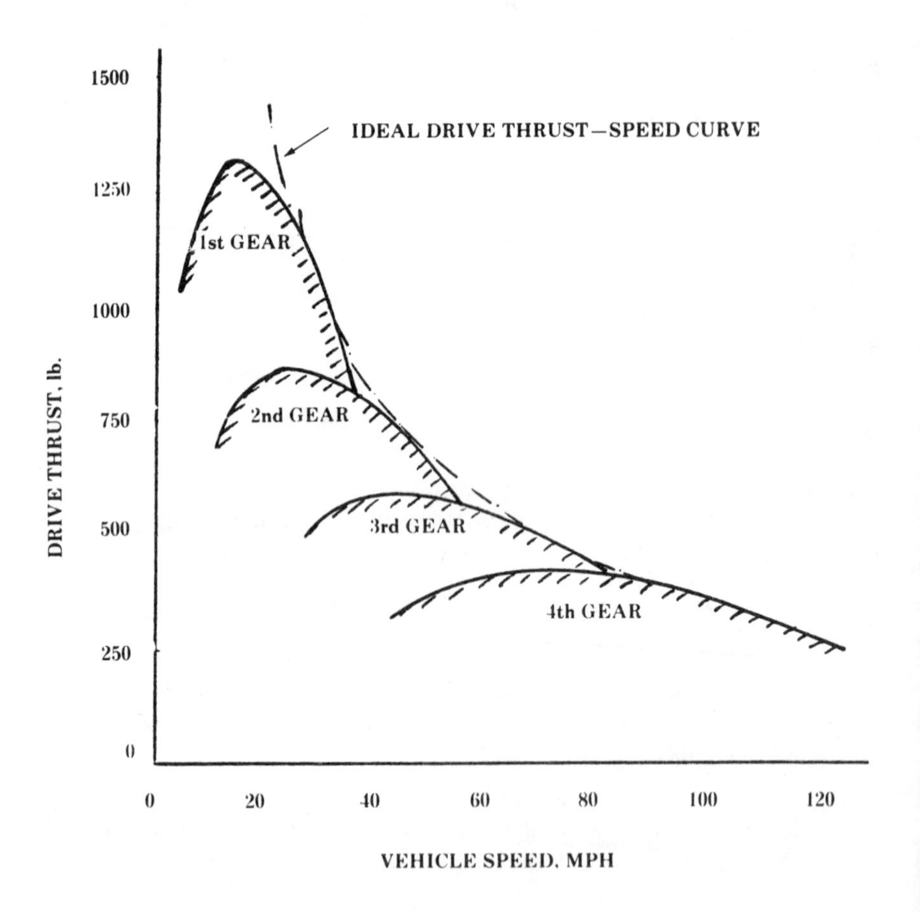

Figure 19–1. Drive Thrust vs. Speed For Four-Speed Transmission

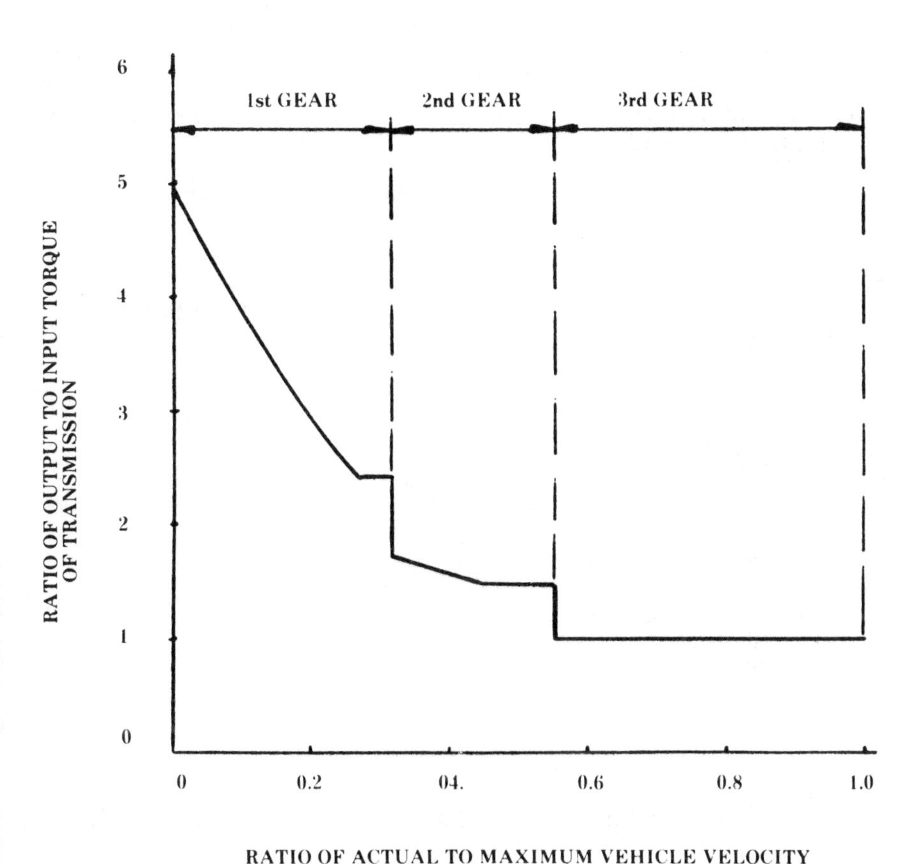

Figure 19-2. Automatic Transmission Characteristics vs. Vehicle Speed

19-4. MAXIMUM SPEED PREDICTION

The maximum speed of a vehicle is limited by the total resistance acting on the vehicle and the drive torque of the engine. The speed may be indirectly determined by using a force consideration:

$$\frac{i\eta\, T_e}{R} = f_R\, W + F_{DD} + R_T\, W \pm W \sin\alpha + C_{AD}\, A\left(\frac{\rho}{2}\right)V^2, \text{ lb} \quad (19\text{–}8)$$

where

i = overall gear ratio, d'less

T_e = engine torque, lb · ft

R = effective radius of driven wheels, ft

η = mechanical efficiency between engine crankshaft and driven wheels, d'less

All terms on the right-hand side of Eq. 19–8 are explained in Sections 19–2.1 through 19–2.7.

A different equation using engine power considerations is

$$\eta N_e\,(1 - s_T) = f_R\, W\, V_{max} \pm W(\sin\alpha)\, V_{max} + F_{DD}\, V_{max} + C_{AD} A\left(\frac{\rho}{2}\right)(V_{max})^3 \ \frac{\text{lb}\cdot\text{ft}}{\text{sec}} \quad (19\text{–}9)$$

where

N_e = maximum engine power, $\frac{\text{lb}\cdot\text{ft}}{\text{sec}}$

s_T = slip of driven tires, d'less

V_{max} = maximum vehicle speed, ft/sec

Example 19–2

Determine the maximum straight-line speed of a Corvette automobile by the use of the data that follow (see Example 19–1 for other data): engine horse power 215 hp, $s_T = 0.15$. $\eta = 0.8$.

By the use of Eq. 19–9 the indirect velocity relationship becomes with 215 hp equal to 215 × 550 lb · ft/sec.

$$(0.8)(215)(1 - 0.15)(550) = (0.049)(3857)\, V_{max} + (6.8)\, V_{max} + (0.36)(20.5)\left(\frac{0.0023}{2}\right)(V_{max}{}^3)$$

or

$$80410 = 189\, V_{max} + 6.8\, V_{max} + 0.0085\, (V_{max}{}^3)$$

Rearranging and dividing each term by 0.0085 yields

$$V_{max}^3 + 23035\ V_{max} - 9{,}460{,}000 = 0$$

Solution by trial and error, i.e., guessing a value for V_{max} and checking by substitution in the equation yields 175.6 ft/sec or 119.7 mph. Since the rolling resistance is speed dependent, an initial value of rolling resistance coefficient must first be computed from the "guessed" velocity. The trial and error procedure must be continued until the computed velocity from the speed equation equals the "guessed" velocity used for computing the rolling resistance coefficient.

The maximum velocity of a motor vehicle is also limited by the maximum crankshaft speed of the engine. Speeds in excess of this limiting speed tend to damage engine components, in particular valve train components.

The limiting speed may be determined by

$$V_{max} = \frac{2\pi R\ n_{max}(1 - s_T)}{i \times 60},\ \text{ft/sec} \qquad (19\text{–}10)$$

where

n_{max} = maximum engine crank shaft speed, RPM
s_T = tire slip, d'less
i = engine crank shaft-to-drive wheel gear ratio, d'less
R = effective driven tire radius, ft

19–5. MAXIMUM SLOPE PREDICTION

The maximum slope a motor vehicle can maneuver is obtained from Eq. 19–8 by solving for the angle α. Maximum slope calculations are important for low speeds and first gear, i.e., aerodynamic resistance, turning resistance and damping resistance are ignored. For slope calculation involving high speeds Eq. 19–8 or 19–9 may be used.

When the slope is expressed in percent rather than degrees, the maximum slope S when operating at low speeds is

$$S = \left(\frac{i_{max}\ \eta\ T_{e,max}}{R \cdot W} - f_R\right) 100,\ \text{percent} \qquad (19\text{–}11)$$

where

$T_{e,max}$ = maximum engine torque, lb · ft
i_{max} = maximum overall gear ratio, d'less
R = tire radius, ft
W = vehicle weight, lb
η = mechanical efficiency, d'less

Eq. 19–11 yields the maximum slope a vehicle can maneuver due to the engine torque provided. However, the tire-ground friction coefficient may be too low or the weight distribution (front-, rear-, or four-wheel drive) may be such that the driven wheels spin.

The coefficient of friction μ between tire and ground must be equal or greater than the values computed below to prevent wheel spinning.

Front wheel drive:

$$\mu_F = \frac{S}{\frac{\ell_R}{\ell} - \left(\frac{h}{\ell}\right)S}, \text{ d'less} \tag{19–12}$$

Rear wheel drive:

$$\mu_R = \frac{S}{\frac{\ell_F}{\ell} + \left(\frac{h}{\ell}\right)S}, \text{ d'less} \tag{19–13}$$

where

h = center-of-gravity height above ground, in.
ℓ = wheel base, in.
ℓ_F = distance from front axle to center-of-gravity, measured along vehicle axis, in.
ℓ_R = distance from rear axle to center-of-gravity, measured along vehicle axis, in.
S = slope, d'less

Example 19-3

Determine the maximum slope a light duty truck can maneuver. Use the data that follow:

$T_{e,\max} = 355$ lb · ft, $i_{\max} = 22$, $\eta = 0.8$, $R = 15$ in., $W = 6000$ lb, $f_R = 0.045$, $\ell = 12$ ft, $\ell_F = 5$ ft, $\ell_R = 7$ ft, $h = 46$ in.

Eq. 19–11 yields

$$S = \left[\frac{(22)(0.8)(355)}{\left(\frac{15}{12}\right)6000} - 0.045\right]100 = 78.8 \text{ percent or } 38 \text{ degrees}$$

The tire-to-ground friction coefficient required to prevent rear wheel spinning by use of Eq. 19–13 is:

$$\mu_R = \frac{0.788}{\frac{5}{12} + \left(\frac{46}{12}\right)\left(\frac{1}{12}\right)(0.788)} = \frac{0.788}{0.667} = 1.18$$

Consequently, a friction coefficient of 1.18 is required for the vehicle to use its maximum hill climbing capability. A friction value of 1.18 is far in excess of what off-road surfaces provide. See Section 19–7 for four-wheel drive analysis.

19–6. MAXIMUM ACCELERATION PREDICTION

When a vehicle is accelerating, the vehicle speed increases and the rotating component such as wheels and shafts increase their rotational speeds. For most vehicles the effect of rotational masses can be neglected. However, in the case of specialty vehicles, large dirt haulers, tanks, etc., the rotational acceleration of rotating components must be considered.

The maximum acceleration a is

$$a = \left[\frac{\dfrac{i \eta T_e}{R} - f_R W - C_{AD} A \left(\dfrac{\rho}{2}\right) V^2}{k W} \right] 32.2, \text{ ft/sec}^2 \qquad (19\text{–}14)$$

where

k = rotational inertia factor of wheels and axles, d'less

Typical values of k are 1.35 for first, 1.15 for second, 1.08 for third, and 1.05 for fourth gear. For acceleration from rest or for acceleration maneuvers involving speeds less than 30 mph the aerodynamic drag term of Eq. 19–14 may be neglected. The appropriate overall gear ratio is designated by i.

The maximum acceleration may be limited by the traction force of the driven wheels involving wheel spinning similar to maneuvering on a slope.

The tire-road friction coefficients required to prevent wheel spinning are

Front wheel drive:

$$\mu_F = \frac{a}{(32.2)\left(\dfrac{\ell_R}{\ell}\right) - \left[\dfrac{h}{\ell} + \left(\dfrac{R}{\ell}\right)(k-1)\right] a}, \text{ d'less} \qquad (19\text{–}15)$$

Rear wheel drive:

$$\mu_R = \frac{a}{(32.2)\left(\dfrac{\ell_F}{\ell}\right) + \left[\dfrac{h}{\ell} + \left(\dfrac{R}{\ell}\right)(k-1)\right] a}, \text{ d'less} \qquad (19\text{–}16)$$

19-7. FOUR-WHEEL DRIVE ANALYSIS

In the four-wheel drive vehicle the engine power available is distributed to all wheels. The vehicle can utilize all available friction for vehicle acceleration or hill climbing since the entire vehicle weight is supported by driven wheels.

The maximum acceleration from rest becomes equal to $a_{max} = (32.2)\mu$, the maximum slope equal to $S_{max} = \mu$.

19-8. PREDICTION OF FUEL CONSUMPTION

In some accident reconstructions involving engine stalling or in which weight considerations are critical, it becomes necessary to compute the fuel consumption of the vehicle.

For the case of constant speed driving, the fuel consumption in miles per gallon MPG may be computed by

$$MPG = \frac{(778)\, \eta_e\, \eta_m\, H}{(5280)\left[(f_R + S)\, W + C_{AD}\, A \left(\frac{\rho}{2}\right) V^2\right]}, \text{ miles per gallon} \quad (19\text{-}17)$$

where

H = combustion energy stored in one gallon of fuel, BTU/gallon

η_e = engine efficiency, d'less

η_m = mechanical efficiency between crank shaft and drive wheels, d'less

Example 19-4

Compute the MPG-value of the Corvette automobile of example 19-1. Use the data that follows:

$$\eta_e = 0.3,\ \eta_m = 0.8,\ H = 154{,}200 \text{ BTU/gallon}$$

Hence,

$$MPG = \frac{(778)(0.3)(0.8)(154{,}200)}{(256)(5280)} = 21.3 \text{ miles}$$

If the Corvette were traveling on a level road instead of downhill, the total resistance to motion would be 458 lb and the MPG-value would decrease to 11.9 miles.

CHAPTER 20
VEHICLE BRAKING ANALYSIS

Braking is an important aspect of highway safety. Federal braking standards regulate hydraulic and airbrake systems for normal and partially failed systems. Approximately 2% of all accidents involve brake malfunctioning as contributing to accident causation. Of these accidents, approximately 90% are related to brake system defects and 10% to vehicle instability during braking. Nearly all brake defects are maintenance caused (see Chapter 42). A detailed braking analysis is found in U.S. Army Engineering Design Handbook entitled Analysis and Design of Automotive Brake Systems by R. Limpert (Ref. 11).

20-1. BRAKE TORQUE AND BRAKE FORCE

The pedal effort produces the hydraulic brake line pressure. In the wheel brakes a friction material is pressed against the brake drum or disc, resulting in brake torque. The brake torque is reacted upon by the tire-to-ground traction force, commonly called brake force.

The hydraulic brake line pressure p_ℓ in the brake line of a non-powered (manual) hydraulic brake system is

$$p_\ell = \frac{F_p \ell_p \eta_p}{A_{MC}}, \text{ psi} \qquad (20\text{–}1)$$

where

A_{MC} = master cylinder area, in.^{2}
F_p = pedal force, lb
ℓ_p = pedal lever ratio, d'less
η_p = pedal lever efficiency, d'less

Typical values for the pedal lever efficiency are 0.8 which includes the efficiency associated with the master cylinder. The brake torque T_B of one brake may be determined by

$$T_B = (p_\ell - p_o) A_{WC} \eta_C BF r, \text{ lb} \cdot \text{in.} \qquad (20\text{–}2)$$

where

A_{WC} = wheel cylinder area, in.^{2}
BF = brake factor, defined as the ratio of drag force on the drum friction surface to the actuating force of one shoe, d'less

p_o = pushout pressure, required to bring the brake shoe in contact with the drum, psi

r = drum or effective disc radius, in.

η_C = efficiency corresponding to frictional losses in the wheel cylinder, d'less

Push out pressures for disc brakes are small (5 psi) and may be neglected. In the case of drum brakes the pushout pressure is determined by the shoe return springs and wheel cylinder area and may assume values as high as 100 psi. The wheel cylinder efficiency is approximately 0.96.

The brake factor, *BF,* is a function of brake type and specific design, i.e., disc brake, leading-trailing, two-leading, or duo-servo brake, and of the lining-to-drum friction coefficient. Typical brake factor versus lining friction curves for the standard drum brakes are shown in Fig. 20–1. Inspection of the curves indicates the duo-servo brake to have the highest brake factor for a given coefficient of brake lining friction, followed by the two-leading and leading-trailing shoe brake. Duo-servo brakes are extremely sensitive to changes in lining friction as indicated by the sensitivity curve. A small change in friction coefficient may cause a significant change in brake factor, and hence brake torque. A decrease of brake factor caused by a decrease of friction is commonly called brake fade.

Wedge brakes of air brake systems exhibit typical unfaded brake factor values of 4.6 as compared to S-cam brakes of 2.3. In the case of passenger cars or light truck drum brakes, a brake factor analysis must be carried out since geometrical factors may vary considerably for different designs.

Equations determining brake factor as a function of brake geometry and lining friction coefficient are straightforward, but algebraically involved and are not repeated here. Many brake factor equations including application are presented in Ref. 11.

For disc brakes without self energizing effect, the brake factor may be determined by

$$BF = 2\mu, \text{ d'less} \tag{20–3}$$

where

μ = coefficient of friction between pad and rotor, d'less

The brake force F_x acting between tire and road surface may be determined from the brake torque and tire radius

$$F_x = \frac{T_B}{R}, \text{ lb} \tag{20–4}$$

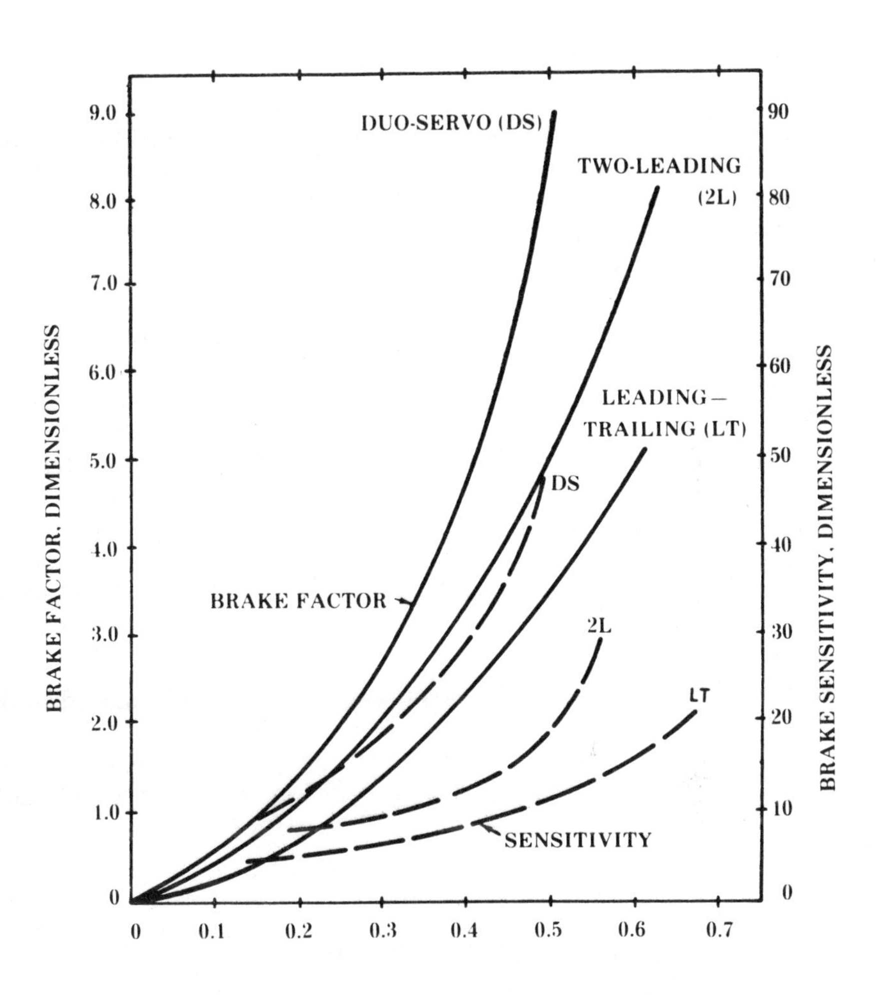

Figure 20-1. Brake Factor—Lining Friction Curves for Typical Drum Brakes

where

$$R = \text{tire radius, in.}$$

20–2. BRAKING DECELERATION

The total brake force is the summation of the brake forces of all braked wheels. The vehicle brake force equals the inertia force acting at the center of gravity of the vehicle or the inclination force in downhill travel. By the use of Eqs. 17–3, 20–1, 20–2, and 20–4 the deceleration of a two-axle vehicle equipped with non-powered brakes may be determined by

$$a = \left(\frac{F_p \ell_p \eta_p}{A_{MC}} - p_o\right)[(A_{WC}BF \cdot r)_F + (A_{WC}BF \cdot r)_R]\frac{(32.2)}{WR}, \text{ ft/sec}^2 \tag{20–5a}$$

The subscripts F and R indicate front and rear axle components.

When a vacuum booster or a pump system is used on the vehicle, the brake system gain is increased, i.e., a smaller pedal force is required to produce the same level of deceleration.

The deceleration of a two-axle vehicle equipped with power assist may be determined by

$$a = \left[\left(\frac{F_p \ell_p \eta_p B}{A_{MC}} - p_o\right)\right][(A_{WC}BF \cdot r)_F + (A_{WC}BF \cdot r)_R]\frac{32.2}{WR}, \text{ ft/sec} \tag{20–5b}$$

where

$$B = \text{booster factor, d'less}$$

The booster factor B may be determined by

$$B = 1 + \frac{F_A}{F_p \ell_p}, \text{ d'less} \tag{20–6a}$$

where

$$F_A = \text{booster force, lb.}$$

Typical booster factors range between 3 and 8, with the higher values frequently employed by U.S. manufacturers.

The booster factor may be obtained from the manufacturer, most often provided in a diagram showing master cylinder output pressure versus master cylinder input force. The booster factor may be determined from the diagram by

$$B = \frac{p_\ell A_{MC}}{F_{in}}, \text{ d'less} \tag{20–6b}$$

where

F_{in} = input force obtained from diagram, lb

p_ℓ = associated brake line pressure obtained from diagram, psi

For example, a brake line pressure of 900 psi, a master cylinder area of 1.23 in^2, and an input force of 250 lb yield a booster factor of 4.42.

20–3. PREDICTION OF STOPPING DISTANCE

The deceleration-time curve of the braking process may be idealized as illustrated in Fig. 20–2. The pedal displacement begins at time zero. After the application time t_a, deceleration begins to increase and the deceleration a_{max} is attained after the buildup time t_b has elapsed.

The distance traveled by a vehicle while braking at a constant deceleration may be determined by Eq. 16–7. The all-wheels locked stopping distance S_μ is obtained by using deceleration $a = 32.2\mu$ in Eq. 16–7, or

$$S_\mu = \frac{V^2}{(2)(32.2)\mu} = \frac{V^2}{(64.4)\mu} \qquad (20\text{–}7)$$

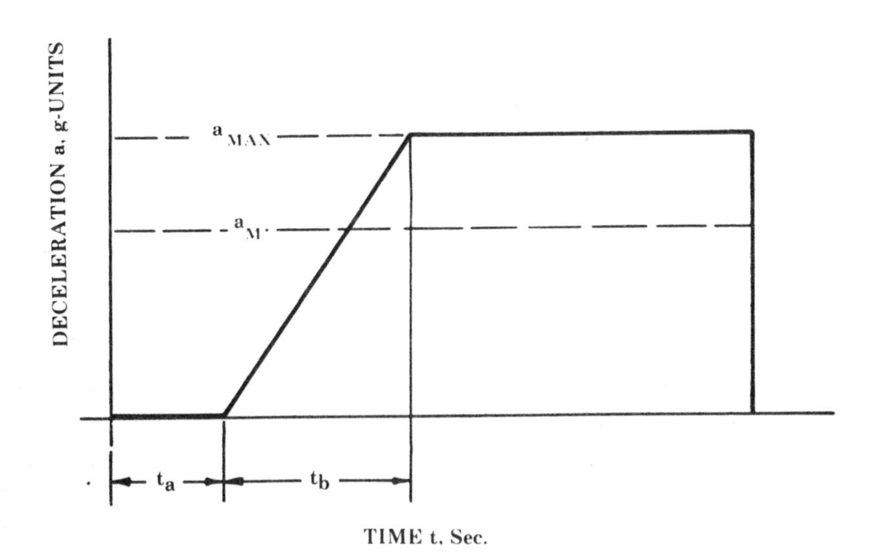

Figure 20–2. Idealized Deceleration Diagram

where

V = vehicle speed, ft/sec²
μ = tire-road friction coefficient, d'less

The stopping distance obtained by Eq. 20–7 represents the minimum possible for the tire-road condition specified by the friction coefficient μ. However, this stopping distance will only be achieved when all wheels approach wheel slide conditions at the same instant. Since this is not the case for a variety of loading, braking, and road conditions, the stopping distance S_a associated with the actual deceleration a computed by Eq. 20–5 is given by

$$S_a = \frac{V^2}{2a}, \text{ ft} \tag{20–8}$$

In Eq. 20–8 the deceleration is assumed to reach its maximum value at the instant of pedal application. The actual stopping distance is also affected by time delays required to apply the brakes and to build up brake force as illustrated in Fig. 20–2. Under these considerations the actual stopping distance may be determined by

$$S_{\text{actual}} = \frac{V^2}{2a} + \left(t_a + \frac{t_b}{2}\right) V, \text{ ft.} \tag{20–9}$$

where

a = deceleration, ft/sec²
t_a = brake application time, sec
t_b = deceleration buildup time, sec
V = velocity, ft/sec

At lower speeds the effects of application and buildup time are more pronounced than at higher speeds. Eq. 20–9 does not include driver reaction time. Any driver reaction time must be added to the application time t_a to determine the driver time effect upon stopping distance (see Chapter 24).

Application time t_a for hydraulic brake systems is very small and usually less than 0.1 sec. A measured delay between brake line pressure buildup and pedal force for a vacuum assisted brake system is shown in Fig. 20–3. Although the pedal force exceeds 100 lb in a rapid application, the brakeline pressure is only approximately 30% of that produced in slow pedal force application. For air brakes 0.25 to 1.0 sec may be required for the farthest brake of a truck-trailer combination (Fig. 20–4, Ref. 15).

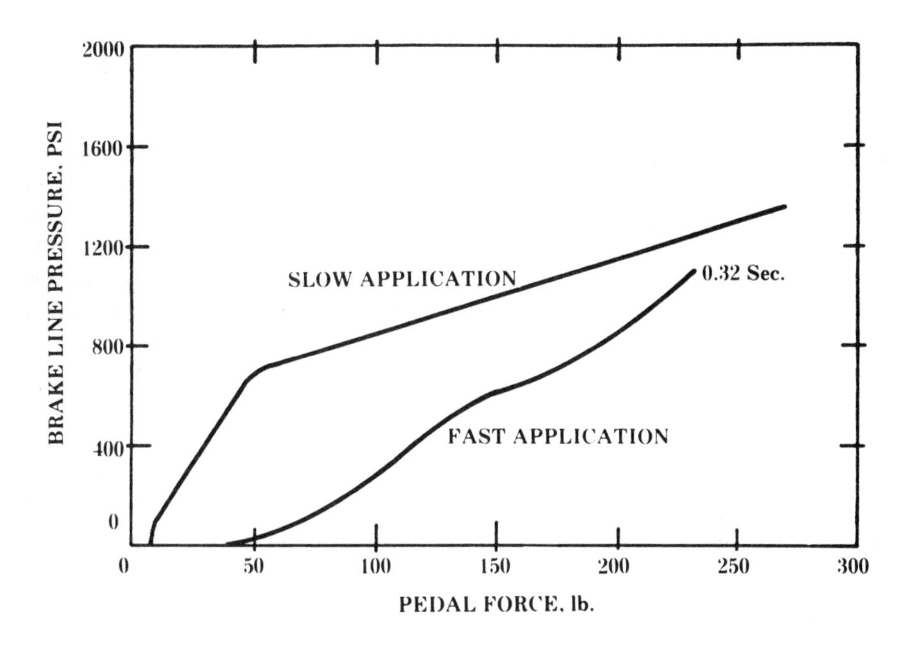

Figure 20-3. Measured Steady-State and Transient Brake-Line Pressure/Pedal Force Response

The deceleration buildup time t_b is basically the time required for the wheel to produce maximum brake force and may be determined by

$$t_b = \frac{s_T I_w \omega_o}{\mu F_z R} + \frac{\mu F_z R}{k}, \text{ sec} \tag{20-10}$$

where

F_z = tire normal force, lb

I_w = mass moment of inertia of wheel, lb · in./sec²

k = brake torque versus time slope, lb · in./sec

R = tire radius, in.

ω_o = initial wheel angular velocity, rad/sec

μ = tire-road friction coefficient, d'less

s_T = tire-slip, d'less

Brake torque rates k may range between 8,000 and 40,000 lb · in./sec with the latter applicable for rapid brake applications. Measured values of mass moment of inertia for different wheels including brake rotor are: '71 Ambassador, '71 Chevrolet Brookwood, and Ford F-100:

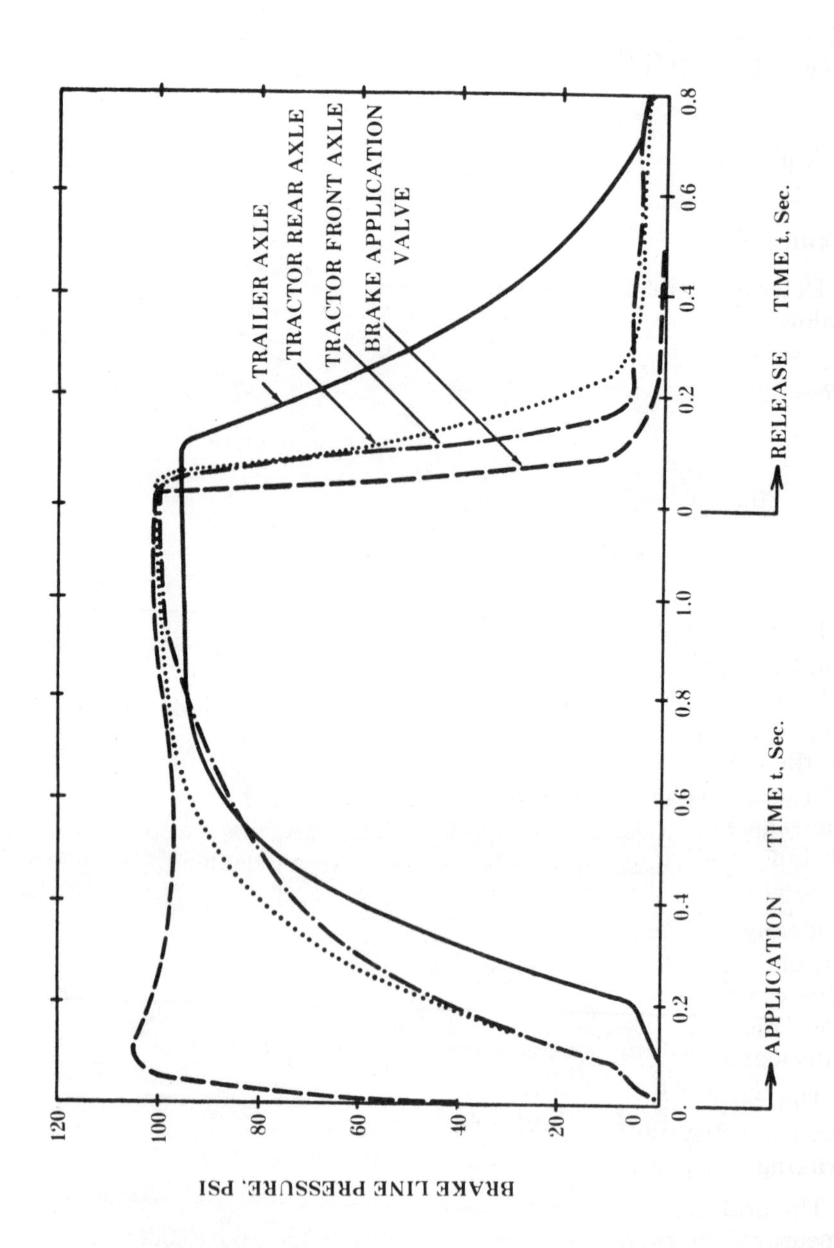

Figure 20–4. Brake Response Times for Tractor-Semitrailer Combination

17 in. lb sec^2; '71 Dodge Coronet, '71 Ford Mustang, and '71 Oldsmobile F-85: 16 in. · lb · sec^2, '71 VW Super Beetle: 15 in. · lb · sec^2; heavy truck tubeless highway tread 15–22.5 tire with brake drum, front wheel: 163 in. · lb · sec^2; driven rear wheels, tandem axle: 205 in. · lb · sec^2 for dual tires.

Example 20–1

Determine the deceleration build up time by use of the data that follow:

$F_z = 1000$ lb, $I_w = 15$ lb · in. · sec^2, $k = 40{,}000$ lb in./sec,
$R = 12$ in., $\omega_0 = 87.9$ rad/sec (corresponds to 60 mph vehicle speed),
$s_T = 0.12$, $\mu = 0.9$. By use of Eq. 20–10, the buildup time becomes

$$t_b = \frac{(0.12)(15)(87.9)}{(0.9)(1000)(1)} + \frac{(1.9)(1000)(1)}{(40{,}000)} = 0.176 + 0.046 = 0.222 \text{ sec}$$

20–4. MINIMUM WHEELS UNLOCKED STOPPING DISTANCE

Eq. 20–7 allows the computation of the stopping distance from the point all wheels are locked until the vehicle comes to rest. Although all wheels are locked in many emergency brake applications, a shorter stopping distance may be achieved when the wheels are modulated by the driver so that no lockup occurs; however, maximum peak friction tones are produced. Since a vehicle is inherently unstable when the rear wheels are locked with the front wheels still rolling, most braking systems are (or should be) designed to cause front wheel locking prior to rear wheel.

Ideally, the driver would modulate pedal force so that the front wheels are just about to lock in a straight-line braking maneuver. This condition forces the front wheels to brake near their peak friction value and the rear wheels to provide close to peak traction with sufficient side force capacity for braking stability.

The capability of a vehicle braking system to use the available friction between tire and road for deceleration is commonly called braking efficiency.

The braking efficiency is defined by the ratio of vehicle deceleration (measured in g-units) to tire-road friction coefficient. A high braking efficiency indicates that a large portion of the tire-road friction is used for wheels unlocked deceleration, a low value would indicate the opposite.

The braking efficiency E_F for the front axle is

$$E_F = \left(\frac{a}{\mu}\right)_F = \frac{1-\psi}{1-\phi-\mu\chi}, \text{ d'less} \tag{20-11}$$

and for the rear axle

$$E_R = \left(\frac{a}{\mu}\right)_R = \frac{\psi}{\phi+\mu\chi}, \text{ d'less} \tag{20-12}$$

where

μ = tire-road friction coefficient, d'less

ϕ = rear axle brake force divided by total brake force, d'less

χ = center of gravity height divided by wheel base, d'less

A graphical representation of Eqs. 20–11 and 20–12 is shown in Fig. 20–5. Inspection of the curve indicates that the front wheels of the empty vehicle are the limiting element for tire-road friction coefficients less than 0.7. For example at $\mu = 0.2$ the braking efficiency is approximately 0.82, yielding a vehicle deceleration of $(0.82)(0.2) = 0.164\ g$ or $(0.164)(32.2) = 5.28$ ft/sec^2. If the driver increases pedal force above that corresponding to 5.28 ft/sec^2, the front wheels will lock rendering the vehicle nonsteerable. Further pedal force increase will lead to rear wheel lockup. When braking on a roadway having a friction coefficient, e.g., of 0.8, the braking of the empty vehicle is limited by rear wheel lockup. On dry road surfaces high deceleration is possible resulting in dynamic load transfer onto the front axle which decreases the danger of premature front wheel lockup. Inspection of Fig. 20–5 indicates a braking efficiency of approximately 0.92 for a friction coefficient of 0.8. The associated rear wheels unlocked deceleration limit is $(0.92)(0.8) = 0.73\ g$ or $(0.73)(32.2) = 23.7$ ft/sec^2. A pedal force increase above that corresponding to a deceleration of 23.7 ft/sec^2 cause first rear wheel lockup and then front wheel lockup. Also shown in Fig. 20–5 is the increase in stopping distance over the minimum possible. For example, when braking on a road having a friction coefficient of 0.2, the actual stopping distance (excluding response time) is approximately 22% longer than the minimum.

Example 20–2

Compute the minimum wheels unlocked stopping distance of a vehicle having the following data: static rear axle load 1500 lb, total weight 3600 lb, center-of-gravity height 31 in., wheel base 132 in., front wheel caliper diameter 3 in. (disc brake), front pad lining friction coefficient 0.4, effective front rotor radius 4 in., rear wheel cylinder diameter 1 in. (drum brake), rear wheel brake factor 2.6, rear drum

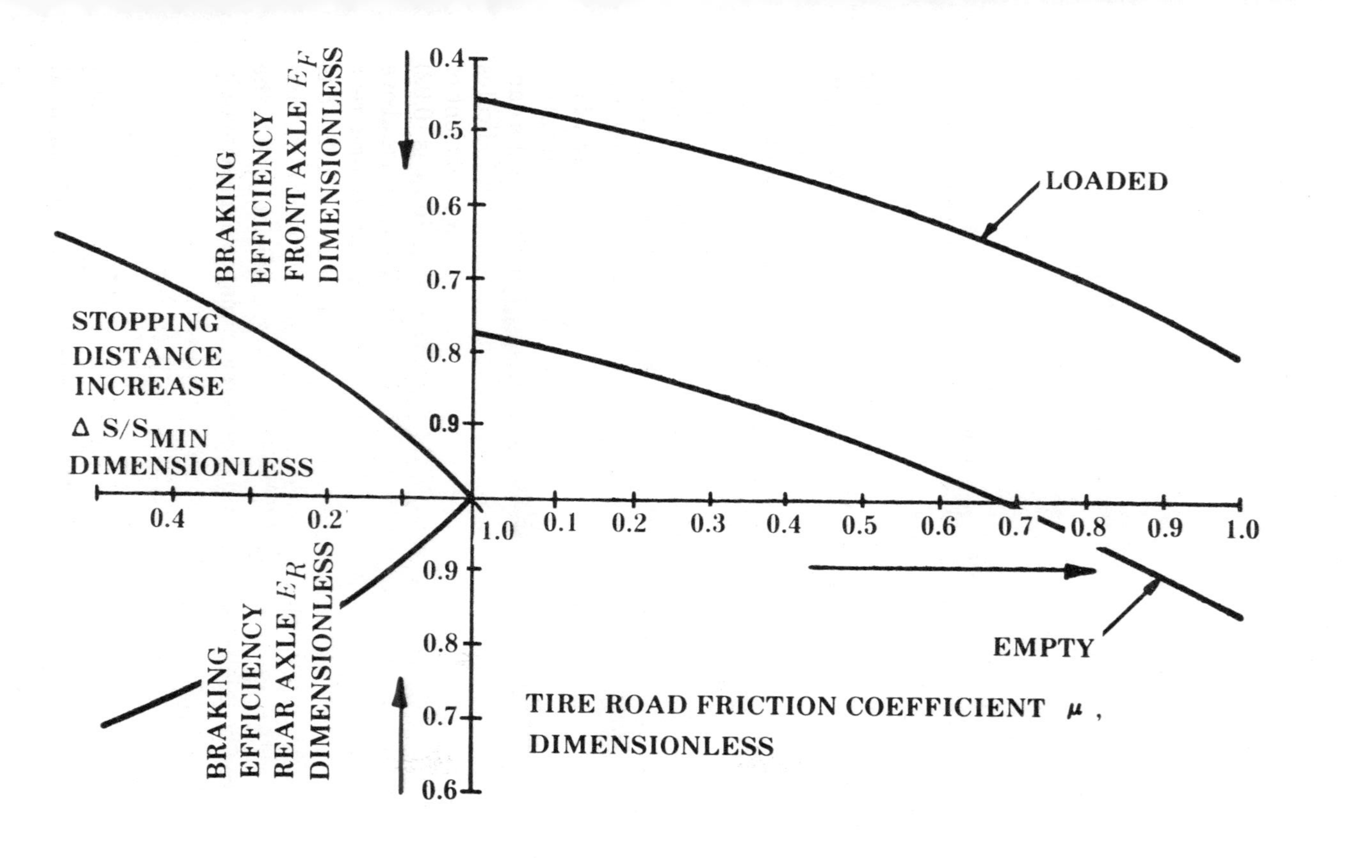

Figure 20–5. Braking Efficiency Diagram

diameter 11 in., application time 0.1 sec., deceleration buildup time 0.2 sec.

Compute the stopping distance from a speed of 40 mph on a dry road surface ($\mu = 0.85$) and a wet polished road surface ($\mu = 0.35$).

The braking efficiency computation requires some preliminary calculations.

Relative rear axle load $\psi = \frac{1500}{3600} = 0.416$, i.e., 41.6% of the total weight is concentrated on the rear axle.

Brake force distribution ϕ is defined by the ratio of rear axle brake force to total brake force.

$$\phi = \frac{(A_{WC}\ BFr)_R}{(A_{WC}\ BFr)_R + (A_{WC}\ BFr)_F}, \text{ d'less} \qquad (20\text{–}13)$$

Substitution of the appropriate values into Eq. 20–13 yields

$$\phi = \frac{[(0.785)(2.6)(5.5)]}{[(7.06)(0.8)(4)] + [(0.785)(2.6)(5.5)]}$$

= 0.33, i.e., 33% of the total braking effort is concentrated on the rear axle.

Relative center of gravity height is defined by the ratio of center-of-gravity height to wheel base,

$$\chi = \frac{31}{132} = 0.23$$

The front wheels generally limit braking on low friction surfaces; hence by the use of Eq. 20–11 the braking efficiency E_F becomes on the front:

$$E_F = \frac{1 - 0.416}{1 - 0.33\text{-}(0.35)(0.23)} = 0.99$$

On the rear by use of Eq. 20–12 the braking efficiency E_R is

$$E_R = \frac{0.416}{0.33 + (0.85)(0.23)} = 0.79$$

Consequently, the maximum wheels unlocked deceleration on the low friction surface is $(0.99)(0.35) = 0.346g$ or 11.1 ft/sec^2. The corresponding deceleration on the dry road is 21.6 ft/sec^2.

By use of Eq. 20–9 the stopping distance on the wet surface becomes

$$S_{\text{actual}} = \frac{[(40)(1.466)]^2}{(2)(11.1)} + \left(0.1 + \frac{0.2}{2}\right)(40)(1.466) = 166.6 \text{ ft}$$

The corresponding stopping distance on the dry surface is 91.3 ft. It is interesting to note that the ratio of wet to dry stopping distance is 1.82 while the ratio of dry to wet friction coefficients is 2.42, indicating the lower braking efficiency on the dry road surface. The reason for the poor braking efficiency stems from a relatively high brake force concentration on the rear axle indicated by $\phi = 0.33$. By appropriate changes of the wheel cylinder sizes front and rear a decrease in rear axle brake force ϕ may be obtained. For example, a brake force distribution $\phi = 0.27$ yields a braking efficiency of 0.89 on both front and rear axle. The corresponding decelerations are 24.6 ft/sec^2 and 10 ft/sec^2 on the dry and wet road surface, respectively. The associated stopping distances are 81.6 and 183 ft. Improvements in braking efficiency are obtained by proportioning valves that automatically adjust the rear wheel braking effort to better match the dynamic conditions.

A minimum wheels unlocked stopping distance maneuver requires a continued pedal force modulation throughout the braking process. Inspection of Eq. 18–4 indicates an increase of tire-road friction coefficient as speed decreases. Consequently, the driver must decrease the pedal force during the maneuver to force the "limiting" axle to operate near peak friction levels. The change in pedal force can be computed by use of Eqs. 20–11 (change in braking efficiency) (or 20–12), 18–4 (change in friction), and 20–5 (deceleration/pedal force).

20-5. DECELERATION ANALYSIS OF NONREGULAR CASES

Frequently collision damage causes one or more wheels to lock due to sheet metal deformation. In other cases a parked vehicle with its parking brakes applied is impacted and slides with the rear wheels locked.

In all these cases Eq. 17–4 must be used to determine vehicle deceleration. The resultant force F_{res} must be determined from a force analysis. The weight W used in Eq. 17–4 is the total weight decelerated by the resultant retarding force F_{res}. Although in most accident reconstructions W is the weight of one vehicle, occasionally two vehicles collide and lock during impact, i.e., the retarding force must decelerate both vehicle weights.

Example 20-3

Determine the stopping distance of a vehicle from 40 mph having the left front wheel locked by sheet metal deformation. Use the pertinent data of example 20–2. The vehicle is equipped with a 327 $in.^3$ gasoline engine, total transmission ratio $\rho = 3$, and a tire radius of 12 in. The roadway is dry.

Eq. 17–4 requires the value of the resultant force acting on the vehicle. The individual forces are acting on the tires. The left front wheel produces sliding friction determined by Eq. 18–7, the remaining three rolling resistance forces determined by Eq. 18–2. The driven wheels are also retarded by engine drag.

The average sliding coefficient of friction of the left front wheel existing between a speed of 40 and zero mph may be determined by Eq. 18–4 as 0.8. The static (without braking) normal force on the left front wheel is $W(1 - \psi)0.5$ or $3600\ (1 - 0.416)(0.5) = 1051.21$ lb. During braking the static normal force on one front wheel increases by one half of the dynamic load transfer. The dynamic load transfer onto the front axle is equal to $\chi a W = (0.23) \times (0.2)(3600) = 165.6$ lb. A deceleration of 0.2 g was initially assumed to be developed by the total retarding force acting on the vehicle in order to compute dynamic load transfer. The correct value will be determined by trial-and-error solution.

The dynamic load transfer onto the left front wheel is one half of that of the front axle, or approximately 83 lb. Consequently, Eq. 18–7 yields a left front wheel retarding force of $(1051 + 83) \times (0.8) = 907$ lb.

The rolling resistance force of the right front wheel is $(1051 + 83)(0.015) = 17$ lb. The rolling resistance coefficient of 0.015 is obtained from Table 18–1.

The rolling resistance force of the rear wheels is equal to the product of rear axle load times rolling resistance coefficient, i.e., $[(3600)(0.416) - 165](0.015) = 20$ lb. In the calculation the dynamic load transfer (165 lb) was subtracted from the static load of the rear wheels.

In addition to the rolling resistance, the rear wheels are also retarded by engine drag. The engine torque is determined by Eq. 19–5 as $(0.0065)(60)(327) = 127.5$ ft · lb. The retarding force at the driven rear wheels is determined by Eq. 19–6 as $F_x = 127.5(3)/[(0.8)(1)] = 478$ lb.

The resultant retarding force acting on the vehicle is the sum of the individual retarding forces, i.e., 1422 lb. The deceleration is determined by Eq. 17–4 as

$$a = \frac{(1422)(32.2)}{3600} = 12.7 \text{ ft/sec}^2$$

The deceleration initially assumed at (0.2)(32.2) = 6.4 ft/sec^2 was too low. Consequently, the normal forces on the wheels change due to higher dynamics load transfer. Instead of 83 lb, the dynamic load transfer onto the left front wheel is (0.23)(12.7/32.2)(3600)(0.5) = 163 lb. The left front wheel normal force becomes (1051 + 163) = 1214 lb, yielding a sliding friction force of 971 lb. The right front wheel rolling resistance force becomes (1214)(0.015) = 18 lb. The rolling resistance of the rear wheels becomes [(3600)(0.416) − 326](0.015) = 18 lb. The engine drag force remains unchanged. The total retarding force is 1485 lb; yielding a deceleration of 13.3 ft/sec^2.

Since the newly computed deceleration of 13.3 ft/sec^2 exceeds the "old" deceleration of 12.7 ft/sec^2, one more iteration may be carried out. The final deceleration is 13.4 ft/sec^2.

The stopping distance may be determined by Eq. 16–7 or 20–8 as

$$S = \frac{[(40)(1.466)]^2}{(2)(13.4)} = 128.3 \text{ ft}$$

The unbalanced retarding force acting on the left front wheel may be sufficiently large to rotate the vehicle in a counter clockwise direction. By the use of Eq. 17–5, the angular acceleration ϵ may be determined. The angular rotation may be determined by Eq. 16–30 when the sliding time is known.

It is interesting to note that the stopping distance would increase to 193 ft when the engine drag is zero, i.e., the transmission lever was in the neutral position.

20-6. STABILITY DURING BRAKING

Accident and vehicle test data, as well as basic engineering analysis, indicate that premature rear wheel lockup of vehicles traveling at higher speeds may result in violent vehicle instability, most frequently causing the vehicle to spin about its verticle axis. Investigations have shown that typical drivers when faced with an unexpected emergency maneuver apply large pedal forces causing wheel lockup to occur and, furthermore, no attempts are made to counteract the initial yaw or rotating motion of the vehicle. The development of vehicle instability due to wheel lockup is as follows. If it is assumed that the front wheels are still rolling or, have not yet approached sliding conditions and that the rear wheels are already sliding, any disturbance due to road grade or sidewind will produce a lateral component at the vehicle center of gravity. The resultant force stemming from the inertia force induced by braking and the lateral force (disturbance force) is now oriented along a disturbance angle measured from the longitudinal vehicle axis. Since the rear wheels are sliding, no tire side force can be produced at the rear (see Section 18–4) and consequently, the side forces developed by the rolling front tires will produce a yawing moment. This moment is directed such as to rotate the vehicle about its vertical axis in a manner that increases the initial disturbance angle. The resulting rotation increases, i.e., the motion is unstable.

If the front wheels are locked, an identical disturbance will be reacted upon by a stabilizing moment produced by the rear wheels. The direction of this moment is such as to rotate the longitudinal axis of the vehicle towards the direction of travel of the center of gravity of the vehicle, thus reducing the initial disturbance angle and rendering the vehicle completely stable.

Different brake forces left and right on the front wheels cause a rotating moment of the vehicle about its vertical axis. The front suspension design has a significant effect upon the vehicle behavior when different brake forces are developed by the front wheels. The scrub radius r_s determines the degree to which a front wheel is forced to rotate about its vertical axis in the presence of front wheel brake force unbalance. Scrub radius is the distance between tire-to-road contact point and wheel assembly steering rotation relative to the ground. A positive scrub radius exists when the intersection A of the tire center plane (line 1 in Fig. 20–6) and wheel assembly steering line (line 2 in Fig. 20–6) is located below the road surface. A negative scrub radius exists when the intersection A is located above the road

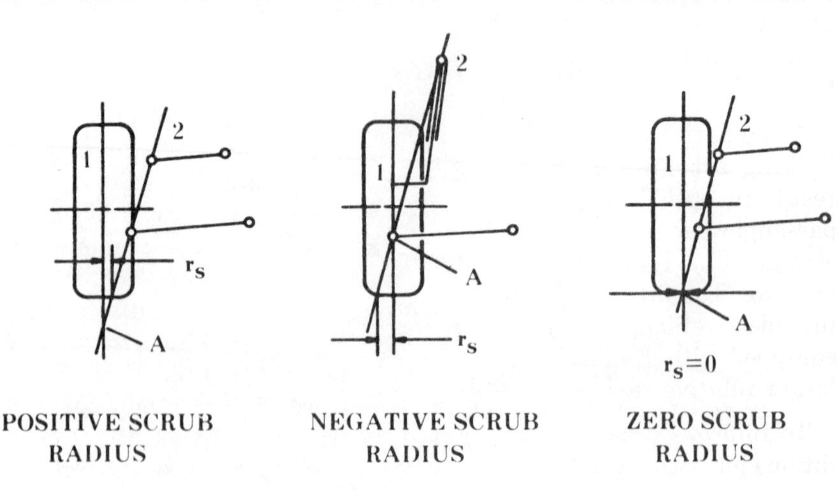

Figure 20–6. Definition of Scrub Radius

surface. The scrub radius is zero when the intersection A is located at the road surface.

A positive scrub radius has the effect of eliminating play in steering linkages during forward travel and wheel vibrations are reduced. Large values of positive scrub radius force the wheel to rotate towards the higher brake force in the event of front wheel brake unbalance. A negative scrub radius forces the wheel to rotate slightly in the direction of the lower brake force thus producing tire slip angles and tire side forces sufficiently to hold the vehicle in a stable controlled stop.

20-7. BRAKING IN A TURN

When braking in a turn, additional load transfer occurs due to the centrifugal force acting at the vehicle center of gravity resulting in increased normal forces at the outer wheels. The tires must also produce side forces to turn the vehicle. This side force requirement reduces the friction available for braking. The braking efficiency and, consequently, the wheels unlocked deceleration is reduced from that associated with the straight-line stop. A typical diagram of a rear braking efficiency as a function of speed and road curvature is illustrated in Fig. 20-7. Inspection of the curves indicates that a road surface friction of 0.6, a curve radius of 300 ft and a velocity of 45 mph yields a braking efficiency of 0.50. The associated deceleration is $(0.50)(0.60)(32.2) = 9.66$ ft/sec^2. The straight-line braking efficiency obtained for an infinite curve radius or straight-line braking is approximately 0.86, the associated wheels unlocked deceleration 16.6 ft/sec^2. When stopping from 50 mph, the associated safe, stable (due to wheels unlocked braking) distances are 278 and 162 ft, respectively.

A comparison of straight and curved braking indicates clearly that braking systems optimized for straight-line braking do not always result in optimum curved braking. Results indicate that a typical passenger car requires a relative rear brake force of 30% for optimum straight-line braking, however, only 25% for optimum curved-line braking. The final choice of brake force distribution depends upon the intended vehicle function and safety standards compliance. Trucks equipped with dual tires on the rear axle generally permit somewhat larger relative rear axle brake forces than passenger cars.

To improve braking performance for a wide range of loading conditions for both straight and curved-line braking, automatic adjustable proportioning valves are used. A detailed discussion and engineering relationships for braking in a turn analysis are found in Ref. 11.

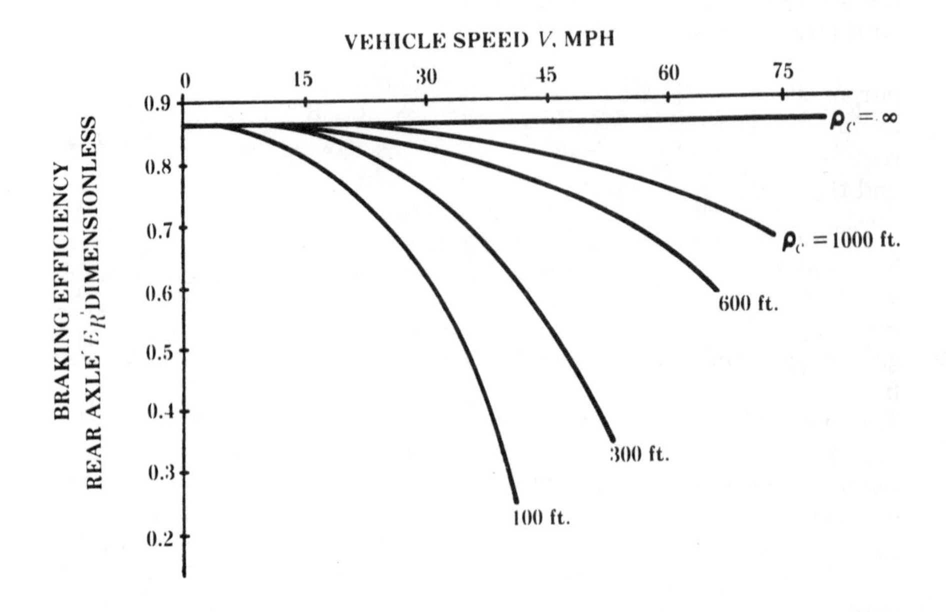

Figure 20–7. Rear Braking Efficiency as Function of Speed and Road Curvature for a Tire – Road Friction Coefficient of 0.6

20–8. BRAKING OF COMBINATION VEHICLES

Braking analysis of tractor-semitrailer or truck-trailers is more complicated than for a two-axle vehicle because the summation of the axle loads of the tractor are not equal to the tractor weight. The tractor axle loads are also a function of the loading and braking of the semitrailer. Engineering equations are available that allow the prediction of braking performance within a 5 to 10% accuracy (Refs. 11, 15, and 16).

A braking in a turn analysis similar to that of solid frame vehicles can be developed which includes the effects of lateral acceleration on the braking efficiency and optimum brake force distribution. The resulting equations are lengthy and are normally evaluated only by means of computer programs (Ref. 17). Lateral acceleration values of trucks and truck/trailer combinations generally are limited to values significantly lower than those achievable by passenger cars. Tests have shown that proper brake systems designs in terms of a brake force distribution causing a sequence of tractor front, trailer, and tractor rear axle lockup will yield minimum stopping distances for both straight and curved braking. A proper brake system design requires consideration of brake torque and wheel lockup sequence. For purposes of "stretching" the combination, the trailer brakes should be applied prior to the tractor brake. In terms of wheel lockup, stability requires that the tractor front axle lock first, the trailer axle second, and the tractor rear axle last.

Test results and accidents have shown that three different types of loss of control of a tractor-semitrailer combination may occur. In the event of front wheel lockup, steering control is lost and the vehicle continues in a straight and stable path. Steering control can be regained by simply lowering the pedal force sufficiently to release the front brakes. In the event of trailer wheel lockup trailer swing occurs. This instability can be overcome by releasing the brakes and stretching the combination by slight acceleration. The reason for trailer swing occurring is the same that causes a passenger car to spin around its vertical axis due to loss of side force on the rear wheels in the event of rear wheel lockup. Violent instability including jackknifing may occur when the tractor rear wheels lock prior to any others particularly when turning. In this case the side forces at the tractor rear wheels are nearly zero and in the event of braking in a turn the side forces on the front tires tend to support the jackknifing action by keeping the tractor front in the intended turn; whereas, the tractor rear axle slides sideways causing the tractor to yaw violently.

Antijackknifing devices have been proposed that would affect the friction at the fifth wheel location. Some extreme devices have been proposed that would lock the tractor rigidly in position relative to the trailer in the event of jackknifing. Such a device could change the articulated vehicle to that of a rigid system without steerability.

Any device affecting the fifth wheel friction would shift the side force requirements lost by the locked tractor rear axle to the front and trailer wheels. This change may cause tire side force saturation at those wheels. In addition, the resulting (rigid) combination vehicle motion may be more severe than the jackknifing alone.

Since the causes of jackknifing are loss of tire side force at the tractor rear wheels, a proper brake force distribution to ensure front wheel lockup first, then trailer wheels and last tractor rear wheels appears to be a proper engineering approach for avoiding jackknifing. Furthermore, with the advances made in antiskid controls for heavy vehicles, tractor rear and trailer wheel lockup is prevented for all loading and road conditions as well as driver skill levels. Federal government regulations (FMVSS 121) necessitate the use of antiskid systems on most axles.

The braking performance of tractor-semitrailers is significantly less than that of passenger cars or a small solid-frame vehicle such as pickup trucks. Reasons for the decreased braking effectiveness of heavy trucks and trailers is due to the lower friction coefficients associated with truck tires and the decreased braking efficiency or braking friction utilization. The decreased utilization of the available friction in terms of vehicle deceleration is caused by dynamic wheel load changes during braking, frequently called brake hop, and the practice of not installing brakes on the front axle in the case of a tandem axle tractor for trucks not required to comply with FMVSS 121, i.e., older vehicles. For example, a loaded tractor-semitrailer may have a front axle load of 11,000 lb in the absence of braking and 15,000 lb when braking at 16 ft/sec^2. Since this weight of 15,000 is not used for the production of retarding friction, the deceleration in *g*-units must always be less than that level of braking associated with the tire-road friction coefficient. In the particular case cited, a friction coefficient of 0.7 could have produced a front wheel retardation of $0.7 \times 15{,}000 = 10{,}500$ lb on the vehicle by the use of front brakes.

Road tests have shown that the maximum decelerations achieved with different truck-trailers are approximately 16 ft/sec^2 for a 3-S2 combination and 17 ft/sec^2 for a 2-S1 combination. The average tire sliding friction coefficients associated with the cited deceleration values are 0.65 at 10 mph, 0.53 at 30 mph, and 0.45 at 40 mph (Ref. 15).

In addition to the decreased braking effectiveness, the response times of air brake systems are greater than those associated with hydraulic brake systems (Fig. 20–4). Typical time delay value for a tractor-semitrailer combination (40 ft trailer) is 0.25 sec for the tractor rear axle brake chamber to reach 60 psi air pressure and 0.3 sec for the trailer brake chamber. The release time delays are 0.30 sec on the tractor rear axle and 0.70 on the trailer axle to decrease to 5 psi air pressure.

20–9. BRAKE FAILURE ANALYSIS

Motor vehicle brake systems are designed to decelerate the vehicle safely. A review of approximately 8000 multidisciplinary accident investigation studies (MDAI) reveals that brake malfunctioning was noted as accident causation factor in less than 2% of all accidents. The brake malfunctioning involved brake failures such as brake line failure, wheel cylinder failure, brake hose failure, defective lining attachment, lining mismatch. A review of the individual case reports revealed that most brake malfunctioning is caused by faulty maintenance or repair (See Section 42–1). A detailed study of degradation of brake system component and the associated performance is found in Ref. 18.

20–9.1. Development of Brake Failure. Failure of braking system components under ordinary driving conditions is likely to occur only if:

1. parts are defective
2. parts become severely worn
3. parts become degraded

A part becomes degraded, e.g., through oil contaminating brake linings. A part becomes severely worn through long-time use, as, e.g., in the case of cups or seals of master cylinders and wheel cylinders. A part is defective when it is designed or manufactured defectively or when it is degraded or worn sufficiently to malfunction.

In friction brakes the linings are designed to take most of the wear. Since wear will increase with time of rubbing, linings and drums in use over a longer period of time are more likely to fail than new ones. Also, master and wheel cylinder housings, pistons, and seals will show increasing wear with time of operation. Excessive wear may cause brake failure. In general, brake or automobile manufacturers will specify permissible wear dimensions of cylinders and drums. Under normal driving conditions failure of brake components of new vehicles is not likely to occur. In most cases brake system failures occur during severe brake application, i.e., during driving maneuvers requiring large pedal forces that severely stress the entire brake system, and as the result of improper repair or maintenance activities.

Degradation of brake components because of corrosion, aging, or environmental factors may also cause brake failure. Investigations have shown that steel and copper coated steel hydraulic brake tubing used on cars and trucks can be a safety hazard. The performance of steel tubing becomes highly erratic after four to six years in service. The age of the vehicle appears to be more significant than mileage relative to brake tube corrosion. Visual inspection of brake tubing does not always give an accurate indication of its performance. Improvements in brake tubing performance is accomplished through different materials, specifically copper alloy. Test results showed that copper alloy tubing material exhibited no significant decrease of tensile strength after 180 days exposure to salt spray, whereas, copper coated steel tubing showed no tensile strength, indicating complete corrosion (Section 20–9.5).

Prior to the development of a partial or complete brake failure, certain conditions exist within the brake system that may indicate the beginning of brake failure. These conditions are different for drum brakes and disc brakes, and hydraulic and air brake systems in several points. Major causes of brake failure are discussed next.

1. Drum Brake System (hydraulic)

Defect	*Causes*
a. Brake pedal travel too long; brake pedal touching floor.	Worn linings; leaking brake system
b. Brake pedal travel long and spongy	Air in brake system; low on brake fluid
c. Brake pedal travel long (after bleeding of brake)	Check valve of master cylinder defective
d. Brake pedal travel long but may be reduced by "pumping"	Check valve of master cylinder not closing; check valve spring too weak; air in brake system
e. Brake pedal can be pushed to the floor after holding initially	Leaking brake lines or seals in master or wheel cylinder
f. Brakes heat up while driving	Compensating port connecting reservoir and master cylinder not open when master cylinder piston is in released position; brake shoe return springs too weak due to aging; rubber seals have grown due to use of wrong fluid in brake system; parking brake not released
g. No or low braking performance	Brake linings contaminated with oil; wrong brake linings; assist unit defective; leak in brake system; defective seals in master cylinder
h. Brake applies without being operated by driver	Same cause as #1 f

i. Brakes develop brake imbalance (left to right)	Brake drum not round; inadequate tires; brake linings contaminated by oil
j. Brakes grab and perform erratically; brakes tend to lock up	Brake linings are not attached securely to shoes; lining rivets contact brake drum; brake drum not round; brake shoe return springs too weak
k. Brake makes noise while braking	Brake drum not round; dirt contamination of linings; lining rivets not securely attached
l. Brake grabs in spite of low pedal force	Improper adjusted brake; brake backing plate not securely attached

2. Disc Brake System (hydraulic)

Defect	*Causes*
a. Excessive pad wear	Pads do not move freely in pad support; caliper pistons do not move freely in wheel cylinder housing; contaminated brake rotor; rotor surface rough; rear brakes (if drum brakes) out of adjustment
b. Excessive brake pedal travel	Brake rotor has excessive axial tolerance; air or not enough brake fluid in brake system; leak in brake system; defective seals in master cylinder
c. Low or no brake force	Same as under 1g; caliper piston pushed too far back during repair

3. Brake Failures Common to Drum and Disc Brake Systems

Defect	*Causes*
a. Soft pedal	Caused by air in the brake system or by vaporization of brake fluid due to excessive temperatures at wheel cylinders

b. Hard pedal and excessive pedal force	Defective vacuum assist unit; wheel cylinder pistons not moving freely; wrong or oily linings
c. Brake pedal vibrations	Caused by waves in brake fluid due to wheel cylinder piston vibrations which are caused by excessive axial play of disc brake rotors or excessive wheel bearing looseness
d. Brake fade	Caused by a reduction in gain (or brake factor) of wheel brakes; fading is more pronounced in drum brakes than in disc brakes due to the greater sensitivity of drum brakes to lining friction coefficient changes
e. Slow braking response	Defective vacuum assist unit

4. Brake Failures of Air Brake Systems

Defect	*Causes*
a. No brake force	No air supply pressure; restricted tubing or hose; defective application valve
b. Low brake force	Low brake line pressure; too much push rod travel at brake chambers due to excessive lining wear; worn linings or drums; leaking chamber diaphragm; slack adjuster out of adjustment; oil on brake linings
c. Slow brake response	Low brake line pressure; linkage binding; too much push rod travel; leaking application valve; leaking brake chamber diaphragm; brake shoe anchor pins frozen; application valve control linkage improperly adjusted
d. Slow brake release	Linkage binding; restriction in brake line; too much push rod travel; defective application valve;

	binding cams or wedges at wheel brakes; weak brake shoe return springs
e. Grabbing brakes	Uneven slack adjuster setting; linkage bindings at one or more wheels; linings worn unevenly; brake shoe return spring weak or related problem; defective brake chamber; unequal springs in brake chambers or between brake shoes
f. Slow pressure buildup in reservoir	Clogged air cleaner; air leak; defective compressor; open or leaking reservoir drain cocks; defective compressor governor.

The brake failures identified in the previous list can be grouped into failures causing (1) insufficient brake force; (2) excessive component wear; and (3) inconvenience to driver.

20-9.2. Brake Failure Analysis. The purpose of a failure analysis is to determine how the original design effectiveness of the brake system, i.e., the deceleration/pedal force relationship is changed if a partial failure should occur within the system (Ref. 19).

Three basic categories of failure are considered in this failure analysis:

1. Loss of line pressure in dual braking systems
2. Loss of vacuum boost in a power boost element
3. Loss of effectiveness exhibited by an overheated brake commonly called fade.

Important in each partial failure mode is the evaluation with respect to its influence on vehicle braking performance and with respect to the resulting consequences for safety—namely, the ability of drivers to achieve the desired levels of deceleration.

Brake Line Failure

A hydraulic brake system is a dual system when the transmission of pedal effort from the master cylinder to the wheel brakes consists of two independent circuits. A power assist unit (vacuum booster) installed in the system does not have to consist of two circuits.

The brake system contains the mechanisms for pedal force application, pedal force transmission, and brake force production. The mechanism for application of pedal force involves a pedal lever ratio such that an increased pedal effort is applied to the master cylinder push rod. The pedal force transmission involves a dual circuit master cylinder, generally termed tandem master cylinder and the hydraulic brake lines between master cylinder and wheel brakes. Connected into the brake lines can be special devices such as metering, proportioning or antiskid modulating valves. The wheel brakes may be divided into those involving one or two actuating mechanisms. The first category includes leading-trailing type drum brakes and single caliper type disc brakes with one wheel cylinder. In the event of a circuit failure no braking action can be developed by this brake. Brakes involving two actuating mechanisms or two wheel cylinders per brake or caliper may be connected to both brake circuits. In the case of one circuit failure the wheel brakes produce a reduced brake force, in most cases a braking action equal to 50% of the nonfailed case.

The six basic possibilities for installing brake lines between master cylinder and wheel brakes to form two independent brake line circuits are shown in Fig. 20–8. System 1 representing the front-to-rear split is the design generally used by vehicles of U.S. manufacture. Mercedes Benz vehicles also use system 1. Systems 2, 4, 5, and 6 exhibit equal braking force for each circuit. In the case of system 1 and 3, a failure of circuit 1 or 2 will result in different braking force. The braking force achievable with system 2 and 6 are identical in the failed mode for either circuit. The effects upon vehicle stability while braking under the partial failure mode, i.e., a failure of circuit 1 or 2 will be different, with system 6 showing an undesirable side-to-side brake unbalance. Since it is obvious that a dual system of type 6 is undesirable, it is not included in any further analysis.

Three measures of partial braking performance for dual brake systems may be identified.

1. Reduced braking force of the vehicle in the partial failure mode due to a decreased brake system gain between master cylinder exit and wheel brake.

2. Changes in brake force distribution front to rear and hence reduced braking efficiency.

3. Increased application times due to longer brake pedal travel. All three measures will cause an increase in stopping distance. In addition to these measures relative to brake force production, the effects of brake force unbalance on vehicle stability must be considered.

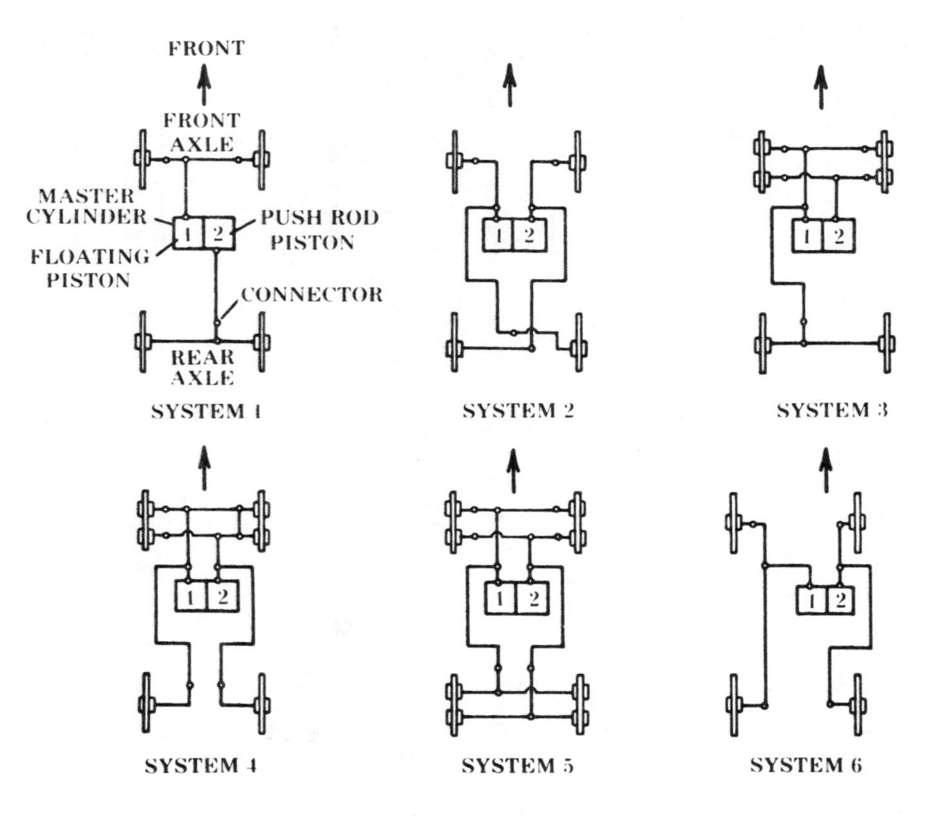

Figure 20-8. Different Dual–Circuit Brake Systems

Complete discussions and engineering equations for the analysis of brake failures are found in Ref. 11.

A comparison of the dual brake systems represented in Fig. 20–8 indicates a different number of connectors and flexible hoses is required for the various systems. For example, system 1 requires 17 connections compared with 34 for system 5.

A leak is more likely to develop in a hydraulic circuit that contains more removable connections, wheel cylinder seals, and other devices such as valves, and control elements. A comparison of the complexity of the different dual circuit splits is shown in Fig. 20–9. All removable connections including T-fittings are represented in Fig. 20–9. The data indicate system 5 to have a higher failure probability based on the number of connections than the remaining systems. Difficulties may also arise in properly installing the flexible hoses near the wheels. Not included in the number of removable connections is the third bleeder screw required for double caliper disc brakes if they are designed as one unit.

The maximum temperature of a brake should be kept below certain limits. High brake temperature may result in: (1) brake fade and increased lining wear, (2) high tire bead temperature, and (3) increased temperature of the brake fluid in wheel cylinders. High brake fluid temperature may cause brake fluid boiling and vaporization, resulting in increased pedal travel and possibly total brake failure. Modern brake fluids boil at approximately 450 deg F. Consequently, continued brake applications, as experienced in prolonged downhill travel, may cause the brake fluid to boil and vapor to develop, and the brake system to fail.

One effect of thermal overloading on circuit failure of the different dual splits is indicated in Fig. 20–10. It is assumed that the front brakes are experiencing excessive temperatures leading to vaporization of brake fluid and hence failure of the circuits connected to the front wheels. Inspection of Fig. 20–10 indicates that only system 1, the front-to-rear split, provides a partial braking capability on the rear wheels with the front brakes failed due to vaporization. If on the other hand a rear wheel exhibits vaporization and hence circuit failure, all but system 1 and 3 will fail completely.

Vacuum Assist Failure

Vacuum assist failure exists when the assist function of the vacuum assist unit is degraded through insufficient vacuum or complete loss of vacuum. For a complete loss of vacuum the equations developed for

BRAKE SYSTEM	SINGLE CIRCUIT SYSTEM	SYSTEM NO.				
		1	2	3	4	5
WHEEL CYLINDER	8	8	8	12	12	16
REMOVABLE CONNECTIONS	17	15	16	25	26	34

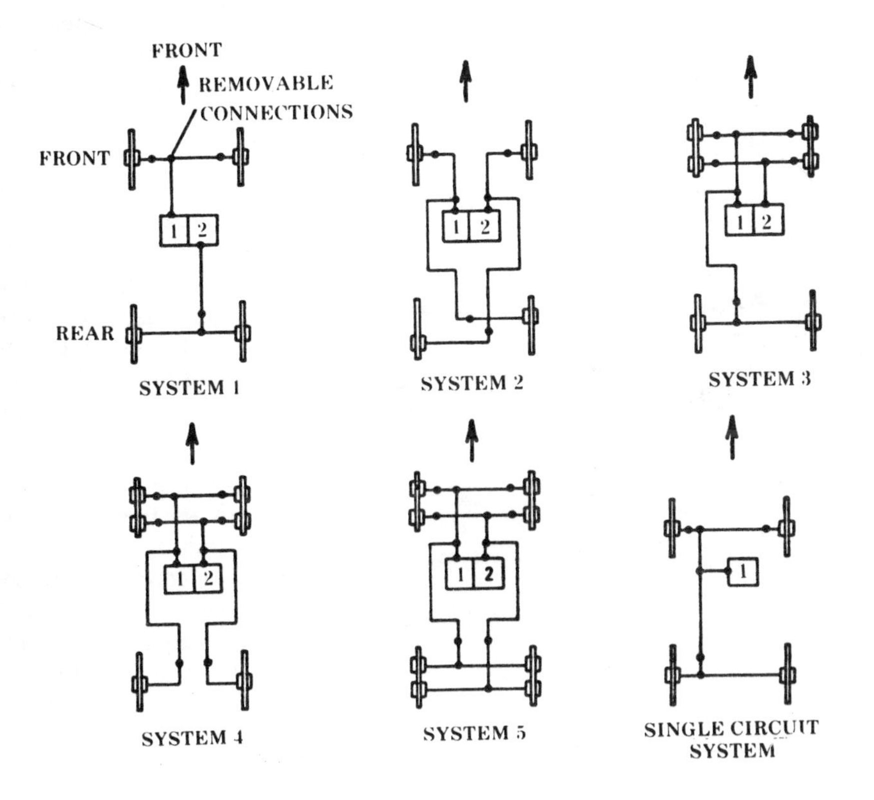

Figure 20-9. Comparison of System Complexity

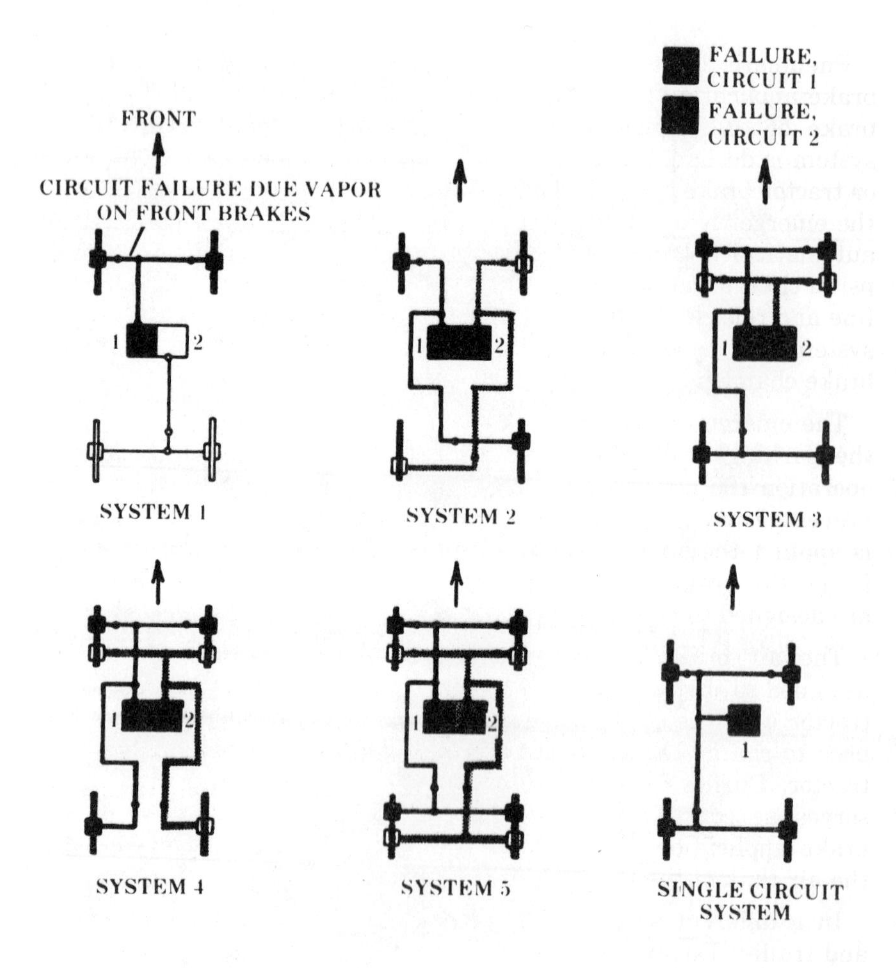

Figure 20-10. Dual Systems, Front Brake Failure Due to Brake Fluid Vaporization

the standard brake system may be used. For partial vacuum failure the reduced booster factor must be used in Eq. 20–5b. A detailed discussion of vacuum assist failure analysis is found in Ref. 11.

Air Brake System Failure

Pneumatic brake systems are designed to provide an emergency brake application in the event the service brake, also called primary brake of the vehicle becomes partially or completely failed. The system is designed to automatically apply the brakes when the truck or tractor brake system supply pressure falls below 45 psi. Whenever the emergency or secondary brakes are actuated, either manually or automatically, truck air system pressure must be built up above 45 psi to charge the trailer (or truck in case of single vehicle) emergency line and release the trailer brake. The secondary or emergency brake system may be actuated by air pressure or by a spring located in the brake chamber.

The emergency or secondary brake of an air brake system becomes the parking brake when the vehicle is stationary. During normal operation the air pressure in the system compresses the spring and prevents contact between brake shoe and drum. As the parking brake is applied, the air is released from the brake chamber and the spring forces the brake shoe against the drum. Parking brakes generally are designed to hold the vehicle stationary on a 20% grade.

The air brake system of a tractor-trailer combination may be designed so that only one brake line connects the brake system of the tractor with the trailer brake system. During nonbraking, the line is used to charge the air tank of the trailer from the compressor of the tractor. During braking the brake line between tractor and trailer serves as control line transmitting the pressure signal from the brake application valve to the trailer brake valve. During braking the air tank of the trailer is not charged.

In a different system, two air lines are installed between tractor and trailer. During braking the air tank of the trailer is charged by the compressor and thus provides an inexhaustible energy source for brake application of the trailer brakes.

Pneumatic brake systems may be designed to provide two independent circuits similar to hydraulic brake systems.

Brake Fade

If a vehicle is subjected to a series of severe stops in rapid succession, in many cases for each successive stop a higher pedal force is necessary to maintain a specified deceleration level. This phenomenon is called brake fade. The phenomenon can be analyzed and predictions of the increase in pedal force can be made provided the variation of the brake factor as a function of the friction coefficient of the lining, and the variation of lining friction coefficient with vehicle speed, pressure between lining and drum, and brake temperature are known. Brake fade may also be caused by excessive speed or lining contamination. Details are found in Ref. 11.

20-9.3. Brake Assembly Failure Due to Excessive Temperature. Brake assembly failure may occur when excessive temperatures are allowed to exist over prolonged periods of time. The thermal capacity of a brake is a function of the allowable temperature of the brake and the surrounding components such as wheel cylinders and brake fluid, tire, and wheel bearings. The temperature of the surrounding components is increased by means of heat transfer through conduction, convection, and radiation. The allowable temperature assumes different values for the individual components. Furthermore, the operating mode of the braking process affects the thermal performance. For an effective stop the surface temperature and the associate temperature gradient are the limiting thermal performance measures. In the case of a continuous brake application, the brake and associated components limit the thermal performance. For repeated brake applications or continued braking, the thermal performance measure is given by the limiting temperature of the brake rotor and brake lining, the wheel cylinder cup and brake fluid, and the tire bead temperature. Maximum allowable temperature of the linings are about 800° F for drum brakes and 1000° F for disc brakes. Special linings may permit higher temperatures, e.g., Apex P 336 GG disc brake pads show little or no fading at temperatures even as high as 1400° F. The maximum allowable temperature of the wheel cylinder is approximately 350° F. Higher temperatures tend to cause damage to seals and vaporization of the brake fluid. The tire bead temperature generally is limited to temperatures near 200° F. If tire bead temperatures are in excess of 200° F, tire unseating may occur during severe braking and/or cornering.

20-9.4. Consequences of Brake Failure. The major effect of the three failure modes (line failure, booster failure, brake fade) is an increase of the pedal force/deceleration gain from the original design point. Longer stopping distances are likely to occur since the driver may not be able to produce the large pedal forces that are necessary to generate the braking forces normally achieved under nonfailure conditions.

In the case of a hydraulic line failure and a standard front-to-rear split, the remaining brakes available for braking must convert the entire kinetic energy of the vehicle into thermal energy which will most likely result in an excessive temperature rise in the friction surfaces or the entire brake assembly. Excessive heating of the brakes, however, may cause a decrease in brake effectiveness due to fading thus compounding the change in pedal force/deceleration gain. The effect of fading due to excessive thermal loading will be more pronounced if the driver tends to achieve high deceleration rates under brake line failure conditions. Another disadvantage of a standard split front-to-rear is that in the case of a line failure the braked axle is likely to overbrake—especially on road surfaces with a low coefficient of friction—rendering the vehicle directionally unstable in the case of rear wheel lockup.

Changes in brake factor due to fading may not be identical for the left and right brakes of the vehicle, possibly resulting in directional instability of the vehicle. It is even possible that an increase in lining friction occurs on the brakes of one side of the vehicle, whereas, the other side experiences a decrease in the coefficient of lining friction due to different temperatures attained by the individual brakes. This may result in an appreciable difference in brake torque developed on each side.

A difference in braking forces at the left and right front wheel, for example, will cause a deflection δ_F of one front wheel as indicated in Fig. 20–11. With a steering stiffness K and tire offset ℓ_o as indicated in

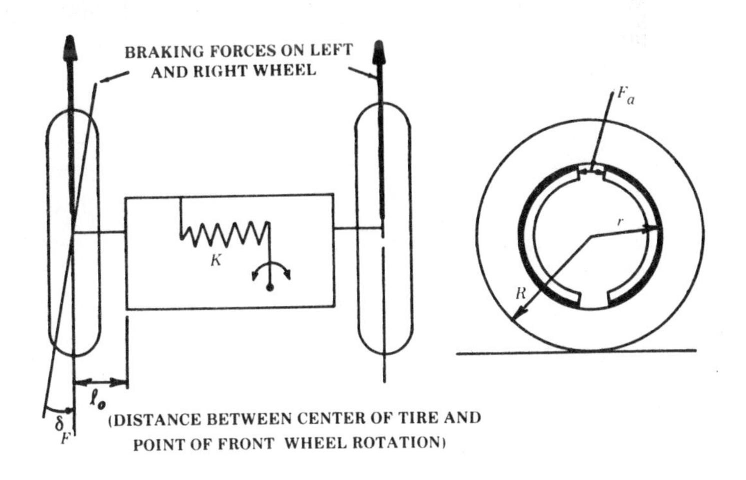

Figure 20–11. Steering Schematic

Fig. 20–11, the front wheel steering angle δ_F is

$$\delta_F = (r/R)(\ell_o/K)F_a(BF_{\text{left}} - BF_{\text{right}}), \text{ deg} \tag{20–14}$$

where

BF_{left} = brake factor of left brake, d'less
BF_{right} = brake factor of right brake, d'less
F_a = application force, lb
ℓ_o = tire offset, in.
K = steering stiffness between pitman arm and kingpin, in lb/deg

From Eq. 20–14 the following can be concluded:

1. Angle δ_F, and hence directional instability will increase with increasing application force F_a, i.e., deceleration.
2. Angle δ_F will be large for a steering with small stiffness.
3. Angle δ_F will be large for more sensitive brakes, i.e., high gain brake such as duo-servo brakes due to larger difference potential between brake factor on the left and right brakes.

Measured values of steering stiffness K are

Vehicle	*Steering Stiffness* (in.lb/deg)
71 Ambassador	1,643
71 Chevrolet Brookward	6,824
71 Dodge Coronet	2,242
71 Ford F-100	3,944
71 Ford Mustang	3,228
71 Olds F-85	4,485
71 VW Super Beetle	2,042
71 Austin America	3,577
Diamond Reo Heavy Duty truck	
4×6, 50,000 lb GVW	41,000
White tractor, 4×6, 46,000 lb GVW	26,600

For example, a difference in brake factor left to right of 5.0 − 3.0 = 2.0, an application force of 2,500 lb, a tire offset of 2 in., a ratio of $r/R = 0.4$, and a steering stiffness of 1643 in.lb/deg. yields an average front wheel steering angle

$$\delta_F = (0.4)\left(\frac{2}{1643}\right)(2500)(2) = 2.43 \text{ deg.}$$

20–9.5. Brake System Component Deterioration. Brake system components that are likely to deteriorate during the life of the motor vehicle are generally designed such that critical elements are replaced periodically. These elements include brake linings, cups, seals, dust boots, and brake fluids. Until approximately 1950 to 1955, the brake lines of hydraulic brake systems significantly limited the overall life of a brake system. Today, this problem has been solved by the use of copper alloy tubing. Tests have shown that the resistance in terms of a decrease in tensile strength of copper alloys remained almost unaffected by a 180 day exposure to salt spray. The tensile strength of copper coated steel tubes rapidly deteriorated after 90 days with essentially no tensile properties remaining after 180 days of exposure to the salt spray. Hydrostatic pressure tests confirm these results. Before the pressure tests, the bursting pressure of the copper alloy tubes ranged from 8500 psi for tubes $^3/_8$ in. diameter to 1700 psi for $^3/_{16}$ in. diameter tubes. Steel tubes (as received) were generally 10% stronger in burst tests than copper alloy tubes. When the steel tubes were exposed to salt spray for 90 days they reduced in their burst strength to about 50%, after 180 days to nearly 90% of their initial burst strength. It is obvious that steel tubing when used in a driving environment subjected to salt sprays could reduce its ability to withstand brake line pressures of 1,500–2,000 psi—frequently obtained in panic brake stops.

Fatigue and impact tests conducted with steel and copper alloy tubes indicated a superior performance of the copper alloy when exposed to a salt spray over an extended period of time.

Specific tests, recommended by the Society of Automotive Engineers (SAE), determine the allowable weight loss of tubing material when exposed to hydraulic brake fluid. Test results show that copper alloys are well within specified ranges.

Other recommended standards published by the Society of Automotive Engineers deal with the minimum performance required, e.g., for air brake hoses, vacuum hoses, hydraulic brake hoses, brake fluid, brake linings and brake pads, structural integrity of the service brake. Of the components mentioned, hydraulic brake fluid deserves further detail. The performance requirements of brake fluid include: (1) Low tendency to absorb water; water in the brake fluid leads to corrosion and decreased boiling temperatures of the fluid and hence brake fluid vaporization during continued braking. For example, motor vehicles operating near large bodies of water such as oceans may absorb enough water to reduce the boiling temperature of the brake fluid from 350 deg F to 300 deg F within one year; (2) high boiling temperature; (3) insensitivity to temperature changes; must operate at arctic conditions; (4) lubrication must be provided for seals and cups under high pressures and temperatures; (5) no corrosion of system components caused by the brake fluid, (6) properties of brake fluid should not be affected by storage time, and high and low temperatures.

Concerning the effect of aging on brake system components, storage or shelf time should not be too long. Components such as master cylinders, wheel cylinders and brake hoses may be stored for three years without exhibiting deterioration. Components such as vacuum assist units and proportioning valves should not be stored for more than two years. Excessive storage times may cause malfunctioning of brake components due to frozen pistons and hardened seals or cups.

20–9.6. Human Factor Considerations. In manual brake systems the driver provides the pedal effort required to press the brake shoes against the drums. Increased pedal forces will result in increased deceleration, provided fade is ignored for the moment. Brake systems using assist devices are primarily designed so that the pedal effort is used to control the assist force and to provide manual pedal effort which produces brake line pressure. Full power hydraulic and pneumatic brake systems use the pedal effort to operate a valve which controls the brake line pressure. The work required for pressing the brake shoes against the drums is stored in the hydraulic accumulator or air tanks and is not affected by pedal effort. For manual systems the pedal force limits braking performance. For this reason it is important to know the foot force capabilities of individuals comprising the driving population.

The maximum force exerted with the right foot for the 5th percentile female is approximately 100 lb; for the male approximately 185 lb. These data were obtained in controlled laboratory conditions. It has been argued that the stress of an emergency situation may enable the drivers to exert higher pedal forces. Satisfactory driver braking performance has been observed in controlled road tests when the lower value of pedal force/deceleration gains is 4.76 lb/g; whereas, the upper value of pedal force/deceleration gain is 83 lb/g. These numbers indicate that not less than approximate 5 lbs pedal force should be required to produce a deceleration of 1g, and that not more than approximately 80 lb pedal force should be required to produce a deceleration of 1g. Too large gain values result in a sensitive brake system where the driver may have difficulties applying the brakes carefully. Too low gain values result in ineffective brakes where the pedal force of the driver may not be sufficiently large to produce an acceptable deceleration. Studies have shown that frequently drivers will not apply sufficient pedal force to decelerate the vehicle in the case of a power assist (vacuum booster) or circuit failure due to increased pedal travel and drastically reduced brake effectiveness.

20–9.7. Effects of Maintenance on Brake Failure. Maintenance has been defined as follows. Maintenance includes all actions necessary for retaining an item in or restoring it to a serviceable condition. Maintenance includes servicing, repair, modification, modernization, overhaul, inspection, and condition determination.

Problems associated with maintenance are:

1. accessibility
2. complexity
3. durability
4. diagnosis

While accessibility and complexity are not directly addressed in physical formulations of the decelerating mechanisms, they certainly are of importance. Critical performance limits of components as well as systems obtained in the braking analysis may be used in assessing critical aspects of durability and diagnosis.

Methods for detecting component defects or degradation that affects brake system performance can be devised. Such techniques use the results of laboratory type brake dynamometers or performance data obtained in actual road tests. These performance related degradations and defects may be associated with brake system gain, system response, front to rear brake force distribution, side-to-side brake balance, brake fade, and pedal travel. Some brake system components can be efficiently and objectively inspected, visually or manually. These components include linkages, brake lines and hoses, and other related mechanisms. Although a diagnosis indicating partial loss of system gain clearly means a loss in braking performance capability, present diagnostic techniques do not identify the source of malfunctioning in all cases. A decrease in system gain could be caused by a change in brake factor, i.e., a change in brake lining/drum friction coefficient, by a loss in power assist performance, or by a decrease in mechanical or hydraulic efficiency. The latter could be caused by frozen wheel cylinder pistons, cams, or wedges. Insufficient system gain in the case of rapid brake applications could indicate severe brake line restrictions or power boost malfunctioning. Excessive pedal travel without evidence of external leakage could indicate large brake shoe travel due to severely worn linings, or internal master cylinder leakage caused by a leaking primary cup in the master cylinder. Excessive pedal travel could also be attributed to large elastic deformation of brake shoes, to soft pad or lining material, and excessive elastic deformations of drums or calipers. However, most of these outages can be monitored with relatively inexpensive gauges so that the cause of any performance related defect or degradation can be identified.

Defects and degradations that do not affect system performance are not easily detectable. In some cases, however, the anticipated failure modes can be categorized in terms of intended or actual vehicle functions. Vehicles operating in typical highway environment will exhibit different wear and hence failure modes than vehicles operating over extended periods of time on unpaved dirt roads. This observation was made in the case of school buses operating in urban and rural environments. Their respective maintenance requirements showed significant differences. In general, basic mechanical engineering considerations may be utilized in assessing the safety criticality of different brake system components. One such application is the prediction of the life expectancy of honed versus rolled master cylinder sliding surfaces as a function of primary seal friction. Furthermore, fixed in place or periodically installed sensors may be efficiently used to obtain information on the expected safety performance of components, information for maintenance purposes, and other related aspects of vehicle inspection. It should be emphasized that this must be done in connection with a proper combination of analysis and parameter evaluation of the braking system. For example, it appears rather useless to measure brake line pressure versus torque in order to determine the safety performance of the brake shoe actuator (wheel cylinder piston, cam, or wedge) without accurate knowledge of the brake factor or internal gain of the foundation brake. Also, a determination must be made if a brake factor decrease is caused by a drop in lining friction, or geometry changes of the brake drum or shoe due to permanent or temporary drum distortion.

CHAPTER 21
VEHICLE VIBRATIONS

Vehicle vibrations are mainly caused by road roughness. The vibrations affect ride comfort and dynamic wheel loads. Excessive wheel loads may result in damage to highways. Safety is significantly reduced when the vibrations cause the dynamic wheel loads to approach zero resulting in a complete loss of tire traction.

21-1. EFFECT OF VEHICLE VIBRATIONS ON HIGHWAY SAFETY

The maximum traction force of a tire is equal to the product of tire-road friction coefficient and the normal force between the tire and road (Eq. 18-7). The dynamic tire normal force varies as the wheels move over road irregularities or wheel imbalances cause wheel vibrations. An example of a dynamic wheel load is shown in Fig. 21-1. Inspection

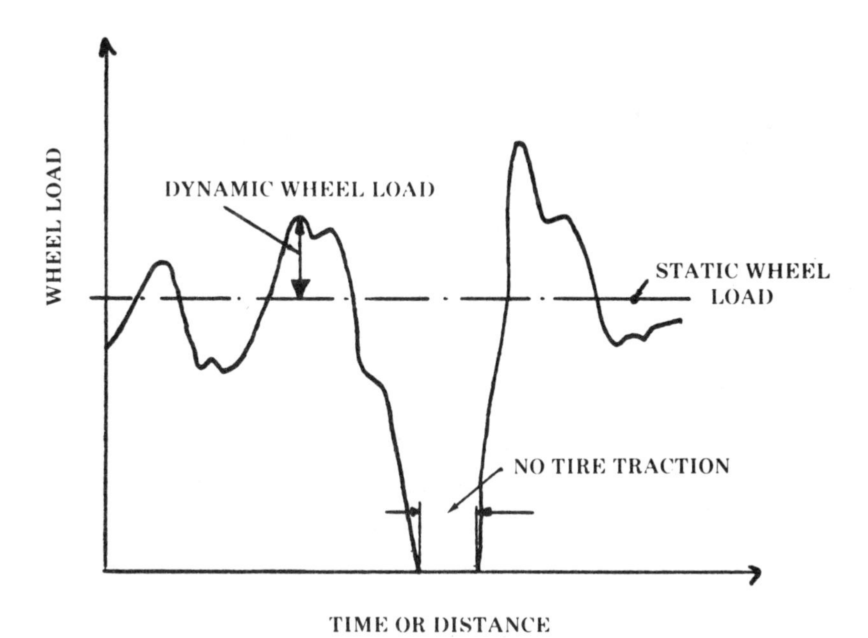

Figure 21-1. Dynamic Wheel Load

of the curve indicates that the dynamic wheel load fluctuates about the static wheel load. During the time period when the dynamic wheel load is zero, no braking, drive, or side forces can be transmitted by the tire. The ratio of dynamic wheel load to static wheel load may be used as a measure of safety. An accurate analysis of the dynamic wheel load generally requires the use of computing machines to evaluate different parameters in combination with complicated differential equations describing the vibrations of vehicle and suspension systems. Dynamic wheel load changes should be kept to a minimum to improve highway safety.

21-2. CAUSES OF VIBRATIONS

Rough roads cause suspension vibrations and associated vehicle vibrations. The vehicle weight supported by suspension springs is commonly called sprung weight. The vibrational inputs from the road are affected by vehicle speed. If the input frequency, i.e., the number of inputs per unit time is in harmony with the natural frequency of the suspension, an extreme dynamic wheel load change may occur, commonly called wheel hop (Refs. 11, 13 and 20).

Wheel load changes may be caused by tire or wheel nonuniformity and wheel imbalances.

Tire nonuniformity is the result of nonuniform elastic properties of the tire. The tire may be thought of as a series of springs entering and leaving the tire-to-ground contact patch. If one of these springs is stiffer than the rest, the wheel axle will be lifted up, resulting in a periodic fluctuation of the wheel load.

Wheel nonuniformity is caused by either an eccentric wheel axle or an oval wheel, i.e., not a perfect circle. Both conditions cause a difference in tire compression and hence result in a periodic wheel lift as the wheel rotates.

Wheel imbalance is the result of a nonuniform distribution of mass. The imbalance increases with the square of vehicle velocity, and may reach extreme effects when the imbalancing input frequency is in harmony with the natural frequency of the wheel/suspension system.

21-3. EFFECT OF VEHICLE WEIGHT

The sprung weight or mass of vehicles varies due to loading. Sprung weight is that portion of the vehicle weight supported by the suspension springs. Sprung mass accelerations and hence ride comfort decrease with increase in vehicle loading. Dynamic wheel loads change little with increased loading. However, since static wheel loads increase also with loading, smaller relative wheel load changes occur and increased vehicle safety results. Consequently, the loaded vehicles exhibit increased comfort and operation safety, when compared to the lightly loaded vehicle. Automobile manufacturers recognize this shortcoming by specifying different levels of inflation pressure, thus adjusting the vertical tire stiffness to the loading condition. Lower tire inflation pressure results in improved vehicle ride and safety near or at wheel hop frequency. It should be recognized that ride comfort is also largely affected by seat stiffness and related parameters. In order to keep ride comfort constant for different loading conditions, the square root of the ratio of suspension stiffness and sprung mass, i.e., sprung mass natural frequency, should be kept constant. The natural frequency of the sprung mass is approximately 1 to 2 cycles per second (Hertz). A constant ratio of static wheel load to tire stiffness would yield nearly constant vehicle safety for different loading conditions. Improved ride comfort may be obtained by keeping damping constant. However, in this case larger dynamic wheel load changes result. Constant sprung mass natural frequency may be achieved through air suspension or progressive springs. Progressive springs involve two sets of springs becoming active at different loads. Automatic variation of tire inflation pressure relative to the loading condition has been attempted in research projects.

21-4. EFFECT OF SUSPENSION STIFFNESS

Changes in spring stiffness produce different values of sprung mass frequency. Values in excess of 2 Hz are above normal for today's passenger cars. Frequency values for empty vehicles range between 1.6 and 1.8 Hz for subcompacts and attain values as low as 1.0 to 1.2 Hz for heavy passenger cars. One reason for the lower values is that heavy passenger cars do not experience as much relative static wheel load changes due to loading as small cars do.

Decreased values of suspension stiffness produce lower levels of vehicle accelerations and hence increased occupant comfort, whereas the dynamic wheels may increase, or decrease depending on the input frequency, i.e., type of road roughness and vehicle speed. Generally, with softer suspensions dynamic wheel load fluctuations decrease at lower frequency values and increase at higher levels. This fact indicates lower safety of a softly sprung vehicle operating at higher speeds. The spring stiffness values are limited by design and intended vehicle function. Suspension leveling devices have been used to keep the distance between wheel axle and vehicle body constant, thus allowing the total suspension travel to be used by dynamic wheel load travels rather than by suspension travel due to vehicle loading.

21-5. EFFECT OF SUSPENSION DAMPING (SHOCK ABSORBER)

With decreasing values of damping both sprung mass acceleration and dynamic wheel loads increase for operation near the sprung mass resonance or natural frequency. Near the suspension resonance frequency only dynamic wheel loads increase whereas sprung mass acceleration decreases with lower values of damping. The damper acts as shock amplifier for the sprung mass at high levels of excitation frequency, i.e., it reduces ride comfort. For the wheel loads it acts as shock reducer, i.e., it increases safety.

Optimum values of damping have to be determined in conjunction with suspension spring stiffness. For example, a constant value of damping in connection with soft suspension springs will improve ride comfort but significantly increase dynamic wheel load and hence reduce crash avoidance safety. Constant damping values as compared to constant spring stiffness require more space for dynamic wheel travel.

21-6. EFFECT OF UNSPRUNG MASS OF WHEEL AND SUSPENSION

Smaller unsprung mass increases the resonance or natural frequency of wheel and associated suspension components. The natural wheel and suspension frequency of passenger cars is approximately 10 to 15 cycles per second. Sprung mass acceleration and hence ride comfort are negligibly affected by changes in unsprung mass. Dynamic wheel loads decrease with lower wheel mass and thus increase vehicle safety by providing better tire-to-road contact. Solid rear axles exhibit a large unsprung weight, and consequently tend to increase dynamic wheel load changes and potential loss of tire traction forces. This problem is partially solved by using higher damping values resulting in reduced ride comfort. An additional problem exists with solid axles, when the left and right wheel is excited with different polarity. This condition exists when the left wheel runs over a bump while the right wheel runs through a pothole. The resulting roll vibrations of the solid axle may increase the dynamic wheel load changes by 30 to 40% over that produced by independent suspensions, such as swing axles and semi-trailing arm suspensions.

21-7. EFFECT OF TIRE CHARACTERISTICS

Tires may be considered as a dynamic system consisting of springs and dampers (Refs. 13 and 21). Softer tires result in lower sprung mass acceleration and dynamic wheel loads at the suspension or wheel hop resonance frequency. The decrease is nearly proportional to tire vertical stiffness. The suspension resonance frequency now occurs at lower values of forcing frequency. Thus, a softer tire has a similar effect on acceleration and wheel loads at the suspension resonance frequency as do softer springs at the sprung mass resonance frequency. Application of softer tires is highly recommended. Low values of vertical tire stiffness may be achieved through larger volume-tires (larger cross-sections) and/or reduced inflation pressures. Changes in tire damping tend to have little effect on overall vehicle damping. Since large values of tire damping produce increased operating temperatures and rolling resistance and hence reduced gas mileage, tire damping should be kept a minimum which in turn results in softer tires when current tire design practices are utilized.

21-8. EFFECT OF FRONT AND REAR SUSPENSION TUNING

In addition to vertical sprung mass acceleration and dynamic wheel load changes vehicle pitch dynamics has to be considered. Investigations have shown that vehicles having a shorter wheel base exhibit larger pitch motion and hence less ride comfort than longer vehicles. Design changes on a given vehicle in form of stiffer rear suspension than on the front, or stiffer rear tires than on the front have shown that subsystems front or rear when properly designed for comfort and safety result in well behaved vertical vehicle dynamics without requiring special efforts on combined tuning. It should be mentioned that the individual suspension design has a significant effect on safety in form of decreased dynamic axle load changes. Proper tuning of a particular suspension design may be achieved through road tests.

As mentioned before, the dynamic wheel load may be divided by the static wheel load thus yielding a factor which, if less than unity would indicate a dynamic wheel load less than the static value. A negative value indicates wheel hop, that is, a complete separation of tire and roadway. Since the static wheel loads change as a result of vehicle loading, an optimum safety design would produce lower dynamic wheel load changes in the empty vehicle condition than in the loaded case in order to keep the effective tire-to-road force near constant.

CHAPTER 22
VEHICLE DIRECTIONAL CONTROL

Included in directional control are all factors which affect the capability of the vehicle to maintain its desired course.

22–1. LATERAL ACCELERATION

In Section 16–3.5 centrifugal acceleration a_c is explained. The acceleration is oriented in a radial direction. In a vehicle turning a corner the acceleration is oriented transverse across the vehicle, i.e., in the lateral direction. The common notation for the lateral direction is the subscript y (see Section 18–4).

The lateral acceleration a_y of a vehicle may be determined by Eq. 16–26

$$a_y = \frac{V_c^2}{r}, \text{ ft/sec}^2 \qquad (22\text{–}1)$$

where:

r = radius of turn, ft
V_c = velocity, ft/sec

The centrifugal force F_c may be determined by Eq. 17–3 as

$$F_c = a_y \left(\frac{W}{g}\right), \text{ lb} \qquad (22\text{–}2)$$

where

W = vehicle weight, lb
$g = 32.2$ ft/sec^2

The force F_c acts at the center of gravity and attempts to push the vehicle toward the outside of the curve and to roll the body on its side. The effect of the centrifugal force can best be visualized by a bath tub turning a corner with the water attempting to spill over the outside tub edge.

Frequently lateral acceleration is expressed in g-units. Eq. 22–1 when divided by g becomes

$$a_y^* = \frac{V_c^2}{rg}, \text{ g-units} \qquad (22\text{–}3)$$

The centrifugal force F_c then is

$$F_c = a_y^* \, W, \text{ lb} \tag{22–4}$$

For example, a lateral acceleration $a_y^* = 0.6$ g equals (0.6)(32.2) = 19.32 fs/sec.

22-2. VEHICLE TURNING

When a vehicle turns, a centrifugal force is produced. The centrifugal force is balanced by the side forces produced by the tires. At vehicle speeds close to zero the centrifugal force may be neglected and only geometrical considerations affect the turning of a vehicle.

22-2.1. Turning Radius at Low Speeds ($a_y \approx$ zero). Frequently it becomes necessary to determine the turning radius and turning space required by a vehicle. This problem exists especially in connection with truck-trailer combinations turning a corner. For a two-axle vehicle the basic turning geometry is illustrated in Fig. 6-1. Not included in Fig. 6-1 are vehicle length and width. The turning geometry of a vehicle including vehicle size is shown in Fig. 22-1. The width

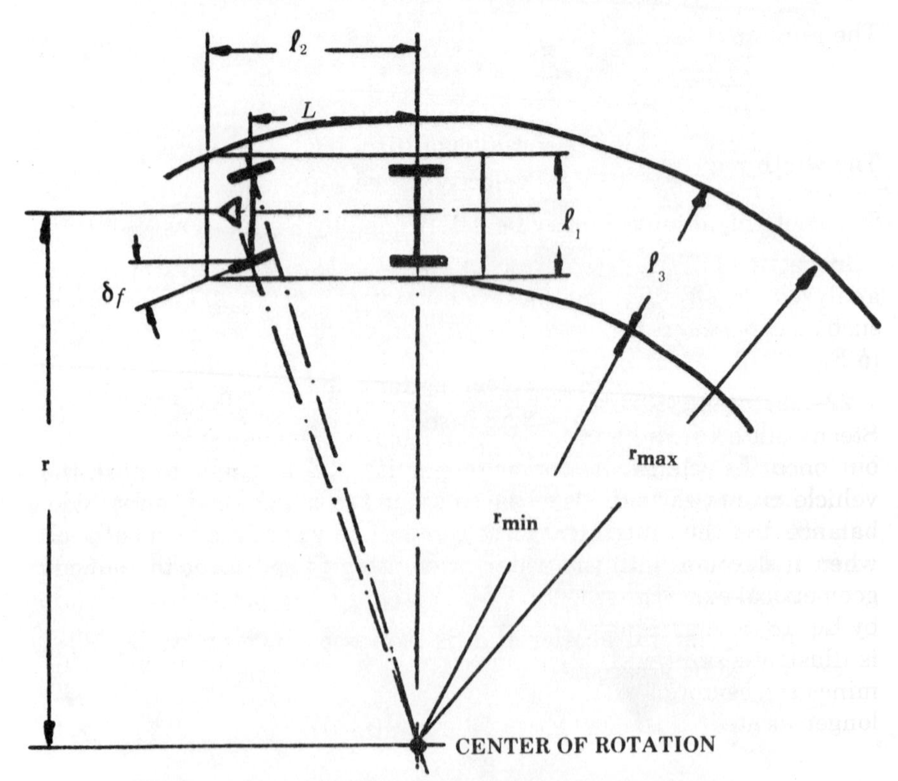

Figure 22-1. Turning Radius Two-Axle Vehicle

requirement and the maximum turning radius define the minimum space requirements (Refs. 13 and 22).

The turning radius r measured to the middle axis is

$$r = \frac{L}{\delta_F}, \text{ ft} \tag{22-4}$$

where

L = wheel base, ft

δ_F = average front wheel steering angle, rad

The steering wheel angle divided by the steering ratio yields the front wheel steering angle δ_F.

The maximum turning radius r_{max} of the two-axle vehicle is

$$r_{max} = \sqrt{\left(\frac{L}{\delta_F} + \frac{\ell_1}{2}\right)^2 + \ell_2^2}, \text{ ft} \tag{22-5}$$

where

ℓ_1 = vehicle width, ft

ℓ_2 = distance from front bumper to rear axle, ft

The minimum turning radius r_{min} is

$$r_{min} = \frac{L}{\delta_F} - \frac{\ell_1}{2}, \text{ ft} \tag{22-6}$$

The width requirement, ℓ_3 is

$$\ell_3 = r_{max} - r_{min}, \text{ ft} \tag{22-7}$$

Inspection of Fig. 22-1 indicates, that the turning geometry can be analyzed graphically. For more complicated vehicle combinations, such as car-trailers a graphical solution is more practical as illustrated in Fig. 22-2.

22-2.2. Steady-State Turning (Constant Forward Velocity). Steady-state turning exists when no steering maneuvers are carried out once the vehicle is turning. The centrifugal force of a turning vehicle increases with the square of the speed. The tire side forces balance the centrifugal force. A tire can only produce a side force when it develops a slip angle between the velocity direction and its geometrical axis. The side force in the linear range may be determined by Eq. 18-8. A turning vehicle with the tire side forces and slip angles is illustrated in Fig. 22-3. The velocity direction of each wheel determines the center of rotation of the vehicle. The center of rotation is no longer located on the extension of the rear axle line.

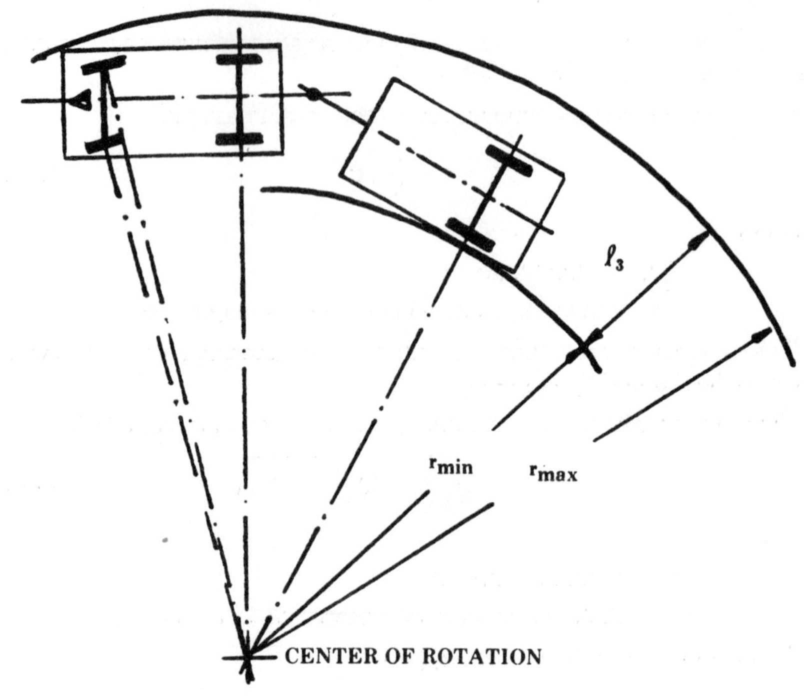

Figure 22–2. Turning Radius Car-Trailer

The turning radius r measured from the middle axis of the vehicle is

$$r = \frac{L}{\delta_F - \delta_R - (\alpha_F - \alpha_R)} r, \text{ ft} \tag{22–8}$$

where

δ_F = average front wheel steering angle, rad
α_R = average rear wheel steering angle, rad
α_F = average front wheel slip angle, rad
δ_R = average rear wheel slip angle, rad

The steering angles δ_F and δ_R are the result of steering wheel rotation and wheel deflection due to suspension travel. Only in rare cases are the rear wheels steered by the driver. For the standard system the turning radius for the motor vehicle is with $\delta_R = 0$ in Eq. 22–8

$$\text{r} = \frac{L}{\delta_F - (\alpha_F - \alpha_R)} r, \text{ ft} \tag{22–9}$$

Inspection of Eq. 18–8 indicates that side force is proportional to slip angle for slip angles less than approximately 5 degrees. The side forces required on front and rear axle generally differ, and would be identical

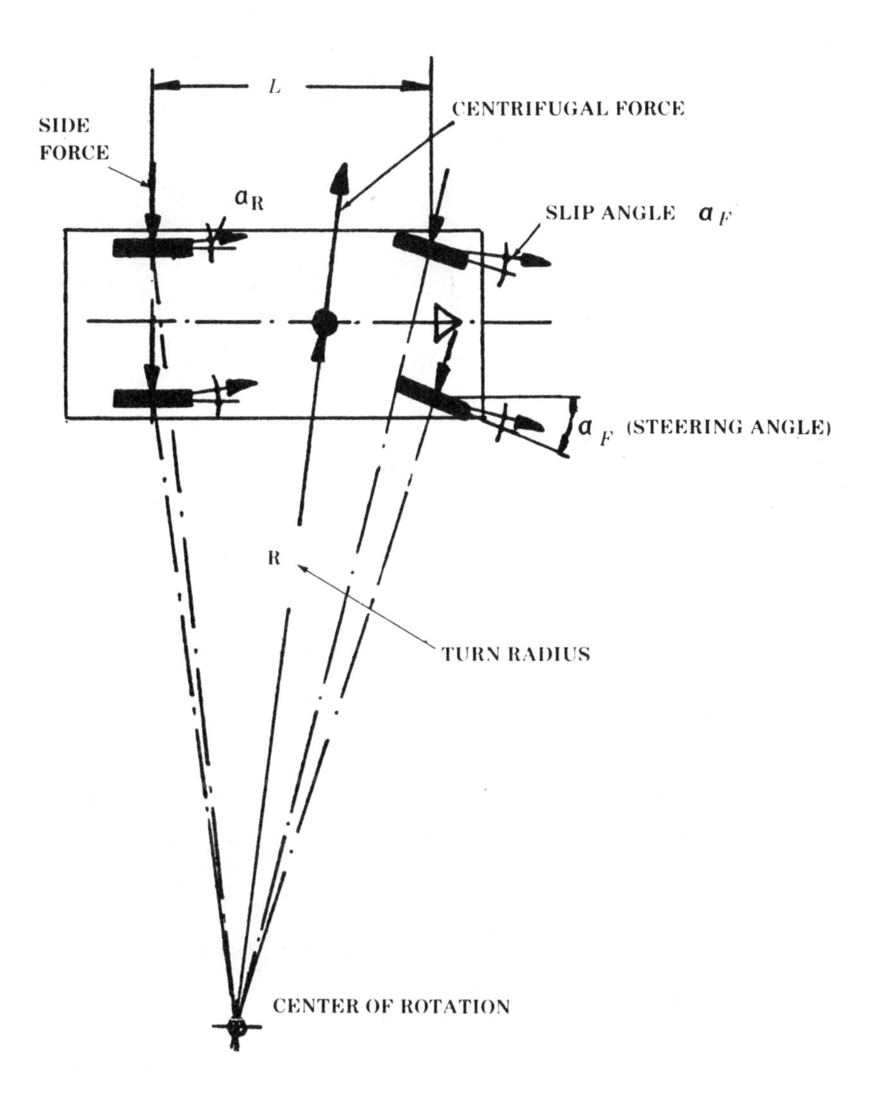

Figure 22-3. Turning Vehicle

only for a vehicle having its center-of-gravity midway between the axles. In general, however, the tires required to produce a higher side force to keep the vehicle in the turn are operating at a higher slip angle as required by Eq. 18–8. The limit of side force traction is exceeded when the entire tire contact patch is sliding and the tire is operating at the low value of sliding friction coefficient.

Three different slip angle regions may be identified.

1. α_F greater than α_R; inspection of Eq. 22–9 indicates that the turning radius increases, i.e., the vehicle tends to travel in a larger circle than demanded by steering wheel angle δ_F.

2. α_F equals α_R; the slip angles have no effect on turning radius which is solely determined by the driver induced steering wheel rotation.

3. α_F less than α_R; the turning radius decreases, i.e., the vehicle tends to travel in a smaller circle than demanded by steering wheel angle δ_F.

Frequently, cases 1, 2, and 3 are designated by under-steering, neutral-steering, and over-steering, respectively. In an under-steering vehicle the front tire contact patch will attain complete sliding first, and consequently the front wheels tend to slide across the roadway. In an over-steering vehicle the rear tire contact patch will attain complete sliding before the front and the rear wheels begin to slide sideways forcing the vehicle into a smaller turn radius.

Frequently it becomes necessary to compute the speed of a turning vehicle when the turning radius is known. The turning radius is most often limited by roadway geometry. In some cases the vehicle tires produce a marking on the roadway that defines the path the vehicle traveled (see Section 39–1.7). The tire markings produced by a turning vehicle are commonly called skuff marks. A turning vehicle may produce skuff marks when operating at or near the limit of tire side force or below this limit. When the inflation pressure is low, for example, skuff marks are produced at lower speeds. However, one fact exists, the tire marking defines vehicle path and hence turning radius. Inspection of Eq. 22–1 indicates that the vehicle speed V_c can be determined when the lateral acceleration a_y is known. A balance of the centrifugal force F_c and the tire force F_y requires $F_c = F_y$. When the simplifying assumption is made that the tire side force equals the weight of the vehicle times the tire-road friction coefficient, then the limiting turning velocity is

$$V_{limit} = \sqrt{a_y g r} = \sqrt{\mu_s g r}, \text{ ft/sec} \qquad (22\text{–}10)$$

where

r = curve radius, ft

μ_s = lateral sliding tire road friction coefficient, d'less.

Eq. 22–10 is only valid in the absence of any driving or braking forces and in the case of low velocities, i.e., small curve radii.

In the derivation of Eq. 22–10 no vehicle design parameters are considered. The sliding braking friction coefficient is not identical to the lateral friction coefficient and generally assumes values that are slightly larger than those associated with side friction (see Eq. 22–32).

A more accurate analysis is obtained by considering the different side forces required on front and rear axle but neglecting lateral load transfer. Although steady state turning generally does not allow braking, braking forces are considered in the following analysis.

A rolling tire can only transmit a maximum shear force equal to the product of tire normal force and tire-road friction coefficient. In the presence of braking (or driving) and side force both forces have to share into the total traction available. Since side and braking force are perpendicular to each other, basic geometry requires that

$$\sqrt{F_x^2 + F_y^2} = F_z \mu, \text{ lb} \qquad (22\text{–}11)$$

where

F_x = braking (or driving) force, lb

F_y = side force, lb

F_z = normal force, lb

μ = tire-road friction coefficient, d'less

Although Eq. 22–11 appears to be simple, the tire-road friction coefficient is also a function of the braking and side forces (F_x and F_y). Eq. 22–11 is more accurate for low friction coefficients since in this case the tire and tread construction have little effect on the braking and side force production.

Upon balancing the tire side forces with the centrifugal force, and by the use of Eqs. 18–8 and 22–9, the demanded side forces on the front and rear axle of a two-axle vehicle are:

Front axle

$$F_{yF} = \frac{(1-\psi)\,\delta_F}{\dfrac{gL}{WV^2} + (1-\psi)/(2C_F) - \psi/(2C_R)}, \text{ lb} \qquad (22\text{–}12)$$

Rear axle

$$F_{yR} = \frac{\psi F_{yF}}{(1 - \psi)}, \text{ lb} \tag{22-13}$$

where

C_F = cornering stiffness of both front tires, (Eq. 18–8), lb/rad
C_R = cornering stiffness of both rear tires, lb/rad
W = vehicle weight, lb
δ_F = average front wheel steering angle, rad
ψ = static rear axle load divided by total vehicle weight, d'less

Typical values for C_F and C_R are 12,000 lb/rad.

The average normal force on the front axle on a level road at the friction limit is related to Eq. 22–11 by

$$\sqrt{F_{xF}^2 + F_{yF}^2} = \mu W(1 - \psi), \text{ lb} \tag{22-14}$$

where

F_{xF} = front axle brake force, lb
F_{yF} = front axle side force, lb

The normal force on the rear axle is

$$\sqrt{F_{xR}^2 + F_{yR}^2} = \mu W\psi, \text{ lb} \tag{22-15}$$

The use of the previous equations is demonstrated by the example that follows.

Example 22–1

Determine the limit speed of a vehicle operating at the following conditions: $\delta_F = 5$ deg, $L = 10$ ft, $W = 3000$ lb, $\psi = 0.4$, $C_F = C_R = 12{,}000$ lb/rad, $\mu_F = \mu_R = 0.9$. Vehicle deceleration $a_x = 0.3g$, brake force distribution $\phi = 0.35$. Neglect rolling resistance and aerodynamic drag.

The longitudinal traction force requirement due to braking on the front tires is

$$F_{xF} = a_x W(1 - \phi) = (0.3)(3000)(1 - 0.35) = 585 \text{ lb}$$

On the rear axle:

$$F_{xR} = (0.3)(3000)(0.35) = 315 \text{ lb}$$

The total traction force on the front axle is (right side of Eq. 22–14)

$$F_{TF} = \mu W(1 - \psi) = (0.9)(3000)(1 - 0.4) = 1620 \text{ lb}$$

The total traction force on the rear axle is (Eq. 22–15)

$$F_{TR} = (0.9)(3000)(0.4) = 1080 \text{ lb}$$

The side forces on front and rear axle may be determined from Eqs. 22–14 and 22–15 by solving for F_{yF} and F_{yR}, respectively.

Front axle:

$$F_{yF} = \sqrt{(1620)^2 - (585)^2} = 1510 \text{ lb}$$

Rear axle:

$$F_{yR} = \sqrt{(1080)^2 - (315)^2} = 1033 \text{ lb}$$

The limit velocity V_{limit} may be determined by Eq. 22–12 by solving for the limit velocity yielding

$$V_{\text{limit}} = \left\{ \frac{\left(\frac{gL}{W}\right)}{\frac{(1-\psi)\delta_F}{F_{yF}} - [(1-\psi)/(2C_F) - \psi/(2C_R)]} \right\}^{1/2}, \text{ ft/sec} \tag{22–16}$$

Substitution of the appropriate values and $F_{yF} = 1510$ lb from above into Eq. 22–16 yields $V_{\text{limit}} = 66.63$ ft/sec or 45.5 mph limited by the front axle. When $F_{yR} = 1033$ lb is substituted into Eq. 22–13, a front axle force $F_{yF} = 1549$ results, resulting in a limiting speed of 65.3 ft/sec or 44.5 mph by use of Eq. 22–16. Since the lower value is the critical, the rear wheels limit the speed of the turning vehicle at 44.5 mph.

In the absence of any braking the limit turning speed increases to 67.3 ft/sec or 46 mph, indicating that the demands of the 0.3 g braking effort on the total traction are small.

The above analysis indicates that weight distribution ψ, brake force distribution ϕ, wheel base L, steering angle δ_F, and cornering stiffness of front and rear tires, C_F and C_R, affect the limit turning velocity.

When lateral load transfer is considered, the analysis becomes more complicated since suspension design parameters must be included. Forces acting on a four-wheel vehicle turning a corner are illustrated in Fig. 22–4. Braking forces are not considered in the analysis that follows. The individual tire normal forces are:

Front, inner wheel

$$F_{zF,i} = (1-\psi)\left(\frac{W}{2}\right) - a_y S_F W_S, \text{ lb} \tag{22–17}$$

Front, outer wheel

$$F_{zF,o} = (1-\psi)\left(\frac{W}{2}\right) + a_y S_F W_S, \text{ lb} \tag{22–18}$$

Rear, inner wheel

$$F_{zR,i} = \psi\left(\frac{W}{2}\right) - a_y S_R W_S, \text{ lb} \tag{22–19}$$

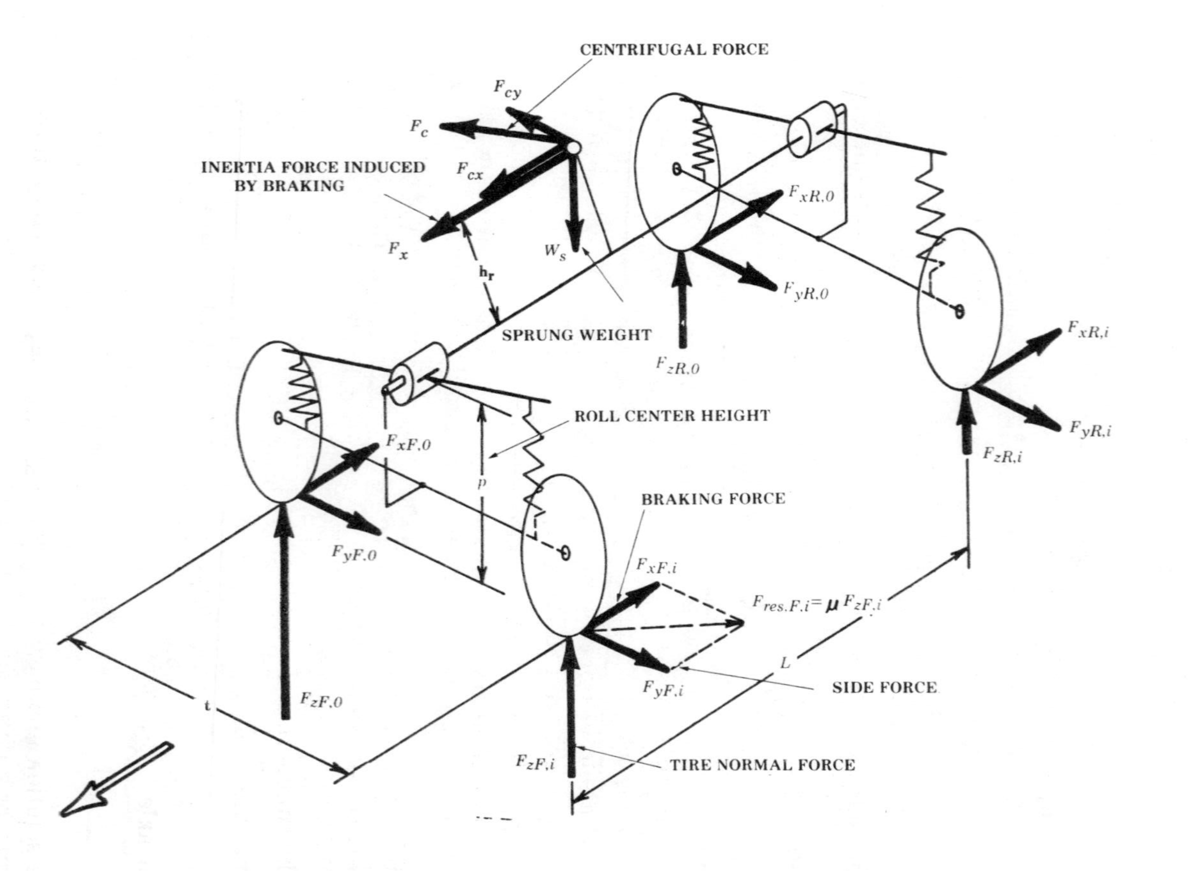

Figure 22–4. Forces Acting on a Braking and Turning Vehicle

Rear, outer wheel

$$F_{zR,o} = \psi\left(\frac{W}{2}\right) + a_y\, S_R\, W_S,\ \text{lb} \tag{22–20}$$

where

a_y = lateral acceleration, g-units
S_F = front suspension normalized roll stiffness, d'less
S_R = rear suspension normalized roll stiffness, d'less
W = total vehicle weight, lb
W_S = sprung vehicle weight, lb

The normalized suspension roll stiffness is, e.g., on the front axle

$$S_F = (1 - \psi)\left(\frac{p_F}{t_F}\right) + \left(\frac{K_F}{K_F + K_R - W_S h_R}\right)\left(\frac{h_r}{t_F}\right) + \left(\frac{W_F}{W_S}\right)\left(\frac{h_F}{t_F}\right),\ \text{d'less} \tag{22–21}$$

where

h_r = distance between center of gravity and roll axis, ft
h_F = center of gravity height of front unsprung mass, ft
K_F = front roll stiffness, ft·lb/rad
K_R = rear roll stiffness, ft·lb/rad
p_F = front roll center to ground distance, ft
t_F = front track width, ft
W_F = front suspension unsprung weight, lb

The rear suspension normalized roll stiffness is obtained from Eq. 22–21 by replacing subscript F by R, and $(1 - \psi)$ by ψ, and using the appropriate rear suspension data.

The summation of inner and outer side forces is

Front axle

$$F_{yF,i} + F_{yF,o} = a_y\, W(1 - \psi),\ \text{lb} \tag{22–22}$$

Rear axle

$$F_{yR,i} + F_{yR,o} = a_y w\ \psi,\ \text{lb} \tag{22–23}$$

The solution approach for computing slip angles and hence turning radius for a given speed is as follows:

1. Use a lateral acceleration a_y and compute individual tire normal force by Eqs. 22–17 through 22–20.

2. Compute the summation of tire side forces on front and rear axle by Eqs. 22–22 and 22–23.

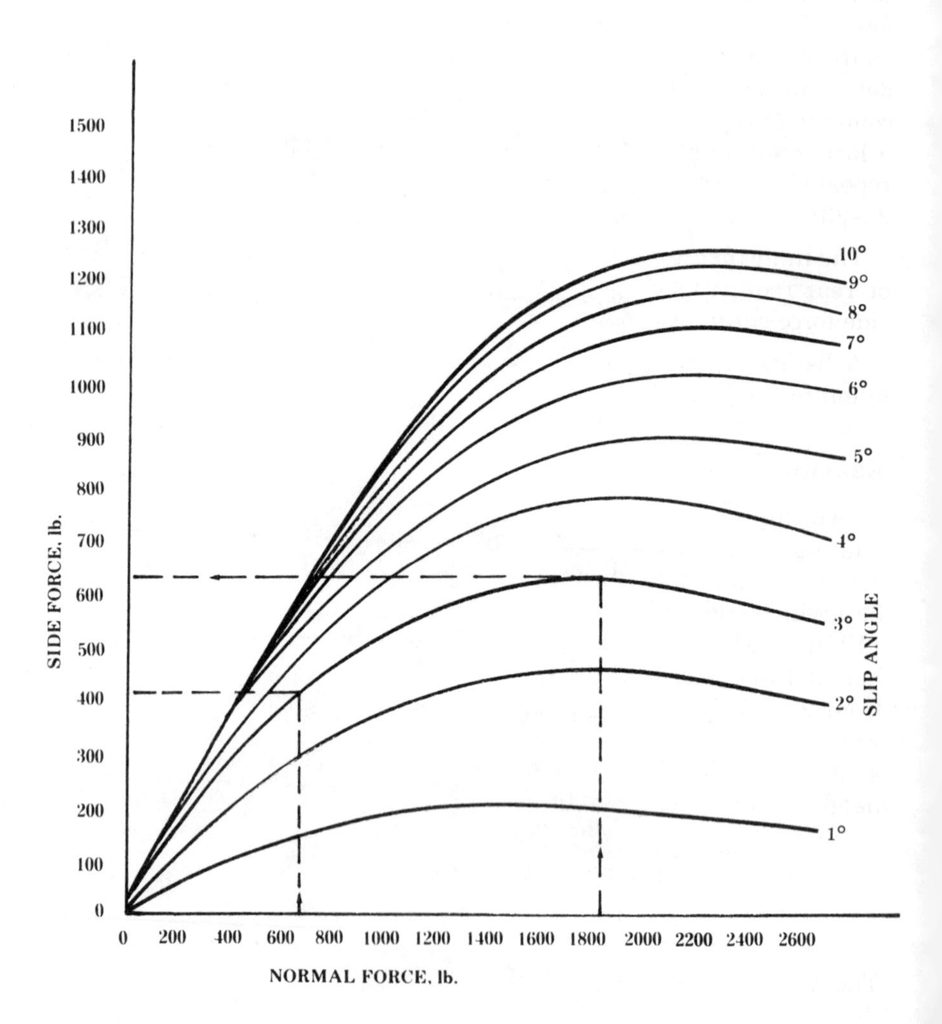

Figure 22-5. Side Force vs. Normal Force for Different Slip Angles for Large Passenger Car Tire

3. Assume an initial slip angle $\alpha_{Fi} = \alpha_{Fo} = \alpha_F$ and obtain the associated side force $F_{yF,i}$ and $F_{yF,o}$ for the corresponding tire normal forces $F_{zF,i}$ and $F_{zF,o}$ from a side force, slip angle, normal force diagram as illustrated in Fig. 22–5. The individual side forces of the front tires determined from Fig. 22–5 must equal the summation of side forces computed by Eq. 22–22 (point 2 above). If the side forces are too small, a larger slip angle must be assumed and the trial and error solution repeated. Carry out the same calculations for the rear tires (Eq. 22–23).

The limit turning performance is achieved when the slip angle front or rear required for sufficient side force production is near or at the side force saturation point.

A listing of vehicle data required for computing vehicle turning is found in Table 22–1.

Example 22–2

Determine the slip angles front and rear of a Chevrolet Impala at a lateral acceleration of 0.5 g with the tire characteristics of Fig. 22–5. The suspension data are found in Table 22–1. The data that follow may be used: Weight 4500 lb, center of gravity height 24 in., wheel base 119 in., track width front 62.5 in., track width rear 62.4 in., roll center height front 0.25 in., roll center height rear 11.75 in., roll stiffness front 27,217 lb · ft/rad, roll stiffness rear 10,772 lb · ft/rad, unsprung weight front 100 lb., unsprung weight rear 150 lb, sprung weight 4250 lb, static rear axle load 2000 lb, unsprung mass center of gravity height 15 in.

The value of h_r required in Eq. 22–21 may be determined by

$$h_r = h - (p_R - p_F)\,\psi = 24 - (11.75 - 0.25)\,\frac{2000}{4500} = 18.9 \text{ in.}$$

The normalized roll stiffness S_F is (Eq. 22–21)

$$S_F = \left(1 - \frac{2000}{4500}\right)\left(\frac{0.25}{62.5}\right) + \left(\frac{27{,}217}{27{,}217 + 10{,}772 - 4250 \times \dfrac{18.9}{12}}\right)$$

$$+ \left(\frac{18.9}{62.5}\right) + \left(\frac{100}{4250}\right)\left(\frac{15}{62.5}\right) = 0.0022 + 0.263 + 0.00567 = 0.272, \text{ d'less}$$

The corresponding roll stiffness value for the rear suspension is $S_R = 0.195$, d'less.

Table 22–1. Vehicle Properties

Vehicle	Weight (loaded)/lb	Weight (empty)/lb	C.g. Height, in.	Wheel base, in.	Suspension Type, (Front)	Static Axle Load, lb (Front)	Trackwidth, in. (Front)	Roll center height, in. (Front)	Roll Stiffness, ft · lb/rad (Front)	Suspension Type (Rear)	Static Axle load lb (Rear)	Trackwidth, in. (Rear)	Roll Center Height, in. (Rear)	Roll Stiffness, ft · lb/rad (Rear)
67 Fiat 124	2471	1776		88.6	2	1138	50.4	0.98	17,395	5	1372	49.3	10.5	15,833
69 BMW 2500	3441	2930	22.9	106	1	1776	57.1	2.21		6	1665	57.5	4.91	
69 VW 411	3263	2264	22.1	98.5	1	1485	54.4	3.59	21,126	6	1778	52.8	3.23	19,716
68 Porsche 911	2681	2370	16.9	87.1	1	1112	52.7	0.96	14,153	6	1569	51.9	1.98	15,414
69 Opel Kadett		1749	20.1	95.1	3	923	49.2	1.4	13,752	7	826	50.2	9.5	9,741
69 Maverick		2534	21.86	103	3	1396	55.5	0.4	18,336	7	1138	55.5	7.8	10,027
69 Camaro		3042	20.76	108	3	1710	59.6	0.25	28,077	7	1332	59.5	8.25	12,606
									28,665					11,460
70 Camaro		3441	20.6	108	3	1980	61.5		14,325		1461	60.5		10,887
67 Toronado	5241	4773		119	4	2904	63.4	1.65	33,721	7	2337	63	10.2	17,648
70 Firebird		3857	19.25	108.5	3	2246	61	1.3	42,688	7	1611	60.5	9.0	27,790
69 Impala		4077	23.8	119	3	2175	62.5	0.25	27,217	7	1902	62.4	11.75	10,772
71 Pinto		2092	20	94	3	1145	55	2.4	12,778	7	947	55.0	9.6	11,918
70 Hornet		2832	21.8	108	3	1616	57.1	2.8	14,153	7	1216	57.4	9.0	11,345

Suspension Type:
1 McPherson Strut
2 Control Arm, Coil Springs
3 Upper and Lower Control Arm, Coil Springs
4 Control Arm, Torsion Bar
5 Solid Axle, Coil Springs
6 Semi Trailing Arms, Coil Springs
7 Solid Axle, Leaf Springs

The normal forces on each wheel are determined by Eqs. 22–17 through 22–20 as follows:

Inner front wheel:

$$F_{zF,i} = (1 - 0.444)\left(\frac{4500}{2}\right) - (0.5)(0.272)(4250)$$

$$= 1251 - 578 = 673 \text{ lb}$$

Outer front wheel:

$$F_{zF,o} = 1251 + 578 = 1829 \text{ lb}$$

Inner rear wheel:

$$F_{zR,i} = (0.444)\left(\frac{4500}{2}\right) - (0.5)(0.195)(4250) =$$

$$= 999 - 414 = 585 \text{ lb}$$

Outer rear wheel:

$$F_{zR,o} = 999 + 414 = 1413 \text{ lb}$$

The summation of side force is determined by Eqs. 22–22 and 22–23 as follows:

Front axle:

$$F_{yF,i} + F_{yF,o} = (0.5)(4500)(1 - 0.444) = 1251 \text{ lb}$$

Rear axle:

$$F_{yR,i} + F_{yR,o} = (0.5)(4500)(0.444) = 999 \text{ lb}$$

The slip angles are determined by trial and error, i.e., a slip angle value is assumed and checked by calculation. The front axle slip angle is determined by use of Fig. 22–5 as follows.

The front normal forces are $F_{zF,i} = 673$ lb and $F_{zF,o} = 1829$ lb; the total front side force is 1251 lb. A slip angle on each front wheel of 3.0 deg is assumed. The side force produced by the inner front wheel with 673 normal force (Fig. 22–5) is $F_{yF,i} = 410$ lb, the side force on the outer front wheel with 1829 lb normal force is $F_{yF,o} = 640$ lb; consequently, the summation of side forces is 1050 lb, i.e., less than that required (1251 lb). The initially assumed slip angle of 3 deg is too small. A new slip angle of 4 deg is assumed to exist on each front wheel. Following the same procedure, a side force of 1260 lb is obtained. Since this value exceeds the required side force slightly, the assumed slip angle exceeds the required by a small amount. The correct slip angle on the front axle is 3.95 deg.

Following the same procedure for the rear axle yields a slip angle of 3.1 deg. Since the difference between front and rear slip angle is positive, the vehicle is under-steering.

The limit turning lateral acceleration can be obtained by increasing the assumed values of lateral acceleration until the front axle (as in this example) or rear axle requires slip angles that are near or at the saturation of sheer force, i.e., at the highest values shown in Fig. 22–5.

A detailed evaluation of the different procedures for determining the limit turning performance of a vehicle reveals that the latter method is the most accurate since it accounts for vehicle geometry, suspension and non-linear tire characteristics. The method involving Eqs. 22–11 through 22–16 yields lateral acceleration values that are approximately 10 to 15% too high. The least accurate method involving Eq. 22–10 yields results that may be in error significantly due to the unknown relationship between lateral acceleration and sliding friction coefficient for the tires involved in the accident.

The effects of different vehicle components on turning performance are summarized below.

Effect of Tire Geometry on Steady-State Turning

Tires may vary widely in their construction. Radial ply tires such as found on many modern cars generally exhibit higher cornering stiffness at lower levels of slip angle than conventional tires (Chapter 18). Most radial tires exhibit also higher maximum cornering stiffness. Radial tires possess two distinct regions of cornering stiffness, a high value up to 4 to 6 deg slip angle and a lower value beyond the transition region. This bilinear behavior may be utilized by the driver as indicator for approaching tire slipping.

Effect of Tire Inflation Pressure

It is common practice to recommend higher inflation pressure for a heavily loaded axle for purposes of increasing tire life and reducing heat build up. Lower inflation pressures are used for lightly loaded axles to reduce wheel hop. Increased inflation pressure allows the tire to produce the required side force at lower values of slip angle. For example, in terms of Eq. 22–9 and its discussion, lower front tire inflation pressure causes an initially neutralsteering vehicle to become understeering. The opposite is true for lower rear wheel inflation pressure.

Effect of Wheel Camber

Many wheel suspensions are designed such that when subjected to a lateral force the wheel is inclined under an angle to the road surface. Positive camber, defined as tilting of the top of a wheel located at the outer turning radius away from the vehicle results in a decrease of side force production. Negative camber yields the opposite effect. This camber phenomenon is similar to that of a motorcycle leaning into a turn. For example, for a motor vehicle a given side force production at zero camber angle may require a slip angle of 2 deg whereas a positive camber angle of 8 deg requires the tire to slip at 3 deg to produce the same side force. Consequently, positive camber on the front wheels (and zero camber on the rear axle) results in an increase of understeering characteristics. Conversely, positive camber on the rear axle tends to decrease the understeering characteristics of a vehicle. Camber changes due to vehicle body roll may be utilized to affect directional control of a vehicle. It should be mentioned, however, that since large values of camber result in large values of slip, tire saturation, i.e., sliding conditions is reached more rapidly. Thus, a tire operating at larger camber angle begins to slide sideways at lower levels of side force than a zero camber tire. Finally, tire construction affects camber side force production. Radial tires have a lesser tendency to affect vehicle directional control through camber changes.

Effect of Compliance Steering of Axles

Of considerable importance in designing suspension systems is their contribution to directional control by means of compliance steer, commonly called roll steer. These steering effects are the result of suspension or wheel motion due to body roll, side force transmission and others. They are not controlled by the driver. Compliance steer effects are included in Eq. 22–8 by the term δ_R indicating the rear axle compliance steer. The front wheel angle δ_F contains both the driver steering input as well as front axle compliance steer, i.e., steering effects due to elastic deflections. Consequently, front axle compliance steer does not affect the front wheel steering rotation for a given turning radius but only the driver steering wheel rotation.

Effect of Drive Thrust

Directional control is significantly affected by drive thrust. For example, a vehicle neutral steering when coasting through a limit turn will show understeering behavior when front wheel drive thrust is applied. Similarly, rear wheel drive thrust will cause the vehicle to become oversteer. This condition is a direct result of the tires being forced to operate at higher levels of slip angle for a certain side force production when also forced to produce drive thrust.

Effect of Lateral Load Transfer

Tire data indicate that increased wheel load initially produces higher levels of tire side force for a given slip angle. Beyond a certain maximum value the side force begins to decline (Fig. 22-5). Thus, for a given limit turning maneuver the axle exhibiting the smaller amount of lateral load transfer will operate at smaller slip angles than the axle having a greater portion of the lateral load transfer. The lateral load transfer distribution between front and rear suspension is a direct function of the roll stiffness of each suspension. Large domestic vehicles have front roll stiffness values nearly twice as large as the corresponding value on the rear axle, thus increasing the understeer characteristics of the vehicle. Properly designed suspension systems may allow increased values of maximum lateral acceleration as much as 15% solely based on optimum roll stiffness distribution between front and rear axle.

So far, lateral load transfer has resulted in a reduced cornering capability of the vehicle, indicated by higher slip angles. This phenomenon may, however, also be utilized to affect the directional control of a vehicle. For example, a rear weight biased vehicle may be altered towards neutral or understeering by increasing front suspension roll stiffness, usually accomplished by installing stiffer springs. As discussed earlier, stiffer suspensions result in higher sprung mass accelerations and hence decreased ride comfort. To obtain increased roll stiffness without affecting ride stabilizer bars are installed. Stabilizers only affect lateral load transfer and are thus a design element for affecting vehicle directional control.

22-2.3. Vehicle Rollover. Rollover of a vehicle occurs when both inner wheels lift off the ground and the subsequent roll motion is sufficient to turn the vehicle on its side, roof or into a multiple rollover. Rollover is closely related to lateral load transfer. Rollover on a flat road surface, when no tripping action occurs by raised curbs or rim to ground contact may be the result of three different types of maneuvers (Refs. 23 and 24).

1. A rapid steering wheel rotation forces the vehicle into a severe turn with the associated centrifugal force sufficiently large to roll the vehicle.

2. The steering wheel is turned repeatedly to the left and right so that the forced vibrations are in harmony with the natural body roll frequency of the vehicle while the vehicle is traveling basically about a straight line.

3. The brakes of a vehicle, initially in a turning maneuver, are rapidly applied to lock all wheels resulting in a marked decrease of side force. A second or so later the brakes are released and the wheels assume maximum side force associated with a rotating wheel. The sudden occurrence of side force may be sufficiently large to "trip" the vehicle into rollover.

All three maneuvers require a tire-road friction sufficiently large to prevent side sliding prior to rollover.

The bead unseating forces may be sufficiently large to force the tire off the rim causing the rim to dig into the pavement and to trip and roll the vehicle. Bead unseating may more easily occur at inflation pressures below recommended levels.

Simplified Rollover Analysis

Only cars and trucks, i.e., solid-frame vehicles will be considered here. Rollover of tractor-semitrailers is presented in Section 22–4.

If each wheel of a turning vehicle exhibits the same "cornering efficiency" (similar to braking efficiency), then the ratio of side force to normal force on each wheel is equal to the coefficient of friction in the side direction. Only under these conditions is Eq. 22–10 valid, and consequently the limit lateral acceleration $a_{y\lim}$ is

$$a_{y\lim} = \frac{V^2}{Rg} \leq \mu_s, \; g\text{-units} \tag{22–24}$$

where

$g = 32.2$ ft/sec^2
$R =$ turn radius, ft
$V =$ vehicle velocity, ft/sec
$\mu_s =$ side or lateral friction coefficient, d'less

When the attempted lateral acceleration exceeds the available friction, the vehicle may slide sideways or roll, i.e., $\mu_s g$ represents the theoretical upper limit of stable turning. In terms of vehicle parameters, an appropriate analysis indicates that a vehicle may only rollover when the following tire-road friction condition exists:

$$\mu_s \geq \frac{t}{2h}, \text{ d'less} \tag{22–25}$$

where

h = center-of-gravity height, in.
t = trackwidth, in.

Eqs. 22–24 and 22–25 may be combined to yield the minimum velocity $V_{\min}$ at which rollover occurs as

$$V_{\min} = \sqrt{\frac{(32.2)rt}{2h}}, \text{ ft/sec}$$

If the actual side friction coefficient is less than that computed by Eq. 22–25, then the vehicle tends to slide sideways when the lateral acceleration exceeds $\mu_s g$. If the actual side friction coefficient is greater than that computed by Eq. 22–25, then the vehicle may roll when the lateral acceleration exceeds a value computed below.

No rollover will occur if at least one inner wheel maintains contact with the ground. In the limit, rollover begins when the normal force between inner wheels and ground becomes zero (Ref. 25).

Eqs. 22–17 through 22–20 may be solved for lateral acceleration a_y at which the normal force $F_{zF,i}$ or $F_{zR,i}$ equals zero, i.e., rollover commences.

Consequently, the lateral acceleration values at which the inner front wheels lift off the ground at the inner front wheel are (Eq. 22–17):

$$a_{yF} = \frac{(1-\psi)\left(\frac{W}{2}\right)}{S_F W_S}, g\text{-units} \quad (22\text{–}26)$$

The normalized roll stiffness S_F is determined by Eq. 22–21. The corresponding value at the inner rear wheel is (Eq. 22–19):

$$a_{yR} = \frac{\psi\left(\frac{W}{2}\right)}{S_R W_S}, g\text{-units} \quad (22\text{–}27)$$

The higher of the two lateral acceleration values computed by Eqs. 22–26 and 22–27 determines the rollover limit in the absence of any braking or driving forces.

When braking occurs during the turning maneuver, then the longitudinal load transfer serves to redistribute the normal forces between tire and ground. The inner front wheel normal force $F_{zF,i}$ when braking at a_x (g-units) is

$$F_{zF,i} = (1-\psi+a_x\chi)\left(\frac{W}{2}\right) - a_y S_F W_s, \text{ lb} \quad (22\text{–}28)$$

The inner rear wheel normal $F_{zR,i}$ is

$$F_{zR,i} = (\psi - a_x \chi)\left(\frac{W}{2}\right) - a_y S_R W_s, \text{ lb} \qquad (22\text{–}29)$$

where

a_x = braking deceleration, g-units

χ = center-of-gravity height divided by wheel base, d'less

The lateral acceleration a_{yF} at which the inner front wheel lifts off the ground is with $F_{zF,i} = 0$ (Eq. 22–28) and solved for a_y

Inner front wheel

$$a_{yF} = \frac{(1 - \psi + a_x \chi)\left(\frac{W}{2}\right)}{S_F W_s}, g\text{-units} \qquad (22\text{–}30)$$

Inner rear wheel (Eq. 22–29):

$$a_{yR} = \frac{(\psi - a_x \chi)\left(\frac{W}{2}\right)}{S_R W_s}, g\text{-units} \qquad (22\text{–}31)$$

Example 22–3

Determine the rollover limit for a Chevrolet Impala (Example 22–2) with and without an 0.3 g braking deceleration.

By use of Eq. 22–25 a tire road friction coefficient of $\mu_s = 1.3$ or more is required to cause rollover, i.e., simulate a tire tripping action. For all regular tires the side friction coefficient is less than 1.3. Special racing tires may develop side friction coefficients in excess of 1.3. Without braking Eqs. 22–26 and 22–27 apply.

The lateral acceleration at which inner front wheel lift off occurs may be determined by Eq. 22–26

$$a_{yF} = \frac{(1 - 0.444)\left(\frac{4500}{2}\right)}{(0.272)(4250)} = 1.08\, g$$

The inner rear wheel lifts off at $a_{yR} = 1.2\, g$ (Eq. 22–27). The higher lift off limit at the rear is mainly caused by a lower rear suspension roll stiffness.

Inspection of the results indicates that both inner wheels have lost ground contact at a lateral acceleration of 1.2 g. However, rollover will only occur if the side friction is equal or greater than 1.2 (and not 1.3 as computed by the approximate relationship Eq. 22–25).

When braking is considered, Eqs. 22–30 and 22–31 yields a_{yF} = 1.21 g and a_{yR} = 1.04g. The load transfer due to braking has decreased the static load on the inner rear wheel resulting in a loss of ground contact at a lower value of lateral acceleration. The basic effect of braking is to redistribute the wheel loads such as to shift wheel lift off to higher values of lateral acceleration. In the case of front heavy cars, braking will cause inner rear wheel lift off to occur at lateral accelerations values as low as 0.3g for longitudinal decelerations of 0.8g. Extremely front heavy vehicles such as found in the Oldsmobile Toronado may experience rear wheel lift off at lateral acceleration as low as 0.2g when braking at 0.8g. In the case of rear heavy cars the braking deceleration tends to balance the normal forces more evenly, resulting in a rollover limit diagram illustrated in Fig. 22–6. Inspection of the curves indicates that for deceleration below a_x = 0.2g the inner front wheel tends to lift off first, for greater decelerations the inner rear wheel. No wheel lift off will occur for conditions below line A, no rollover for the conditions below line B.

Frequently it becomes necessary to determine the approximate limit turning lateral acceleration from a known value of skidding

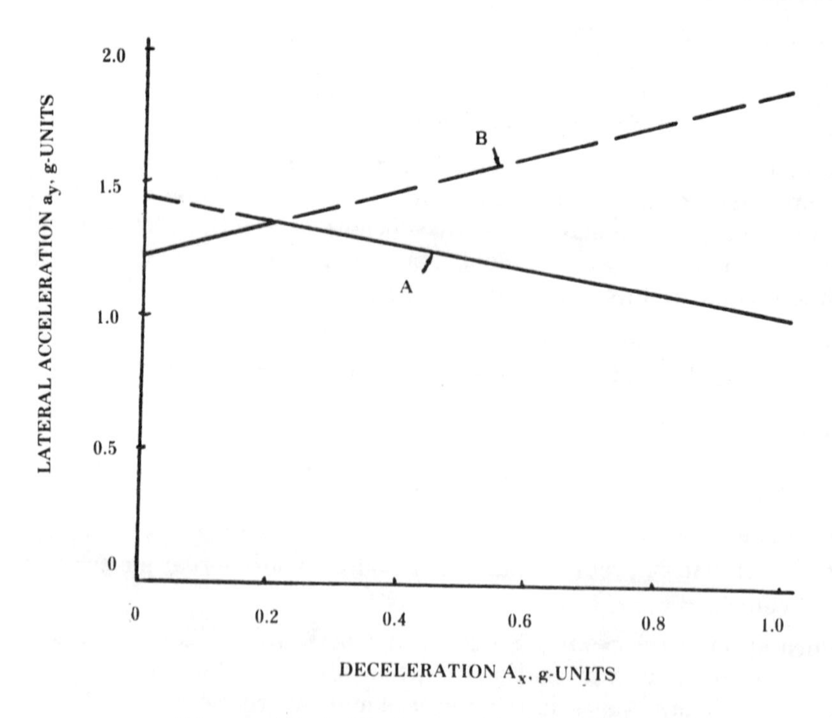

Figure 22–6. Rollover Limit with Braking

friction and an assumed wheels unlocked braking deceleration. This is explained in the discussion that follows.

A surface having a tire-road friction coefficient of $\mu = 1.0$ is capable of producing a maximum vehicle deceleration of 1.0 g. The maximum lateral acceleration capability of the same vehicle in the absence of any braking is usually less than 1.0 g. Reasons for this are caused by differences in mechanisms involved in producing braking and side forces. A tire/road surface having a braking friction coefficient of 0.9 and thus a_x (max) $= 0.9g$ tends to produce only about 0.7 g lateral acceleration. The friction circle concept does not accurately describe the relationship between limit braking and turning performance for a given tire-road surface condition.

To describe this behavior more accurately, a relationship

$$a_x^2 = \mu^2 - (m a_y)^2 \tag{22–32}$$

is proposed. The coefficient m is the ratio of a_{xo} to a_{yo}, where a_{xo} designates the maximum braking in the absence of any lateral acceleration and thus is equal to the conventional tire/road friction coefficient, μ, and a_{yo} designates the maximum lateral acceleration in the absence of any braking. The value of m for most tires and dry road surfaces ranges between 1.1 and 1.2.

When the vehicle slides sideways as shown in Fig. 22–7 and impacts a curb or similar object, rollover may occur when the vehicle possesses sufficient kinetic energy prior to impact. The linear kinetic energy of the vehicle is changed into rotational kinetic energy after impacting the curb. Rollover will occur when the kinetic energy prior to impact is sufficient to lift the center of gravity over the point of rotation or curb impact point. The minimum side sliding speed V_S required for rollover when striking a curb is

$$V_s > 45.5\sqrt{\left(\frac{I_{\text{roll}}}{Wh}\right)\left\{\sqrt{1 + \left(\frac{t}{2h}\right)^2} - 1\right\}} \text{ ft/sec} \tag{22–33}$$

where

I_{roll} = mass moment of inertia of vehicle about point of rotation, ft · lb · sec²

h = center of gravity height, ft

t = track width, ft

W = vehicle weight, lb

Values for I_{roll} may be determined by

$$I_{\text{roll}} = I_{\text{roll,c.g}} + \left(\frac{W}{32.2}\right)\left[h^2 + \left(\frac{t}{2}\right)^2\right], \text{ ft} \cdot \text{lb} \cdot \text{sec}^2 \tag{22–34}$$

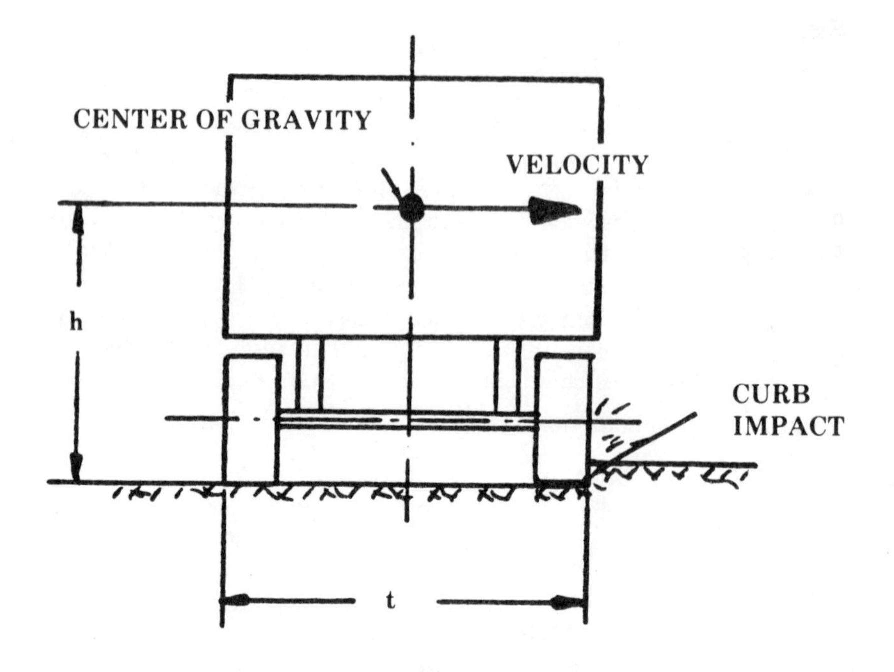

Figure 22-7. Rollover by Tripping

where

$I_{roll,c.g}$ = mass moment of inertia about longitudinal axis of vehicle, $ft \cdot lb \cdot sec^2$

Important dynamic vehicle parameters for rollover computation are found in Table 22-2.

Table 22-2. Dynamic Vehicle Parameters

Vehicle	W (lb)	$I_{roll,c.g.}$ ($ft \cdot lb \cdot sec^2$)	t (ft)	h (ft)
71 VW Super Beetle	1,966	214	4.5	1.94
71 Ambassador	3,721	330	5.0	2.11
71 Chevrolet Brookwood Station Wagon	4,702	488	5.34	2.04
71 Ford F-100	3,703	326	5.20	2.49
71 Oldsmobile F85	3,623	331	4.94	2.02
Diamond Reo 4x6 heavy truck	21,400 / 45,200	2,916 / 3,317	6.67	3.8 / 4.6
Tractor-Semitrailer	74,300	–	6.67	5.5

Example 22–4

Determine the minimum side sliding velocity of a Chevrolet Brookwood station wagon and a VW Beetle required to cause rollover when striking a curb.

The velocity V_s may be determined by Eq. 22–33. The mass moment of inertia I_{roll} about the tripping contact (curb or rim to ground contact) is determined by Eq. 22–34 (Chevrolet data are used first):

$$I_{roll} = 488 + \left(\frac{4702}{32.2}\right)\left[(2.04)^2 + \left(\frac{5.34}{2}\right)^2\right] = 2136 \text{ ft} \cdot \text{lb} \cdot \text{sec}^2$$

The minimum velocity (Eq. 22–33) is

$$V_s = 45.5 \sqrt{\frac{2136}{(4702)(2.04)}\left\{\sqrt{1 + \left[\frac{5.34}{(2)(2.04)}\right]^2} - 1\right\}}$$

$$= 17.3 \text{ ft/sec or } 11.8 \text{ mph}$$

Substitution of the appropriate data into Eqs. 22–34 and 22–33 yields a minimum side sliding velocity of 10 mph for the VW Super Beetle.

Frequently super elevation is used to increase the limit turning speed of vehicles.

Eq. 22–24 may be expanded to include super elevation:

$$\frac{V^2}{Rg} = a_y \leq \frac{\mu_s + \tan\alpha_e}{1 - \mu_s \tan\alpha_e}, \; g\text{-units} \qquad (22\text{–}35)$$

where

α_e = transverse slope of super elevation, deg

μ_s = side friction coefficient, d'less

tan = mathematical operator, d'less

For example, for $\mu_s = 0.7$ and $\alpha_e = 0.1$, i.e., 10% super elevation the result is

$$\frac{V^2}{Rg} = \frac{0.7 + 0.1}{1 - (0.7)(0.1)} = 0.86\, g$$

The result indicates that a flat road without super elevation having a friction coefficient of 0.86 is equivalent to a road super elevation of 10% having a friction coefficient of 0.7.

22–2.4. Steering Wheel Moment. The subjective evaluation of the dynamic responsiveness of a vehicle by a driver is affected by lateral acceleration, body roll, vehicle side slip angle, that is, the angle between vehicle longitudinal axis and velocity direction, steering wheel moment and several other parameters. Of considerable influence is the steering wheel feed back provided by the steering wheel moment and the associated steering wheel deflection to negotiate a given turn. In emergency type situations the steering wheel moment is often utilized as feed back by the motor forces of the driver directly without first going through perceptual-decision making process. Consequently, proper matching of steering wheel dynamics to other response parameters of the vehicle becomes necessary.

A detailed analysis of steering wheel moments and displacements is a function of a host of suspension and tire parameters and is beyond the scope of this book.

However, steering wheel moment requirements may be analyzed individually for turning at zero speed as found during parking maneuvers, as well as during low speed, and high speed turning. A complete analysis requires extensive information on tire forces and moments as the front wheels are steered. Since driver input forces are limited, the steering wheel moment during parking generally determines the steering gear ratio or makes the installation of a power steering necessary.

During low speed turning the analysis reveals that little or no differences exist for front or rear wheel driven automobiles with otherwise identical geometrical design parameters. Steering systems force the steering wheels back to a neutral position by means of the forces and moments produced on the wheels. Of significance is the friction present in the steering system. Probably the single most important element is associated with the king pin design. A negative moment about the king pin results in an increased wheel rotation due to normal wheel load, that is, it produces an undesirable effect. A steering mechanism exhibiting this characteristic tends to have an unstable behavior. Both toe-in and camber may be utilized to affect the steering wheel return into a straight ahead position.

In the case of turning at high speed the effect of lateral acceleration must be considered. The understeer-oversteer characteristics of a vehicle has a significant effect on the development of steering wheel moment as a function of lateral acceleration. Due to the non-linear behavior of pneumatic tires, the steering wheel moment may reach a maximum for moderate levels of lateral acceleration and then decrease for high values of lateral acceleration. Important additional design parameters are pneumatic trail and inflation pressure. Pneumatic trail is distance between the wheel center vertical line and the line of action of the side force. Generally speaking, larger values of pneumatic trail require greater moments whereas increased inflation pressures reduce the steering moment required to negotiate a given turn. The influence of drive thrust location, i.e., front or rear wheel drive, becomes more pronounced as the limit turning performance with drive thrust application is attained. Not only the steering wheel moments are affected but also directional control of the vehicle through the development of tire slip angles. For example, when negotiating a turn at excessive speed the release of the accelerator pedal and hence release of drive thrust should decrease the understeering behavior of the vehicle. Under these conditions the vehicle attempts to turn at a smaller radius of curvature without steering wheel corrections by the driver. Such a selfsteering effect appears to be highly desirable for accident avoidance purposes.

Disturbances on steering wheel moment may result from road surface irregularities, front wheel force unbalance stemming from different braking forces left-to-right or differential rolling resistances when one wheel is traveling off the shoulder. Important design considerations are associated with the coulomb friction exhibited by the steering system. Horizontal disturbance forces are transmitted to the steering wheel when they are greater than the friction forces of the system. Large values of friction are undesirable since they would also eliminate steering sensitivity. However, possible solutions exist by having low friction for the moment transmission from the steering wheel to the front wheel whereas the moment transmission originating from the front wheels to the steering wheel is kept a maximum. Research data suggests that the steering wheel force of the unassisted steering system should not exceed 15 lb.

22–2.5. Steering Wheel Rotation. When a normal turning maneuver is conducted, the driver steering wheel inputs generally do not present any difficulties. In an accident avoidance maneuver, the steering wheel angle may be important since too large values may limit the driver in his maneuver action.

The steering wheel angle may be determined from an analysis involving Eq. 22–16 which is applicable to both turning and braking. Frequently, no braking is attempted in a steering maneuver and the steering wheel angle SW may be determined by

$$SW = \frac{(57.3)\, iL}{R}\left\{1 + \left[\frac{C_R(1-\psi) - C_F\psi}{L\, C_F\, C_R}\right]\left(\frac{W}{g}\right)V^2\right\}, \text{deg} \quad (22\text{–}36)$$

where

C_F = cornering stiffness of both front tires, lb/rad

C_R = cornering stiffness of both rear tires, lb/rad

g = 32.2 ft/sec^2

i = steering ratio, d'less

L = wheel base, ft

R = radius of turn, ft

V = vehicle speed, ft/sec

W = vehicle weight, lb

Example 22–4

Determine the steering wheel angle SW for the following data: $L = 12$ ft, $W = 4500$ lb, $C_F = C_R = 10{,}000$ lb/rad, $i = 17$, $\psi = 0.4$, $V = 50$ mph, $R = 200$ ft.

Substitution of the data into Eq. 22–36 yields $SW = 131$ deg., i.e., a steady-state turn at the described conditions requires a steering angle of 131 deg. If a much tighter turning radius is required, the steering wheel angle would increase significantly. For example, $V =$ 24 mph and $R = 45$ ft yields $SW = 334$ deg., an angle which requires repeated hand application to be accomplished.

If the vehicle in the tight turn were neutral steering, i.e., $C_R(1-\psi) = C_F\,\psi$ in Eq. 22–36, a steering angle $SW = 260$ deg would be required. An oversteering vehicle, indicated by $C_F\,\psi > C_R(1-\psi)$, say $\psi = 0.58$ would require $SW = 200$ deg.

22–2.6. Vehicle Steering Coefficient. The steering characteristic of a vehicle is briefly discussed in Section 22–2.2 in terms of understeering, neutralsteering and oversteering. Each of the three modes is discussed in terms of a slip angle difference.

A steering coefficient C_s may be defined by

$$C_s = 1 + \left[\frac{C_R(1-\psi) - C_F\,\psi}{L\,C_F\,C_R}\right]\left(\frac{W}{g}\right)V^2, \text{ d'less} \qquad (22\text{–}37)$$

The different steering modes are

1. Understeering when $C_s > 1$
2. Neutralsteering when $C_s = 1$
3. Oversteering when $C_s < 1$

Eq. 22–37 may be used to examine the effect of speed on the basic steering characteristic of the vehicle. For an oversteering vehicle Eq. 22–37 may be solved for a critical velocity for which $C_s = 0$, or in light of Eq. 22–36, the turn radius R must be zero, i.e., the vehicle rotates about its vertical axis. The critical turning velocity is:

$$V_{\text{critical}} = \sqrt{\frac{C_F C_R L}{[\psi C_F - (1-\psi)\,C_R]\left(\frac{W}{g}\right)}}, \text{ ft/sec} \qquad (22\text{–}38)$$

If the actual vehicle speed exceeds the critical speed, small side force disturbances caused by wind or road effects may initiate a path deviation of the vehicle. This deviation is the result of a slip angle development and can usually be corrected by the driver through a steering input. An important factor is the time duration during which the deviation develops, giving the driver sufficient time to respond.

22–2.7 Turning of a Car-Trailer Combination. In a motor vehicle trailer combination the towing vehicle determines the direction of travel while the trailer places certain demands upon the directional control potential of the tow vehicle. During steady-state turning the hitch point forces affect the tow vehicle in the same manner as rearward displacement of the center-of-gravity would have in a single vehicle (oversteering).

Similar to the critical speed of an oversteering vehicle, a limiting speed of a turning car-trailer combination can be determined by

$$V_{\text{critical}} = \left[\frac{(LC_F + eC_R)(aC_F - bC_R) + (C_F + C_R)(\ell aC_F - ebC_R)}{\left(\frac{W_c}{g}\right)(e + b)(C_F + C_R) - M(LC_F + eC_R)}\right]^{1/2}, \text{ ft/sec} \qquad (22\text{–}39)$$

where

$$M = \frac{W_c}{g} - \left(\frac{W_t}{g}\right)\left(\frac{c}{d + c} - 1\right), \text{ lb}$$

C_F = cornering stiffness of tow vehicle front tire, lb/rad

C_R = cornering stiffness of tow vehicle rear tire

$L = a + b$

W_c = car weight, lb

W_t = trailer weight lb

All other symbols are illustrated in Fig. 22–8. Typical cars and trailers weighing $W_c = 5000$ lb and $W_t = 4000$ lb, respectively may yield limit speeds between 40 and 60 mph, depending on center of gravity locations and tire stiffness values.

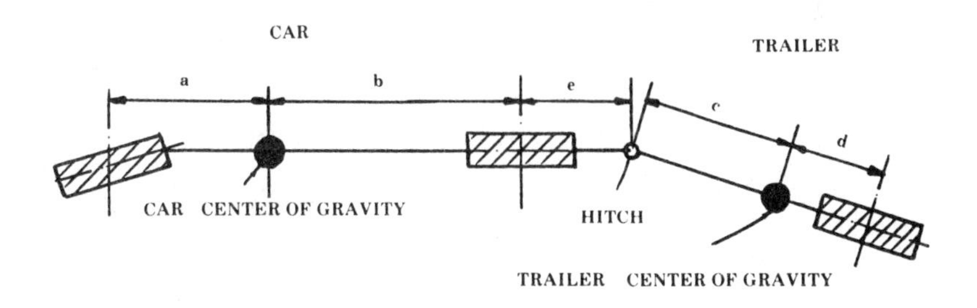

Figure 22–8. Car-Trailer Geometry

22–3. VEHICLE CONTROL

22–3.1. Vehicle Handling. The term vehicle handling, as normally used, describes those vehicle properties that allow a driver to negotiate maneuvers successfully. Since the term handling includes driver characteristics, the interpretation of handling qualities varies almost as much as an interpretation of driver skills. In the past, handling has been defined as: "A general term covering all aspects of the driver-vehicle control relationship embracing all probable maneuvers and motions." Others describe handling as: "The term handling refers to the behavior of the car-man combination in real driving situations and thus embraces a wide variety of possible maneuvers and environmental and roadway conditions." A third approach defines handling in terms of the constituent elements as, "The term handling quality is used to describe the way in which driver control characteristics interact with vehicle response characteristics to produce overall driver-vehicle performance in the lateral-directional sense."

When defining vehicle handling, a significant difference between "safety" or "dynamic" oriented performance requirements exists. For example, in a lane-change maneuver, the width of the lane geometry may be adjusted to the particular size of the vehicle tested. Such an approach tends to emphasize dynamic rather than safety attributes of the driver-vehicle combination. If safety qualities are examined, then a lane geometry of constant width should be favored.

Vehicle handling is thought of in terms of those qualities of the driver-vehicle combination that allow a successful negotiation of a desired course utilizing driver skill capabilities representative of the total driver population.

Vehicle handling is a control process in which the driver, the vehicle, and the environment form a closed loop. When the loop is interrupted by the driver, the vehicle, or the environment (roadway), the normal driving process does not exist anymore. An example would be premature rearwheel lockup resulting in violent vehicle spin. In this case the vehicle interrupted the normal driving loop.

In accident reconstruction it is necessary to isolate the contributions of driver, vehicle, and/or environment to accident causation. The design and mechanical condition of a vehicle affects the contribution of the vehicle. The term vehicle dynamics is used to describe the response of a vehicle to forces, with the driver effects generally excluded.

22-3.2. Straight Line Running Stability. A vehicle is stable when a disturbance force causes an initial path deviation and the vehicle subsequently returns to its original travel direction. Frequently body roll oscillations in combination with the associated directional effects may cause a drastic reduction in safe straight running speed.

Application of basic mechanics to a moving motor vehicle requires for stability that certain limits are placed upon maximum speed.

One basic unstable condition involves a vehicle driving backward. The slightest disturbance may result in divergent, i.e., increasing path deviation.

For forward straight line travel the critical speed V_{crit} is

$$V_{crit} = \sqrt{\frac{C_{Fo} C_{Ro} L}{\frac{W}{g}[(1-\psi)\, C_{Ro} - \psi C_{Fo}]}}, \text{ ft/sec} \qquad (22\text{–}40)$$

where

C_{Fo} = cornering stiffness of both front tires evaluated at zero slip angle, lb/rad

C_{Ro} = cornering stiffness of both rear tires evaluated at zero slip angle, lb/rad

For example, $L = 7.82$ ft, $\psi = 0.45$, $C_{Fo} = C_{Ro} = 10{,}000$ lb/rad, $W = 2730$ lb yields $V_{crit} = 66$ mph. The actual upper safe speed may be somewhat higher since a certain amount of damping assists straight running stability.

During straight-running vehicle travel, steering wheel inputs are required to correct path deviation caused by a disturbance force. If the disturbance force F_S is acting at the center of gravity of the vehicle perpendicular to the direction of travel, the steering wheel angle SW to maintain the intended direction is

$$SW = (57.3) i F_s \left(\frac{1-\psi}{C_F} - \frac{\psi}{C_R} \right), \text{ deg} \qquad (22\text{–}41)$$

where

F_S = side force disturbance, lb

i = steering gear ratio, d'less

The alignment moment of the front tires is neglected in the derivation of Eq. 22–41. Even if the ψ, C_F and C_R values are such that the bracket of Eq. 22–41 is zero, and consequently, $SW = 0$, the alignment moment results in a small steering wheel angle. If the line of action of the side force does not go through the center-of-gravity of the vehicle and acts on a lever arm r about the center of gravity, the steering angle SW required to correct the path deviation is

$$SW = (57.3) i F_s \left(\frac{1-\psi}{C_F} - \frac{\psi}{C_R} + \frac{r}{LC_F} + \frac{r}{LC_R} \right), \text{ deg} \qquad (22\text{–}42)$$

Inspection of Eq. 22–42 indicates that $r = 0$, i.e., no disturbance moment (only force) yields Eq. 22–41.

22–3.3. Transient Response of a Two-Axle Vehicle to a Steering Input. In an emergency accident avoidance maneuver the response of a vehicle to assume a different path is of critical importance. The conditions analyzed involve a vehicle initially traveling in a straight path (Fig. 22–9) when at time zero a ramp steering input is provided as illustrated in Fig. 22–10. The steering input rates are obtained by dividing the steering wheel angular rate by the steering gear ratio.

The path followed by the center-of-gravity of the vehicle responding to the steering input is given as the ratio of unity to the variable

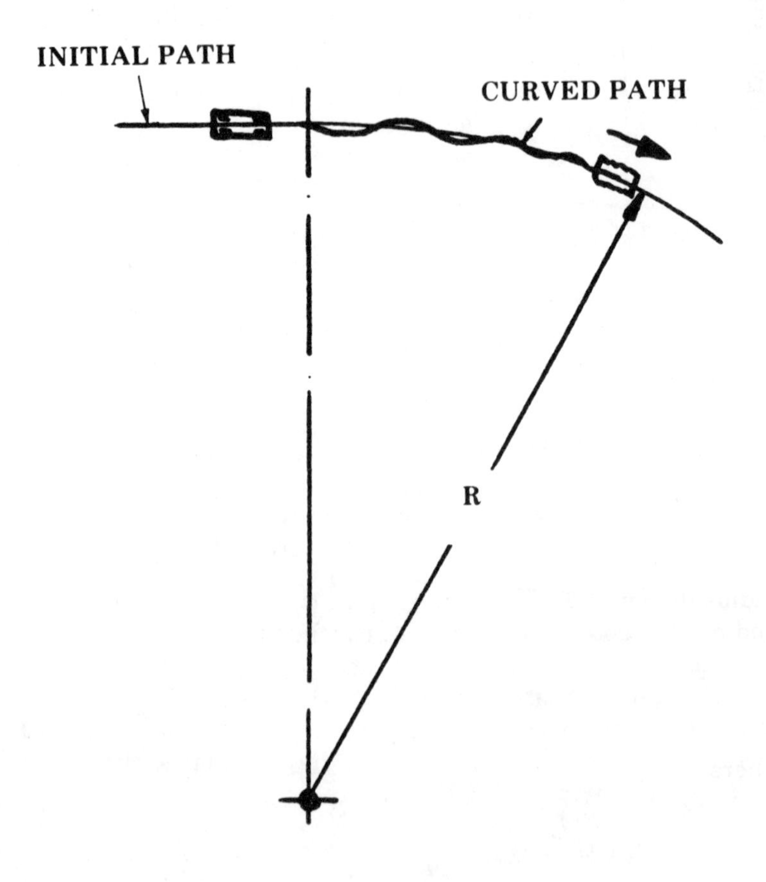

Figure 22–9. Vehicle Path in Response to Steering

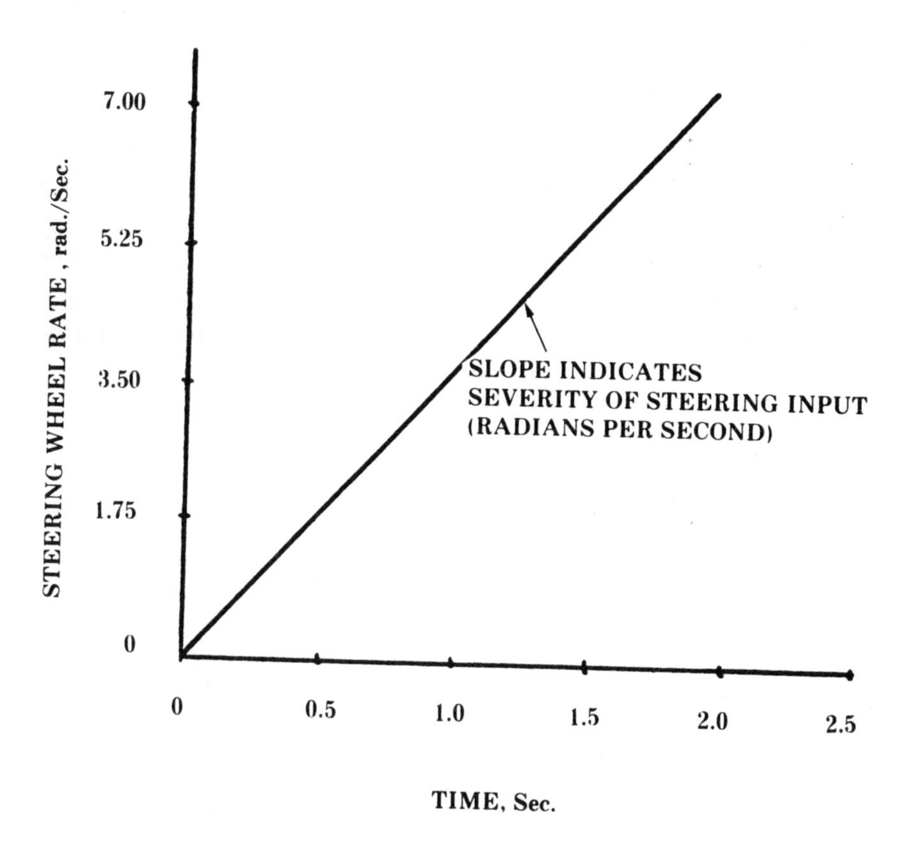

Figure 22–10. Steering Input

radius, R, i.e., $1/R$. The ratio $1/R$ is commonly called path curvature and may be determined by a rather lengthy equation:

$$\left(\frac{1}{R}\right)_t = Ae^{M_1 t} + Be^{M_2 t} + Dt + E, \ \frac{1}{\text{ft}} \qquad (22\text{–}43)$$

where

$$A = \frac{EM_2 - D}{M_1 - M_2}, \ \frac{1}{\text{ft}} \qquad (22\text{–}44)$$

$$B = \frac{EM_1 - D}{M_2 - M_1}, \ \frac{1}{\text{ft}} \qquad (22\text{–}45)$$

$$D = \frac{F}{G} S, \frac{1}{\text{ft sec}} \tag{22–46}$$

$$E = \left(HS - \frac{KFS}{G}\right)\left(\frac{1}{G}\right), \frac{1}{\text{ft}} \tag{22–47}$$

$$F = \frac{C_F\, C_R\, L^2 g}{I\, W\, V^2}, \left(\frac{1}{\text{sec}}\right)^2 \tag{22–48}$$

$$G = F + \frac{C_R(1 - \psi)L - CF\psi L}{I}, \left(\frac{1}{\text{sec}}\right)^2 \tag{22–49}$$

$$H = \frac{L^3(1 - \psi)\, C_F\, C_R\, g}{I\, W\, V^3}, \text{ d'less} \tag{22–50}$$

$$K = \frac{C_F(\psi L)^2 + C_R(1 - \psi)^2 L^2 + (C_F + C_R) I \left(\frac{g}{W}\right)}{IV}, \frac{1}{\text{sec}} \tag{22–51}$$

$$M_1 = -\frac{K}{2} + \sqrt{\left(\frac{K}{2}\right)^2 - G}, \frac{1}{\text{sec}} \tag{22–52}$$

$$M_2 = -\frac{K}{2} = \sqrt{\left(\frac{K}{2}\right)^2 - G}, \frac{1}{\text{sec}} \tag{22–53}$$

I = vehicle yaw mass moment of inertia, lb·ft·sec²

$$S = \frac{SW}{Lt}, \frac{rad}{\text{ft sec}}$$

L = wheel base, ft

Eqs. 22–43 through 22–53 are algebraically straightforward but show the lengthy computations required even for the simple model used to describe the automobile.

The transient response of an understeering and a neutral steering vehicle is shown in Fig. 22–11. Inspection of the curves indicates that the understeering vehicle responds more rapidly to a moderate steering input than the neutral steering vehicle, however, the oscillations are more violent during the turning maneuver (Refs. 13, 26, 27, 28 and 29).

Typical I-values are: 71 Ambassador 2437 lb·ft·sec²; 71 Chevrolet Brookwood Stationwagon 3470; 71 Dodge Coronet 2250; 71 Ford F-100 2408; Ford Mustang 1875; 71 Oldsmobile F-85 2346; 71 VW Super Beetle 869.

22–3.4. Transient Response of a Car-Trailer Combination to a Steering Input. In a car-trailer combination it is important to analyse the articulation angle between car and trailer to determine any significant increases, i.e., excessive trailer swing.

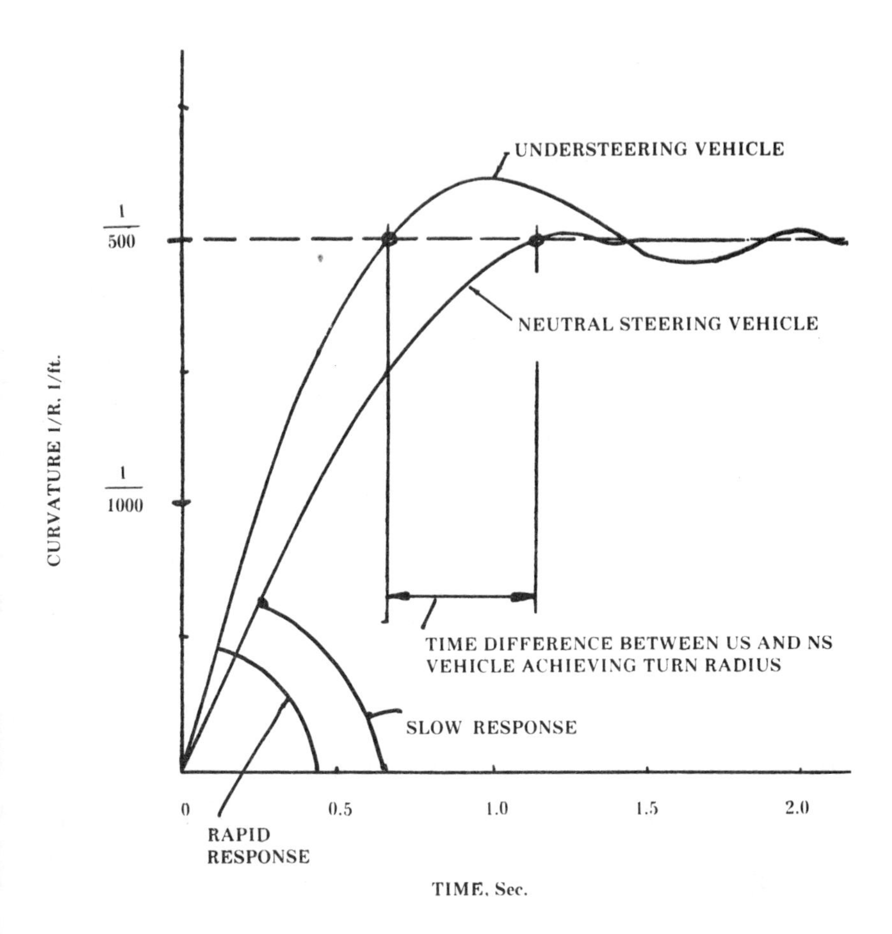

Figure 22-11. Transient Vehicle Response Entering a 500 ft Turn

The geometrical relationships are indicated in Fig. 22-12. The equation describing the articulation angle between car and trailer as a function of time is similar to those describing the response of a car to a steering input. In the analysis a disturbing force F_S acting a distance ℓ_s behind the hitch point produces a disturbing moment M_S about the vertical trailer axis. The resulting angle γ_o may be determined by

$$\gamma_o = \frac{(57.3)M_S}{2\,C_T\,\ell_T} \qquad (22\text{-}54)$$

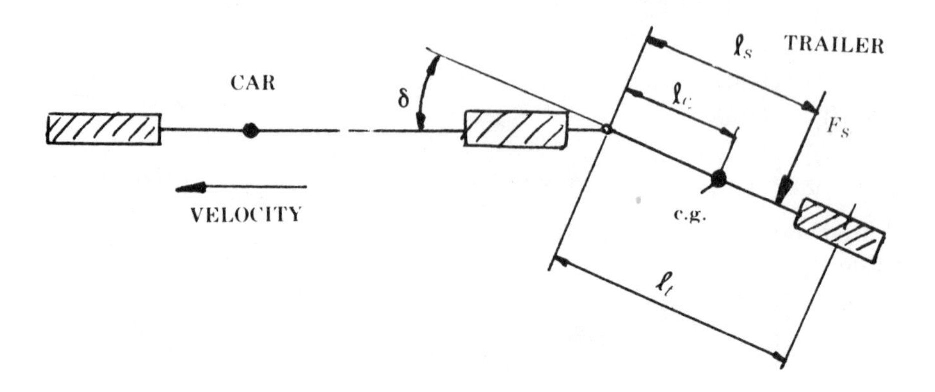

Figure 22–12. Car-Trailer Description

where

M_S = disturbing moment = $F_S \cdot \ell_S$, ft. lb
C_T = cornering stiffness of all trailer tires, lb/rad
ℓ_T = trailer wheel base, ft

The transient trailer angle $\gamma(t)$ is again a lengthy equation:

$$\gamma(t) = \frac{\gamma_{in} - \gamma_o}{1 - \dfrac{M_1}{M_2}} \left[e^{M_1 t} - \left(\frac{M_1}{M_2}\right) e^{M_2 t} \right] + \gamma_o \text{, deg} \qquad (22\text{–}55)$$

where

$$M_1 = -\frac{A_1}{2} + \sqrt{\left(\frac{A_1}{2}\right)^2 - A_2}$$

$$M_2 = -\frac{A_1}{A_2} - \sqrt{\left(\frac{A_1}{2}\right)^2 - A_2}$$

$$A_1 = \frac{2\, C_T\, \ell_T^{\,2}}{\left(I_T + \dfrac{W_T}{g}\, \ell_c^{\,2}\right) V}$$

$$A_2 = \frac{2C_T(\ell_T)^2}{\left[I_T + \dfrac{W_T}{g}(\ell_c)^2\right]}$$

γ_{in} = initial trailer angle if combination is turning, deg
γ_o = computed by Eq. 22–56, deg

ℓ_c = horizontal distance between trailer center-of-gravity and hitch point, ft

ℓ_T = trailer base, ft

I_T = trailer yaw mass moment of inertia, lb·ft·sec²

W_T = trailer weight, lb

g = 32.2 ft/sec²

V = velocity, ft/sec

Trailer swing can only occur if the forward speed exceeds a critical value V_{crit}

$$V_{crit} \geq \sqrt{\frac{C_T \ell_T^3}{2\left[I_T + \left(\frac{W_T}{g}\right)\ell_c^2\right]}}, \text{ ft/sec} \qquad (22\text{–}56)$$

If the actual velocity is less than $V_{critical}$, then the disturbance angle γ_o will decrease automatically to zero as time increases without any oscillations. If the actual velocity exceeds $V_{critical}$, then trailer angle oscillation does occur. The angular trailer oscillation may dampen out and the trailer angle return to zero as time increases. Under those conditions the trailer angle will never exceed the initial disturbance angle γ_o.

Divergent trailer swing, i.e., an unstable driving condition may occur at higher speeds since the damping of the trailer decreases with increasing speed. Oscillatory instability is more likely to occur with low trailer tire cornering stiffness, short trailer, high trailer weight and mass moment of inertia, and a trailer-center of gravity location on or behind the trailer axle. A detailed analysis of trailer swing and the determination of the critical velocity at which oscillatory instability occurs would require the use of computers. In a trailer-accident reconstruction where the actual speed exceeded the critical speed computed by Eq. 22–56, a computer analysis may show instability particularly when a rearward trailer center of gravity existed and the inherent damping was reduced by high speed.

For example, the results of such a computer analysis show that a trailer with its center of gravity located directly over the trailer wheels becomes unstable at a speed of 65 mph. At lower speeds the trailer would not be unstable due to the increased damping at lower speeds.

22–4. TRACTOR-SEMITRAILER ROLLOVER ANALYSIS

Rollover of cars and trucks is discussed in Section 22–2.3. A simplified procedure for determining the limit turning speed of a vehicle when curve radius, track width, and center-of-gravity weight are known was presented. Although speed may be predicted at which rollover occurs within 5 to 10% accuracy, the effects of different vehicular design and loading parameters cannot be evaluated.

The tractor-semitrailer combination consists of a tractor and a trailer that is connected to the tractor by the fifth wheel or king pin. The fifth wheel is a plate attached to the tractor. The front end of the trailer rests on the plate and may rotate about the king pin. The fifth wheel allows certain motions to take place between tractor and trailer, the most important one being articulation.

The rollover behavior of the tractor-semitrailer is mostly determined by the geometrical and loading characteristics of the trailer. The load of the trailer may be such that oscillations can occur. Trailers carrying liquids frequently have partitioned tanks to prevent undesirable slushing of the load. In some cases the load is not located midway between the wheels, i.e., more toward one side of the trailer. Some trailers carry loads hanging from the ceiling of the trailer and load swinging may occur. The effects of suspension design on limit turning speed must be considered in certain cases. Super elevation of roadways should always be included in the rollover analysis since it has a significant effect on the limit turning speed.

22–4.1. Fixed Load Rollover. A fixed load is securely located in the trailer. The rollover of a tractor-semitrailer on a flat surface (as compared with rolling off into an embankment) always starts with the trailer. As the trailer rollover motion continues the play in the fifth wheel connection is taken up and the trailer attempts to roll the tractor over. At this instant the total tractor-trailer track width becomes effective in resisting rollover. Prior to this point only the width of the fifth wheel plate and the trailer rear axle is resisting trailer rollover.

The rollover limit of the trailer defined by the inside trailer wheels losing ground contact in terms of the lateral acceleration a_{yT} is determined by

$$a_{yT} = \frac{0.5\, W_T\, t_{\text{rel}} - W_{TS}\,[h_r\, \alpha_T + S_L\,(1 - 0.1\, \alpha_T) \pm h_{TS}\, \alpha_e]}{W_{TS}\,[h_{TS} - (0.1\, h_r + S_L)\, \alpha_T] + W_{UT}\, h_{UT}}; \text{ g-units} \tag{22–57}$$

$$t_{\text{rel}} = \ell_5 \cos\gamma + \left(\frac{\ell_{cg}}{\ell_t}\right)(t_T - \ell_5 \cos\gamma), \text{ ft} \tag{22–58}$$

$$h_r = h_{TS} - \frac{h_5 + p_T}{2}, \text{ ft} \tag{22–59}$$

where:

a_{yT} = limit lateral acceleration, g-units
h_r = distance between roll axis and center-of-gravity, ft (Eq. 22–59)
h_{TS} = trailer center-of-gravity height, ft
h_{UT} = center-of-gravity height of unsprung trailer weight, ft
h_5 = distance between ground and fifth wheel, ft
ℓ_{cg} = horizontal distance from fifth wheel to center-of-gravity of trailer, ft
ℓ_T = horizontal distance from fifth wheel to trailer rear axle, ft
ℓ_5 = width of fifth wheel plate measured transversely, ft
p_T = roll center height of trailer suspension, ft
S_L = transverse distance between longitudinal trailer center line and center-of-gravity of trailer (off-center distance), ft
t_{rel} = relative track width of trailer at trailer center-of-gravity, ft
t_T = trailer track width, ft
W_T = trailer weight, lb
W_{TS} = sprung weight of trailer, lb
W_{UT} = unsprung weight of trailer, lb
α_e = transverse road slope angle or super elevation, radians
α_T = roll angle of sprung weight of trailer, radians
γ = articulation angle between tractor and trailer, deg (Fig. 22–12)

The plus-sign in front of the $h_{TS}\ \alpha_e$-term is used when the road slopes down to the outside of the curve. The negative-sign is used when the road slopes down toward the inside, i.e., a curve favoring higher speeds.

The determination of the roll center height of trailer suspensions using elliptical leaf springs and solid axles is a lengthy and difficult task. The roll center is located between the height of the frame eyes carrying the spring ends and the upper surface of the axle carrying the spring package. For softer springs the roll center is located closer to the axle, for harder springs closer to the frame eyes, i.e., slightly higher.

The articular angle γ and the trailer length ℓ_T determine the approximate radius of the curve. The curve radius r may be determined by

$$r = \frac{57.3\ \ell_T}{\gamma},\ \text{ft} \tag{22–60}$$

where

$$\gamma = \text{articulation angle, deg}$$

The approximate steering wheel angle required by the driver to negotiate the turn is

$$SW = \frac{57.3\, L\, i}{r}, \text{ deg} \qquad (22\text{–}61)$$

where

i = steering gear ratio, d'less
L = tractor wheel base, ft

For example, an articulation angle $\gamma = 4$ deg and $\ell_T = 36$ ft yield a turn radius of $r = 516$ ft. The steering wheel angle for $L = 14$ ft and $i = 28$ is 44 deg.

When the turn radius is known from the road geometry or tire markings, then the articulation angle γ may be determined by Eq. 22–60 and substituted into Eq. 22–58.

The limit speed at which the trailer inside wheels left off the ground may be determined by Eq. 22–10 with a_y obtained by Eq. 22–57 and the radius r measured or determined by Eq. 22–60.

Example 22–5

Determine the limit lateral acceleration and turning speed of a tractor-semitrailer traveling through a turn of radius $r = 390$ ft. Use the data that follow:

$h_{TS} = 7$ ft, $h_5 = 40$ in., $\ell_5 = 40$ in., $p_T = 26$ in., $\ell_{cg} = 16$ ft, $\ell_T = 34$ ft, $t_T = 7.5$ ft, $W_T = 55{,}000$ lb, $W_{TS} = 52{,}000$ lb, $W_{UT} = 3{,}000$ lb, $h_{UT} = 26$ in., $S_L = 0$ (and 1 ft), $\alpha_T = 0$ (and 6 deg), $\alpha_e = 0$ deg, i.e., no super elevation (and 5 deg.).

The articulation angle γ to be used in Eq. 22–58 may be determined by Eq. 22–60 as

$$\gamma = \frac{(57.3)(34)}{390} = 5 \text{ deg.}$$

Substitution of the appropriate values into Eq. 22–58 yields $t_{\text{rel}} = 5.871$ ft. This result indicates that the effective trailer track width at the location of center-of-gravity of the trailer is 5.871 ft and not 7.5 ft, the track width.

Use of Eq. 22–57 yields a limit lateral acceleration $a_{yT} = 0.435$ g. The limit speed may be determined by Eq. 22–10 as

$$V_{\text{limit}} = \sqrt{(0.436)(32.2)(390)} = 74 \text{ ft/sec}$$

or 50 mph.

If the load is not located midway between the wheels, the limit speed for $S_L = 1$ ft becomes with $a_{yT} = 0.292$g 41 mph.

When the trailer roll motion has progressed sufficiently far to attempt to roll the tractor, $t_{\text{rel}} = 7.5$ ft yields a limit speed of 57 mph. The limit speeds associated with a trailer sprung weight roll angle of 6 deg (instead of zero) are 47 mph (instead of 50), 37 mph (41), and 54 mph (57).

Inspection of the results shows that the sprung weight roll angle effect is approximately 12% for a typical roll angle $\alpha_T = 10$ deg.

The effect of the road slope $\alpha_e = 5$ deg can be evaluated by means of Eq. 22–57. A transverse road slope of 5 deg corresponds to a road-slope of $5/57.3 = 0.087$ radians. Upon substituting this value along with the previous data in Eq. 22–57 and using the minus-sign in front of the $h_{TS}\ \alpha_e$-term yields an increased limit speed of 55 mph as compared to 50 mph without super elevation.

22–4.2. Swinging Load Rollover. When the load is hanging from the trailer ceiling and allowed to swing sideways, the limit lateral acceleration a_{yT} may be determined by

$$a_{yT} = \frac{0.5\, W_T\, t_{\text{rel}} - [W_o\, h_{ro} + W_L\, (h_{rL} + \ell)]\ \alpha_T}{(W_{os} + W_L)\, p_T + [W_{os}\, h_{ro} + W_L\, (h_{rL} + \ell)]\ (1 - 0.1\ \alpha_T) + W_{UT}\, h_{UT}}, \quad \text{g-units} \qquad (22\text{–}62)$$

where:

h_{rL} = distance between load attachment point and roll axis, ft

h_{ro} = distance between empty trailer center-of-gravity and roll axis, ft

ℓ = distance between load attachment point and center-of-gravity of swing load, ft

W_L = weight of swing load, ft

W_o = weight of empty trailer, lb

W_{os} = sprung weight of empty trailer, lb

Example 22–6

Determine the limit lateral acceleration for a tractor-semitrailer carrying a swinging load. Use the data of Example 22–5 and those that follow: $h_{rL} = 6$ ft, $h_{ro} = 2$ ft, $\ell = 3$ ft, $W_o = 7{,}000$ lb, $W_L = 45{,}000$ lb, $\alpha_T = 6$ deg.

Substitution of the appropriate data into Eq. 22–62 yields a limit lateral acceleration of 0.219 g or a limit speed of 36 mph. The result indicates that the limit turning speed is significantly reduced for a trailer carrying swinging loads.

22-5. MOTORCYCLE STABILITY

Application of basic dynamics to the motion of a motorcycle yields a number of complicated equations whose discussion is beyond the scope of this book (Ref. 30).

The control of the motorcycle in a turning maneuver may be accomplished by body lean and/or roll stabilization. The stability of the motorcycle itself is the result of the gyro effect of the wheels. The centrifugal force attempts to right the motorcycle, when the motor cycle is leaned into the turn. Stability is improved when the mass moment of inertia about the steering axis is large, while steering axis inclination angle, castor, and center-of-gravity location are of lesser importance.

PART 3

ACCIDENT AVOIDANCE ANALYSIS

Part 3 presents the physical concepts involved in accident avoidance. In a large number of accidents it is important to determine the extent to which a driver could have avoided or mitigated a collision, and furthermore, are the driving skills necessary for accident avoidance within the driver's capability? Fundamentals of passing and driver view field analysis are also presented.

CHAPTER 23

ACCIDENT AVOIDANCE CONCEPTS

Accident avoidance is the attempt by a driver to avoid or mitigate a collision through braking, steering, or both and by acceleration. The accident maneuver may be a braking, turning or lane changing maneuver. Frequently a passing maneuver must be analyzed for accident avoidance considerations. The passing maneuver may be carried out with an essentially constant velocity or an increasing velocity during the passing process.

Automobile-pedestrian and two or multiple vehicle-collisions frequently require a view obstruction analysis in which the view fields of drivers are analyzed and stationary and moving obstructions are considered.

Accident avoidance is significantly affected by driver experience. Since collision avoidance generally involves an emergency situation, driver behavior will vary with accident type and threat. Factors such as age, physical disability, emotional stress, experience and others play an important role for a driver to provide the appropriate avoidance control input. Significant is the integration capability or judgement of the driver to understand the precrash conditions and to initiate the correct accident avoidance measure. Driver judgement is greatly influenced by age, alcohol and drug consumption.

The avoidance of a collision most generally involves the drastic reduction of vehicle speed or redirection of vehicle heading angle. The three driver control inputs are braking, steering and acceleration. The driver control inputs can be applied with the vehicle initially traveling in a straight or curved path. The braking maneuver may involve lockup of all or some wheels. The steering maneuver may involve only turning or complete lane changing with a reversal of steering wheel rotation. Braking and steering may be applied at different times during the accident avoidance maneuver or simultaneously.

Accident avoidance is significantly affected by driver response time and the capability of the driver to recognize a hazard. Since both factors are influenced by alcohol use, more information is presented in the next chapter.

Frequently, driver reaction to an accident threat must be analyzed in terms of time. Although drivers differ in their delay time, an average value based on measured data may be established. Test data showed that drivers between the ages of 25 and 40 produced the following average values (laboratory and road tests) (Ref. 13). The drivers reacted to the brake lights of a lead vehicle in the following way:

Of the drivers tested 10% required less than 0.88 sec, 50% less than 1.04 sec, and 90% less than 1.27 sec. The time was measured from the instant of brake light appearance to the instant of brake pedal movement on the test vehicle. The height difference between accelerator and brake pedal was 3 in. When the height difference is 5 in., the corresponding response time values are 0.89 sec, 1.06 sec, and 1.32 sec, and for zero pedal height difference 0.85 sec, 1.01 sec, and 1.24 sec, respectively.

The time required to produce a certain pedal force is related to brake system design, and in particular brake pedal travel, and is important in poorly adjusted brakes or in the event of a hydraulic brake line failure of a dual circuit brake system.

The test drivers produced pedal forces between 25 to 80 lb resulting in a deceleration of 16 ft/sec^2 as follows: of the drivers tested 10% required less than 0.06 sec, 50% less than 0.13 sec, and 90% less than 0.36 sec.

The total time delay ranges between 0.91 sec to 1.68 sec. An average value of 1.00 sec is used most often. It must be recognized that a difference exists between what a person can do in a laboratory experiment without any accident threat, and what a person will do in a real accident situation.

CHAPTER 24
ALCOHOL EFFECTS ON HUMAN RESPONSE TIME

The alcohol in the blood generally reduces the response time of the operator of a vehicle. The amount of alcohol is measured in terms of percent blood alcohol. The percent blood alcohol level is caused by the amount of alcohol and not so much by the type of drink, e.g. beer or wine. Other factors determining the blood alcohol level are weight of the person, resorption rate, i.e., the transmission of the alcohol into the blood, and the rate of alcohol reduction.

The reduction rate is mostly a function of time and is approximately 0.017% per hour. A typical alcohol reduction curve is illustrated in Fig. 24-1. Female drinkers exhibit a reduction rate which is on the average approximately 15% less than that observed for male drinkers.

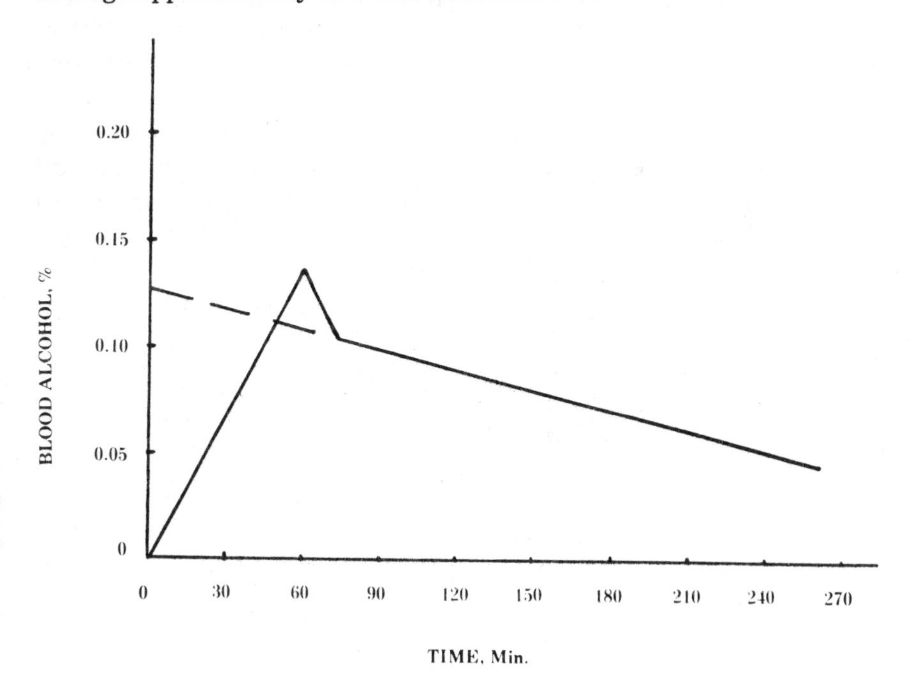

Figure 24-1. Blood Alcohol Reduction

Furthermore, alcohol from beer is reduced at a slightly higher rate than alcohol from hard liquor.

The percent blood alcohol level $(BA)_{ACC}$ at the time of the accident may be determined from the approximate relationship

$$(BA)_{ACC} = (BA)_M + rt, \% \tag{24-1}$$

where

$(BA)_M$ = percent blood alcohol measured at some time t after the accident, %

r = reduction rate %/hour
0.017%/hr for male
0.015%/hr for female

t = time between accident and time blood alcohol was measured, hour

For example, a blood alcohol level of $(BA)_M = 0.08\%$ measured 3 hours after the collision indicates a blood alcohol level $(BA)_{ACC}$ at the time of the accident of

$$(BA)_{ACC} = 0.08 + (0.017)(3) = 0.131\%$$

The corresponding female BA level would be 0.125%.

The effect of blood alcohol in terms of a reduced response time varies greatly. Laboratory tests have shown that an upper and lower bound on response time increase can be determined as shown in Fig. 24–2. The average response time t_a with alcohol in the blood may be determined by

$$t_a = [1 + 1.5\ (BA)_{ACC}](t_{\text{nor}}), \text{ sec} \tag{24-2}$$

where

t_{nor} = normal, i.e., without alcohol in the blood, response time, sec

For example, a $(BA)_{ACC}$ value of 0.131% increases a normal response time of 0.75 sec to (1.196)(0.75) = 0.90 sec.

The test data associated with the development of Eq. 24–2 were collected on a number of subjects in laboratory conditions. Each person knew what the response test consisted of and was mentally prepared for it. In real accident situations the actual response time of intoxicated drivers may increase significantly above that computed by Eq. 24–2. Although the response time may only increase by a small amount, the hazard recognition and judgment time may be largely

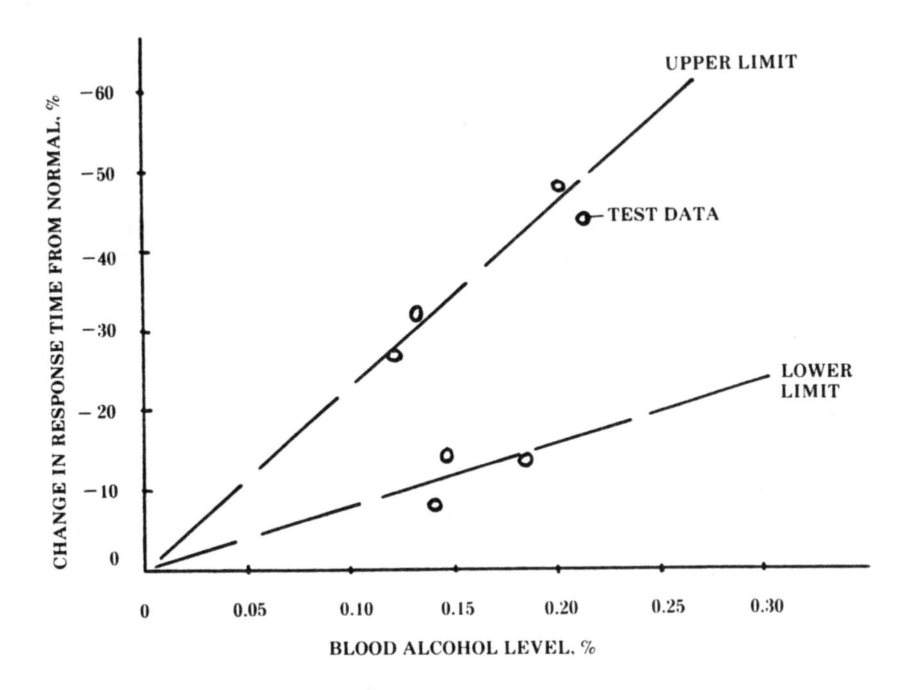

Figure 24–2. Response Time Change vs Blood Alcohol From Laboratory Results

affected. Studies show that the risk of a serious accident is increased significantly with higher blood alcohol levels, as indicated below

BA(%)	*Accident Risk Increase*
0.05	2 times normal
0.08	6
0.11	10
0.15	25
0.17	50

CHAPTER 25

PREDICTION OF ACCIDENT AVOIDANCE CAPACITY

The driver of a vehicle may attempt to avoid an accident by either braking, steering or combined braking and steering. In some cases accelerating the vehicle may result in accident avoidance. Most frequently, drivers will apply the brakes to avoid or mitigate the collision. Accident statistics indicate that approximately 20% of the drivers involved in accidents apply the brakes during the precrash phase (Section 42–2). Only about 9% of the drivers that did have an accident attempted to avoid the collision by steering. Between 6 and 15% of the drivers conducted a combined braking and steering maneuver to avoid the collision. Inspection of the statistical data indicates that as much as two-thirds of the drivers did not provide any accident avoidance control inputs in form of steering and/or braking.

For the proper preparation for trial and detailed questioning of drivers and witnesses before and during trial it is essential to determine the accident avoidance potential that was available to a particular driver and vehicle. The information developed allows the determination of the contribution of the vehicle, driver or environment to accident causation.

25–1. STRAIGHT-LINE BRAKING MANEUVER

The distance required by a vehicle to come to a stop from a given speed may be computed accurately provided the deceleration of the vehicle is known. Since this section addresses the minimum distance required for collision avoidance, i.e., how close to an obstacle located in the roadway can a vehicle come when traveling at a given speed and still come to a complete stop by the use of braking, certain valid constraints are placed upon vehicle deceleration. To achieve minimum distance the driver may lock all wheels to reduce time delays. When traveling on dry roads, no significant differences exist between the peak and sliding friction coefficient of most tires. When braking on wet and slippery road surfaces, the peak and sliding friction values are significantly different. Consequently, the achievement of minimum stopping distances on wet road surfaces requires a careful pedal force modulation to prevent wheel lockup.

For a roadway with a constant coefficient of friction μ between tire and pavement, the stopping distance S_b due to braking may be determined by Eq. 20–9. Since road slope frequently is involved in accident reconstruction, Eq. 20–9 is rewritten to include road slope α (see Section 19–2.7):

$$S_b = \frac{V^2}{2 \times 32.2\ (\mu \pm \sin\alpha)} + t_R V,\ \text{ft} \qquad (25\text{–}1)$$

where

V = vehicle speed at instant when wheels are locked, ft/sec

t_R = delay time between recognition of hazard and full brake force development, sec ($t_R = t_a + t_b/2$)

α = road incline, deg

μ = tire-road friction coefficient, d'less

The plus-sign in front of the sine-term is used for a vehicle traveling uphill, the minus-sign for downhill travel.

In the derivation of Eq. 25–1 retarding forces due to aerodynamic and rolling resistance are neglected. For speeds in excess of 50 mph aerodynamic effects must be included (Section 19–2.5). Tire rolling resistance also increases with speed and must be considered on a case by case basis depending on the tire type and inflation pressures involved (Section 18–3). The delay time t_R assumes different values for different drivers and is strongly connected to driver reaction time. An average value of 1.00 sec is assumed in most accident analyses.

The use of Eq. 25–1 is illustrated by the following example. A vehicle is traveling downhill on a dry concrete road surface on a 6 deg incline at 50 mph. Upon recognizing an obstacle in the roadway, the driver locks all four wheels. What distance is required to stop the vehicle? Accident site investigations showed a tire-road friction coefficient of $\mu = 0.8$.

Substitution of these values into Eq. 25–1 yields

$$S_b = \frac{(50 \times 1.466)^2}{(2)(32.2)(0.8 - 0.1045)} + 1.00\ (50 \times 1.466) = 119.9 + 73 = 192.9\ \text{ft}$$

Inspection of the results indicates that the vehicle travels 119.9 ft with its wheels locked. A distance of 73 ft is traveled during which the driver reacts and before the full braking force is developed.

25-2. LANE CHANGING—STRAIGHT PATH INITIALLY

Many collisions could be prevented if a steering input were provided by the driver as compared with braking only. Lane changing is a maneuver in which the driver provides a steering wheel rotation to one side and then returns the steering wheel to the straight-ahead position.

Although the detailed mathematical treatment of a lane changing vehicle results in complicated equations, the overall performance may be expressed in a simple equation. The lane change schematic is illustrated in Fig. 25–1. The minimum distance between vehicle and obstacle required by a vehicle to accomplish a safe lane change maneuver from a given initial speed is

$$S_{\ell} = 0.45\, V \sqrt{\frac{\ell}{a_y}} + t_R\, V, \text{ ft} \qquad (25\text{–}2)$$

where

a_y = average lateral acceleration, g-units
ℓ = lateral displacement of the vehicle required for obstacle avoidance, ft
V = vehicle speed, ft/sec

The value of the average lateral acceleration used in Eq. 25–2 is the average value produced by the vehicle for the particular accident avoidance maneuver. Indepth investigations of automobile accidents indicate that drivers rarely exceed lateral acceleration values of 0.25 to 0.30 g and thus stay within the side force capability of most tires when operating on wet or dry road surfaces. Review of research data shows lower values of limit lateral acceleration levels of approximately 0.6 g for today's automobiles, the average to be near 0.7 g (Ref. 23).

The use of Eq. 25–2 is illustrated by the following example. A vehicle is traveling at 50 mph when approaching a parked vehicle in the driver lane. For $\ell = 10$ ft and a normal lane change maneuver with $a_y = 0.2$ g, what distance between point of lane change initiation and parked

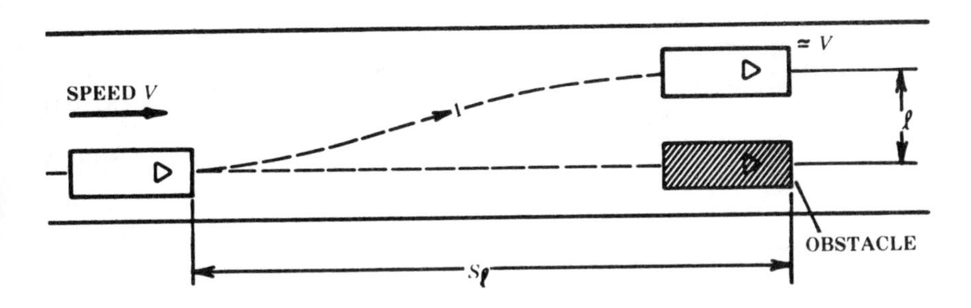

Figure 25–1. Lane Changing Accident Avoidance Maneuver on Straight Roadway

vehicle is required for a safe lane change maneuver. Substitution of the data into Eq. 25–2 yields

$$S_\ell = 0.45\ (50 \times 1.466) \sqrt{\frac{10}{0.2}} + 1.00\ (50 \times 1.466) = 233 + 73 = 306 \text{ ft.}$$

The result indicates that the driver of a vehicle traveling at 50 mph and attempting to avoid a 10-ft wide obstacle with a lane change maneuver of severity $a_y = 0.2g$ must recognize the obstacle 306 ft prior to the point where the obstacle is located. The result furthermore indicates that 73 ft are required to recognize the obstacle, react and to develop the initial steering wheel rotation.

When a lane change accident avoidance maneuver is attempted, it is important to determine the steering wheel angle required for such a maneuver. If the required angle is large, then the driver may not be able to turn the steering wheel within the time available. The steering wheel angle required may be determined by Eq. 22–36. The turn radius R required in Eq. 22–36 may be determined by Eq. 16–26, i.e., $R = V^2/a_y$. The initial turning angle of the steering wheel has to be provided within the time available for recognizing the hazard and full side force production of the tires. Consequently, a typical driver has 1.00 sec available for the steering wheel rotation; a slow responding driver has correspondingly less. If one assumes a driver reaction time of 0.3 sec during which no driver action occurs, then a time of 0.70 sec is available for producing the required steering wheel rotation.

For a steering wheel angle SW the steering wheel angular velocity RSW is

$$RSW = \frac{SW}{t}, \text{ deg/sec} \tag{25–3}$$

For example, if $SW = 100$ deg is required to produce the desired turn, then the steering wheel angle rate is $RSW = 100/0.70 = 143$ deg/sec. This value has to be compared with the steering wheel angle rate the driver can produce. If this information is not available, the results must be compared with the steering rates typical drivers are capable of producing. Some research data indicate that the upper limit of highly skilled drivers is approximately 500 deg/sec (Ref. 24).

25-3. TURNING MANEUVER – STRAIGHT PATH INITIALLY

The accident avoidance schematic is illustrated in Fig. 25–2. The maneuver involves a vehicle attempting to avoid a collision by a single steering input only, i.e., the vehicle is turning to one side only.

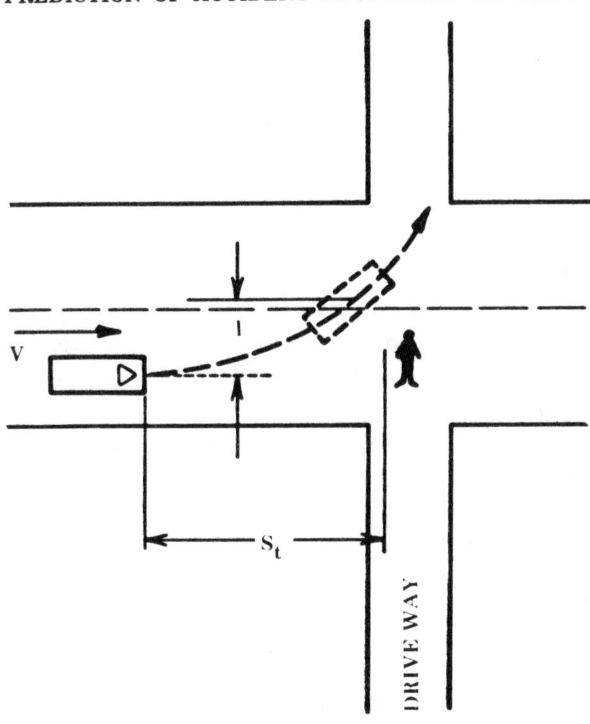

Figure 25-2. Turning Accident Avoidance on Straight Roadway

The basic equations presented in Section 25-2 may be modified for the turning maneuver. The minimum distance between vehicle and obstacle required by a vehicle to accomplish a safe turning maneuver from a given initial speed is

$$S_t = 0.225\ V \sqrt{\frac{\ell}{a_y}} + t_R\ V, \text{ ft} \qquad (25\text{–}4)$$

The units and definition of the parameters in Eq. 25-4 remain unchanged from those of the previous paragraph.

25-4. BRAKING OR STEERING TO AVOID A COLLISION

A driver is often faced with the decision of either braking or steering to avoid a collision. Prior to applying the brakes or to turning the steering wheel, the driver must judge whether a steering-only or braking-only maneuver will have a higher probability of leading to a successful accident avoidance maneuver. The equations presented in Sections 25-1 and 25-2 may be used to develop the information required to decide for what precrash conditions braking or steering would be a more desirable driver control input for collision avoidance.

Eq. 25–1 determines the distance required to avoid a collision when only the brakes are applied. Eq. 25–2 determines the distance required to avoid a collision when a lane change maneuver without braking is carried out. If the precrash conditions are such that both Eq. 25–1 and 25–2 predict the same accident avoidance distance, then braking and lane changing have the same collision avoidance potential. The vehicle speed existing in the case when both distances predicted by Eq. 25–1 and 25–2 are identical may be designated as critical speed. The critical speed is illustrated in Fig. 25–3. The curved line is a graphical representation of Eq. 25–1 and represents the distances required in braking maneuvers as a function of speed. Inspection of this curve indicates that stopping distance increases rapidly as speed increases. The straight line is a graphical representation of Eq. 25–2 and represents the lane change distance required for accident avoidance of a given obstacle with width ℓ. At the point where the braking and lane change curves intersect, both distances are identical for a single value of vehicle speed. This value of speed is designated as critical speed. A closer inspection of Fig. 25–3 indicates that for speeds below the critical speed a braking maneuver requires shorter distances than a lane changing maneuver. For speeds greater than the critical value a lane change maneuver requires less distance for accident avoidance. This is in agreement with the general observation that steering maneuvers have a higher probability of accident avoidance at high speeds than braking maneuvers. For low speeds braking maneuvers tend to be more successful for collision avoidance.

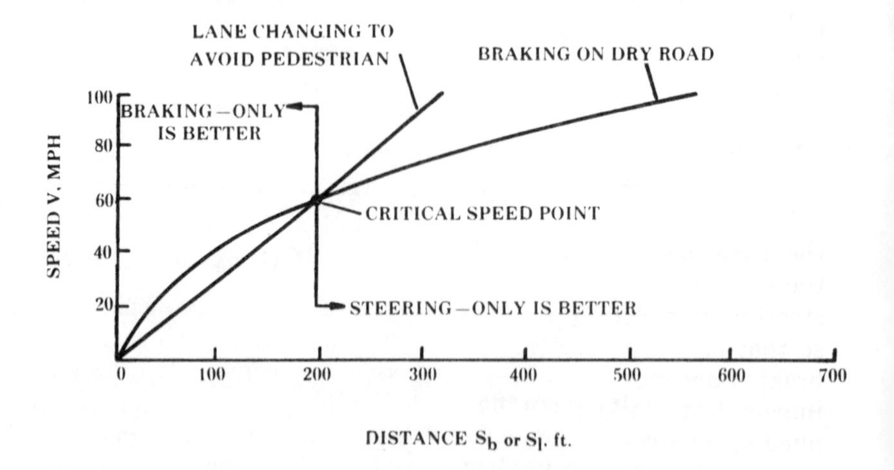

Figure 25–3. Criterion for Steering or Braking Accident Avoidance Maneuver

The critical speed may be determined analytically by equating Eqs. 25–1 and 25–2 and solving for speed V. The result is

$$V_{\text{critical}} = 29\ (\mu \pm \sin\alpha)\ \sqrt{\frac{\ell}{a_y}},\ \text{ft/sec} \qquad (25\text{–}5)$$

Eq. 25–5 determines the critical speed for a given tire-road friction coefficient μ and hence locked-wheel braking maneuver, road incline α, and a certain obstacle width ℓ and lane change severity a_y. The plus-sign is used for a vehicle traveling uphill, the minus-sign for downhill travel.

Assume the following accident facts exist: $\mu = 0.7, \alpha = 4$ deg downhill slope, $\ell = 5$ ft, $a_y = 0.2$ g, actual vehicle speed prior to collision is 40 mph. Determine if a steering or braking maneuver would have higher accident avoidance potential. Substitution of the appropriate data into Eq. 25–5 yields a critical speed of 62.3 mph. The results indicate that for speeds less than 62.3 mph a braking application would have a higher probability of collision avoidance than a steering maneuver. Since the actual speed is less than the critical a braking maneuver should be attempted. If the vehicle is traveling in excess of 62.3 mph, say 70 mph, then a steering wheel control input by the driver and the following lane change maneuver has a higher probability of collision avoidance. The reasons for a steering maneuver to be more successful at high speeds are related to the characteristics of Eq. 25–1 and 25–2. Eq. 25–2 is a linear equation with speed. A linear relationship means that a given increase in speed results in a proportional increase in required accident avoidance distance. Eq. 25–1 is a nonlinear equation indicated by the V^2-term. The distance increases rapidly as speed increases. For example, doubling the speed results in four times the distance.

25-5. BRAKING AND LANE CHANGING—STRAIGHT PATH INITIALLY

In a combined braking and steering accident avoidance maneuver the driver has to provide both braking and steering control inputs. In the case of large pedal forces and resulting front wheel lockup, the steering capability of the vehicle is lost. If the brakes are modulated so that no wheel lockup occurs, the driver may attempt a combined braking and steering maneuver to avoid a collision or to mitigate the impact. If it is assumed that both steering and braking inputs are applied at the same instant, then Eq. 25–2 may be modified to yield the required lane change distance

$$S_{\ell,b} = 0.45\ V\ \sqrt{\frac{\ell}{a_y}} + t_R\ V - 2E\mu\left(\frac{\ell}{a_y}\right),\ \text{ft} \qquad (25\text{–}6)$$

where

$$E = \text{braking efficiency, d'less}$$

The braking efficiency E expresses the extent to which a given tire-road friction coefficient is used for vehicle retardation (see Section 20–4 and 20–7).

An E-value of unity would indicate complete use of the available road friction. Braking efficiency values are influenced by driver skill. For accident analysis purposes an E-value between 0.4 and 0.5 may be assumed for standard braking systems, especially in view of the fact that combined braking and steering maneuvers require skillful pedal force modulation in order to avoid wheel lockup. Tests conducted under controlled conditions indicate braking efficiency of 80% of modern automobiles with standard brakes when driver effects were eliminated. Four-wheel antiskid systems may exhibit large values of braking efficiency ranging as high as 0.95 (Section 7–4).

The use of Eq. 25–6 is illustrated next. A vehicle traveling initially at 50 mph and attempting to avoid a 10-ft obstacle by lane changing at 0.2 g and braking at $E = 0.5$ on a dry road surface ($\mu = 0.8$) requires a lane change distance of

$$S_{\ell,b} = 0.45(50 \times 1.466)\sqrt{\frac{10}{0.2}} + 1.00\ (50 \times 1.466) - 2 \times 0.5 \times 0.8 \left(\frac{10}{0.2}\right)$$

$$= 233 + 73 + 40 = 266 \text{ ft}$$

Inspection of the results indicates that the braking action reduces the safe lane change distance by 40 ft from that of the nonbraking distance.

25-6. BRAKING AND TURNING—STRAIGHT PATH INITIALLY

The required distance is determined by

$$S_{t,b} = 0.225\ V\sqrt{\frac{\ell}{a_y}} + t_R\ V - E\mu\left(\frac{\ell}{a_y}\right), \text{ ft} \tag{25–7}$$

Eq. 22–7 predicts one half of the distance computed by Eq. 25–6 when $t_R = 0$.

25-7. BRAKING IN A TURN

When the initial path is a curve, the accident avoidance distance may be computed from equations developed in previous sections. The lateral acceleration for accident avoidance is decreased due to the demand placed upon the traction side force by the initial turning maneuver.

The lateral acceleration a_y used in previous equations can be modified to include the curved path effect by

$$a_y\text{, modified} = a_y\left(1 - \frac{\ell}{R}\right)\text{, } g\text{-units} \qquad (25\text{–}8)$$

where

R = turning radius, ft

CHAPTER 26

PASSING MANEUVER

A passing maneuver consists of three phases: (1) the lane change, (2) the passing, and (3) the lane change back to the original lane.

A passing maneuver may involve no velocity change of the passing vehicle, or an increase of velocity of the passing vehicle. In the first case the passing vehicle approaches the slower vehicle at a speed that is higher than that of the vehicle being passed. This type of passing maneuver requires sufficient view toward oncoming traffic. In the second passing maneuver the passing vehicle travels behind the slow vehicle at the speed of the slow vehicle. The lane change, passing, a return-lane change are carried out with increasing velocity.

26-1. CONSTANT VELOCITY PASSING

The passing maneuver requires a minimum distance in which the lane change, passing, and return lane change have to be accomplished. The passing maneuver distance S_p may be determined by

$$S_p = V_1 \left[\left(\frac{L_1 + L_2 + L_s}{V_1 - V_2} \right) + 0.9 \sqrt{\frac{\ell}{a_y}} \right], \text{ ft} \qquad (26\text{–}1)$$

where

a_y = average lateral acceleration of lane change and return lane change, g-units

L_1 = length of passing vehicle, ft

L_2 = length of vehicle being passed, ft

L_s = safety distance between vehicles before and after passing, ft

ℓ = lateral distance, determined by summation of one-half width of both cars and lateral safety distance, ft

V_1 = velocity of passing vehicle, ft/sec

V_2 = velocity of vehicle being passed, ft/sec

The time required for the passing maneuver is

$$t_p = \frac{S_p}{V_1}, \text{ sec} \qquad (26\text{–}2)$$

Example 26–1

Determine the distance and time required for a passing maneuver by the use of the following data: $V_1 = 60$ mph, $V_2 = 50$ mph, $L_1 = 17$ ft, $L_2 = 60$ ft (truck-trailer combination), $L_s = 2 \times 20 = 40$ ft, $\ell = 12$ ft, $a_y = 0.2\,g$. Substitution of the data into Eq. 26–2 yields with $V_1 =$ 87.9 ft/sec and $V_2 =$ 73.3 ft/sec a passing maneuver distance $S_p =$ 1317 ft. The time required for the passing maneuver is 14.98 sec.

26–2. PASSING WITH ACCELERATION

The passing maneuver distance may be determined by a piecewise calculation of the lane change, passing, and return lane change distance of the maneuver. With the acceleration of the passing vehicle known, the velocity at the end of each phase may be determined and the distances for each phase be computed. Before commencement of passing both vehicles travel at the same speed.

The distance of the first change may be determined by

$$S_{\ell 1} = 0.45 \sqrt{\frac{\ell}{a_y}} \left(\frac{V_o + V_1}{2}\right), \text{ ft} \qquad (26\text{–}3)$$

where

$V_0 =$ speed of passing vehicle and vehicle being passed before passing maneuver commences, ft/sec

$V_1 =$ speed of passing vehicle when first lane change is completed and passing commences, ft/sec

The speed V_1 is computed by

$$V_1 = 0.45 \left(\sqrt{\frac{\ell}{a_y}}\right) a + V_0, \text{ ft/sec} \qquad (26\text{–}4)$$

where

$$a = \text{vehicle acceleration, ft/sec}^2$$

The distance $S_{\ell 2}$ required for the passing phase is

$$S_{\ell 2} = \left(\frac{L_1 + L_2 + L_s}{\frac{V_1 + V_2}{2} - V_0}\right)\left(\frac{V_1 + V_2}{2}\right), \text{ ft} \qquad (26\text{–}5)$$

where

$V_2 =$ speed of passing vehicle when passing phase is complete, ft/sec

The speed V_2 is computed by

$$V_2 = \sqrt{V_1^2 + 2a\,S_{\ell 2}}, \text{ ft/sec} \qquad (26\text{–}6)$$

The analysis of the passing phase, i.e., Eqs. 26–5 and 26–6 requires a trial and error solution. The distance $S_{\ell 3}$ required for the return lane change is

$$S_{\ell 3} = \left(0.45\sqrt{\frac{\ell}{a_y}}\right)\left(\frac{V_2 + V_3}{2}\right), \text{ ft} \qquad (26\text{–}7)$$

where

V_3 = speed of passing vehicle at completion of return lane change, ft/sec

The speed V_3 is computed by

$$V_3 = 0.45\left(\sqrt{\frac{\ell}{a_y}}\right)a + V_2, \text{ ft/sec} \qquad (26\text{–}8)$$

Example 26–2

Determine the passing maneuver distance for the following data: $V_0 = 20$ mph, $L_1 = 17$ ft, $L_2 = 60$ ft, $L_s = 40$ ft, $a = 3$ ft/sec^2, $\ell = 12$ ft, $a_y = 0.2g$. The speed at the end of the first lane change with 20 mph = 29.3 ft/sec is (Eq. 26–4):

$$V_1 = 0.45\left(\sqrt{\frac{12}{0.2}}\right)3 + 29.3 = 39.8 \text{ ft/sec}$$

The distance of the first lane change is (Eq. 26–3)

$$S_{\ell 1} = 0.45\sqrt{\frac{12}{0.2}}\left(\frac{29.3 + 39.8}{2}\right) = 120.4 \text{ ft}$$

The distance required for the passing phase is determined by initially assuming a value for V_2 in Eq. 26–5 and then checking it by use of Eq. 26–6.

A first value of $V_2 = 65$ ft/sec is assumed and Eq. 26–5 yields

$$S_{\ell 2} = \left(\frac{117}{\frac{39.8 + 65}{2} - 29.3}\right)\left(\frac{39.8 + 65}{2}\right) = 265 \text{ ft}$$

The velocity V_2 is computed by Eq. 26–6 as

$$V_2 = \sqrt{(39.8)^2 + (2)(3)(265)} = 56.3 \text{ ft/sec}$$

The assumed value of 65 ft/sec is greater than the computed one (56.3 ft/sec^2). A new value of $V_2 = 58$ ft/sec is assumed. The use of Eq. 26–6 yields a velocity $V_2 = 57.8$ ft/sec.

The assumed and computed values of V_2 are approximately equal, and consequently, $S_{\ell 2} = 291$ ft may be determined by Eq. 26–5. The distance for the return lane change is determined by Eq. 26–7. The velocity V_3 at the completion of the return lane change maneuver is (Eq. 26–8),

$$V_3 = \left(0.45\sqrt{\frac{12}{0.2}}\right) 3 + 58 = 68.5 \text{ ft/sec}$$

Consequently, the return lane change distance is (Eq. 26–7)

$$S_{\ell 3} = \left(0.45\sqrt{\frac{12}{0.2}}\right)\left(\frac{58 + 68.5}{2}\right) = 220 \text{ ft}$$

The time required for the passing maneuver may be determined by an application of Eq. 16–9 to each phase. For example, the time Δt required for the passing phase is

$$\Delta t = \frac{2S}{V_t + V_0} = \frac{(2)(291)}{(54 + 58)} = 5.2 \text{ sec}$$

The total time required for the maneuver is 12.2 sec. The total distance is $S_{\ell 1} + S_{\ell 2} + S_{\ell 3} = 631$ ft.

CHAPTER 27
DRIVER VIEW FIELD ANALYSIS

The accident avoidance analysis frequently requires the determination of time at which a vehicle becomes first visible to the other driver. In the view analysis the effects of moving and stationary obstructions are examined. The geometry of the obstruction has to be known, such as trees, bushes, buildings, signs, hills, or other vehicles. Also important but not considered here are view obstructions caused by vehicle design (A-posts, hood shape), by lack of maintenance (broken or soiled windshield), or by sun glare.

27-1. CONSTANT VELOCITY CASE

A typical intersection with a corner building is illustrated in Fig. 27-1. Vehicle 1 and 2 are approaching the intersection at constant velocity V_1 and V_2, respectively. If the time of impact is designated as zero time, the time t_b before impact at which both vehicles first entered into the view field, i.e., became visible to each other (Fig. 27-2 with $\alpha = 0$) may be determined by

$$t_b = \frac{L_2}{V_1} + \frac{L_1}{V_2}, \text{ sec} \tag{27-1}$$

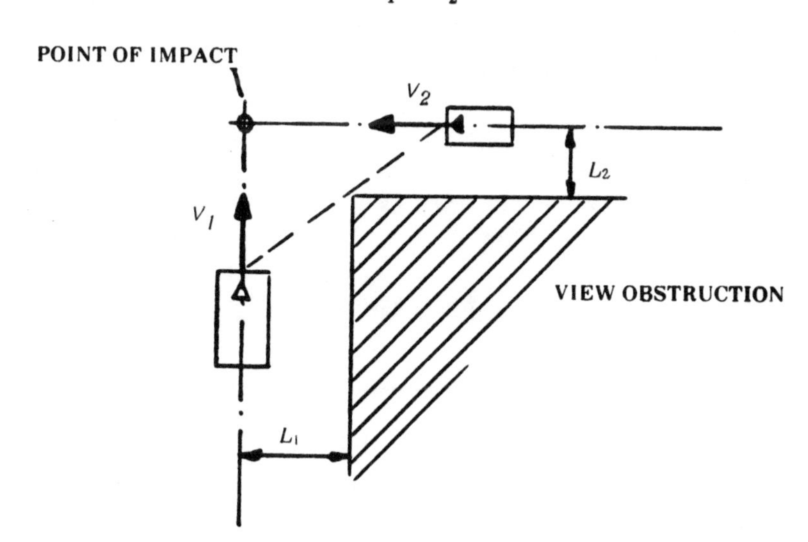

Figure 27-1. View Field Right Angle Travel

where

L_1 = perpendicular distance of point of impact from building (Fig. 27–1), ft

L_2 = perpendicular distance of point of impact from building (Fig. 27–1), ft

V_1 = velocity of vehicle 1, ft/sec

V_2 = velocity of vehicle 2, ft/sec

If the vehicles are not traveling at a right angle to each other as illustrated in Fig. 27–2, the time t_b may be determined by

$$t_b = \frac{L_2}{V_1 \cos\alpha} + \frac{L_2 \tan\alpha}{V_2} + \frac{L_1}{V_2}, \text{ sec} \qquad (27\text{–}2)$$

where angle α, deg is identified in Fig. 27–2.

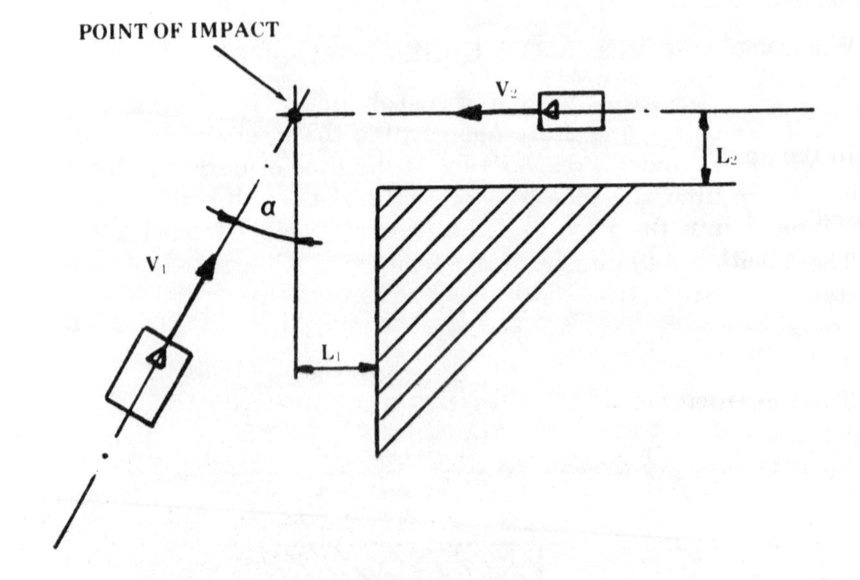

Figure 27–2. View Field Oblique Angle Travel

Example 27–1

Determine the time at which two vehicles enter their view field by the use of the following data: $L_1 = 12$ ft, $L_2 = 40$ ft, $\alpha = 45$ deg, $V_1 = 40$ mph, $V_2 = 25$ mph.

Substitution of the appropriate data into Eq. 27–2 yields with $V_1 =$ 58.6 ft/sec and $V_2 = 36.6$/sec

$$t_b = \frac{40}{(58.6)\cos 45} + \frac{(40)\tan 45}{(36.6)} + \frac{12}{36.6}$$
$$= 2.385 \text{ sec}$$

The result indicates that both vehicle drivers could see each other's vehicle 2.385 sec prior to arriving at the point of impact.

If the vehicles were traveling at a right angle to each other, i.e., $\alpha = 0$, then the view time would be $t_b = 1.01$ sec. The same result can be obtained by use of Eq. 27–1. The time is shorter since vehicle no. 1 is now traveling parallel and closer to the building, i.e., it is "hiding" longer.

27–2. DECREASING VELOCITY CASE

When one or both vehicles are braking prior to the collision, the skid marks, brake system response time, and driver reaction time have to be considered in the view field analysis.

In the analysis that follows vehicle no. 1 is assumed to be decelerating with its wheels locked while vehicle no. 2 travels at a constant speed.

The following data identify the required parameters: $s_1 =$ skidding distance of vehicle no. 1, $a_1 =$ sliding deceleration of vehicle no. 1, $V_{11} =$ velocity of vehicle no. 1 immediately before impact, $V_1 =$ velocity of vehicle no. 1 at instant driver no. 1 recognizes the hazard.

The time required to decelerate the vehicle from V_1 to V_{11} may be determined Eq. 16–17 (if V_1 is known), or Eq. 16–16 (if V_{11} is known). If V_{11} is known, Eq. 16–16 yields

$$t_{\text{slide}} = -\frac{V_{11}}{a_1} + \sqrt{\left(\frac{V_{11}}{a_1}\right)^2 + \frac{2S_1}{a_1}}, \text{ sec} \qquad (27\text{–}3)$$

where

$a_1 =$ deceleration of vehicle 1, ft/sec²
$V_{11} =$ impact speed of vehicle no. 1, ft/sec
$s_1 =$ sliding distance of vehicle no. 1, ft

The velocity at initiation of sliding may be determined by Eq. 16–19, i.e.,

$$V_{1,\text{begin}} = \sqrt{V_{11}^2 + 2a_1s_1}, \text{ ft/sec} \qquad (27\text{–}4)$$

The velocity at the initiation of braking, i.e., the deceleration begins to rise from zero, may be determined by

$$V_1 = V_{1,\text{begin}} + \left(\frac{a_1}{2}\right) t_b, \text{ ft/sec} \quad (27\text{–}5)$$

where

t_b = deceleration buildup time, sec

The deceleration buildup time may be determined by Eq. 20–10. Rapid brake application from moderate speeds rarely exceeds 0.2 sec.

The reaction time of driver no. 1 t_{R1} marks the time interval during which the driver recognized the hazard and initiated the control response (braking). The total time elapsed between hazard recognition and impact is

$$t_t = t_{\text{slide}} + t_b + t_{R1}, \text{ sec} \quad (27\text{–}6)$$

During this total time (t_t) vehicle no. 2 was traveling at a constant velocity V_2. At the instant driver no. 1 recognized the hazard, vehicle no. 2 was $s_2 = V_2 \, t_t$ (ft) from the point of impact. The total distance traveled by vehicle no. 1 is $s_{\text{slide}} + s_b + s_R$.

The distance traveled during the deceleration buildup is

$$s_b = V_1 \, t_b - \left(\frac{a_1}{2}\right) t_b^2, \text{ ft} \quad (27\text{–}7)$$

The distance traveled during the reaction time of driver no. 1 is

$$S_{R1} = V_1 \, t_{R1}, \text{ ft} \quad (27\text{–}8)$$

Example 27–2

Develop the view field analysis for an intersection with $L_1 = 12$ ft, $L_2 = 80$ ft, $\alpha = 45°$. Use the vehicle and accident data that follow: $V_{11} = 25$ mph, $s_1 = 90$ ft, $a_1 = 26$ ft/sec^2 (corresponds to a sliding friction coefficient of about 0.8), $t_b = 0.2$ sec, $t_{R1} = 0.6$ sec, $V_2 = 65$ mph (constant).

The total time traveled by vehicle no. 1 from hazard recognition to impact must be determined first.

Eq. 27–3 yields with $V_{11} = 25$ mph $= 36.7$ ft/sec $t_{\text{slide}} = 1.57$ sec. The total time is $1.57 + 0.2 + 0.6 = 2.37$ sec. During this time vehicle no. 2 traveled $2.37 \times 95.29 = 225.8$ ft as illustrated in Fig. 27–3. The distance (in addition to 90 ft sliding) traveled by vehicle no. 1 is determined by Eq. 27–7 and Eq. 27–8. The velocity V_1 is determined by Eq. 27–5 with Eq. 27–4.

Consequently,
Eq. 27–4 yields $V_{1,\text{begin}} = 77.6$ ft/sec (53 mph)
Eq. 27–5 yields $V_1 = 80.2$ ft/sec (54.7 mph)
Eq. 27–6 yields $s_b = 15.86$ ft
Eq. 27–7 yields $S_{R1} = 48.12$ ft

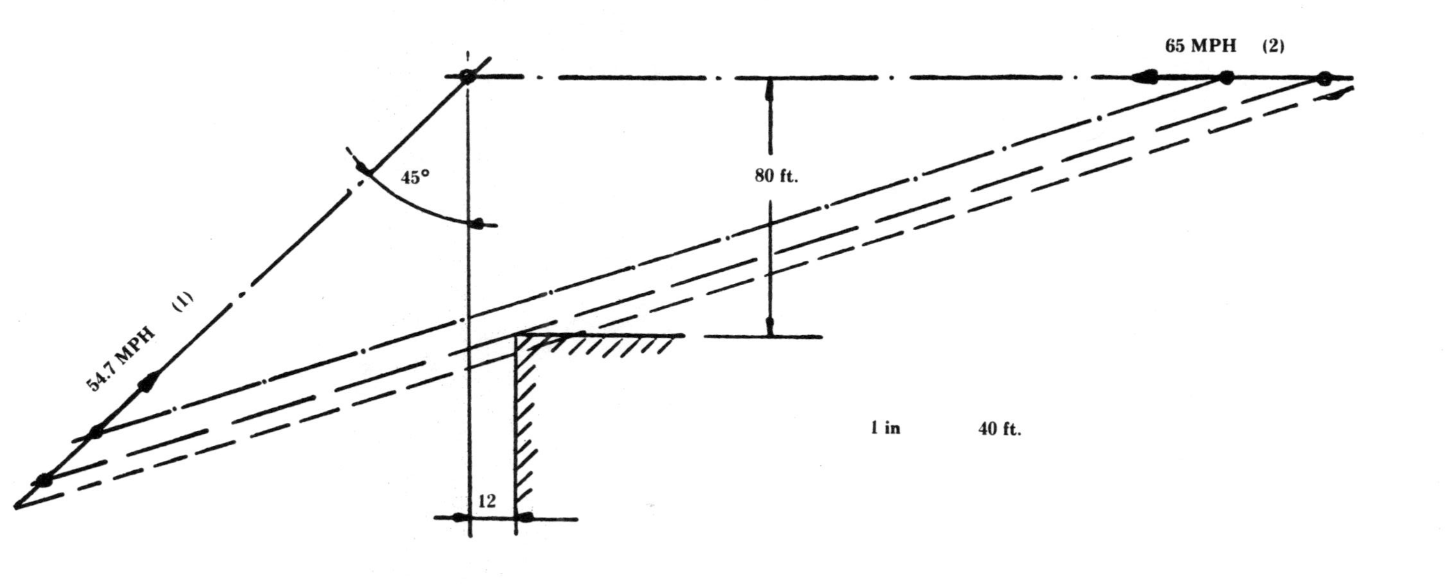

Figure 27-3. View Analysis One Vehicle Braking

Hence, the total travel of vehicle no. 1 is 153.98 ft. Inspection of Fig. 27–3 indicates that driver no. 1 recognized vehicle no. 2 a short period after it became visible. The earliest time vehicle no. 2 became visible can be determined by trial and error using the geometrical information of the diagram.

Assume a first value of additional time, say 0.5 sec. Vehicle no. 1 was located an additional 40.1 ft further back, vehicle no. 2 47.6 ft as shown in Fig. 27–3 by the dotted line. Inspection indicates obstruction still exists. After several trials an additional time of 0.3 sec is found. Consequently, the total view time for this case is 2.67 sec and vehicle no. 1 was located $153.9 + 0.3 \times 80.2 = 177.96$ ft, vehicle no. 2 $225.8 + 0.3 \times 95.29 = 254.38$ ft from the point of impact.

PART 4

COLLISION ANALYSIS

Part 4 presents the concepts associated with collision analysis. The physical laws describing vehicle motions, tire force production, and vibrations remain valid for collision analysis. Important physical relationships analyzing vehicle-to-vehicle and fixed object impacts are presented. Approximate relationships developed from crush deformation for determining vehicle impact speed are included. Occupant kinematics and the effects of vehicle design on collision performance are reviewed.

CHAPTER 28
IMPACT ANALYSIS

The objective of impact analysis is the computation of the velocities of the colliding vehicles immediately before and/or after impact.

28–1. IMPACT FUNDAMENTALS

When two bodies collide the process is called impact. The impact is the transmission of force from one body to another within a very short interval of time. During this time interval the colliding bodies experience an elastic and/or plastic deformation. Collision modes may be divided according to the type of impact such as headon, right angle or oblique collision. For a straight central impact the impact force goes through the center of gravity without causing postcrash vehicle rotation.

The forces transmitted between the two colliding bodies are equal and opposite. The impact force may be determined by Eq. 17–1 with the definition of acceleration equal to velocity ΔV divided by time change Δt (Eq. 16–2)

$$F = m\left(\frac{\Delta V}{\Delta t}\right), \text{ lb} \qquad (28\text{–}1)$$

where

$$m = \text{mass}, \frac{\text{lb} \cdot \text{sec}^2}{\text{ft}}$$

The mass may be computed by Eq. 17–2,

$$m = W/g, \frac{\text{lb sec}}{\text{ft}}$$

Eq. 28–1 may be rewritten to reveal important impact concepts, as

$$F\Delta t = mV \qquad (28\text{–}2)$$

The left hand side of Eq. 28–2 is called impulse. It represents the thrust or force input F over the (short) time interval Δt. The right hand side of Eq. 28–2 represents the momentum. The total momentum for both bodies is conserved during the impact phase. In other words, the momentum of all bodies before impact equals the momentum of all bodies after impact.

The impulse I of a body of Eq. 28–2 may be expressed as

$$I = m(V_1 - V_2), \text{ lb} \cdot \text{sec} \quad (28\text{–}3)$$

where

V_1 = velocity before impact, ft/sec

V_2 = velocity after impact, ft/sec

The impact and momentum equation are not valid when the impact occurs over an extended time interval as in the case of a vehicle sliding alongside a bus.

28–2. STRAIGHT CENTRAL IMPACT

For the straight central impact of two bodies of mass m_1 and m_2 the conservation of momentum yields with Eq. 28–3 ($I_{\text{before}} = I_{\text{after}}$)

$$m_1V_{11} + m_2V_{21} = m_1V_{12} + m_2V_{22}, \text{ lb} \cdot \text{sec} \quad (28\text{–}4)$$

In Eq. 28–4 the first subscript designates the vehicle (or body), the second before (1) or after (2) impact. For example, V_{12} is the velocity of body 1 identified by (1) immediately after impact identified by (2).

During the deformation phase of the collision the velocities of the colliding bodies will change so that at maximum deformation both bodies have the same velocity. Since momentum is conserved, this velocity may be determined by Eq. 28–4 as

$$V = \frac{m_1V_{11} + m_2V_{21}}{m_1 + m_2}, \text{ ft/sec} \quad (28\text{–}5)$$

The impulse during the deformation period is

$$I_{\text{def}} = m_1(V_{11} - V) = m_2(V - V_{21}), \text{ lb} \cdot \text{sec} \quad (28\text{–}6)$$

If the deformation is partially or completely elastic, a period of restitution follows in which the bodies will either return to their original shape (elastic deformation) or will remain somewhat permanently deformed. The restitution depends primarily upon the materials and geometries of the colliding bodies as well as impact speed. The impulse during the period of restitution is

$$I_{\text{res}} = m_1(V - V_{12}) = m_2(V_{22} - V), \text{ lb} \cdot \text{sec} \quad (28\text{–}7)$$

The ratio of I_{res} to I_{def} is called the coefficient of restitution e,

$$e = \frac{I_{\text{res}}}{I_{\text{def}}}, \text{ d'less} \quad (28\text{–}8)$$

Eq. 28–6 and 28–7 in connection with Eq. 28–8 may be used to derive a more useful equation for the coefficient of restitution as

$$e = \frac{V_{22} - V_{12}}{V_{11} - V_{21}}, \text{ d'less} \qquad (28\text{–}9)$$

Eq. 28–9 indicates that the ratio of the difference of velocity of body 2 and 1 after impact to the difference of velocity of body 1 and 2 before impact equals the coefficient of restitution.

In the case of an elastic impact $e = 1.0$. For a plastic impact $e = 0$ resulting in $V_{12} = V_{22} = V$, i.e., both bodies remain in contact and have a common velocity V after impact. In real accident situations vehicles generally separate after impact even if the impact was completely plastic. The coefficient of restitution may be determined from an evaluation of vehicle crash data in which velocities are measured. A value $e = 0.2$ may be assumed for passenger cars and impact speeds of 25 mph or less. For higher impact speeds the coefficient of restitution may easily assume a value of zero, i.e., that associated with plastic deformation. Elastic deformation ($e = 1.0$) may be assumed at low impact speeds with damage free bumpers, or tire-to-vehicle contact.

In a particular case the coefficient of restitution was determined from crash tests in which vehicle speeds were recorded electronically. The tests involved an Audi 50 impacting an Audi 100 headon. The Audi 50 traveled 37.5 mph prior to impact and bounced back at 5.9 mph. The Audi 100 traveled 18.8 mph before and 0.9 mph after impact, both in the same direction. Substitution of the velocity values into Eq. 28–9 yields $e = 0.088$. The test weights were 2886 lb and 1776 lb for the Audi 100 and 50, respectively.

In a straight central impact such as a headon or a rearend collision the coefficient of restitution must be known to compute the speeds of both vehicles before impact. If one speed prior to impact is known from witness statement or other information, the other speed may be computed by Eq. 28–4 without the use of the coefficient of restitution.

When one of the bodies is stationary prior to impact, Eq. 28–4 reduces to, e.g., with $V_{21} = 0$:

$$m_1 V_{11} = m_1 V_{12} + m_2 V_{22} \qquad (28\text{–}10)$$

When one of the bodies is a fixed object, i.e., its mass may be considered infinite, then e.g., with $m_2 = \infty$ and $V_{21} = 0$ one obtains $V_{22} = V = 0$, i.e., the impacting body has no velocity after impact.

The difference in velocities of the bodies before and after the collision indicates the change in kinetic energy into thermal energy, strain or deformation energy, and creation of sound. This change in kinetic energy may be determined by

$$\Delta KE = \left(\frac{m_1}{2}\right)(V_{11}^2 - V_{12}^2) - \left(\frac{m_2}{2}\right)(V_{21}^2 - V_{22}^2), \text{ ft} \cdot \text{lb} \tag{28-11}$$

Eq. 28–11 does not indicate how the energy is distributed to both bodies or vehicles.

Example 28–1

Determine the velocities after impact of two bodies colliding headon by the use of the following data: $W_1 = 3000$ lb, $W_2 = 1800$ lb, $V_{11} = 25$ mph, $V_{21} = -35$ mph, $e = 0.2$. It should be noted that the velocity of a vehicle traveling in the opposite direction receives a minus sign. Compute the "loss" in kinetic energy. The momentum equation alone is not sufficient. The relationship containing the coefficient of restitution must also be used. The solution requires the computation of V_{11} and V_{21}. Thus Eqs. 28–4 and 28–9 may be used giving two equations and two unknowns. Assume the velocity direction of vehicle no. 1 positive, that of vehicle no. 2 is negative. Substitution of the data into Eq. 28–4 with $m_1 = 3000/32.2 = 93.16$ lb · lb sec²/ft, $m_2 = 55.9$ lb sec²/ft, $V_{11} = 36.65$ ft/sec and $V_{21} = -51.3$ ft/sec yields

$$(93.16)(36.65) + (55.9)(-51.3) = (93.16)(V_{12}) + (55.9)(V_{22}) \text{ or,}$$

$$3414 - 2868 = 93.16\, V_{12} + 55.9\, V_{22}$$

where V_{12} and V_{22} are unknown.

Substitution of the known velocities and $e = 0.2$ into Eq. 28–9 yields

$$0.2 = \frac{V_{22} - V_{12}}{(36.65) - (-51.3)}$$

Rearranging yields

$$V_{22} - V_{12} = 17.6$$

Both numerical equations may be solved for V_{12} and V_{22} by the method of substitution yielding $V_{12} = -2.93$ ft/sec or -2.0 mph, and $V_{22} =$ 14.6 ft/sec or 10.0 mph. The results indicate that vehicle no. 1 is traveling with a negative velocity, i.e., backwards whereas vehicle no. 2 is now traveling with a positive velocity, i.e., it is also traveling backwards relative to the precrash motion. The change in kinetic energy into deformation energy by use of Eq. 28–11 is

$$\Delta KE = \left(\frac{93.16}{2}\right)[(36.65)^2 - (2.93)^2] - \left(\frac{55.9}{2}\right)[(51.3)^2 - (14.6)^2]$$

$$= 62{,}167 - 67{,}598 = -5431 \text{ ft} \cdot \text{lb}$$

A two-vehicle intersection collision is presented in Section 40–6.

28-3. OBLIQUE CENTRAL AND STRAIGHT NON-CENTRAL IMPACT

The oblique central and straight non-central impacts are special cases of the oblique non-central impact most frequently encountered in motor vehicle collisions. Oblique central and straight non-central impacts are not discussed specifically. See Section 40–5 for an oblique central impact reconstruction.

28-4. OBLIQUE NON-CENTRAL IMPACT

The initial contact position of two vehicles is illustrated in Fig. 28–1. Vehicle no. 2 impacts vehicle no. 1 at the left side under an angle.

For each of the vehicles the following impulse components in the X and Y direction may be derived (Ref. 22):

Impulse in the x-direction:

$$I_x = \frac{a(\Delta V_x) + c(\Delta V_y)}{ab - c^2}, \text{ lb} \cdot \text{sec} \quad (28\text{–}12)$$

Impulse in the y-direction:

$$I_y = \frac{c\Delta V_x + b\Delta V_y}{ab - c^2}, \text{ lb sec} \quad (28\text{–}13)$$

where

$$a = \frac{1}{m_1} + \frac{1}{m_2} + \frac{\ell_{1x}^2}{I_1} + \frac{\ell_{2x}^2}{I_2}, \frac{\text{ft}}{\text{lb sec}^2} \quad (28\text{–}14)$$

$$b = \frac{1}{m_1} + \frac{1}{m_2} + \frac{\ell_{1y}^2}{I_1} + \frac{\ell_{2y}^2}{I_2}, \frac{\text{ft}}{\text{lb sec}^2} \quad (28\text{–}15)$$

$$c = \frac{\ell_{1x}\ell_{1y}}{I_1} + \frac{\ell_{2x}\ell_{2y}}{I_2}, \frac{\text{ft}}{\text{lb sec}^2} \quad (28\text{–}16)$$

$$\Delta V_x = V_{21,x} - V_{11,x}, \text{ ft/sec} \quad (28\text{–}17)$$

$$\Delta V_y = V_{21,y} - V_{11,y}, \text{ ft/sec} \quad (28\text{–}18)$$

In general, the difference velocities ΔV_x and ΔV_s may be determined graphically from the velocity diagram. The difference velocity diagram is obtained by using velocities prior to impact. For a straight impact Eqs. 28–17 and 28–18 may be used. In Fig. 28–1 ΔV_x is negative, ΔV_y, positive.

The distances ℓ_{1x}, ℓ_{1y}, ℓ_{2x}, and ℓ_{2y} locating the center of gravities relative to the point of vehicle-to-vehicle contact must be given plus or minus signs. The distances are always measured *from* the center of

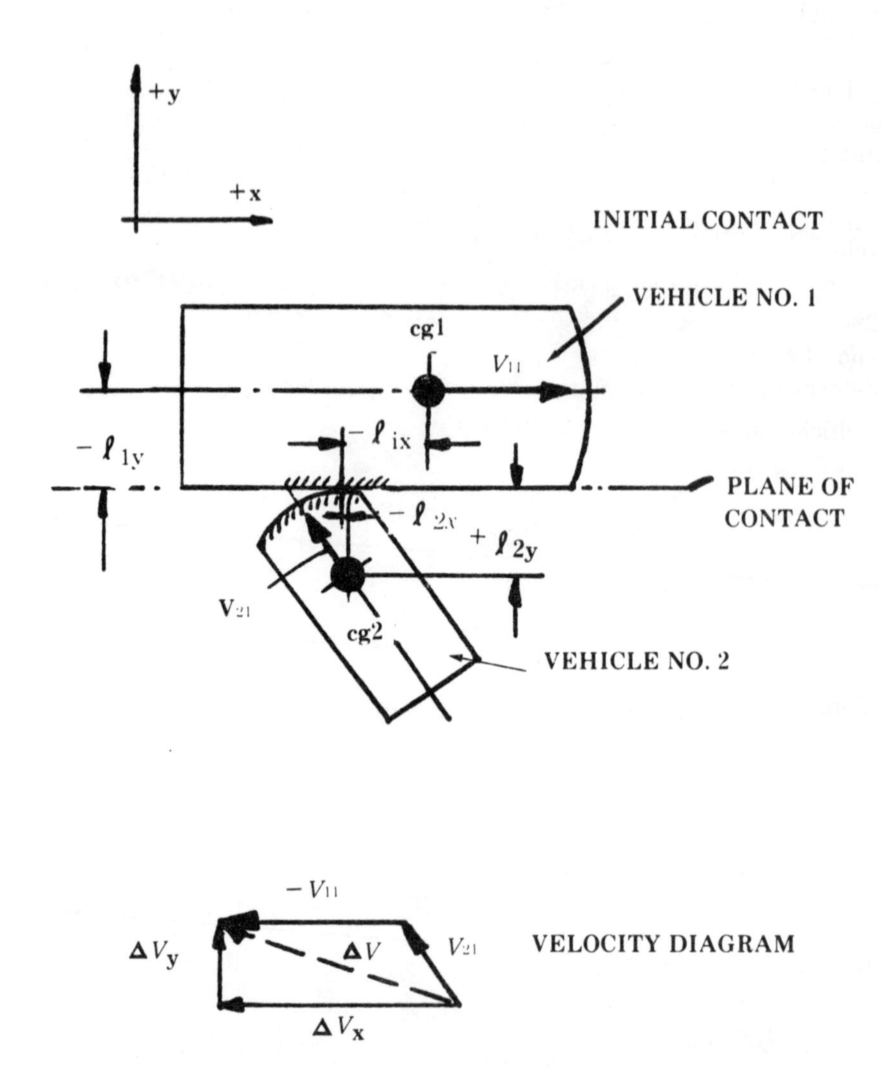

Figure 28–1. Impact Geometry and Velocity Difference

gravity *to* the point of contact. Measuring up and to the right receives a plus sign, measuring down or to the left receives a minus sign. For example, in Fig. 28–1 only ℓ_{2y} will be positive, all three other distances will be negative.

The velocity diagram is constructed by drawing the initial velocity of vehicle no. 2 to scale and direction. At the tip (arrow) of V_{21} the initial velocity of vehicle no. 1 is drawn to scale, however in the opposite direction to its true condition. The beginning (origin) of arrow V_{21} and the end of V_{11} are connected, yielding the desired difference velocity.

When the impulse components are determined by Eqs. 28–12 and 28–13 the velocity components of the centers of gravity of each vehicle and the angular velocities of each vehicle after the impact may be determined as follows.

Vehicle no. 1:

$$V_{12x} = \frac{I_x}{m_1} + V_{11x}, \text{ ft/sec} \qquad (28\text{–}19)$$

$$V_{12y} = \frac{I_y}{m_1} + V_{11y}, \text{ ft/sec} \qquad (28\text{–}20)$$

$$\omega_{12} = \frac{(\ell_{1x} I_y - \ell_{1y} I_x)}{I_1} + \omega_{11}, \frac{\text{rad}}{\text{sec}} \qquad (28\text{–}21)$$

Vehicle no. 2:

$$V_{22x} = V_{21x} - \frac{I_x}{m_2}, \text{ ft/sec} \qquad (28\text{–}22)$$

$$V_{22y} = V_{21y} - \frac{I_y}{m_2}, \text{ ft/sec} \qquad (28\text{–}23)$$

$$\omega_{22} = \frac{(\ell_{2y} I_x - \ell_{2x} I_y)}{I_2} + \omega_{21}, \frac{\text{rad}}{\text{sec}} \qquad (28\text{–}24)$$

where

I_1 = mass moment of inertia of vehicle 1, lb · ft · sec^2

I_2 = mass moment of inertia of vehicle 2, lb · ft · sec^2

See Section 22–3.3 for values of mass moment of inertia. If one or both vehicles are rotating prior to the collision due to, e.g., loss of control or cornering, this rotation is included in Eqs. 28–21 and 28–24 by the terms ω_{11} and ω_{21}, respectively.

Practical solutions of accident reconstruction problems usually involve a combination of graphical and numerical analysis. For example, the x and y components of the individual velocities before or after impact may be determined by a velocity diagram. The collision analysis has been programmed for computer use.

Example 28–2

Determine the velocities and their directions and the angular velocities immediately after impact of the Chevrolet Brookwood station wagon and Volkswagen Super Beetle impacting as illustrated in Fig. 28–2. The vehicles have no initial angular velocities, i.e., $\omega_{11} = \omega_{21} = 0$. Use the following data: The VW Beetle is designated by subscript 1, the Chevrolet by 2, $W_1 = 1966$ lb, $I_1 = 869$ lb · ft · sec², $\ell_{F1} = 4.358$ ft, $\ell_{R1} = 3.583$ ft (center of gravity location between front and rear axle), $V_{11} = 36.6$ ft/sec (25 mph); $W_2 = 4703$ lb, $I_2 = 3471$ lb · ft · sec², $\ell_{F2} = 5.557$ ft, $\ell_{R2} = 4.850$ ft, $V_{21} = 70.3$ ft/sec (48 mph).

Examination of the vehicle damage and skidmarks prior to the collision were used to draw the collision diagram (Fig. 28–2).

The collision point measurements are taken from the collision diagram as

$$\ell_{1x} = 6.6 \text{ ft}, \ \ell_{1y} = -2.6 \text{ ft}$$
$$\ell_{2x} = 0.53 \text{ ft}, \ \ell_{2y} = 10.9 \text{ ft}$$

The difference velocities may be determined next by the velocity diagram shown in Fig. 28–3. The velocity diagram is constructed from the known velocities and positions prior to contact, i.e., angle $\alpha = 69°$ (frequently the velocities after impact are known). The difference velocities are $\Delta V_x = -11.4$ ft/sec and $\Delta V_y = 66.6$ ft/sec (Fig. 28–3). Substitution of the appropriate data into Eqs. 28–14 through 28–16 yields with $m_1 = 61$ lb sec²/ft and $m_2 = 146$ lb sec²/ft, $a = 0.0734$ ft/(lb · sec²), $b = 0.0653$ ft/(lb sec²), and $c = 0.0214$ ft/(lb · sec²).

The impulse components are determined by Eqs. 28–12 and 28–13 as $I_x = -454$ lb sec and $I_y = 1007$ lb sec. The magnitude and direction of the resultant impulse may be drawn in the contact diagram as shown. The magnitude may also be computed by

$$I = \sqrt{I_x^2 + I_y^2} = \sqrt{454^2 + 1007^2} = 1105 \text{ lb sec}$$

The angle of impact β of the impulse is 65.7 deg as shown on Fig. 28–2.

The unknown velocity components of each vehicle may now be determined by Eqs. 28–19 through 28–24. In this case $V_{11x} = V_{11} = 36.6$ ft/sec, $V_{11y} = 0$, $V_{21x} = 26.5$ ft/sec, $V_{21y} = 66.6$ ft/sec (Fig. 28–3)

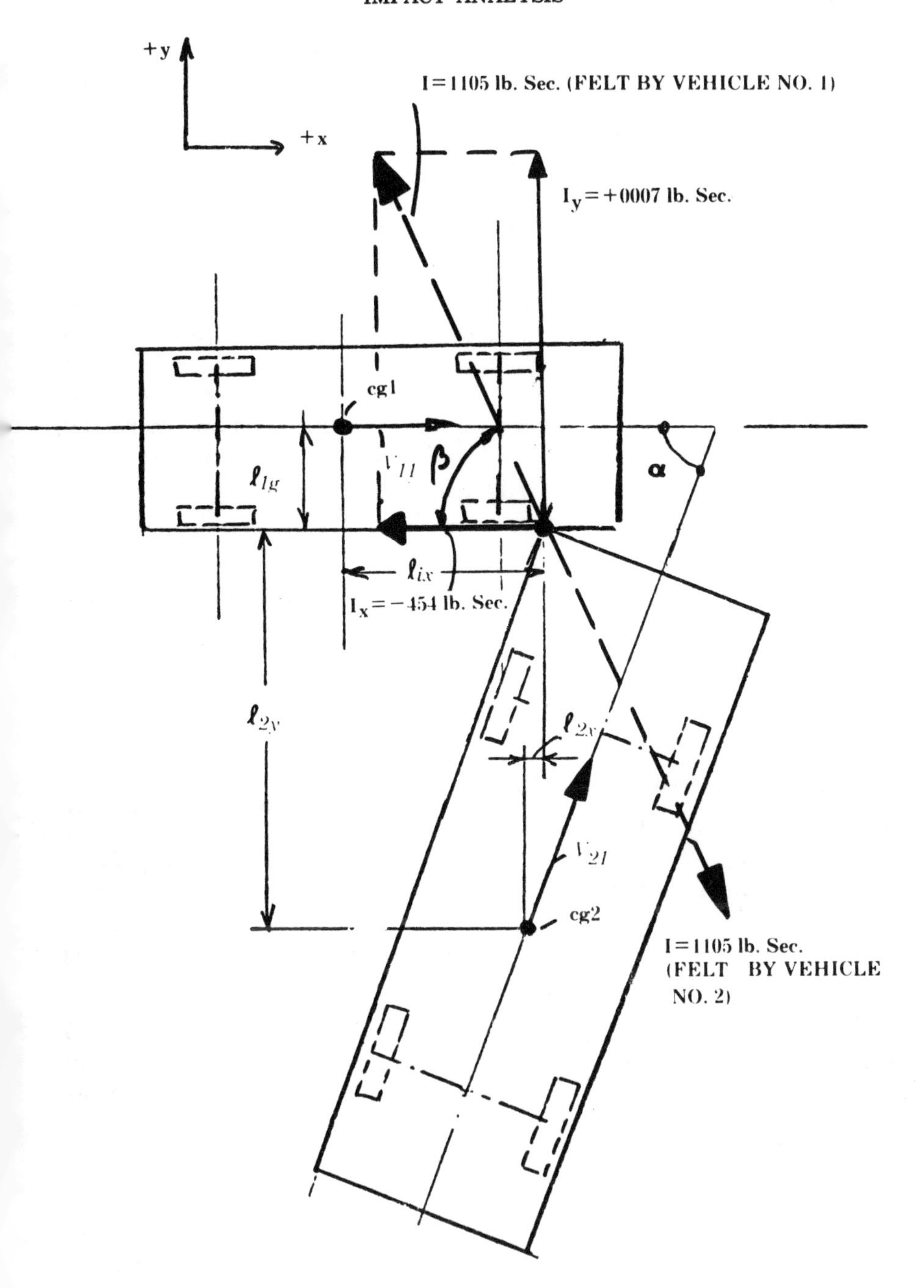

Figure 28-2. Initial Contact Diagram, Example 28-2

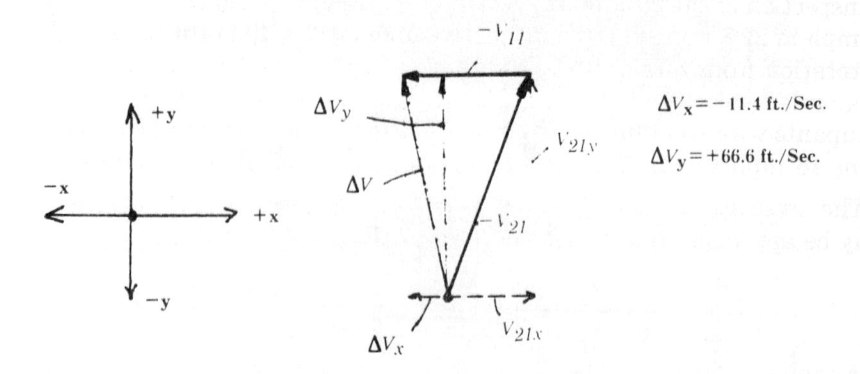

Figure 28-3. Velocity Diagram, Example 28-2

Vehicle 1 velocity components. (Eqs. 28–19 through 28–21):

$$V_{12x} = \frac{-454}{61} + 36.6 = 29.2 \text{ ft/sec}$$

$$V_{12y} = \frac{1007}{61} + 0 = 16.5 \text{ ft/sec}$$

Angular velocity of vehicle no. 1:

$$\omega_{12} = \frac{(6.6)(1007) - (-2.6)(-454)}{869} = 6.28 \frac{\text{rad}}{\text{sec}} \text{ or } 360.3 \text{ deg/sec}$$

A positive value of angular velocity ω_{12} indicates a counterclock wise rotation or spinning of the vehicle.

Vehicle 2 (Eqs. 28–21 through 28–23):

$$V_{22x} = 26.5 - \frac{(-454)}{146} = 28.3 \text{ ft/sec}$$

$$V_{22y} = 66.6 - \frac{1007}{146} = 58.8 \text{ ft/sec}$$

$$\omega_{22} = \frac{(10.9)(-454) - (0.53)(1007)}{3471} = -1.58 \frac{\text{rad}}{\text{sec}} \text{ or } -90.6 \text{ deg/sec}$$

The resulting velocity of vehicle 1 after impact is

$$V_{12} = \sqrt{29.7^2 + 16.5^2} = 33.5 \text{ ft/sec or } 22.8 \text{ mph}$$

The resulting velocity of vehicle 2 after impact is

$$V_{22} = \sqrt{(28.3)^2 + (58.8)^2} = 65.3 \text{ ft/sec or } 44.5 \text{ mph}$$

Inspection of the results indicates a decrease of speed of the VW from 25 mph to 22.8 mph. However, more significantly is the rapid increase in rotation from zero at a rate of 360 deg per second. This high value of angular velocity causes high centrifugal forces and impact of the occupants with the interior. The Chevrolet reduces its forward velocity from 48 mph to 44.8 mph while assuming a lower angular rotation.

The average impact force F_{av} transmitted between both vehicles may be approximated for impact durations Δt less than 0.2 sec by

$$F_{av} = \frac{I}{\Delta t}, \text{ lb} \tag{28-25}$$

For example, for $\Delta t = 0.15$ sec, $F_{av} = \frac{1105}{0.15} = 7366$ lb.

28-5. DETERMINATION OF IMPACT SPEEDS FROM DAMAGE DIMENSIONS

The kinetic energies of two colliding vehicles before and after impact are not equal (Eq. 28-11). The difference in energy (ΔKE) produces the damage of the vehicles and environment, and the injuries to the occupants.

Frequently attempts are made to predict the impact speeds or differences of impact speeds from damage dimensions. The question to be answered is: can the impact speeds be computed from crush depth? To find the answer, the law of conservation of energy must be considered. It states that the energy of a system, e.g., two colliding cars after impact has to equal the energy before impact minus (or plus) the work done by (or put into) the system during impact. In the case of two colliding vehicles the kinetic energy of both vehicles after impact must equal the kinetic energy before impact minus the deformation work associated with the vehicle damage. It is obvious that the work involved in deforming each vehicle component such as fender, hood, frame, engine block, radiator, and drive shaft is different for each component due to its difference in strength. Consequently, the individual forces involved are unknown, although the approximate deformations of each component may be measured from the damaged vehicle. The specific resistance to deformation is not constant and varies with the rate of deformation, thus compounding the problem. If these deformation forces were known, then crush energy ΔKE may be determined from the summation of all products of force and crush depth, and the difference in impact speeds may be determined by the use of Eqs. 28-4, 28-9, and 28-11. Since there are four unknowns (the velocities of vehicle no. 1 and 2 before and after impact, i.e., V_{11} and V_{12}, and V_{21} and V_{22}), however only three equations are available, the solution can only be obtained in terms of the difference of impact speeds.

28–5.1. Elastic Deformation. When the impact is elastic, i.e., no permanent deformation occurs, then the analysis is considerably simplified, provided the maximum elastic deformation can be determined. Specialty vehicles and modern automobiles frequently are equipped with rubber or elastic bumpers which absorb the entire low speed crush without plastic deformation.

Under these conditions the impact speed V of the moving rigid object upon a stationary elastic target may be determined by

$$V = 5.67\,\ell\sqrt{\frac{k}{W}},\ \text{ft/sec} \tag{28–26}$$

where

ℓ = maximum elastic deformation, ft
k = spring stiffness of target structure, lb/ft
W = impacting weight, lb

Example 28–3

Determine the speed of a 2-year old child impacting the back of the front seat of a station wagon. Approximate the speed of the station wagon prior to impact. All rear seats were folded down. Examination of the damage of the front seat rest due to child head impact indicated a permanent crush depth of 6 in.

Force deflection tests conducted on a similar backrest showed an elastic spring stiffness of approximately 3600 lb/ft. The backrest could be deflected elastically, i.e., without permanent deformations upon force removal, to 2.8 in. The weight of the child is 21 lb.

Substitution of the appropriate data into Eq. 28–26 yields

$$V = (5.67)\left(\frac{2.8}{12}\right)\sqrt{\frac{3600}{21}} = 17.3\ \text{ft/sec}$$

or

$$11.8\ \text{mph}$$

The result shows that the impact speed of the child with the back rest was at least 11.8 mph. The actual impact speed was greater, since permanent seat back deformation occurred, i.e., more impact energy was available.

The minimum speed of the station wagon prior to impact may be determined by Eq. 16–19. The coefficient of friction between the sliding child and the station wagon surface, and the sliding distance of the child in the vehicle must be known. Using a friction coefficient of 0.5 and a sliding distance of 7 ft yields a vehicle speed of 15.6 mph prior to impact.

28–5.2. Elastic/Plastic Deformation. Impact speeds and damage dimensions in controlled passenger car crashes have been measured. The results are presented in Figs. 28–4, 28–5, and 28–6 for front, side, and rear impacts, respectively. Inspection of Fig. 28–4 indicates that small vehicles exhibit a larger crush for a given impact speed than large vehicles. For example, a frontal crash depth of 20 in. on a small car may be the result of an impact speed ranging from 28 to 38 mph. The corresponding speed values for large cars range between 22 and 32 mph. The average impact speed for all vehicles evaluated is approximately 30 mph for a crush depth of 20 in.

For side impacts a 20 in. crush depth indicates an average impact speed of approximately 45 mph (Fig. 28–5).

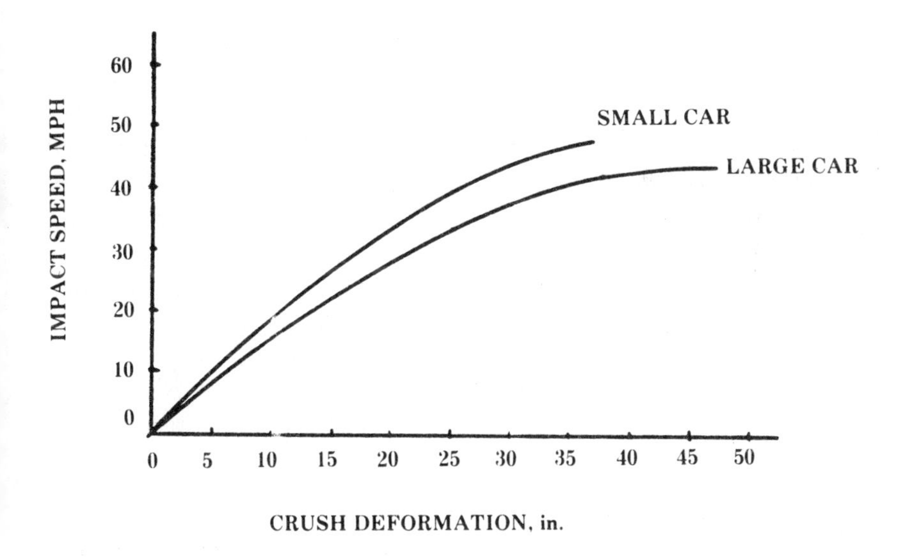

Figure 28–4. Frontal Impact Speed vs. Crush Deformation

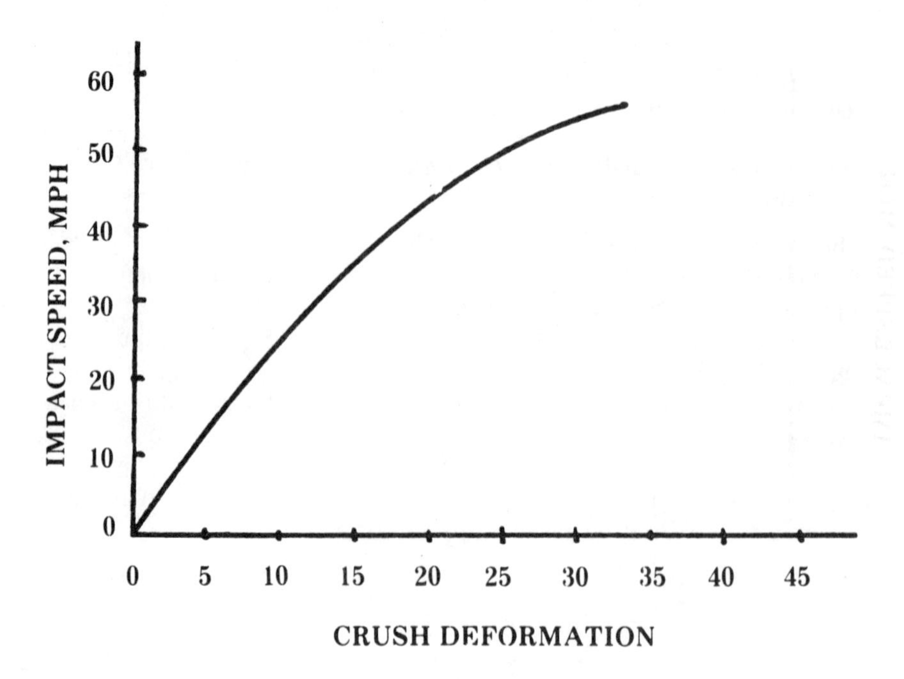

Figure 28–5. Side Impact Speed vs. Crush Deformation

For rear impacts a 20 in. crush depth indicates an average impact speed of approximately 26 mph (Fig. 28–6).

The information contained in Fig. 28–4 may be expressed by an equation showing impact speed as a function of crush depth.

For the average vehicle the impact speed V_f in a frontal crash is

$$V_f = -14.2 + 9.4\sqrt{\ell + 2.62}, \text{ mph} \qquad (28\text{–}27)$$

where

$$\ell = \text{frontal crush depth, in.}$$

For small vehicles the average frontal impact speed V_f is

$$V_f = -22.6 + 11\sqrt{\ell + 4.18}, \text{ mph} \qquad (28\text{–}28)$$

For large vehicles the average frontal impact speed V_f is

$$V_f = -11.6 + 8.4\sqrt{\ell + 1.92}, \text{ mph} \qquad (28\text{–}29)$$

The information contained in Fig. 28–5 may also be expressed by an equation. The average side impact speed V_s of passenger cars as a function of crush depth ℓ is

$$V_s = 551 - 46.8\sqrt{139 - \ell}, \text{ mph} \qquad (28\text{–}30)$$

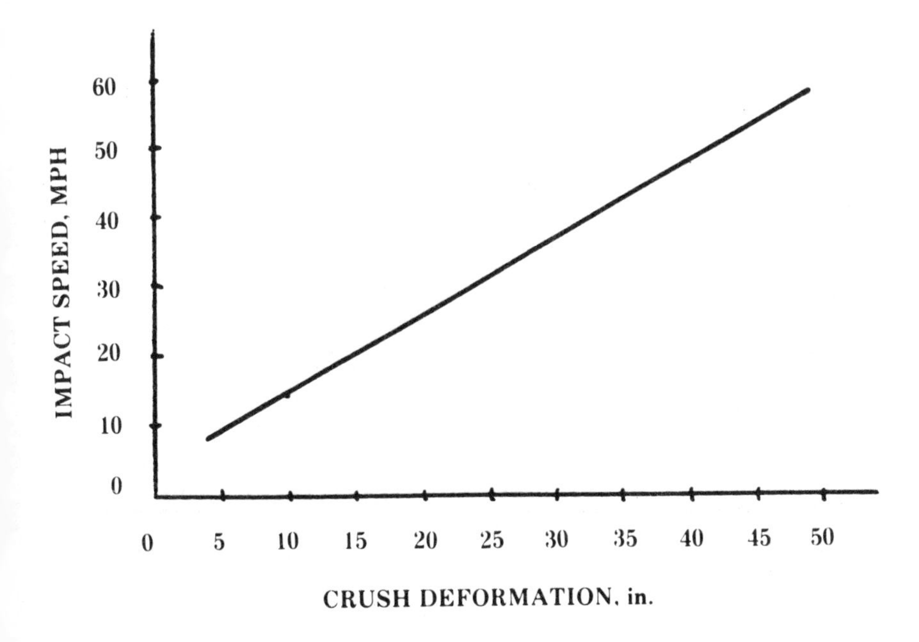

Figure 28-6. Rear Impact Speed vs. Crush Deformation

In passenger car rear end collisions the approximate average impact speed V_r as a function of crush depth ℓ is

$$V_r = 1.133\,\ell + 2.67, \text{ mph} \tag{28-31}$$

The accurate use of Eqs. 28-27 through 28-31 or the information contained in Figs. 28-4 through 28-6 is limited by the differences existing between the conditions associated with the accident under consideration and the controlled crash tests. Consequently, results obtained by the equations relating damage dimensions to speed prediction should be applied with care. The results may be used to obtain a range of impact speeds. If necessary, appropriate indepth investigations of accidents must be reviewed or a controlled crash test must be conducted.

CHAPTER 29
POST CRASH MOTION ANALYSIS

In many accident reconstructions post crash tire markings, vehicle positions and distances traveled may be used to compute the vehicle speeds immediately after impact. These speeds may then be used in the collision analysis to compute vehicle speeds immediately before impact.

29–1. STRAIGHT LINE VEHICLE TRAVEL WITHOUT ROTATION

When the post crash motion of a vehicle is a straight line, Eq. 16–7 may be used to determine the velocity immediately after impact. Minimum wheels unlocked stopping distance calculations are found in Section 20–4. Unusual cases involving unbalanced brake forces are presented in Section 20–5.

29–1.1. Skidding After Impact. The velocity immediately after impact may be determined by Eq. 20–7 rewritten as

$$V = \sqrt{(64.4)\,\mu\, S}, \text{ ft/sec} \qquad (29\text{–}1)$$

where

S = skidding distance, ft

μ = tire-road friction coefficient, d'less

The skidding distance S may not always be identical to that shown by the tire markings. When skidding on concrete surfaces, the visible skidding distance should be used in computing speed by Eq. 29–1. When skidding on asphalt surface, a tire sliding distance of approximately 8 ft is necessary to produce a visible tire skidmark. Eq. 29–1 may be rewritten as

$$V = \sqrt{30\,\mu\, S}, \text{ mph} \qquad (29\text{–}2)$$

where S is measured in ft and μ d'less. Eqs. 29–1 and 29–2 are identical except for the units of velocity.

29–1.2. Braking Without Skidding After Impact. The tires are not locked and consequently, no easily visible tire markings are present. The deceleration produced by the vehicle braking system may be determined by Eq. 20–5a or 20–5b. If appropriate, resistance forces to vehicle motion as discussed in Section 19–2 must be considered. In some cases the minimum wheels unlocked stopping distance as discussed in Section 20–4 may be used in accident reconstruction. The result would be a limiting value of velocity after impact in the absence of any tire markings.

29–2. VEHICLE SKIDDING WITH ROTATION

When all tires are locked due to over-braking or fender damage, the tire-road friction may be assumed to be independent of sliding direction. The occupant kinematics frequently is such that the pedal force is increased during the crash resulting in a continued wheel lockup.

A vehicle moving after impact is illustrated in Fig. 29–1. The four-wheeled vehicle is simplified by collapsing left and right wheel to one wheel, respectively, yielding the so-called bicycle model. The vehicle immediately after impact slides with a velocity V_x in the x-direction and rotates with an angular velocity ω about its center of gravity. The motion is resisted by the tire drag forces F_F and F_R on the front and rear tires, respectively.

Force equilibrium requires that the inertia force equals the tire drag forces:

$$m\left(\frac{dV_x}{dt}\right) + F_F \cos\gamma_F + F_R \cos\gamma_R = 0 \qquad (29\text{–}3)$$

Moment equilibrium requires that the inertia moment equals the moment produced by the tire drag forces:

$$I\left(\frac{d\omega}{dt}\right) + F_F\,\ell_F \cos\delta_F + F_R\,\ell_R \cos\delta_R = 0 \qquad (29\text{–}4)$$

where

I = mass moment of inertia of vehicle, lb·ft·sec²

m = vehicle mass, $\frac{\text{lb}\cdot\text{sec}^2}{\text{ft}}$

Angles as defined in Fig. 29–1.

The angles γ and δ found in Fig. 29–1 may be determined from the velocity diagram at front and rear wheel as

$$\tan\gamma_F = \frac{\omega\,\ell_F \cos\varphi}{\omega\ell_F \sin + V_x}, \text{ d'less} \qquad (29\text{–}5)$$

$$\tan\gamma_R = \frac{\omega\ell_R \cos\varphi}{V_x - \omega\ell_R \sin\varphi}, \text{ d'less} \qquad (29\text{–}6)$$

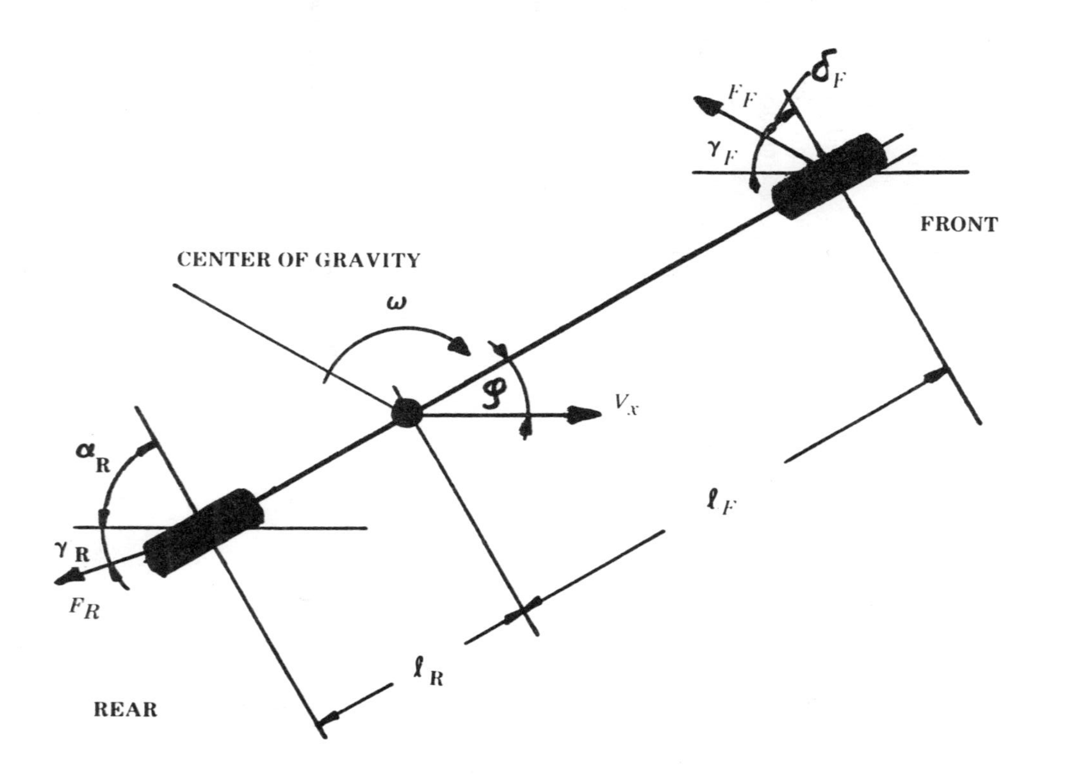

Figure 29–1. Vehicle Model, Skidding After Impact

$$\tan \delta_F = \frac{V_x \cos\varphi}{\omega\ell_F + V_s \sin\varphi}, \text{ d'less} \tag{29–7}$$

$$\tan \gamma_R = \frac{V_x \cos\varphi}{V_x \sin\varphi - \omega\ell_R}, \text{ d'less} \tag{29–8}$$

Eqs. 29–1 through 29–8 can best be solved by a finite difference procedure. This procedure involves the use of small time intervals Δt during which average values of angular rotation φ are used to predict the associated change in velocity V_x and ω.

Example 29–1

Outline the solution approach for the determination of distance traveled and the angle rotated by a VW Beetle after impact similar to Example 28–2. Use the appropriate vehicle data of Example 28–2. The total velocity is 43.4 ft/sec designated as V_X in the post impact motion analysis. The post impact angular velocity is $\omega = 7.69$ rad/sec. The angle $\varphi = 16$ deg. Initial velocity and angular velocity are slightly different from those computed in Example 28–2.

The solution involves a piecewise computation of a new velocity (and angular velocity) from known velocities at a previous time. At time equal to zero, the known velocity equals the initial velocity (43.4 ft/sec and 7.69 rad/sec). A table is best used to organize the solution. The solution proceeds with the known data at the initial conditions, i.e., immediately after impact. The initial angle $\varphi = 16$ deg, the velocity $V_x = 43.4$ ft/sec and the angular velocity $\omega = 7.69$ rad/sec are used to compute the angles γ_F, γ_R, δ_F, and δ_R by Eqs. 29–3 through 29–8. These values are then used to compute $\frac{dv_x}{dt}$ and $\frac{d\omega}{dt}$ in Eqs. 29–1 and 29–2, respectively. The value of $\frac{dv}{dt}$ is then used to compute a new velocity V_x' at a time step Δt later by

$$V_x' = V_x + \left(\frac{dv_x}{dt}\right)\Delta t, \text{ ft/sec} \tag{29–9}$$

where

V_x = old velocity, ft/sec

Δt = small time interval, arbitrarily chosen, sec

The value of $\frac{d\omega}{dt}$ is used to compute a new angular velocity at a time step Δt later by

$$\omega' = \omega + \left(\frac{d\omega}{dt}\right)\Delta t, \frac{\text{rad}}{\text{sec}} \tag{29–10}$$

where

$$\omega = \text{old angular velocity, rad/sec}$$

The distance traveled by the vehicle during the time interval Δt is

$$\Delta S = \left(\frac{V_x + V_x'}{2}\right)(\Delta t), \text{ ft} \tag{29–11}$$

The rotation of the vehicle during the time interval Δt is

$$\Delta\varphi = \left(\frac{\omega + \omega'}{2}\right)(\Delta t), \text{ rad} \tag{29–12}$$

In the paragraphs that follow the numerical calculations are demonstrated. Using the initial conditions as the old values, Eq. 29–3 yields for $\tan \gamma_F$

$$\tan \gamma_F = \frac{(7.69)(4.358) \cos 16}{(7.69)(32.2) \sin 16 + 43.4} = \frac{32.2}{52.6} = 0.612$$

or

$$\gamma_F = 31.5 \text{ deg}$$

The corresponding values for the other angles are $\gamma_R = 36.5$ deg, $\delta_F = 42.5$ deg, $\delta_R = -69.5$ deg.

The value of $\frac{dV_x}{dt}$ may be determined by Eq. 29–3 as

$$\frac{dV_x}{dt} = -\left(\frac{F_F}{m}\right) \cos \gamma_F - \left(\frac{F_R}{m}\right) \cos \gamma_R \tag{29–13}$$

where

F_F = total front axle skid resistance, lb
F_R = total rear axle skid resistance, lb

The value of F_F may be determined from moment equilibrium as

$$F_F = \frac{W_1\, \mu\, \ell_R}{\ell_R + \ell_F} = \frac{1966 \times 0.7 \times 3.583}{3.583 + 4.358} = 621 \text{ lb.}$$

The value of F_R is determined by

$$F_R = \frac{W_1\, \mu\, \ell_F}{\ell_R + \ell_F} = \frac{1966 \times 0.7 \times 4.358}{3.583 + 4.358} = 755 \text{ lb}$$

A tire-road sliding friction coefficient $\mu = 0.7$ was assumed. Substitution of the appropriate values into Eq. 29–13 yields

$$\frac{dV_x}{dt} = -\left(\frac{621}{61}\right)(\cos 31.5) - \left(\frac{755}{61}\right)(\cos 36.5) =$$

$$= -8.68 - 9.95 = -18.8 \frac{\text{ft}}{\text{sec}^2}$$

The results indicate a deceleration of 18.6 ft/sec² during the first time interval.

Eq. 29–9 now yields with a time interval of 0.5 sec a new velocity existing (after 0.5 have elapsed) of

$$V_x' = 43.4 - 18.6 \times 0.5 = 34.1 \text{ ft/sec}$$

The distance traveled by the center of gravity of the VW Beetle is by use of Eq. 29–11

$$\Delta S = \left(\frac{43.4 + 34.1}{2}\right) 0.5 = 19.4 \text{ ft}$$

The rotation is computed by Eq. 29–4, solving for the value of $\frac{d\omega}{dt}$, yielding

$$\frac{d\omega}{dt} = -\left(\frac{F_F}{I}\right) \ell_F \cos \delta_F - \left(\frac{F_R}{I}\right) \ell_R \cos \delta_R \qquad (29\text{–}14)$$

Substitution of the appropriate data into Eq. 29–14 yields

$$\frac{d\omega}{dt} = -\left(\frac{621}{869}\right) \times (4.358)(\cos 42.5) - \left(\frac{755}{869}\right)(3.583)[\cos(-69.5)]$$

$$= -3.38 \text{ rad/sec}^2$$

The result indicates that the rotation decreased at a rate of 3.38 rad/sec² during the first time interval. Eq. 29–10 yields a new angular velocity

$$\omega' = 7.69 - 3.38 \times 0.5 = 6.00 \text{ rad/sec}$$

The angle rotated by the vehicle during the first time interval of 0.5 sec is with Eq. 29–12

$$\Delta\varphi = \left(\frac{7.69 + 6.00}{2}\right) \times 0.5 = 3.42 \text{ rad or } 196 \text{ deg}$$

One-half second after impact the center of gravity of the vehicle has traveled 19.4 ft and the vehicle has rotated through 196 deg.

The next step in the solution uses the newly computed velocity $V_x = 34.1$ ft/sec and angular velocity $\omega = 6.00$ rad/sec as old values in the appropriate equation and the process is repeated. Instead of $\varphi = 16$ deg an average value of $(16 + 196)/2 = 106$ deg is used. The result is a new velocity V_x' and angular velocity ω' after an additional time interval of 0.5 sec (or a total of 1.0 sec after completion of impact) has elapsed. The entire computational process is repeated several times until the final new velocity V_x is approximately zero or first becomes negative. If the angular velocity is not zero at this time, the process is continued with $V_x' =$ zero, until the new angular velocity is approximately zero. At this time both forward velocity and spinning motion are zero, i.e., the vehicle is stationary.

The results of the complete calculations of Example 29–1 show that the rotation of the vehicle stops after the forward velocity is zero at 2.05 sec after impact. The total angle of rotation is approximately 344 deg, the distance traveled by the center of gravity of the vehicle is approximately 44 ft.

The analysis may be employed when distance traveled and vehicle rotation after impact are known to compute vehicle speed and angular velocity immediately before impact. The procedure is capable of using different friction coefficient when, for example, the vehicle transverses surfaces exhibiting different friction coefficients.

When Eq. 20–7 is used, a stopping distance $S = 41.78$ ft is obtained. A comparison of the stopping distance of 44 ft obtained by finite difference method with the distance of 41.78 ft indicates that the average deceleration with rotation is slightly lower than the value indicated by the friction coefficient.

29–3. WHEELS UNLOCKED MOTION

The analysis of vehicle motion involving turning without wheel lock is beyond the scope of this book. The solution involves the development of equations of motion using wheels unlocked braking forces, tire side forces, and inertia effects. For small tire slip angles, the side force may be determined by Eq. 18–8. For vehicle cornering near tire limit performance, a side force-slip angle diagram must be used. The solution is similar to that of Section 29–2 involving small time intervals and a time-step type computation of new values of forward velocity, angular velocity and the associated vehicle travel. The analysis usually requires the use of computers since manual calculations are too time consuming and possess a high probability of numerical error. A computer program for the analysis of wheels unlocked postcrash motion has been developed by the author.

CHAPTER 30
COLLISION ANALYSIS BY COMPUTER

The computer is a machine that is capable of carrying out complex calculations in an extremely short period of time. A computer does exactly what it has been "told" by the programmer, i.e., the computer uses the program prepared beforehand. Refinements are possible to improve the use and eliminate errors. But the core of any computer program simulating a physical process is the mathematical description of the model idealizing the actual process. If the idealization is too far removed from reality, the computer will produce only an approximate solution. Since the computer can carry out many calculations rapidly, collision analyses may include a large number of vehicle and road parameters bearing upon the collision performance of impacting vehicles.

30–1. SIMULATION MODEL OF AUTOMOBILE COLLISION (SMAC)

The SMAC program was developed by the Calspan Corporation for the National Highway Traffic Safety Administration of the U.S. Department of Transportation. Several research institutions have implemented the SMAC program for collision reconstruction purposes.

30–1.1. Vehicle Model Description. The program uses two basic models: one for the collision analysis, another one for the single vehicle trajectory calculations after impact. The collision analysis includes the following assumptions.

1. In the collision calculations each vehicle is treated as a rigid body, surrounded by a layer of elastic-plastic material.

2. The mechanical pressure between contacting vehicles increases linearly with crush depth.

3. The coefficient of restitution varies as a function of maximum deflection.

4. The vehicle motions are limited to a horizontal plane, i.e., body roll and pitch are neglected.

The model used to analyze the post impact trajectory assume the following:

1. The vehicle motion is limited to a horizontal plane, i.e., vehicle roll and pitch are neglected.

2. The surface on which the vehicle travels is flat, i.e., no road surface irregularities are considered.

3. Vehicle suspension effects are neglected.

4. Lateral load transfer is neglected.

5. The tire-road friction coefficient is assumed to be decreasing linearly with increasing speed.

6. The tire side force is a nonlinear function of slip angle.

7. The friction circle concept is used to describe the relationship between side force and braking or driving force of a tire.

8. Braking or drive thrust may be considered.

Refinements of the SMAC program and special programs to facilitate the use of the program have been developed.

30-1.2. Computer Analysis Accuracy. The accuracy of the collision and post crash trajectory simulation depends largely on the correlation between model and actual conditions. If the crash performance parameters chosen in the program are identical to those exhibited by the impacting vehicles, then the computed data should correlate well with measured collision data.

Similarly, the computer post crash trajectory will correlate well with measured accident data only when the accident and vehicle conditions are accurately described by the model forming the basis of the program. When, for example, a rough terrain surface causes loss of tire to ground contact, and the loss of all traction forces the resulting vehicle motion is not accurately evaluated by the program.

The iterative use and the results of the program aid significantly in the reconstruction of a large number of collisions, and although no special accident reconstruction skills are required for the proper application of the program, certain judgments have to be made to determine whether or not a particular accident can reasonably accurately be reconstructed by the SMAC program.

CHAPTER 31
OCCUPANT DYNAMICS

The objectives of occupant dynamics are the determination of the forces and motions of the occupants during the collision and the correlation between injury and occupant contact.

31-1. THE UNRESTRAINED OCCUPANT

During impact the velocity of a vehicle is suddenly changed. The occupant maintains his forward velocity until he hits the interior of the vehicle or is ejected through an opening. At this instant of interior contact the occupant speed is reduced drastically and his kinetic energy is changed into deformation of vehicle interior and injuries to the occupant. An unrestrained occupant may impact several parts of the interior during the collision and post impact phase of the accident. Frequently the occupant is ejected through a vehicle opening such as door or window.

31-1.1. Occupant Kinematics. The motion of the occupant during a collision without reference to forces is accomplished by a kinematic analysis. The purpose of this analysis is to correlate occupant injuries with vehicle interior damage or points of contact. Occupant kinematics requires an understanding of the vehicle motion during the accident and frequently provides an independent check on the accuracy of the vehicle motion analysis itself. For example, onscene investigations and subsequent vehicle examination and a review of medical records may reveal certain data that indicate, for example, that the right front passenger impacted the upper right door frame with his head. The production of this damage requires an acceleration of the passenger into the door, most likely accomplished by a sudden displacement of the vehicle toward the left. Occupant size and weight must be considered in the kinematic analysis.

31-1.2. Forces Sustained by the Occupant. The forces sustained by the occupant during the collision may be approximated by using data determined in the impact analysis (Chapter 28).

The impulse computed by Eqs. 28-12 and 28-13 may be used to determine an average impact force produced between the impacting vehicles when the duration of impact is known (see Example 28-2).

The impact duration is extremely small and usually does not exceed 0.5 sec. A careful examination of vehicle damage in general produces maximum crash data, i.e., the distance required by the colliding vehicles to change their speeds from the preimpact values to those associated with post impact conditions.

The approximate impact time interval may be determined by Eq. 16–9, rewritten as

$$\Delta t = \frac{2\,S_i}{V_{i1} + V_{i2}}, \text{ sec} \qquad (31\text{–}1)$$

where

S_i = maximum crush of vehicle no. i, ft

V_{i1} = velocity of vehicle no. i before impact, ft

V_{i2} = velocity of vehicle no. i after impact, ft/sec

For example, the impact duration associated with the conditions of Example 28–2 for a measured crash of $S_2 = 1.0$ ft would be $\Delta t = 0.27$ sec.

The average impact force F_{av} may be determined by Eq. 28–25.

The average acceleration a_i experienced by vehicle no. i may be determined by Eq. 17–1, solved for acceleration a_i

$$a_i = \frac{F_{av}}{m_i}, \text{ ft/sec}^2 \qquad (31\text{–}2)$$

where

$$m_i = \text{mass of vehicle } i, \frac{\text{lb} \cdot \text{sec}^2}{\text{ft}}$$

The occupant motion may now be analyzed by considering that he maintains his forward velocity until he is stopped by the vehicle interior. The time after which this occupant impact occurs may be determined by the free space between body and interior and the relative motion of the vehicle with respect to the occupant caused by a change in vehicle speed during the impact. See Section 28–5.1 for example calculations.

Frequently, the injury potential is related to the kinetic energy exhibited by the occupant during various phases of the collision.

31-2. THE RESTRAINED OCCUPANT

An occupant may use active restraints such as seat belts or passive restraints such as air bags to reduce the likelihood of severe injuries in a collision. The restraints in combination with the padded interior of the vehicle prevent large impact forces between the occupant and vehicle components. The function of a restraint system is to "gently" decelerate the occupant (or accelerate in the case of a rear end collision) as the car is stopped by avoiding body contact with injury producing interior components.

In the design of the restraint system the crash characteristics of the vehicle must be considered.

The deceleration of the occupant should not lag behind the deceleration of the vehicle, otherwise the occupant deceleration occurs during high levels of vehicle deceleration. For example, commencement of occupant deceleration 0.015 sec after the beginning of vehicle deceleration yields good injury protection whereas, e.g., a 0.040 sec delay may cause significantly larger forces to the occupant. Crash tests involving two small passenger cars showed a maximum shoulder belt force of 2382 lb for a lag time of 0.039 sec as compared to 1991 lb for a lag time of 0.018 sec.

The occupant using a lap belt only may impact the steering wheel, dash or windshield at a high level of speed due to the pivoting action at his hips and the sudden deceleration of the hip point, i.e., the seat and seat belt assembly associated with the crashing vehicle.

The velocity of the occupant's head hitting the vehicle interior may be determined by

$$V = \left(\frac{0.41\,R}{K_0}\right)\sqrt{(32.2)r_{cg}\,(1 - \cos\theta) + a r_{cg}\sin\theta},\ \text{ft/sec} \qquad (31\text{–}3)$$

where

a = vehicle deceleration, ft/sec^2

K_0 = radius of gyration, in.

R = distance from hip point to interior component impacted by occupant head, in.

r_{cg} = distance from hip point to center of gravity of upper torso, i.e., the body part that rotates, in.

θ = angle rotated by upper torso from initial seating position to interior component, deg

Example 31–1

Determine the speed at which an occupant's head impacts the dashboard or steering wheel; use the data that follow:

$$R = 29 \text{ in.},\ r_{cg} = 16 \text{ in.},\ K_0 = 21 \text{ in.}$$
$$a = 30g,\ \theta = 50 \text{ degrees}$$

Substitution of the appropriate data in Eq. 31–3 yields the velocity of the occupant's head relative to the vehicle at the location of the dashboard.

$$V = \frac{(0.41)(29)}{21}\sqrt{(32.2)(16)(1 - cos 50) + (32.2)(30)(16) sin 50^{\circ}}$$

$$= 61.1 \text{ ft/sec or } 42 \text{ mph}$$

The result indicates that the occupant impacts the dashboard or steering wheel at a velocity of 42 mph which is also the relative velocity between occupant head and vehicle.

Equations similar to Eq. 31–3 may be derived for different conditions of relative motion between occupant and vehicle interior.

The average deceleration sustained by the head during impact with the dashboard may be determined by Eq. 16–7 when the crash deflection of the dashboard due to head impact is known. For example, for a crush distance $S = 3$ in., the average deceleration of the head is 295 g. This head deceleration is far in excess of the probable survival level. Measured deceleration of head impacts against steering wheels ranged between 50 to 180 g for crashes into a wall at 30 mph. A discussion of human tolerances to impact loading is found in Chapter 32.

CHAPTER 32

HUMAN TOLERANCE TO IMPACT LOADING

Human tolerance to impact is a complicated medical problem and a detailed discussion is beyond the scope of this book.

32–1. BASIC CONSIDERATIONS

Human tolerance levels may be divided into several categories as a function of the test under consideration, such as voluntary tolerance level, or injury-threshold tolerance level.

The voluntary tolerance level is that level to which a volunteer will subject himself.

The no-injury threshold level is that level of exposure which is at or below the severity required to produce injury.

The injury threshold level is that level of exposure which is severe enough to produce reversible or irreversible injuries.

The factors that affect the tolerance level, i.e., the severity of injury are

1. Impact location on the body
2. The impact area, i.e., localized or distributed impact load
3. The direction of impact force
4. The duration of the impact force
5. The surface roughness in contact with the body
6. The relative displacement induced by the impact

Impact loading may result in bone fracture, soft-tissue injuries, or internal organ injuries.

Bone fracture tolerance levels can be established relatively easily by measurement. Fractures can be detected from X-rays.

Soft-tissue injuries are divided into several categories depending upon the severity of the impact force. Bruises and contusions are generally the result of low severity impact by a blunt object. If the blunt object impact is too severe, internal soft-tissue damage occurs accompanied by tearing of muscles and connecting tissues. Lacerations are caused by impact of sharp edges from metal, glass, or rough surface, e.g., when the occupant is ejected onto the road surface.

Internal organ injuries are caused by severe impact loadings or relative displacements. The internal organs may be damaged by contusion, laceration, or rupture and such injuries are particularly dangerous since no external indications of damage may be visible.

32-2. HUMAN TOLERANCE LEVELS

The development of accurate tolerance levels is a difficult and expensive task. Obviously, no volunteer can be subjected to sustain severe injuries in a laboratory. However, a combination of test data, clinical analysis, and accident data have been used to develop certain tolerance levels of various body components. Federal standards relating to expected injury levels in certain crash tests require that specific computed values of human tolerance levels are not exceeded.

The frequently injured body parts are the head, chest, and legs when a regularly seated occupant in a crashing vehicle is considered.

The fracture load of the head ranges between 1100 lb and 2400 lb, of the ribs between 300 lb and 1300 lb, and the human skin develops a tensile strength of approximately 1000 psi.

The static load carrying capacity of various body parts does not indicate the injury potential in a dynamic force application. Since both peak value and duration of the deceleration affect the injury severity, specific injury criteria are computed from measured deceleration-time histories.

The head injury criteria (HIC) requires that the computed HIC value must not exceed a value of 1000. The resultant acceleration exhibited by the center of gravity of the head is critical when it exceeds a value of $80g$. Peak values exceeding $80g$ cannot last more than a cumulative time interval of 3 millisec.

The severity index (SI) of the upper thorax or chest computed from measured acceleration time histories must not exceed a value of 1000. The resultant acceleration of the chest must not exceed a value of 60 g. The peak values exceeding $60g$ must not last more than a cumulative time interval of 3 millisec.

The force transmitted axially through each upper leg must not exceed 1700 lb.

Other human tolerance levels to impact loading have been measured. Since the test data are affected by the properties of the test device, the results may not be applicable directly to the case under consideration.

Several human tolerance levels are discussed. For head impact with padded deformable metal dashboard: velocity 60 ft/sec peak acceleration 165*g*, no fracture, probable brain damage (cadaver test).

Shoulder impact with steering wheel rim, 36 ft/sec, 500 lb, no fracture (cadaver test).

Chest impact with steering wheel with collapsable column, 36 ft/sec 1800 lb, no fracture (cadaver test).

Knee, thigh, hip (seated) impact with 6-in diameter unpadded target, 1500 lb, patella fracture (similar fracture in a different test), 1500 lb (cadaver test).

32–3. DEFINITION OF INJURY SEVERITY

For purposes of categorizing injury severity, injuries have been coded and designated by numbers 0 through 9 in terms of an abbreviated injury scale (AIS). Numbers of 6 or higher indicate single or multiple fatal injuries.

ATS 0 Uninjured

AIS 1 Minor Injuries: Superficial abrasion, contusion, laceration, cervical spine injury, complaint without anatomical or radiological evidence, thoracic and/or lumbar strain, digit sprain, fracture and/or dislocation

ATS 2 Moderate Injuries: Deep and/or extensive laceration, basilar or linear fracture, no loss of consciousness, closed rib fracture without respiratory embarrassment, minor compression fracture (abdomen), undisplaced longbone or pelvic fracture.

AIS 3 Severe (Not Dangerous) Injuries: Laceration involving major nerves and/or vessels, loss of eye, avulsion of optic nerve, hemothorax or pneumothorax, contusion of abdominal organs, displaced and/or open fractures of a single limb.

AIS 4 Severe (Dangerous, Survival Probable) Injuries: Second or third degree burns (31% to 50% body surface), closed and displaced or depressed skull fracture, severe neurological injury, open chest wound, avulsion of the genitals, amputation of limbs.

AIS 5 Critical (Survival Uncertain) Injuries: C-4 or lower cervical spine injury with cord transection, aortic laceration (chest), rupture, avulsion or extensive laceration of intraabdominal vessels or organs except kidney, spleen or ureter, open fractures of multiple limbs.

AIS 6 Maximum Severity Injuries: Second or third degree burns (80% or more body surface, including incineration), crush injuries or lacerations of the brain stem or upper cervical spine, transection of the torso.

AIS 7 8,9, 10 Identify fatal injuries in one or more regions. AIS 10 designates fatal injuries with unknown cause.

32-4. FIRE INJURY SEVERITY

The injuries sustained by high environmental temperatures vary as result of exposure, i.e., protective clothing and duration of exposure. In most cases a skin surface temperature of 180° F or above will lead to fatal injuries in 50% of the cases when 50% or more of the human skin has been exposed to the high temperature.

Protective clothing which exhibits flame resistant characteristics has been developed and is frequently used by race car drivers.

In laboratory tests in which the temperature at the outside of the clothing and at the inside of the clothing immediately adjacent to the skin of a hog leg was measured, a skin temperature of 284° F was obtained after 10 sec of exposure to a flame temperature of 1500° F. Gasoline and synthetic fuel flame temperatures achieve levels of approximately 1500° F.

The protective clothing examined was a two-layer Nomax suit with Nomax underwear.

The test data can reasonably well be expressed by an equation of the form

$$T_{\text{skin}} = \left(\frac{T_{\text{Flame}} - 700}{40}\right)t + 84, \ ^\circ\text{F} \qquad (32\text{-}1)$$

where

T_{Flame} = flame or ambient temperature, °F

t = time of exposure, sec

Eq. 32-1 is only valid for skin temperature computations associated with the protective clothing tested.

PART 5

GOVERNMENT HIGHWAY SAFETY STANDARDS

The objective of Part 5 is a brief review of Federal Standards relating to crash avoidance, crashworthiness, and highway safety programs. The Federal Safety Defects program is reviewed. Detail information may be found in appropriate government publications.

CHAPTER 33
FEDERAL MOTOR VEHICLE SAFETY STANDARDS

The objectives of this chapter are to provide a brief review of existing federal regulations on motor vehicle safety standards. The standards are continually reviewed and improved by the government to provide an optimum level of highway safety.

In September of 1966, the National Traffic and Motor Vehicle Safety Act was signed into law. This law directs the Secretary of Transportation, and in particular the National Highway Traffic Safety Administration (NHTSA) to issue meaningful and objective safety standards resulting in a reduction of deaths, injuries and property losses. In 1972 the Motor Vehicle Information and Cost Saving Act was issued. This law requires the promulgation of property loss reduction standards and odometer disclosure statements.

The National Highway Traffic Safety Administration also has authority to investigate alleged vehicle defects and to enforce recall programs and to test for compliance with existing standards.

The Federal Highway Administration has among others authority to issue standards relating to the safety of commercial transportation.

To improve traffic safety, the National Highway Traffic Safety Administration has authority to issue highway safety program standards which relate to vehicle operation including motor vehicle inspection, vehicle registration, driver education, and driver licensing.

Recently the NHTSA has been authorized to issue fuel efficiency standards for motor vehicles.

33-1. STANDARDS FOR CRASH AVOIDANCE

Crash avoidance standards involve design improvements and safer operation of motor vehicles to reduce the frequency of accidents.

33-1.1. Std. 101 – Control Location, Identification, and Illumination. The standard specifies requirements for location, identification, and illumination of motor vehicle controls. The purpose is to ensure the accessibility of controls and to facilitate their selection under day and nightime conditions to reduce hazards associated with driver diversion. When seated in a specified position, the driver must be able to operate a number of specified controls.

33–1.2. Std. 102—Transmission Shift Lever Sequence, Starter Interlock, and Transmission Braking Effect. This standard specifies requirements for the transmission shift lever sequence, starter interlock for automatic transmission vehicles, and for engine retardation effect of automatic transmission vehicles. No starter interlock is required for vehicles equipped with a manual transmission. The standard applies to passenger cars, multipurpose vehicles, trucks, and buses.

33–1.3. Std. 103—Windshield Defrosting and Defogging Systems. The standard specifies requirements for windshield defrosting and defogging systems of passenger cars, multipurpose vehicles, trucks and buses. The purpose is to increase driver visibility and thereby increase traffic safety.

33–1.4. Std. 104—Windshield Wiping and Washing Systems. The standard specifies requirements for windshield wiping and washing systems of passenger cars, multipurpose vehicles, trucks and buses. The standard requires that motor vehicles are equipped with windshield wiping and washing systems and that specified windshield areas are wiped, with the area determined by the overall width of the vehicle.

33–1.5. Std. 105—Hydraulic Brake System. The standard specifies requirements for the hydraulic service brake and associated parking brake system of passenger cars, multipurpose vehicles, trucks and buses. A hydraulic brake system is defined as a system that uses hydraulic fluid as a medium for transmitting force from a service brake control (brake pedal) to the service brake (wheel brakes). It may incorporate a brake power assist (vacuum booster) or power unit (full pump power).

The standard specifies performance requirements of the service brake in terms of minimum stopping distances and fade performance for a variety of conditions, stopping distances for partially failed brake conditions, inoperative power assist parking brake performance, wet brake recovery, and spike stops. In addition a number of design requirements are provided, including warning lights, and the use of friction type brakes.

33–1.6. Std. 106—Hydraulic Brake Hoses. The standard specifies requirements for hydraulic brake hoses and air and vacuum hoses that will reduce brake failure.

33–1.7. Std. 107—Reflecting Surfaces. The standard specifies requirements of reflecting surfaces for certain vehicle components in the driver's field of view. The purpose is to reduce the hazards associated with the reflection of the sun or bright lights into the driver's eyes from shiny surfaces. The standard requires that windshield wiper arms, inside windshield moldings, horn rings, and the frames and brackets of rear view mirrors have a dull surface.

33-1.8. Std. 108—Lamps, Reflective Devices, and Associated Equipment. The standard specifies requirements for lamps, reflective devices and associated equipment for signaling to ensure safe operation during darkness and other conditions of reduced visibility. The standard is applicable to passenger cars, multipurpose vehicles, trucks, buses, motorcycles and trailers. Extension of the standard includes replacement equipment.

33-1.9. Std. 109—New Pneumatic Tires. The standard specifies passenger car tire dimensions and laboratory test requirements for bead unseating resistance, strength, endurance, and high speed performance. The standard also defines load ratings and specific labeling requirements.

33-1.10. Std. 110—Tire Selection and Rims. The standard specifies requirements for tire and rim selection to prevent overloading. The requirements include labeling relating to load distribution and rim performance under conditions of tire deflation.

33-1.11. Std. 111—Rear View Mirrors. The standard specifies requirements for rear view mirrors to provide the driver with a clear and reasonably unobstructed view to the rear. The standard requires an outside rearview mirror on the driver side, and when the inside mirror does not provide a sufficient field of view, an additional outside mirror on the passenger side. The inside mirror must be designed to reduce the likelihood of injury on impact.

33-1.12. Std. 112—Headlamp Concealment Devices. The standard specifies requirements for headlamp concealment devices such that the device shall remain fully opened when any loss of power in or to the device occurs and/or when the wiring or electrical supply for controlling the device malfunctions.

33-1.13. Std. 113—Hood Latch Systems. The standard specifies the requirements for providing a hood latch system or systems on passenger cars, multipurpose vehicles, trucks, and buses. The standard requires that front opening hoods that may obstruct a driver's forward view during inadvertent opening must be equipped with a second latch position.

33-1.14. Std. 114—Theft Protection. The standard specifies requirements for theft protection of passenger cars. The standard requires a key locking system, that with the key removed prevents normal engine starting, steerability and/or forward self-mobility of the vehicle.

33-1.15. Std. 115—Vehicle Identification Numbers. The standard specifies requirements for vehicle identification numbers to reduce the incidence of accidents resulting from unauthorized use of passenger cars. The identification number must be embossed upon a part that is designed not to be removed by repair. Identification numbers of two vehicles of the same manufacture shall not be identical for a period of ten years.

33-1.16. Std. 116—Hydraulic Brake Fluids. The standard specifies requirements for brake fluids for use in hydraulic brake systems, brake fluid containers, and brake fluid container labeling.

The purpose of the standard is to reduce failures in the hydraulic brake system due to manufacture or use of improper or contaminated brake fluid.

33-1.17. Std. 117—Retreaded Pneumatic Tires. The standard specifies requirements on performance, labeling, and certification for retreaded pneumatic passenger car tires. The purpose of the standard is to require retreaded tires to perform similarly to new pneumatic tires.

33-1.18. Std. 118—Power-Operated Window Systems. The standard specifies requirement for power-operated window and partition systems to reduce the likelihood of death or injury from their accidental operation. The standard requires that the window is inoperative when the ignition is in the off position or when the key is removed.

33-1.19. Std. 119—Tires for Vehicles Other Than Passenger Cars. The standard specifies requirements in terms of strength, endurance, and high speed performance and markings for new pneumatic tires of multipurpose vehicles, trucks, trailers, buses, and motorcycles.

33-1.20. Std. 121—Air Brake Systems. The standard specifies performance requirements and equipment for braking systems on vehicles equipped with air brakes. It applies to trucks, buses, and trailers equipped with air brakes.

The standard requires specific equipment such as air compressor and its capacity, reservoirs and size, tow vehicle protection system, pressure gauge, and warning signals and lights.

The braking performance is specified in terms of stopping distances for a variety of conditions. Brake application and release times must be below 0.25 sec and 0.60 sec, respectively. Wheel brakes when tested on a dynamometer must provide a certain retardation force for specified brake chamber pressures. Fade and recovery brake performance requirements are specified for ten consecutive decelerations (snubs). Emergency braking capabilities are specified.

33–1.21. Std. 122 – Motorcycle Brake Systems. The standard specifies performance requirements for motorcycle brake systems. The standard applies to two-wheeled and three-wheeled motor cycles. Each motor cycle must have either a split hydraulic service brake system or two independently actuated service brake systems. Performance requirements are specified in terms of stopping distances.

33–1.22. Std. 123 – Motorcycle Controls and Displays. The standard specifies requirements for the location, operation, identification and illumination of motorcycle controls and displays, and requirements for motorcycle stands and footrests.

33–1.23. Std. 124 – Accelerator Control Systems. The standard specifies requirements for the return of a vehicle's throttle to the idle position when the accelerator control is released, or in the event of a disconnection in the accelerator control system.

33–1.24. Std. 125 – Warning Devices. The standard specifies requirements for portable devices that are used to warn approaching traffic of the presence of a stopped vehicle, except for devices designed to be permanently affixed to the vehicle. The standard specifies shape, size and performance requirements for reusable day and night warning devices that can be erected on or near the roadway. It applies only to devices that do not have self-contained energy sources.

33–1.25. Std. 126 – Truck-Camper Loading. The standard specifies requirements for label identification of slide-in campers. The label must show certification, identification and proper loading and to provide more detailed loading information in the owner's manual. The purpose of the standard is to reduce overloading and improper load placement in truck camper combinations.

33–2. STANDARDS FOR INJURY REDUCTION

The standards in this section deal with prevention and reduction of injuries produced in a collision.

33–2.1. Std. 201 – Occupant Protection in Interior Impact. The standard specifies requirements for instrument panels, seat backs, protrusion, sunvisors, and arm-rests to afford impact protection for passenger cars. Specific head acceleration limits are established when certain areas of the instrument panel or seat back are impacted by a 15 pound, 6.5 in. diameter head form at a relative velocity of 15 mph.

Performance requirements for side door latch systems are established.

33-2.2. Std. 202 – Head Restraints. The standard specifies requirements for head restraint (or head rests) to reduce the severity of neck injury in rear-end collisions of passenger cars. A head restraint must be provided at each outboard front seat with the location and adjustment limits prescribed in the standard. When loaded with 200 lb the head restraint must not deflect more than 4 in. In a dynamic test involving the forward acceleration of the structure supporting the seat certain displacement limits must be met.

33-2.3. Std. 203 – Impact Protection for the Driver From the Steering Control System. The standard specifies requirements for steering control systems of passenger cars that will reduce injuries to chest, neck and face of the driver in frontal impacts. The performance requirements state that at a relative impact velocity of 15 mph the force developed on the chest of the body transmitted to the steering wheel and column assembly shall not exceed 2,500 lb. During normal driving maneuvers no steering components shall catch the driver's clothing or jewelry.

33-2.4. Std. 204 – Steering Control Rearward Displacement. The standard specifies requirements limiting the rearward displacement of the steering assembly into the passenger compartment to reduce the likelihood of chest, neck, or head injuries. The standard requires that in a 30 mph barrier collision test the maximum rearward displacement is less than 5 in.

33-2.5. Std. 205 – Glazing Materials on Passenger Cars, Multipurpose Vehicles, Motorcycles, Trucks, and Buses. The standard specifies requirements for glazing materials for use in motor vehicles and equipment. The purpose is to reduce injuries resulting from impact to glazing surfaces, to ensure transparency, and to minimize the possibility of occupant ejection through windows. The glazing materials with some exceptions must conform to the American National Standard Safety Code for Safety Glazing Materials. Chemical resistance is tested with certain chemicals, plastics must conform in certain tests, and specific markings to identify manufacturer and type of glazing must be provided.

33-2.6. Std. 206 – Door Locks and Door Retention Components. This standard specifies requirements for side door locks and side door retention components including latches and hinges to reduce the likelihood of occupant ejection as a result of impact. The standard applies to passenger cars, multipurpose vehicles, and trucks. Specific requirements state that a door must not separate in the fully latched position when loaded by a longitudinal load of 2,500 lb. When in the secondary latched position, the door latch and striker plate shall not separate when a longitudinal load of 1,000 lb is applied. When in the fully latched position no separation shall occur when a transverse load of 2,000 lbs is applied, or when a longitudinal or transverse inertia load of 30g is applied. Load carrying requirements not resulting in door separation are specified for hinges and locks of cargo and sliding doors.

33–2.7. Std. 207 – Seating Systems. This standard specifies requirements for seats, seat attachments and installation to reduce the possibility of seat failure during impact. The standard applies to passenger cars, multipurpose vehicles, trucks and buses. The requirements are stated in terms of specific loads applied to the seat structure or inertia forces at 20g.

33–2.8. Std. 208 – Occupant Crash Protection. The standard specifies performance requirements for the protection of vehicle occupants in crashes. The purpose of the standard is to reduce the number of fatalities and the severity of injuries of vehicle occupants by specifying vehicle crashworthiness requirements by means of force and acceleration levels on anthropomorphic dummies in test crashes.

The restraints include seat belts and may be extended to passive protection systems such as passive seat belts or air bags that do not require any action by the vehicle occupants to be effective.

The protection must be demonstrated in frontal barrier crashes, lateral moving barrier crashes, and rollover tests. During each test the calculated injury criteria must stay below certain levels (see Section 32–2). Adjustment of seat belts, warning systems and test procedures are specified.

33–2.9. Std. 209 – Seat Belt Assembly. The standard specifies requirements for seat belt assemblies of passenger cars, multipurpose vehicles, trucks and buses. The seat belt is the device designed to secure an occupant in a vehicle to mitigate the results of a collision. Requirements include lap and shoulder belt, release mechanism performance, webbing width and strength and other factors. Load carrying capacities and elongations vary as a function of seat belt type, e.g., lap belt, combination belt or child restraint.

33–2.10. Std. 210 – Seat Belt Assembly Anchorages. The standard specifies requirements for seat belt assembly anchorages to ensure their proper location for effective occupant restraint and to reduce the likelihood of belt anchorage failure. The anchorage assembly must support certain levels of force when tested in specific procedures.

33-2.11. Std. 211 – Wheel Nuts, Wheel Discs, and Hub Caps. The standard specifies geometry of wheel nuts, wheel discs, and hub caps to reduce the likelihood of injury to pedestrians and cyclists. The standard applies to passenger cars, multipurpose vehicles and related equipment and basically states that wheel assemblies must not incorporate winged projections.

33-2.12. Std. 212 – Windshield Mounting. The standard specifies requirements for windshield retention. During a 30 mph barrier crash each windshield mounting must retain at least 75% of the windshield periphery or not less than 50% of that portion of the windshield periphery on each side of the vehicle longitudinal center line, when an unrestrained 95th percentile adult male dummy is seated in each outboard front seating position.

33-2.13. Std. 213 – Child Seating Systems. The standard specifies requirements for child seating systems to reduce the likelihood of death and injury to children in collisions, sudden stops by ejection, contact with the vehicle interior, or excessive forces from the restraint system. The requirements include labeling, adjustment, installation, head restraints, impact load carrying capacity, webbing, and hardware.

33-2.14. Std. 214 – Side Door Strength. The standard specifies strength requirements for side doors of passenger cars to reduce the likelihood of injuries by intrusion into the passenger compartment in a side impact collision. When tested in specific procedures, the peak crush resistance shall not be less than twice the vehicle weight or 7000 lb, the intermediate crush resistance not less than 3,500 lb, the initial value not less than 2,250 lb. The crush deformation associated with the peak resistance force shall not exceed 18 in.

33-2.15. Std. 215 – Exterior Protection. The standard specifies requirements for the impact resistance and the configuration of front and rear vehicle surfaces. The purpose of the standard is to prevent low-speed collisions from impairing the safe operation of vehicle systems, and to reduce the frequency of override or underride in higher speed collisions of passenger cars. The vehicle must withstand certain impact tests without damage to lighting, fuel, exhaust, cooling or hood latching systems.

33-2.16. Std. 216 – Roof Crush Resistance. The standard specifies strength requirements for the passenger compartment roof. The purpose is to reduce death and injury due to crushing of the roof into the occupant compartment in rollover accidents. In specific tests the crush shall not exceed 5 in. when a load of 1.5 times the vehicle weight or 5000 lb, whichever is less, is applied at different locations at the roof.

33-2.17. Std. 217—Bus Window Retention and Release. The standard specifies requirements for the retention of windows in buses and establishes operating forces, opening dimensions, and markings for push-out bus windows and other emergency exits. The purpose of the standard is to reduce the likelihood of occupant ejection through windows, and to provide a means of readily accessible emergency egress.

33-2.18. Std. 218—Motorcycle Helmets. The standard specifies requirements for helmets for use by motorcyclists. The standard provides for test procedures, impact attenuation, penetration, and retention, peripheral vision clearance and labeling.

33-3. FLAMMABILITY STANDARDS

33-3.1. Std. 301—Fuel System Integrity. This standard specifies requirements for integrity and security of fuel tanks, fuel tank filler pipes, and fuel tank connections to reduce fire hazards as a result of a collision. Test procedures include both impact and rollover test during which the fuel discharge must remain below 1 ounce per minute.

33-3.2. Std. 302—Flammability of Interior Materials. The standard specifies burn resistance requirements for material used in the occupant compartments of motor vehicles to reduce deaths and injuries caused by vehicle fires. Test procedures and requirements provide for a burn rate less than 4 in. per minute across the surface.

CHAPTER 34
HIGHWAY SAFETY PROGRAM STANDARDS

The National Highway Traffic Safety Administration of the U.S. Department of Transportation has issued a number of standards relating to improving highway safety through a common approach by federal, state, and local government. Only the major categories are listed below. Details may be obtained from NHTSA or state transportation departments.

The program standards are:

1. Periodic motor vehicle inspection
2. Motor vehicle registration
3. Motorcycle safety
4. Driver education
5. Driver licensing
6. Codes and traffic laws
7. Traffic courts
8. Alcohol in relation to highway safety
9. Identification and surveillance of accident locations
10. Traffic records
11. Emergency medical services
12. Highway design, construction and maintenance
13. Pedestrian safety
14. Traffic control devices
15. Police traffic services
16. Debris hazard control and cleanup
17. Pupil transportation safety
18. Accident investigation and reporting

CHAPTER 35
OTHER REGULATIONS

A number of regulations have been published by the National Highway Traffic Safety Administration relating to the official conduct of its business with the public.

Other regulations dealing with certain aspects of traffic safety are briefly listed below.

Part 555: Temporary exemption from motor vehicle safety standards.

Part 566: Manufacturer identification

Part 567: Certification regulation

Part 568: Vehicles manufactured in two or more stages

Part 569: Regrooved tires. This standard allows only tires designed for the regrooving process to be regrooved. Labeling and dimensions and conditions after regrooving are specified.

Part 570: Vehicle in use inspection. The standard specifies procedures for the inspection of hydraulic brake systems, steering and suspension systems, and tire and wheel assemblies of motor vehicles in use. It is intended to be implemented by the states for vehicles with a gross vehicle weight rating of 10,000 lb or less.

Part 572: Anthropomorphic test dummy

Part 573: Defect reports. The standard specifies manufacturer requirements for reporting safety related defects to the National Highway Traffic Safety Administration.

Part 574: Tire identification and record keeping

Part 575: Consumer information of passenger cars and motorcycles to provide information on vehicle stopping distance, tire reserve load, and acceleration and passing ability. Manufacturers of trucks that are capable of accommodating slide-in campers are required to provide cargo weight ratings, and longitudinal limits within which the center of gravity for the cargo weight should be located.

Part 577: Defect notification. The standard specifies requirements for the format and contents of manufacturer notification to first purchasers and warranty holders of motor vehicles of a defect relating to motor vehicle safety or a noncompliance with a federal motor vehicle safety standard.

Part 580: Odometer disclosure. The standard requires a person who transfers ownership of a motor vehicle to give the new owner a written disclosure of the mileage traveled by the vehicle.

CHAPTER 36
MOTOR VEHICLE DEFECTS INVESTIGATIONS

The National Highway Traffic Safety Administration (NHTSA) regularly conducts investigations of alleged motor vehicle defects. Investigation reports are furnished to the Consumer Product Information Center, Pueblo, Colorado. The reports may be obtained upon written request in single copies from the above address.

Persons having information bearing on current investigations are invited to write to: The Office of Consumer Services, U.S. Department of Transportation, National Highway Traffic Safety Administration, 400 Seventh St. SW, Washington, D.C. 20590. Information provided should indicate the make, model, year and serial number (VIN) of the vehicle, and all pertinent facts relating to the failure. Summary findings of NHTSA investigations in terminated cases, or the public files for suspended cases, may be reviewed in the technical reference room of the NHTSA at the above address.

Persons wishing to report automobile safety-related defects, request vehicle information or obtain information on activities of NHTSA may use the NHTSA Auto Safety Hotline, toll free at 800-424-9393. Washington, D.C. residents may call 426-0123.

The December 1976 defect investigation cases report contained among others 67 active investigations, 35 surveys and audits, and 13 terminations, dealing with all facets of motor vehicle safety.

CHAPTER 37

MOTOR CARRIER SAFETY REGULATIONS

The Federal Highway Administration of the U.S. Department of Transportation has issued regulations concerning highway safety of commercial vehicles. The regulations are briefly reviewed.

37-1. PART 390–GENERAL

Part 390 of the Motor Carrier Safety Regulations specifies definitions of such terms as motor vehicle, vehicle, bus, gross weight.

37-2. PART 391–QUALIFICATIONS OF DRIVERS

This regulation specifies requirements for qualification or disqualification of a driver, written and medical examinations, and driver records.

37-3. PART 392–DRIVING OF MOTOR VEHICLES

The regulation specifies requirements on driver factors such as ill or fatigued operator, schedules to conform with speed limits, equipment, inspection and use, safe loading, on driving of vehicles on special locations such as railroad grade crossings, drawbridges, on hazardous conditions, and on use of seat belts, on stopped vehicles such as emergency signals, dangerous cargo, on accidents, on fueling precautions, and on prohibited practices, such as towing or pushing loaded buses or use of vehicle when carbon monoxide is detected.

37-4. PART 393–PARTS AND ACCESSORIES NECESSARY FOR SAFE OPERATION

This regulation specifies equipment and performance requirements of lighting, reflectors and electrical equipment, of brake systems, fuel systems, coupling devices and towing methods and miscellaneous parts such as tires, heater, windshield wipers.

37-5. PART 394 – RECORDING AND REPORTING OF ACCIDENTS

This regulation specifies format and requirement of accidents reporting. It defines recordable accidents, provides format, and specifies reporting procedures for fatal accidents and annual accident reports.

37-6. PART 395 – HOURS OF SERVICE OF DRIVERS

This regulation specifies requirements of driving schedules, maximum driving and on-duty time, driver's daily log, adverse driving conditions, and emergency conditions.

37-7. PART 396 – INSPECTION AND MAINTENANCE

The regulation specifies requirements of vehicle inspection and maintenance, lubrication, inspection of motor vehicles in operation, inspection of damaged vehicles, and vehicle condition reports.

37-8. PART 397 – TRANSPORTATION OF HAZARDOUS MATERIALS; DRIVING AND PARKING RULES

The regulation specifies requirements on safety inspections of vehicles carrying hazardous materials, e.g., every 2 hours or 100 miles, and driving and parking rules of vehicles carrying hazardous materials.

PART 6

ACCIDENT INVESTIGATION

Part 6 presents important factors relating to accident investigation. Special emphasis is placed upon identification of data required for proper accident reconstruction by use of equations found in previous chapters.

35-4

upon the

at the

vehic

Frequently

removed

35-5

gas, exami

ing

follow

of an

accident

process

during

related

Whether

the investigation

must be recorded

CHAPTER 38
ACCIDENT INVESTIGATION PREPARATION

38–1. LEVELS OF INVESTIGATION

Investigations may be divided into several categories depending upon the data available.

On-scene investigations involve an examination of facts as found at the accident scene. The accident scene is defined as the locations of vehicles, persons and debris existing immediately after the collision. Frequently, injured persons and/or vehicles have been relocated or removed prior to the investigation.

In many cases an accident reconstruction is requested weeks, months, or even years after the date of the accident. Information generally is available through witness statements, vehicle examination or photographs, photographs of accident scene, and accident site examination. The accident site is defined as the location of an accident occurrence.

Frequently, accident reconstructions rely entirely upon written material and photographs. Inadequate photographs and incomplete sketches or descriptions make it extremely difficult or impossible to provide a meaningful reconstruction of the accident.

38–2. PREPARATION

An efficient and complete accident investigation requires specific preparation. On-scene investigations are conducted by the investigating officer responsible for the investigation. Other investigators must follow instructions of the investigating officer. Main requirements of on-scene investigations are complete and accurate collection of accident data before changes occur. Accident data collection is improved when the investigator can formulate the accident events during the investigation. As different pieces of accident data can be related to the entire accident, overall accuracy can be improved. Whether or not a formulary of the accident can be developed during the investigation, all data appearing to be related to the collision must be recorded.

CHAPTER 39
ON-SCENE INVESTIGATION

39–1. ENVIRONMENTAL FACTORS

Environmental factors relate to the conditions of roadway geometry, road surface, sight obstructions, driver distractions, and ambient conditions. Environmental conditions such as tire markings change their appearance with time. Others may be affected by ambient conditions. Road surfaces alter their characteristics due to traffic, weather, and maintenance efforts.

39–1.1. Road Geometry. The roadway geometry provides a description of the collision site, including name and other identification of the road, straight or curved, width of pavement, pavement traffic markings, road crown, slopes, super elevation, off-road surfaces, and guard rails.

The roadway geometry, if necessary, may be illustrated in a site diagram. It is helpful when the diagram is drawn to scale and that, in the case of a trial, no conclusions or opinions are placed on the diagram that may result in a rejection of the exhibit by the court.

39–1.2. Road Surface Conditions. The conditions of the road surface contains a description of the material used such as concrete, asphalt, gravel and its condition such as coarse or polished, and any road surface irregularities (pot holes, bumps). The coefficient of friction may be used to describe the traction capability of the road surface. If the tire-road friction coefficient has not been measured, the coefficient to be used for reconstruction purposes may be determined by Eq. 18–4.

39–1.3. Traffic Controls. The controls used for directing vehicle traffic are described including speed limit(s), location of warning and regulatory signs, traffic lane and markings, raised medians, traffic lights.

39–1.4. Non-Roadway Environment. The general nature of the environment of the accident site is described including trees, poles, billboards, private and public accesses, use of adjacent land, and description of possible sight obstructions and driver distractions.

39–1.5. Ambient Conditions. The ambient conditions are described including weather (sun, rain, snow, dust), wind gusts, noise (e.g., airplanes), temperature and time of day.

39–1.6. Visibility Obstructions. The partial or complete visibility obstruction(s) is described including moving vehicles, trees, buildings, darkness, fog, smoke, hill or curve, glare from sun or other road users, and off-road objects.

39–1.7. Accident Caused Markings. The markings made by the vehicle(s), ejected occupants, or other objects to the road surface and roadway environment are described. These markings include tire skid marks (wheels locked), tire scuff marks, (tire slipping while rolling), tire prints (rolling wheel), gauge marks from metal to road contact, oil, gasoline, and water from ruptured engine components, and loose debris such as broken glass and mirrors and paint transfer.

All markings must be measured accurately to provide sufficient information on vehicle motion before, during, and after impact.

An example of the usefulness of road markings is illustrated in Fig. 39–1. The tire markings immediately after impact may be used

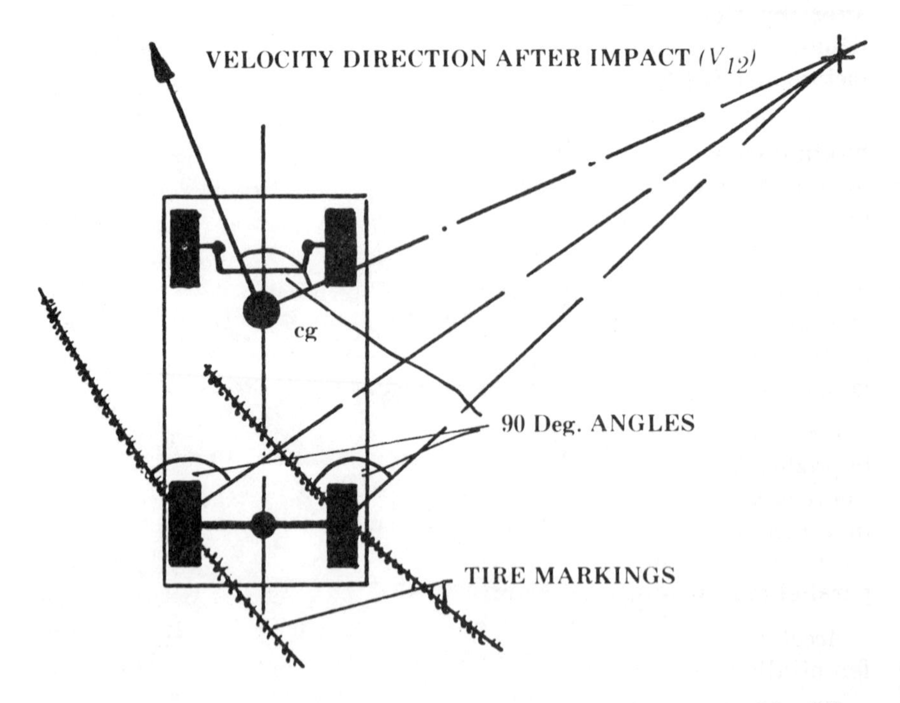

Figure 39–1. Determination of Velocity from Tire Markings

to determine the position and direction of motion of the vehicle after impact. The markings made by the tread pattern may be used to determine vehicle position.

Since tire markings are a significant factor of accident reconstruction, some details will be presented next.

Skidmarks are produced by tires that are not rotating due to brake application or sheet metal deformation. A wheel sliding sideways may also produce a skidmark even if it is free to roll. The friction is the result of adhesion, hystersis damping, i.e., internal damping, viscous damping, and tearing.

The skidding motion may occur on clean or contaminated road surfaces. The basic mechanism of skidmark production involves the relative sliding motion of the tire contact patch over the road surface. In the process road material may be embedded in the rubber to grind the pavement as the tire continues to slide (pavement grinding) or particles of tire rubber may be deposited onto the road surface (tire grinding). The latter requires hard aggressive surfaces. Since pavement grinding involves a change of road surface conditions it may occur on wet surfaces and usually is visible for a long period of time after the accident. Rubber particles deposited onto the road surface usually disappear shortly after the accident due to environmental factors and due to other road users.

A sliding tire may smear the road surface due to softening of the bituminous material of the roadway, or due to melting of the rubber at higher temperatures. A sliding distance of 8 to 10 ft may be required to mark the pavement due to surface melting.

Tire imprints are produced by a tire rolling on a soft surface, or by deposition of material by the tire tread picked up previously. An example of the latter is found when a tire rolls over wet paint, or an oil spot. Since tire tread geometry is accurately marked, tire imprints generally may be used to clearly define vehicle position.

Tire scuff markings are produced by a rolling tire, slipping sideways to produce a side force while turning. Circumferential slipping can be the result of a braking or accelerating tire. A tire producing side force in a cornering vehicle is partially side slipping. When the side slipping motion is sufficiently severe, striations may become visible as narrow, parallel markings.

Acceleration skid markings are produced by a tire slipping circumferentially due to excessive drive thrust.

Tire markings are affected by inflation pressure. Under inflation results in a higher concentration of tire-road contact pressure under the edges of the contact patch. Tire markings produced by under inflated tires generally show two dark parallel lines separated by a distance equal to the tire width. Overinflated tires exhibit a concentration of tire-road contact pressure at the center. The associated tire markings show a single line having a width less than the tire width.

A tire sliding on a road surface contaminated by dust, dirt, or water produces an erasor-type marking, generally barely visible. The wet wiping action usually disappears a short time after the accident. When the skidding distance is sufficiently long to heat the tire, the water may evaporate under the tire and the road surface may be partially or completely dry. Subsequently water may run back onto the skid marking.

A tire sliding on snow or mud may not produce pronounced tread pattern due to the deposit of snow or mud into the tread cavities, thus performing closely to that of a bald tire.

Gouges are produced by metal to road contact. Gouges are frequently produced during the collision, or by a vehicle having rolled. Collisions involving motorcycles usually show gouge markings produced by the motorcycle sliding on its side. On-the-road-single-vehicle rollovers frequently are the result of rim-to-ground contact, indicated by a groove in the pavement and corresponding rim damage and possibly tire bead unseating.

39-2. VEHICLE FACTORS

Examination of the vehicle including damage, mechanical condition, and loading may provide information on how the accident happened and what caused it.

39-2.1. General Data. General data include vehicle identification numbers (VIN), mileage, safety inspection information, weight data, engine, transmission, steering and brake information, safety equipment, maintenance records, color, tire type and size, gear position and amount of fuel. The objective of the general data is to be used to cross-reference other data required for accident reconstruction such as tire radius, weight distribution, or transmission ratio without the necessity of actually measuring detailed data.

39-2.2. Precrash Factors. The examination of an accident vehicle relative to precrash factors provides data that may indicate why the accident happened. Due to vehicle damage a complete precrash evaluation may be impossible or difficult to conduct. All factors relating to precrash vehicle conditions must be evaluated. These factors include tire condition and inflation pressure, shock absorbers, steering system, lighting and signals, windshield transparency, brake system, and vehicle loading condition. Frequently, maintenance factors may indicate a possible defect such as a partially used can of brake fluid stored in the trunk. Important precrash factors to be determined are proper functioning of the lights, precrash tire flats, and braking and steering effectiveness.

39–2.3. Collision Damage. The collision damage evaluation provides data that may be used to determine direction of impact, relative position of vehicles and relative motion prior to contact, and sometimes impact speeds.

The dimensions of the damage must be measured as illustrated in Fig. 39–2. The crush distance measured may be compared to crush distances obtained in controlled test with the impact speed measured.

The damage may be caused by direct contact with another vehicle or object, or may be induced by a part of the vehicle or by inertia effects. Consequently, damage may be found at a location that was not in contact with any other "foreign" object. For example, the fender may buckle at a location distant from the contact point.

Induced damage of windshields results in parallel or cross-hatched cracks, whereas direct impact, e.g., by the head of an occupant, results in radial and circular cracks.

39–2.4. Brake System. The lack of skid marks may sometimes indicate a possible brake system defect. However, a detailed visual inspection of the brake system including wheel brakes, master cylinder, reservoir, brake linings or pads, and hydraulic brake lines and hoses generally reveals a possible brake defect. A hard pedal in most cases indicates that the transmission of pedal force to the brake shoes is in good mechanical condition. If fade or degraded lining friction is suspected, the wheels and drums must be taken off the vehicle for closer inspection. The SAE friction code designated by two letter, e.g., FF, should be read off the linings and recorded for braking effectiveness calculations. Section 20–9 provides more detail on brake failure analysis.

39–2.5. Steering System. Damage to the vehicle may be so severe that the steering system is damaged during the collision and an examination may be difficult. Failure of the steering system may be caused by a fracture of linkage components connecting the pitman

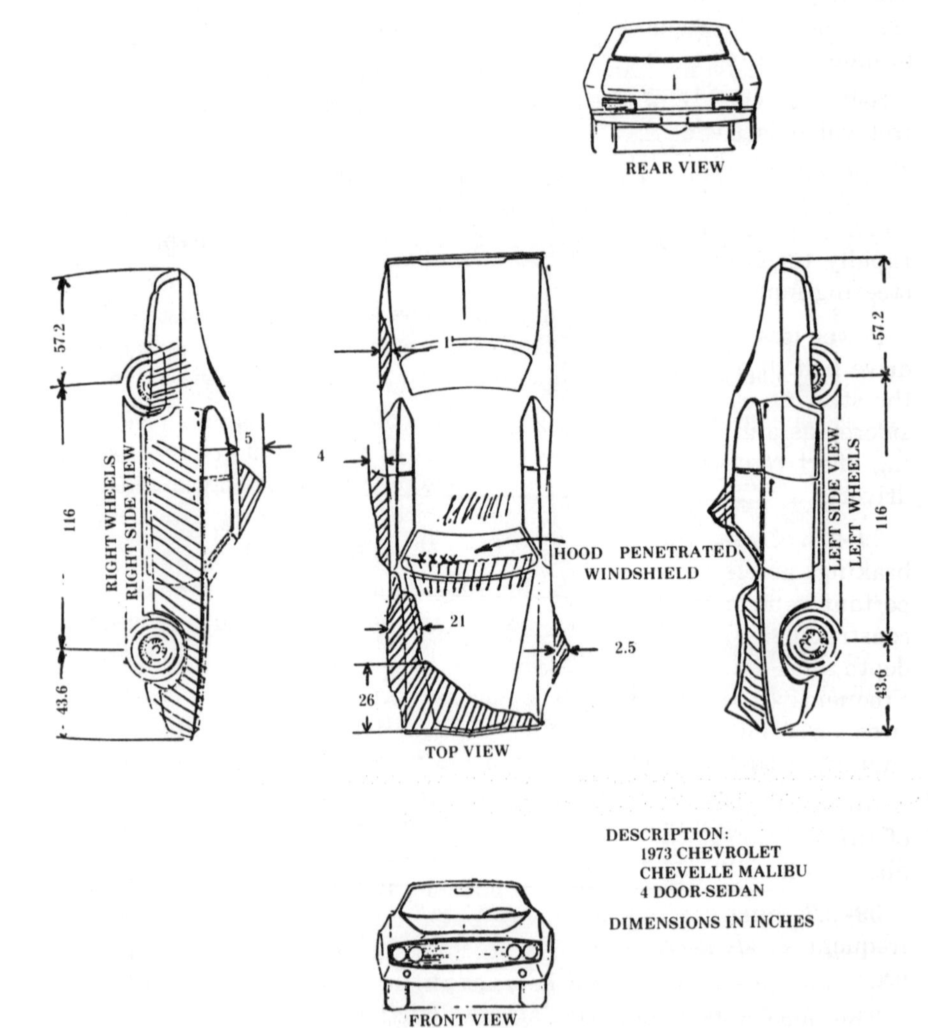

Figure 39–2. Vehicle Damage Diagram

arm to the front wheels, by self-steering of the power steering system, or by a failure of the power steering assist.

Fracture of a steering system component or separation due to bolt loosening occurs infrequently when proper vehicle safety inspections are conducted. Sometimes defective manufacturing may cause a fatigue fracture.

Self-steering due to malfunction of the power steering assist control valve is a rare event but does occur. If possible, the steering system should be tested in the vehicle prior to disassembly. If the engine is damaged, an electric drill motor may be used to drive the steering pump. Self-steering is evident when the steering wheel rapidly turns to the left or right end position without prior driver steering inputs.

Power loss may result from pump defect, lack of oil, or a damaged drive belt. If a power loss occurs at medium to higher vehicle speeds, the steering effectiveness may not be degraded sufficiently to be considered as a major accident causation factor. At low speeds the steering effort required to negotiate turns may be beyond that of many drivers.

39–2.6. Tires. The tires are the vehicle components that produce braking, acceleration, and cornering forces and are one of the important vehicle safety elements. In the examination of the tires the construction type, manufacture, model, inflation pressure, tread depth, and unusual wear pattern should be obtained for each wheel. Frequently, the mismatch of tire types, e.g., radial and conventional tires on front and rear axle may significantly alter the handling characteristics of a vehicle.

An insufficient tread depth may cause hydroplaning, i.e., total loss of tire traction on a wet road surface. Improperly inflated tires may alter the handling characteristics of a vehicle.

39–2.7. Suspension. Suspension failure due to fracture is an infrequent accident causation factor. If suspension component fracture occurs, fatigue due to defective manufacturing may be suspected.

The mechanical condition of the shock absorbers significantly affects the road holding of a vehicle. When intermittent skidmarks are found at the accident site, degraded shock absorbers may be suspected. Frequently, tandem axles of semitrailers develop "brake hop" during severe braking, indicated by intermittent skid marks.

Suspension characteristics change when the maximum wheel travel is exhausted and the suspension travel is arrested by the stop.

On-the-road-rollover with or without tripping due to rim-to-ground contact generally requires a detailed examination of suspension geometry for possible rollover causation.

39-2.8. Lighting System. In accidents occurring during darkness it may be necessary to determine whether the head or taillights were illuminated when the collision occurred. An examination of the filaments may indicate whether or not the lights were on when the glass of the light bulb was broken. The space inside the glass bulb is a vacuum, and consequently, no oxidizing of the hot filament occurs during lights-on operation. When the filament is cold prior to bulb fracture, the filament remains bright after it is exposed to the oxygen of the air. A hot filament may heat an unlighted filament sufficiently to cause its discoloring when exposed to air. Filament examination may be done on headlights, brake and tail lights, and emergency flashers.

The impact forces during a collision yield inertia forces acting on the filament. A hot filament is less resistant and may elongate more than a cold one and thus may indicate whether or not the lights were illuminated at the time of the collision.

During the vehicle examination light switches should not be operated to prevent inadvertent destruction of accident data.

39-2.9. Vehicle Trailers. Trailers in car-trailer combinations alter the handling characteristics of the tow-vehicle. Important trailer parameters to be determined in a trailer examination are (see Section 22-3.4) tire characteristics, trailer wheel base, distance between hitch point and center-of-gravity of loaded trailer, weight, and mass moment of inertia.

39-3. HUMAN FACTORS

Human factors involve all aspects of occupant influence on accident avoidance, collision damage, injury production and injury reduction by means of restraint systems.

39-3.1. General Occupant Data. Included in the occupant data are occupant position prior to impact, weight, height, age and sex. If appropriate, other information such as driver education, driving experience, familiarity with the transportation network near the accident site, use of drugs must be included.

39-3.2. Occupant Injuries. A detailed description of injuries and causes of fatal injuries requires substantial medical knowledge. In accident reconstruction it is important to determine what interior vehicle components caused the injuries and the direction of occupant impact. This information may be used to determine the occupant kinematics during the collisions when matched with the associated interior vehicle damage.

In collisions involving occupant ejection the injuries sustained inside and outside the vehicle must be separated.

39–3.3. Driver Response Time. Accident avoidance analysis frequently involves the determination of the time prior to impact at which a driver control input must be provided to avoid the collision. In addition to the time required to decelerate or turn the vehicle, the response time of the driver to the accident threat has to be considered. Although a driver response time of 1.00 sec for reaction and control input is assumed in many reconstructions, observations of the driver in post accident interviews may reveal larger values, particularly in older or handicapped people.

39–4. DATA MEASUREMENT

Measurement of accident data is a critical element to accident reconstruction. The results are used to locate vehicles at impact, determine vehicle speeds, represent accident scene and vehicles, give vehicle damage, and provide any other information forming a basis for the reconstruction and cause analysis of the accident.

39–4.1. Measuring Equipment. The equipment for measuring on-scene accident data must be light and compact so that it can be transported easily. As a minimum, the items that follow should be available:

1. 100-foot steel tape
2. 10-foot steel tape
3. Depth gauge (tire tread)
4. Hand level or angle measuring device
5. Chalk
6. Camera
7. U-tube or dial gauge decelerometer (1g)
8. Lever-type weight scale (to weigh each wheel load of the accident vehicle—passenger car)

In addition, the investigator should have available a number of empty envelopes to store paint samples, metal chips, etc., and a number of small glass or plastic bottles to store samples of brake fluid, fuel or oil.

The vehicle damage is more accurately recorded if a vehicle diagram sheet is used that shows the general outline of the passenger car (or truck) in all essential views. It is helpful to use a complete check list covering all items that must be inspected and recorded during the vehicle examination. Included in this check list are vehicle identification number, safety inspection sticker data, maintenance data, and data on all essential components such as engine transmission, brakes, steering, seatbelts, lighting, tires, and suspension.

39–4.2. Measurement of Accident Data. Important consideration in data measurement is that the data as recorded can be used for accident reconstruction without any modification or guessing.

Tire markings should be measured in terms of their actual geometry, i.e., length and shape. Photographs of tire marking should (ideally) contain some information that may be used to determine the size and length of the skidmarks from the photograph. For example, the intermittent white line dividing a highway, light poles, or a building front may be used to relate the geometry of the skid mark to a known length. Scene and site photographs should contain similar information.

Photographs of vehicles should contain information such as tire diameter, that may be used later to determine other vehicle dimensions. Vehicles should be photographed to permit an evaluation of crush deformation. A number of photographs must be taken in a direction perpendicular to the side. For example, if a vehicle has front end damage, the photographs must be taken at a right angle from the side and front of the vehicle. Frequently, the crush deformation can be recorded on the photograph by using a "stick" tape with a half or quarter inch division placed on the vehicle. Since photographs represent a valuable data bank, it usually pays to take a sufficient number including top and interior views of the vehicle.

Road friction measurement should ideally be conducted immediately following the removal of the accident vehicles. On dry road surfaces the tire-road friction coefficient may be approximated by brake testing of a vehicle having tires that are similar to those of the accident vehicle. The approximate friction coefficient can be determined by a skid test in which the test vehicle is decelerated with all wheels locked from a known speed. The resulting stopping distance is measured and the average friction coefficient is determined by

$$\mu = \frac{V^2}{30S}, \text{ d'less} \tag{39–1}$$

where

S = skidding distance, ft

V = vehicle speed at instant sliding begins, mph

It is apparent from an inspection of Eq. 39–1 that speed has a significant effect on the computed friction coefficient due to the V-squared relationship. For example, the speed read off the speedometer of the test vehicle may have ranged between 28 and 32 mph for a tire skidding distance of 50 ft. Under these conditions the computed friction coefficients may vary between 0.52 and 0.68, i.e., a significant difference may exist due to the speed variance. Since both velocity and distance measurements involve inaccuracies, several tests should be conducted and an average friction coefficient computed.

Decelerometers using the inertia effect may be used to measure the deceleration of a skidding vehicle. These decelerometers may involve a U-tube filled with a liquid, or a pendulum. The deceleration is measured in feet per second-squared or g-units. The coefficient of friction is obtained by dividing the deceleration (ft/sec^2) by 32.2. When measured in g-units, the friction coefficient equals the numerical value in g-units.

In critical cases the tires of the accident vehicle must be used on the test vehicle to measure the friction coefficient more accurately.

If the road surface is wet, tires of the accident vehicle or tires having a near identical tread pattern and tread depth should be used. Since wet road friction is greatly affected by tread geometry and water depth, extreme care must be taken in conducting the test to ensure reasonable data accuracy.

In some cases a skid trailer may be used that measures the sliding friction of a tire at different speeds. Skid trailers may be equipped to measure both peak and sliding friction values.

Since the tire-road friction coefficient is an important parameter in accident reconstruction, all necessary steps should be undertaken to measure the value existing at the time of the accident or at a similar condition.

The *actual weight* and weight *distribution* of the accident vehicle is an important measure of accident reconstruction. The weight of a vehicle (passenger car) can easily be determined by a lever scale. The scale is placed under the rim contour and the lever pressed down until the tire lifts off the ground. A hydraulic cylinder and pressure gauge system permit the reading of the wheel load. Repeated for each wheel yields total vehicle weight and longitudinal center of gravity location.

The distance of the center of gravity from the front wheel ℓ_F is

$$\ell_F = \frac{F_{zR} \cdot \ell}{W}, \text{ ft} \qquad (39\text{–}2)$$

where

$$F_{zR} = \text{static rear axle wheel load, lb}$$
$$\ell = \text{wheel base, ft}$$
$$W = \text{vehicle weight, lb}$$

The vertical location of the center of gravity may be determined by raising one axle relative to the other and measuring the difference in wheel load exhibited by the non-raised axle. The raising of one axle simulates down hill driving and the associated load transfer. The vertical height of the center of gravity above ground h (with the rear end raised) is

$$h = r_F + \frac{(F_{zF,r} - F_{zF})\,\ell\,[\ell^2 - (a - r_f)^2]^{1/2}}{W(a - r_f)}, \text{ ft} \qquad (39\text{–}3)$$

where

a = raised vertical distance between rear axle center and ground, ft
F_{zF} = front axle load without raising rear axle, lb
$F_{zR,r}$ = front axle load with rear axle raised, lb
ℓ = wheel base, ft
r_F = front wheel radius, ft

Frequently road curvature or vehicle turning radius must be completed from accident data. The radius r is given by

$$r = \frac{4d^2 + c^2}{8d}, \text{ ft} \qquad (39\text{–}4)$$

where

c = cord length, ft; a straight line connecting beginning and end of skuff markings
d = maximum perpendicular distance between cord and skuff markings, ft

PART 7

ACCIDENT RECONSTRUCTION

The objective of Part 7 is to apply the material of previous chapters to actual accidents to give the reader a better understanding of the use of engineering analyses, and to provide a list of different accident modes that may serve as a guide in the reconstruction of similar accidents under study by the reader.

The reconstruction details presented in the following paragraphs in terms of the mathematical depth vary. However, in most cases the equations and data to be used and the results are presented. In some cases a complete reconstruction including mathematical numerical equations are presented to provide the inexperienced reader an opportunity to follow the analyses without any difficulties.

CHAPTER 40
RECONSTRUCTION OF ACTUAL ACCIDENTS

40-1. TWO-VEHICLE COLLISION WITH BRAKING

This reconstruction is carried out in greater detail and involves braking application by one of the drivers.

On January 16, 1974 at 3:30 P.M., a 1966 Cadillac four-door hardtop was stopped on an asphalt paved road, waiting for a car in front of the Cadillac to make a left turn. The driver of the Cadillac was 51 years old, male. The passenger in the right front seat was 16 years old, female. The roadway had an uphill slope of 2.3 deg. A 1970 Volkswagen Type 113 (Beetle) was approaching the Cadillac from behind. The driver of the VW was an 18-year old female. The road surface was dry, the weather was clear, the road was straight, no alcohol or drugs was involved.

The VW collided with the rear of the Cadillac, pushing it several feet forward. The front bumper of the VW and the rear bumper of the Cadillac remained connected during the post-impact motion of the vehicles. The driver of the VW applied the brakes prior to impact, however no visible skid marks were produced on the pavement.

Inspection of the vehicles indicates no damage to the rear end of the Cadillac and a 2-in dent to the VW bumper near the center and a minor dent in the trunk lid. The Cadillac was equipped with a trailer hitch which first damaged the VW bumper and then produced a slight dent in the trunk lid of the VW. The braking action of the VW caused the front end of the VW to dip down, thus permitting the trailer hitch to slip over the bumper.

The driver of the VW sustained no injuries. The driver of the Cadillac had a history of prior back and neck injuries, however the whiplash sustained in the collision caused additional pain and probable injuries.

The reconstruction of the accident requires the determination of the impact speed of the VW and the force exerted on the head of the driver of the Cadillac due to the whiplash.

The Volkswagen is denoted by number 1. The environment had no effect on the motion of vehicle no. 1 (V1), and consequently is not considered. Driver no. 1 applied the brakes during the precrash motion. The severity of the brake application cannot be determined from accident facts except it may be stated that the level of braking was not sufficiently high to lock some or all wheels. In this particular accident the effect of the road is two fold, considered in terms of the tire-road friction coefficient and the uphill slope. Since the wheels were not locked on the VW, the sliding tire friction coefficient is of no significance except that it defines an upper boundary of deceleration below which the VW must have been braking. The particular road geometry did not affect the behavior of the driver. An example would be a very rough road or misleading roadway marking which may adversely affect driver control or judgment.

The engineering equations relating pedal force to vehicle braking or road slope are presented in detail in Chapter 20.

The pedal force F_p applied by the driver causes a braking force to be developed between tires and road which is proportional to the gain of the brake system. The calculation of brake system gain is discussed in Chapter 20. The braking force produced by the vehicle brake system causes the vehicle to slow down at a certain deceleration a_B. The deceleration experienced by the vehicle will depend upon vehicle weight W. These interactions may be expressed by a single equation as (see Eq. 20–5).

$$a_B = \frac{F_p G}{W/g}, \text{ ft/sec}^2 \qquad (40\text{–}1)$$

where

a_B = vehicle deceleration on a level road due to braking ft/sec^2
G = brake system gain, d'less
g = 32.2 ft/sec^2 (gravitational constant)
F_p = pedal force, lb
W = vehicle weight, lb

The effect of the road slope on the vehicle is an additional retarding force. This retarding force produces an additional deceleration of the vehicle and may be expressed as (see Eq. 19–7).

$$a_S = g(\sin\alpha), \text{ ft/sec}^2 \qquad (40\text{–}2)$$

where

a_S = vehicle deceleration due to slope, ft/sec^2
g = 32.2 ft/sec^2, gravitational constant
α = slope angle, deg

The term sin(e) is a mathematical notation defining a certain mathematical operation on the angle α. For example, sin (30 deg) is 0.5. Other values may be obtained from tables or electronic calculators. The combined effect of the road slope and vehicle braking produces a vehicle deceleration of $a = a_B + a_S$.

In this case the Volkswagen exhibited a certain speed upon impact. The impact velocity may be related to the initial velocity V, i.e., the velocity at which the VW began to brake at a deceleration a, and the distance S traveled from initiation of braking to impact by the equation (see Eq. 16–15).

$$V_2 = \sqrt{V_1^2 - 2aS}, \text{ ft/sec} \tag{40–3}$$

where

a = vehicle deceleration, ft/sec^2
S = distance traveled, ft
V_1 = initial velocity, ft/sec
V_2 = impact velocity, ft/sec

Examination of accident and vehicle data and information gained from interviews with driver no. 1 yield the following numerical values for the precrash analysis.

The VW traveled two to three car lengths or approximately 40 ft from the instant braking began to the point of impact. The VW driver estimates prebraking speed at 25 mph. The Cadillac was pushed forward approximately 3 to 5 ft by the impact. The Cadillac including driver weighs approximately 4780 lb, the VW approximately 2230 lb. The brake system gain of the VW is 13.8 (detailed discussions are presented in Chapter 20 and Ref. 11). During interviews with driver no. 1 no specific information concerning pedal force level could be obtained. The driver only indicated "that she hit the brake". "Hitting" the brake without causing wheel lock to occur may indicate poor mechanical condition of the brakes, or simply that driver no. 1 was traveling at a high speed and no sufficient time was available to lock the wheels prior to impact, or the estimated distance of 40 ft was actually much less to yield sufficient time for wheel lock to occur. The upper deceleration in g-units is equal to the sliding tire-road friction coefficient. Inspection of the roadway surface indicated a sliding friction coefficient of approximately 0.60 to 0.70, yielding an upper deceleration limit of (0.60 to 0.70) times 32.2 or 19.3 to 22.5 ft/sec^2. A second lower limit of braking exists due to the fact that for most braking conditions either the front or the rear wheels lock up first. The determination of this fact can be accomplished easily by the use of engineering analysis and is discussed in detail in Chapter 20. Here it is sufficient to indicate that the front wheels tend to lock at a deceleration of approximately 0.75 (also called braking efficiency) times (19.3 to 22.5) or 14.5 to 16.9 ft/sec^2.

If, on the other hand, the driver of the VW claimed that she applied a pedal force as large as she could, then this information may be compared with human factors data on pedal force capabilities, and an upper pedal force limit may be established. Research data indicate that only 5% of female drivers produce pedal forces in excess of approximately 85 lb. Upon using a pedal force of 85 lb, a gain of 13.8, and a vehicle weight of 2230 lb in Eq. 40–1, a deceleration due to braking of 16.9 ft/sec^2 is obtained.

Comparison of the deceleration limited by tire-road friction with the maximum pedal force induced deceleration shows that both are approximately equal indicating that the VW driver may have braked hard. A moderate brake application involves pedal forces of female drivers up to approximately two-thirds of 85 lb or 56 lb. The corresponding deceleration of the VW would be 11.1 ft/sec^2. In the actual reconstruction a value of 12.8 ft/sec was used.

The retardation of the VW due to the uphill slope is (32.2) (0.0406) = 1.31 ft/sec^2 when a slope angle of 2.33 deg is used in Eq. 40–2. Consequently, a resulting deceleration of $12.8 + 1.31 = 14.1$ ft/sec^2 is obtained.

The impact speed of the VW may now be determined by Eq. 40–3 as

$$V_2 = \sqrt{(25 \times 1.466)^2 - (2)(14.1)(40)} = \sqrt{216} = 14.7 \text{ ft/sec}$$

or

$$14.7/1.466 = 10 \text{ mph}$$

Consequently, the computed impact speed of the VW is 10 mph. Since the calculation involved the use of some assumptions on pedal force, the impact speed of the VW was determined more accurately by experiment. The identical bumper hitch was mounted to a vehicle weighing 4780 lb. A 1970 VW bumper was installed on a vehicle weighing 2230 lb. The rear end collision simulation tests were conducted on a uphill slope approximately equal to 2.3 deg. The stationary vehicle was rear ended by the lighter vehicle. The damage sustained by the VW bumper in several tests was analyzed and compared to the damage exhibited by the actual bumper. Both damage geometries appeared to be approximately equal for impact speeds between 9 and 10 mph. Comparison of the computed and "measured" impact speed indicates good agreement. It should also be noted that the evaluation of the movie taken of the rear end crash indicated a forward displacement of the heavy test vehicles of approximately four feet, indicating basic agreement with driver no. 1 observation.

In the actual trial a 10 mph impact speed was permitted as evidence and subsequent post trial jury review revealed that all jury members believed a 10 mph speed to be a realistic impact speed of the VW.

In the case of a two-car collision a similar analysis will yield the engineering equation describing the precrash motion of vehicle no. 2. In this particular accident vehicle no. 2 (1966 Cadillac) was stationary and consequently no precrash analysis is required.

The collision analysis for the general case involves a number of complicated computations. Fortunately, however, the actual collision phase of many collisions occurs over a very short time period. During this small time external forces produced by tire-to-road contact, body components sliding along each other and road slopes may be neglected. Details of collision analysis are discussed in Chapter 28. The crash phase of the Cadillac/VW collision can be analyzed by engineering equations relating the straight line velocities immediately before and after the central impact. Eq. 28–4 may be rewritten in terms of vehicle weights as

$$\left(\frac{W_1}{g} V_1 + \frac{W_2}{g} V_2\right)_{\text{before}} = \left(\frac{W_1}{g} V_1 + \frac{W_2}{g} V_2\right)_{\text{after}} \qquad (40\text{–}4)$$

Eq. 40–4 may be simplified by eliminating g and by remembering that both vehicles were connected after the impact, i.e., the velocity of vehicle no. 1 equals the velocity of vehicle no. 2 after the impact. Hence, Eq. 40–4 becomes

$$(W_1 V_1 + W_2 V_2)_{\text{before}} = (W_1 + W_2)\, V_{\text{after}} \qquad (40\text{–}5)$$

Furthermore, since the Cadillac was stationary prior to the impact, i.e., $V_{2\,\text{before}} = 0$, the final expression becomes

$$(W_1 V_1)_{\text{before}} = (W_1 + W_2)\, V_{\text{after}} \qquad (40\text{–}6)$$

Eq. 40–6 indicates that the post crash forward momentum represented by the right hand side of Eq. 40–6 is produced by the momentum of vehicle no. 1 before the crash, represented by the left hand side of Eq. 40–6.

Eq. 40–6 may be solved for the common velocity after impact V_{after}, yielding

$$V_{\text{after}} = \frac{W_1 V_1}{W_1 + W_2}, \text{ mph} \tag{40-7}$$

By the use of $V_1 = 10$ mph, $W_1 = 2230$ lbs, and $W_2 = 4790$ lbs a velocity of 3.2 mph immediately after impact is obtained for the Cadillac (and the VW connecting to the Cadillac).

The motion analysis of the postcrash phase is similar to that of the precrash analysis. In general, the postcrash accident data provide more accurate information such as tire-road friction since the driver influence is removed in most severe collisions and only vehicle and road factors have to be considered which are subject to more accurate engineering calculations. In this particular accident only the VW driver braked after the impact and produced the major retarding force for both the VW and the Cadillac. If the VW driver continues to brake at the same pedal force, then the resulting deceleration of Cadillac and VW is 4.2 ft/sec^2. The Cadillac acts only as an additional weight without contributing to braking.

The force imposed upon the head of driver no. 2 can be determined from the acceleration of vehicle no. 2 and the particular seating geometry of driver no. 2. Vehicle no. 2 was not equipped with a head rest and consequently the head and chest positions associated with driver no. 2 must be considered in the calculations of the forces to the head. It is sufficient to indicate here that vehicle no. 2 (Cadillac) accelerated from zero to 3.2 mph over a distance of approximately 0.5 feet as indicated by the damage of vehicle no. 1. This damage data in connection with the speed increase yields an acceleration of vehicle no. 2 and hence the driver (neglecting rotational effects) of 22 ft/sec^2. In terms of force, this acceleration is equivalent to approximately 7.5 lb horizontal force when a weight of 11 lb is considered for a human head (Eq. 17–3: $7.5 = (11/32.2)(22)$.

It appears that this force is not excessively large to produce any undue damage. However, it must be remembered that damage is the result of stress and/or strain and even a small force may cause damage if the load carrying characteristics of certain tissues or muscles are weakened.

The application of the general formulation to the particular accident under consideration was carried out in a chronological order, i.e., followed the events as they occurred during the collision. In most accidents, however, the postcrash accident data such as skidding distance or distance rolled after impact are used to compute the speed of the vehicles immediately after impact. The equations of momentum then yield the speeds immediately before impact.

40-2. SINGLE VEHICLE IMPACT—ACCELERATING VEHICLE

Vehicle

Intermediate, yellow with black top, 1968 Mercury Cougar, two-door hardtop; odometer reading: 41,860 miles; power steering, power front-disc brakes, automatic transmission; padded instrument panel and sunvisors; lap and shoulder restraints for front occupants, lap restraints for rear occupants, head restraints; no mechanical defects noted; damage due to direct impact to the front of the vehicle, 30-inch maximum rearward crush, buckled hood and front fenders, cracked windshield due to occupant contact.

Occupant

Driver, 65 year old male, 5′9″ tall, 200 lb, trip plan from home to church meeting; collision occurred two blocks from origin; familiar with vehicle and road; possible unstable health condition; not using available restraints; heart failure prior to accident (possibly death causation); injuries caused by accident: head lacerations and contusions, chest injuries, fracture of ribs, internal lacerations with hemorrhage.

Standards

The following Federal Motor Vehicle Safety Standard (FMVSS) was relevant to this case:

FMVSS 203—Impact protection for the driver from the steering control system. Driver suffered fatal injuries from steering column.

Description

Pre-crash phase: Driver of Cougar was attempting to make left turn; he probably suffered heart attack and lost control over his vehicle as he entered Green Street; Cougar began rolling towards right side of street; no evidence of braking or sudden turning.

Crash phase: (Fig. 40-1) Cougar climbed right sidewalk, continued on it for 150 ft; went back on road crossing it diagonally for 130 ft and climbed left sidewalk onto lawn; Cougar hit some small trees and bushes and struck the corner of house at approximately 36 mph; inspection of accident site showed acceleration skid marks at various locations. Occupant was thrown forward impacting steering wheel and windshield; he suffered fatal injuries to the chest in addition

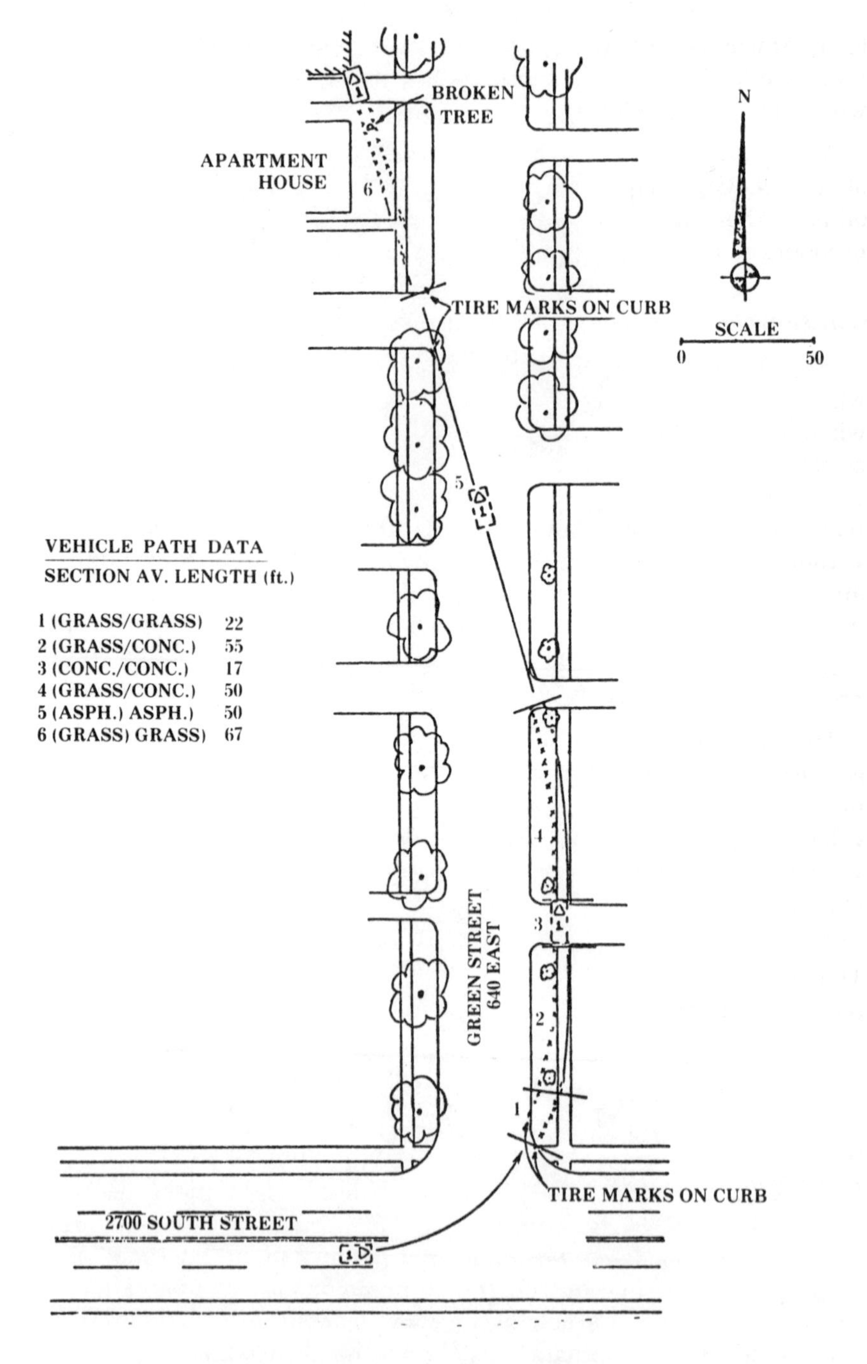

Figure 40-1. Collision Diagram, Single Vehicle Collision

to the initial possibly fatal heart attack. Front of Cougar was crushed rearward 30 inches; hood and front fenders were buckled rearward and windshield was cracked.

Post crash phase: The Cougar came to rest three feet from the point of impact. Oil leakage was present due to a probable rupture of the oil pan. The driver was taken to a hospital by ambulance where he was pronounced dead on arrival.

Collision Calculation

Inspection of the accident site showed acceleration tire spin marks when the vehicle was traveling over grass and no tire markings when traveling on concrete or asphalt. On grass the maximum acceleration is limited by a low value of tire-road friction, and may be determined by solving Eq. 19–16 for acceleration a for a given tire-road friction coefficient. On dry pavement the vehicle acceleration without wheel spinning is determined by engine torque and gear ratio, and may be determined by Eq. 19–14. Aerodynamic effects may be neglected at the low velocities existing in this case.

It appears that the driver, due to heart problems, inadvertently depressed the accelerator pedal.

An initial velocity of 15 mph is assumed prior to depressing the acceleration control. The vehicle's automatic transmission remained in second gear, the transmission ratio decreased exponentially as velocity increased from a high value of 2.8 to 1.0. The engine developed 210 hp at 4400 rpm, the vehicle weighed 3600 lb, the rear axle load is 1440 lb.

The vehicle's path was subdivided into six segments (Fig. 40–1). The vehicle rolled over concrete, grass, and asphalt. Assumed effective coefficients of friction are:

concrete: 0.4
grass: 0.1 (wet from prior rainfall)
asphalt: 0.4

Segment	*Right Rear Tire*	*Left Rear Tire*	*S(feet)*
1	grass	grass	22
2	concrete	grass	55
3	concrete	concrete	17
4	grass	grass	50
5	asphalt	asphalt	150
6	grass	grass	67

The increase of velocity may be determined from a repeated application of Eq. 16–10, solved for the velocity V_t at the end of the segment. For example, at the end of the first segment the new velocity V_t is

$$V_t = \sqrt{V_o^2 + 2aS} = \sqrt{22^2 + (2)(1.28)(22)} = 23.2 \text{ ft/sec or } 15.8 \text{ mph}$$

The acceleration is determined by Eq. 17–4, the driving force determined by Eq. 18–7. The details are $F_x = 0.1 \times 1440 = 144$ lb, i.e., the vehicle experiences a forward drive thrust of 144 lb. The acceleration is $a = (144)(32.2)/3600 = 1.28$ ft/sec^2.

When traveling on split coefficient surfaces, i.e., one rear wheel is on grass and the other on dry pavement, the lower friction coefficient is used for determining drive thrust due to the differential characteristics.

Repeated application of the procedure yields the velocity increments for each road segment. The acceleration associated with segment 5 where both rear tires were driving at equal force is determined by Eq. 19–14. The engine torque T_e may be determined from engine horsepower. The impact speed is determined by the use of the appropriate tire radius R, overall mechanical efficiency, and the decreasing overall gear ratio i, the final velocity at impact is determined at 36 mph.

Inspection of crush data where the impact speed is known or by the use of Eq. 28–29 indicates an impact speed of 35.8 mph for the large passenger vehicle (see Section 28–5).

40–3. SINGLE VEHICLE IMPACT–TURNING VEHICLE

Collision Vehicle

Pickup truck with camper, green 1974 Ford F-100; odometer reading: 5181 miles; inspection expired October 1974; standard V-8 engine; power steering, power front-disc brakes, automatic transmission; padded instrument panel and sunvisors; lap belts for outboard passengers; good mechanical condition; direct center-front impact damaged entire engine and occupant compartments, camper shell, frame, and buckled rear sheetmetal; 44-inch rearward crush vehicle crash.

Occupant

Driver, collision vehicle: 41-year-old married male; 5′8″ tall, 190 lbs; chauffeur's license; truck driver by profession; drives 12,000 miles per year in personal vehicle; no driver's education; familiar with collision vehicle and route, nervous driver; drove to Salt Lake from California day before accident; apparent poor mental condition, possible suicidal motives; alcohol; not using available restraints; suffered multiple, extreme injuries, injury severity: fatal (AIS-9).

Standards

The following Highway Safety Program Standards (HSPS) and Federal Motor Vehicle Safety Standards (FMVSS) were relevant to this case:

HSPS 8 – Alcohol in Relation to Highway Safety – driver had been drinking
HSPS 12 – Highway Design, Construction and Maintenance – protective barrier around bridge columns
FMVSS 113 – Hood Latch Systems
FMVSS 201 – Occupant Protection in Interior Impact
FMVSS 203 – Impact Protection for the Driver from the Steering Control System
FMVSS 204 – Steering Control Rearward Displacement
FMVSS 206 – Door Locks and Door Retention Components
FMVSS 208 – Occupant Crash Protection
FMVSS 212 – Windshield Mounting

Application of Standards FMVSS 113 through 212 to trucks may have resulted in nonfatal injuries to the driver.

Pre-Crash Phase

The weather at the time of the accident was clear with a temperature of 17° F and wind from the northeast at 4 mph. The roadway was dry. The pickup was traveling west on 600 North in lane no. 2 (inside lane). Approximately 100 ft east of the overpass column, the vehicle crossed lane no. 1 (outside lane) and the shoulder lane, heading directly toward the support column (Fig. 40–2). No braking effort or skid marks were visible at the scene to indicate that the driver attempted to avoid contact with the support column.

Crash Phase

The pickup truck struck the support column at the front center of the vehicle. Upon impact, steam from the engine, as well as dust

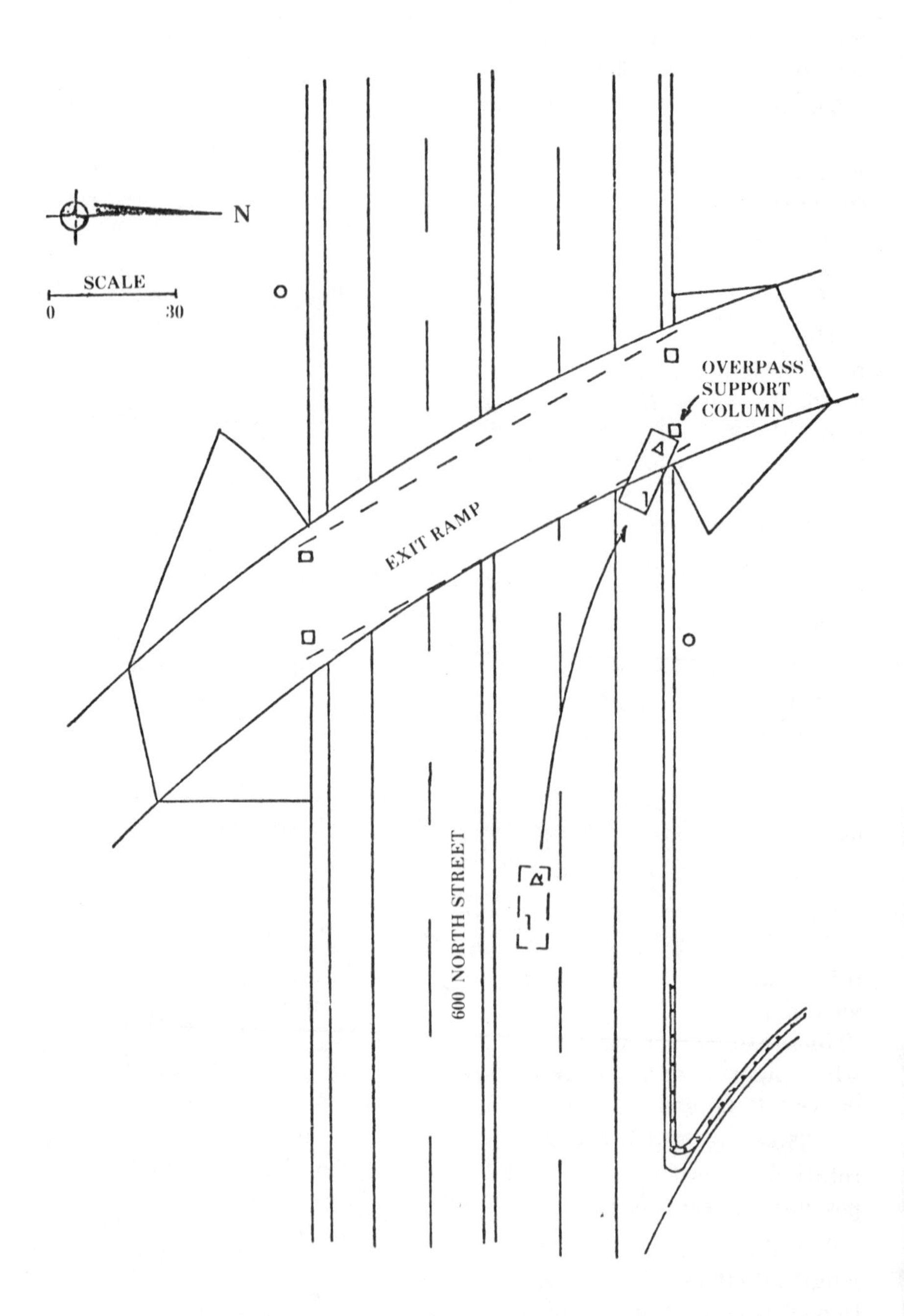

Figure 40-2. Collision Diagram, Single Vehicle Collision

and debris, flew into the air. The vehicle came to rest after crushing the front end three to five feet inward.

The driver of the pickup was thrown forward, impacting the steering wheel. His head contacted the windshield and the window frame. His head then snapped backwards impacting the rear of the occupant compartment. As the occupant compartment decreased in size, the driver was pinned against the seat and steering wheel and column.

Post-Crash Phase

The pickup did not move in any direction after the impact. It came to a complete stop against the support column. A witness to the accident attempted to rescue the driver, but realized he was dead. Upon the arrival of police and ambulance personnel, the witness's tow truck was used to move the pickup back away from the support column. The deceased driver, pinned in the occupant compartment, was then removed by people on the scene.

Collision Calculations

The following information is available:

(a) Witness stating that the pickup executed a definite right turn prior to impact.

(b) Witness estimated the velocity at approximately 40 mph.

(c) No tire marks were produced due to either braking or turning.

(d) Vehicle wheel base = 127 in.

The following assumptions were made:

(a) The driver of the pickup provided a single steering wheel input limited between 45 and 80 degrees.

(b) The lateral acceleration value was above $0.3g$ but below $0.5g$. The two values are reasonable due to the fact that the turn was definite ($0.3g$), however, without producing tire skidmarks ($0.5g$). Eq. 22–9 relating curve radius r, vehicle wheelbase L, front wheel steering and tire slip angle on the front α_F and rear tires α_R may be used to determine the approximate radius of turn.

The front wheel rotation is determined by the steering wheel rotation and steering ratio. Using a steering ratio of 17:1 yields a possible front wheel rotation of 2.65 to 4.7 degrees.

The difference in slip angle front to rear is mostly the result of longitudinal location of the center of gravity. For a lateral acceleration of $0.4g$ and 65% loading on the front axle ($\alpha_F - \alpha_R$) is approximately equal to 1.5 degrees. Substitution of the above values into

Eq. 22–9 yields an average curve radius of 365 feet. The associated velocity for an average lateral acceleration of 0.35 to 0.45 g ranges between 44 and 50 mph.

Comparison of the crush depth in frontal impacts with known impact velocities indicates an average impact speed of 43 mph (Eq. 28–29).

The assumption of a lateral acceleration value for computing vehicle velocity may be undesirable. A more accurate computation of vehicle velocity for a given steering wheel angle range and turn radius may be accomplished by the use of Eq. 22–36. Solving for velocity V and using typical tire cornering stiffness values of 12,000 lb/rad (light pickup truck heavy truck tires may go as high as 30,000 lb/rad for axle cornering stiffness) and weight distribution data yields an average velocity 54 mph for an input angle of 62.5 degrees.

40–4. TWO-VEHICLE REAR END COLLISION–ONE VEHICLE PARKED

Vehicles

Vehicle No. 1: Light duty white-on-red 1970 Chevrolet C-20 pickup; odometer reading: 44,112 miles; V-8 engine; power steering and brakes, manual transmission; lap restraint for two passengers; padded sunvisors and instrument panel; rear tires worn above average; first impact sustained to left front and left side causing sheet metal structural damage 8-in. crush; rollover caused roof crush into cabin 12 in.

Vehicle No. 2: Subcompact pink 1972 Ford Pinto two-door sedan; odometer reading: 9277 miles; manual steering, brakes, and transmission; lap restraints for all seating positions, upper torso and integral head restraints for front outboard positions; padded instrument panels; good mechanical condition; entire car crushed from rear, total loss.

Occupant

Driver, Vehicle No. 1: 37-year-old divorced male, 6′2″ tall; 170 lbs; drives about 20,000 miles per year; traveling to work; driver's education through company; familiar with vehicle and route; poor physical condition, on minor medication due to hospitalization two weeks prior to accident; using lap restraint; suffered contusions to arms, chest, and thigh; lacerations of face and wrist, fractured ribs, injury severity: dangerous, serious (AIS-4). No occupants in vehicle no. 2.

Standards

The following Highway Safety Program Standards (HSPS) and Federal Motor Vehicle Safety Standards (FMVSS) were relevant to this case:

HSPS 8 – Alcohol in Relation to Highway Safety – driver of pickup had been drinking; blood test showed driver above allowable blood alcohol level

HSPS 11 – Emergency Medical Services – driver of pickup trapped for 20 minutes in vehicle

FMVSS 113 – Hood Latch System – hood hinge on pickup did not hold in rollover

FMVSS 201 – Occupant Protection in Interior Impact – driver of pickup struck rear of cab and dash area with parts of body

FMVSS 203 – Impact Protection for the Driver from the Steering Control System – driver of pickup struck steering apparatus with chest

FMVSS 205 – Glazing Materials – windows and windshield of pickup shattered in rollover, injuring driver

FMVSS 206 – Door Locks and Door Retention Components – doors on pickup held during rollover

FMVSS 208 – Occupant Crash Protection – driver of pickup was using lap restraint

FMVSS 212 – Windshield Mounting – mounting crushed during pickup rollover

FMVSS 216 – Roof Crush Resistance – roof of pickup crushed during rollover; part of roof of Pinto crushed from rear impact

FMVSS 301 – Fuel Tanks, Fuel Tank Filler Pipes, and Fuel Tank Connections; Tank on Pinto did not break loose, but heavily bent

Description

Pre-Crash Phase: (Fig. 40–3) Pickup traveling north on 1300 East at 50–55 mph, driver reached across seat to close right door, swerved along roadway; driver had been drinking, was unable to control vehicle; Pinto parked on east side of roadway, facing north; pickup swerved off roadway.

Crash Phase: Left front of pickup impacted right rear of Pinto; Pinto careened to left side of 1300 East, came to rest 135 feet north of

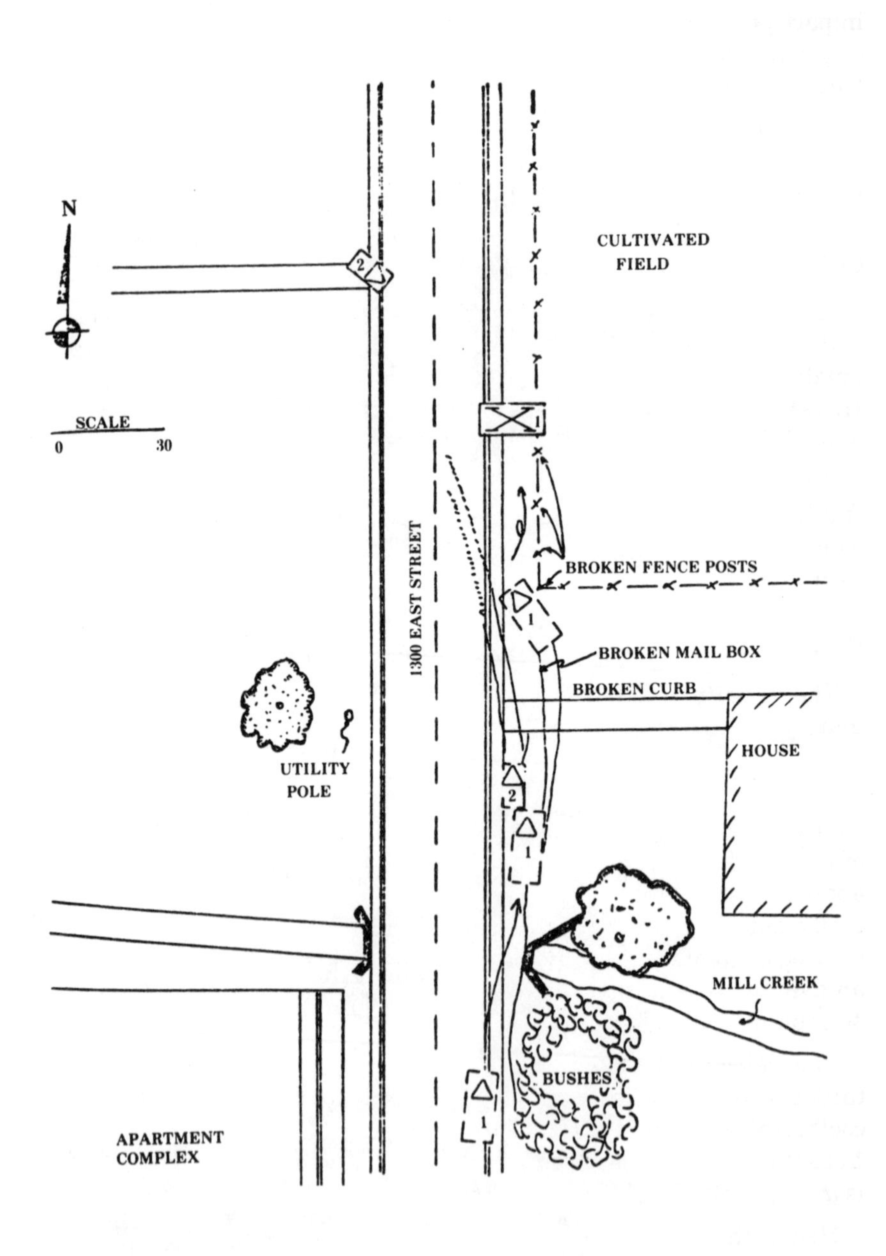

Figure 40–3. Collision Diagram, Two-Vehicle Collision

impact point; pickup slid sideways, began to roll perpendicular to its original direction of travel, rolled twice, came to rest on its top, 116 feet from impact point.

Post-Crash Phase: Driver of pickup trapped in vehicle for 20 minutes; taken to hospital by ambulance; gasoline leaking from vehicle was washed down by fire department.

Collision Calculation

Inspection of Fig. 40–3 indicates a 90-deg rotation of the truck (and rolling onto the roof) and a 180-deg rotation of the Pinto. Due to the small values of rotation relative to the large longitudinal distances traveled by the vehicles after impact, a central impact mode is assumed, i.e., rotational effects are neglected.

Accident data: The Pinto (vehicle no. 2) traveled approximately 135 ft after impact with its rear wheels locked (parking brake application). The truck traveled approximately 116 ft after impact including rollover motion. Truck weight is 4800 lb, Pinto weight is 2475 lb.

Vehicle Speeds Immediately After Impact

The velocity of vehicle no. 1 (truck) V_{12} may be determined approximately by Eq. 29–2, i.e.,

$$V_{12} = \sqrt{(30)(0.5)(108)} = 40 \text{ mph}$$

An average friction coefficient of 0.5 was assumed. Detailed inspection of the accident site revealed that vehicle no. 1 produced tire markings approximately 48 ft long prior to rollover. Upon assigning a friction coefficient of 0.3 for that retardation process, a vehicle speed of 21 mph may be computed at the instant rollover commenced. Upon assuming an average retardation coefficient during tire sliding of 0.7, a speed of 40 mph may be determined by use of Eq. 16–15.

The velocity of vehicle no. 2 (Pinto) V_{22} is determined by the retardation of the locked rear wheels. Upon assuming a tire-road friction coefficient of 0.7 and a rear axle load of 1110 lb, a retarding force of $1110 \times 0.7 = 777$ lb is obtained (Eq. 18–7). The associated deceleration is $a = (777)(32.2)/2475 = 10.1$ ft/sec^2 (Eq. 17–4).

Hence the velocity of vehicle no. 2 becomes (Eq. 16–7 solved for speed):

$$V_{22} = \sqrt{(2)(10.1)(135)} = 52.2 \text{ ft/sec or } 35.6 \text{ mph}$$

Impact Speed Immediately Before Impact

The impact speed of vehicle no. 1 V_{11} may be determined by Eq. 28–4 with $V_{21} = 0$, solved for V_{11}

$$V_{11} = \frac{m_1 V_{12} + m_2 V_{22}}{m_1} = \frac{\left(\frac{4800}{32.2}\right) 40 + \left(\frac{2475}{32.5}\right)(35.6)}{\left(\frac{4800}{32.2}\right)} = 58 \text{ mph}$$

The truck traveled at approximately 58 mph prior to impact.

The mass m of the vehicles is determined by Eq. 17–2, solved for m. Inspection of the numerical values indicates that dividing by 32.2 is not necessary (see Example 40–1).

40–5. TWO-VEHICLE NON-CENTRAL HEAD-ON COLLISION

In this example only the collision calculations are presented.

Description

Vehicle no. 1 (1964 Rambler Classic) drifted across highway and impacted vehicle no. 2 (1971 Cutlass Oldsmobile) head-on as illustrated in Fig. 40–4. The left front of vehicle no. 1 collided with the left front of vehicle no. 2. The vehicle speeds prior to impact were 40 mph (no. 1) and 50 mph (no. 2).

Vehicle Data

Vehicle Weights: No. 1 (Rambler): 2980 lb; No. 2 (Cutlass): 4100 lb.

Vehicle dimensions: (length × width × height)
Vehicle No. 1: 15.1 × 5.9 × 4.5 (ft)
Vehicle No. 2: 17.1 × 6.4 × 4.6 (ft)

Inspection of the initial contact diagram (Fig. 40–4) indicates the following contact point geometry:

$$\ell_{1x} = 5.3 \text{ ft}, \ \ell_{1y} = 1.7 \text{ ft}$$
$$\ell_{2x} = -8 \text{ ft}, \ \ell_{2y} = -2.1 \text{ ft}$$

Collision Calculations (See Section 28–4)

The impact is straight non-central. The difference velocity (prior to impact) (Eq. 28–17) is $V_x = V_{21} - V_{11}$, i.e., it is identical to the relative velocity of the two vehicles. No difference velocity component in the y-direction exists, i.e., $\Delta V_y = 0$.

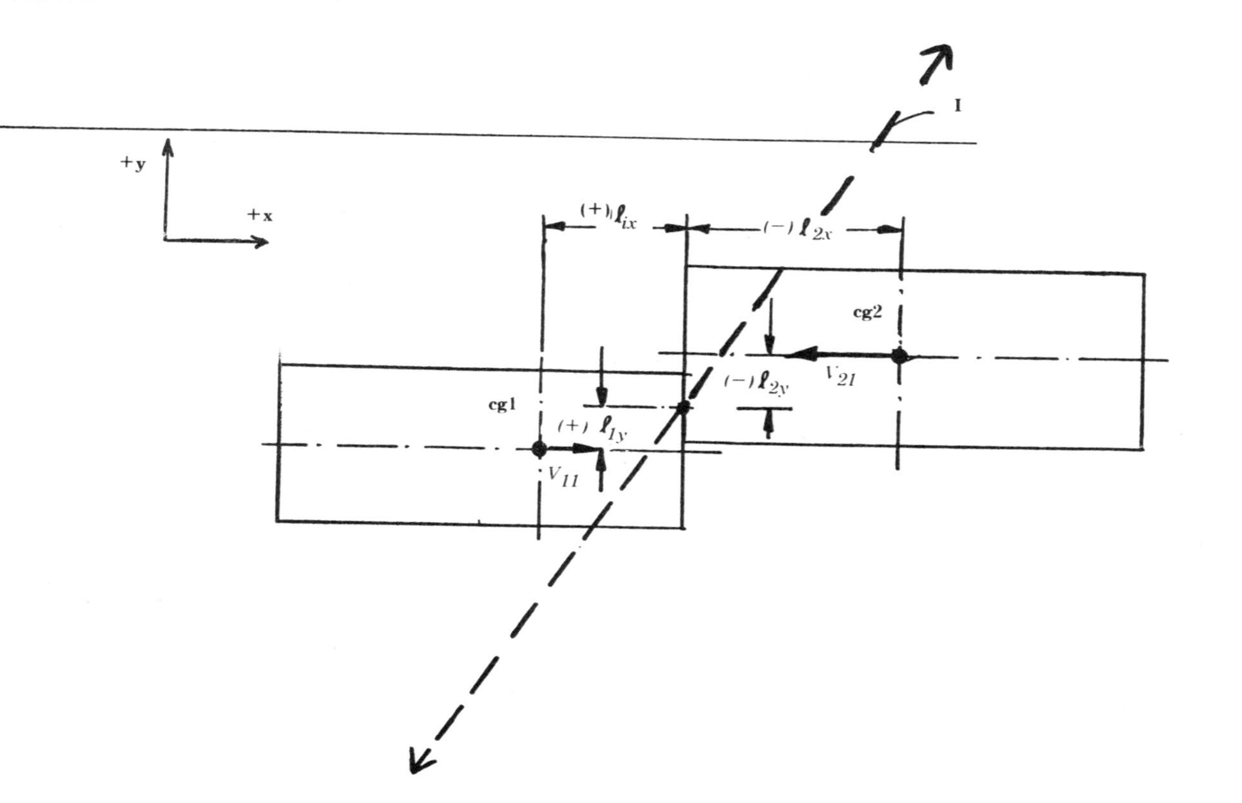

Figure 40–4. Initial Contact Diagram, Head-on Collision

By the use of the sign convention of Fig. 40–4, $\Delta V_x = -50 - 40 = -90$ mph or -132 ft/sec.

The impulses I_x and I_y may be determined by Eqs. 28–12 and 28–13, respectively. Although V_y is zero, the impulse I_y in the y-direction is not zero.

The parameters a, b, and c are determined by Eqs. 28–14, 28–15 and 28–16. The mass moment of inertia I_1 of vehicle no. 1 (Rambler) is approximately 1700 lb·ft·sec² that of vehicle no. 2 2100 lb·ft·sec². The mass of vehicle no. 1 is $2980/32.2 = 92.5$ lb sec²/ft, that of vehicle no. 2 $4100/32.2 = 127.3$ lb sec²/ft.

The impulse components are: $I_x = -6678$ lb sec and $I_y = -1352$ lb sec (Eqs. 28–12 and 28–13).

The total impulse is

$$I = \sqrt{6678^2 + 1352^2} = 6813 \text{ lb sec}$$

as illustrated in Fig. 40–4.

The velocity components of vehicle no. 1 immediately after impact are (Eqs. 28–19 and 28–20):

$$V_{12x} = -\frac{6678}{92.5} + 58.6 = -13.50 \text{ ft/sec}$$

$$V_{12y} = -\frac{1352}{92.5} + 0 = -14.6 \text{ ft/sec}$$

As expected, the center-of-gravity of vehicle no. 1 moves to the left (minus x) and down (minus y), the resultant velocity is

$$V_{2l} = \sqrt{(13.5)^2 + (14.6)^2} = 19.9 \text{ ft/sec}$$

or 13.5 mph under an angle of 47 deg to the longitudinal x-direction.

The angular velocity of vehicle no. 1 after impact is (Eq. 28–21) $\omega_{12} = 141$ deg/sec and rotates counterclockwise (plus sign).

The corresponding values of vehicle no. 2 are $V_{22x} = -20.9$ ft/sec, $V_{22y} = 10.6$ ft/sec, $\omega_{22} = 87.4$ deg/sec. The resultant velocity is 23.4 ft/sec or 16 mph under an angle of 55 deg.

The post crash motions may be analyzed by use of the equations found in Chapter 29.

40–6. TWO-VEHICLE INTERSECTION COLLISION

The collision involved the right angle side impact of a Ford Mach 1 with an Oldsmobile Delta 88. Although important factors in the total accident reconstruction, no injury production, occupant dynamics, and view obstruction analysis is presented. The investigating officer determined a speed of 65 mph for the Ford vehicle at the instant of wheel lock.

A witness of the accident stated that the speed of the Ford vehicle was "very high."

The maximum speed of the Ford must be computed.

Vehicle Data

Vehicle weights: No. 1 (Olds): 5040 lbs. No. 2 (Ford): 3450 lb.

Accident Data

The collision diagram is shown in Fig. 40–5. The approach angles are $\alpha_{11} = 30$ deg (Olds) and 0 deg (Ford). The angles after impact are $\alpha_{12} = 41$ deg (Olds) and $\alpha_{22} = 12.9$ deg (Ford). The Oldsmobile slid 59.2 ft, the Ford 64.2 ft after impact on their tires. The Ford produced a braking skid of 105.3 ft before impact.

Collision Calculations

The impact is oblique non-central. Due to the small values of rotation involved in the actual collision, rotation is neglected in the collision analysis. Since the directions of vehicle travel before and after impact are located under different angles, the different linear momenta must be analyzed separately in the x and y direction. Conservation of momentum in each direction yields the following equations (Eq. 28–4):

y-direction (Vehicle weights are used instead of mass since $g = 32.2$ cancels)

Only the velocity components in the y-direction may be used. Hence,

$$W_2V_{21} - W_1V_{11} \sin \alpha_{11} = W_1V_{12} \sin \alpha_{12} + W_2V_{22} \cos \alpha_{22} \quad (40\text{–}7)$$

x-direction

$$W_1V_{11} \cos \alpha_{11} = W_1V_{12} \cos \alpha_{12} + W_2V_{22} \sin \alpha_{22} \quad (40\text{–}8)$$

The velocity of the Ford before impact V_{12} must be computed from Eqs. 40–7 and 40–8.

Velocities after impact:

The velocities after impact may be determined by Eq. 29–2:

Vehicle No. 1 (Olds):

$$V_{12} = \sqrt{(30)(0.3)(59.2)} = 23 \text{ mph}$$

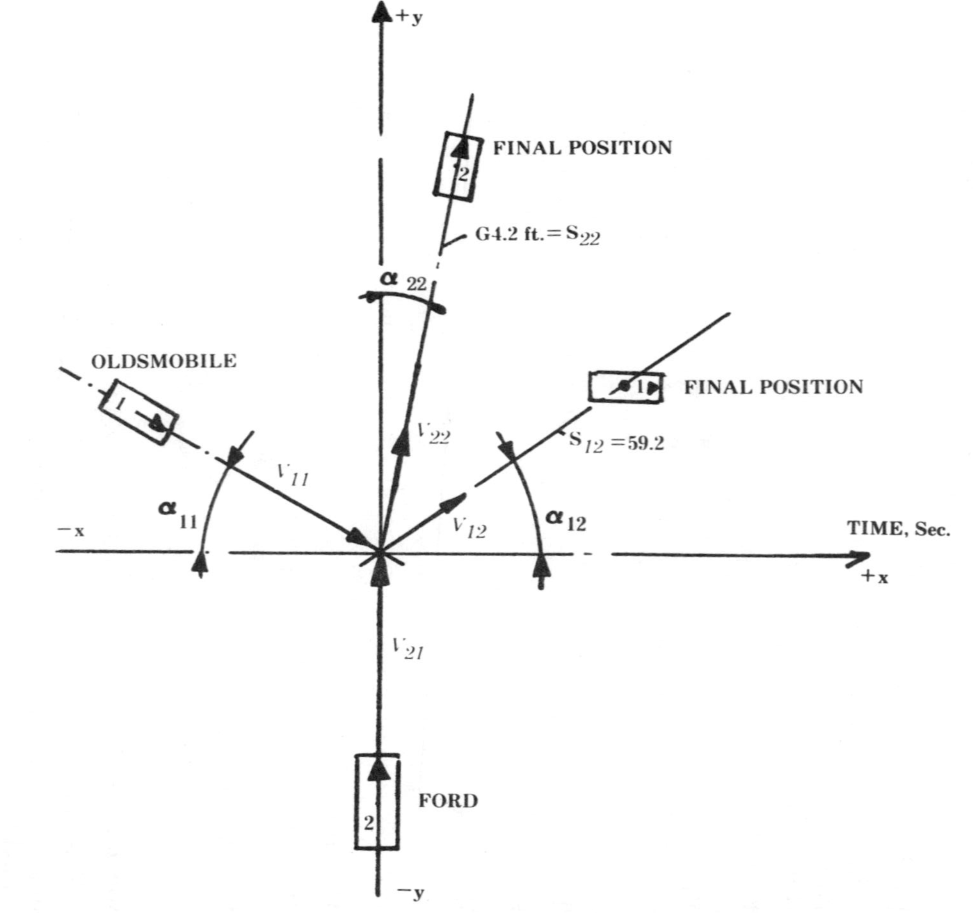

Figure 40-5. Collision Diagram, Two-Vehicle Collision

A friction coefficient of 0.3 was used since vehicle no. 1 was sliding on dirt surface.

Vehicle No. 2 (Ford):

$$V_{22} = \sqrt{(30)(0.6)(64.2)} = 34 \text{ mph}$$

A friction coefficient of 0.6 was assumed since the right wheels were partially off right-lane surface.

Eq. 40–8 may now be solved for velocity V_{11} (Oldsmobile before impact) and substituted into Eq. 40–7. Eq. 40–7 may then be solved for the unknown velocity V_{21}.

From Eq. 40–8:

$$V_{11} = \left(\frac{W_2}{W_1}\right) V_{22} \left(\frac{\sin \alpha_{22}}{\cos \alpha_{11}}\right) + V_{12} \left(\frac{\cos \alpha_{12}}{\cos \alpha_{11}}\right)$$

$$= \left(\frac{3450}{5040}\right)(34)\left(\frac{\sin 11.3°}{\cos 30°}\right) + 23\left(\frac{\cos 41°}{\cos 30°}\right) = 25 \text{ mph}$$

The speed of the Oldsmobile before impact is $V_{11} = 25$ mph.

From Eq. 40–7

$$V_{21} = V_{22} \cos \alpha_{33} + \left(\frac{W_1}{W_2}\right)(V_{12} \sin \alpha_{12} + V_{11} \sin \alpha_{11})$$

$$= (34)[\cos (11.3°)] + \left(\frac{5040}{3450}\right)(23 \sin 41° + 25 \sin 30°) = 74 \text{ mph}$$

The result shows that the Ford was traveling 74 mph at impact. The velocity at the instant of wheel lockup may be determined by Eq. 16–19 as

$$V_{2\text{skid}} = \sqrt{(V_{21})^2 + 2aS} = \sqrt{(108.4)^2 + (2)(25.7)(105.3 + 12)}$$
$$= 133.4 \text{ ft/sec or } 91 \text{ mph}$$

A friction coefficient of 0.8 or a deceleration of $0.8 \times 32.2 = 25.7$ ft/sec^2 was measured at the accident site.

The actual stopping distance was numerically increased by 12 ft to account for aerodynamic drag. The aerodynamic drag may be determined by Eq. 19–4, yielding an effective stopping distance increase of 12 ft.

The velocity at the instant of deceleration initiation (approximately pedal force application begin) may be determined by Eq. 16–11 when both sides of the equation are divided by t, yielding ($V = S/t$):

$$V_{2\text{pedal}} = 133.4 + \frac{25.7}{2}(0.2)$$

$$= 135.9 \text{ ft/sec or } 92.7 \text{ mph}$$

A deceleration buildup time of $\Delta t = 0.2$ sec was assumed from the free rolling to the locked wheel condition.

40-7. TRUCK-ANIMAL IMPACT

The accident involved the straight non-central impact between a small light truck and a steer. The animal weight is 1000 lb, the truck weight is 3200 lb. The mass moment of inertia of the truck is 1500 lb·ft·sec^2. The road surface is slippery wet and no skid marks are found. The truck driver states that his brakes were locked approximately 3 feet prior to impact and during the entire post crash motion. The truck speed prior to impact was 55 mph. The light truck impacted the animal with its right front corner. A second fatal collision was caused by the truck crossing over into the oncoming traffic lane.

One phase of the accident reconstruction detail requires the computation of the time elapsed between animal impact and the truck crossing laterally 5 ft into the oncoming traffic lane.

The time may be computed by Eq. 16–20, once the velocity after impact and the direction of velocity have been determined.

The velocity difference prior to impact is $\Delta V_x = -80.6$ ft/sec (Eq. 28–17, $\Delta V_y = 0$, $V_{\text{animal}}, = 0$).

The parameters a, b, and c are 0.1, 0.045, and 0.013, respectively. ($I_{\text{animal}} = 400$ lbs·ft·sec^2, $_{1x} = 7.5$ ft, $\ell_{1y} = -2$ ft, $_{2x} = 3$ ft, $\ell_{2y} = 0$, Eqs. 28–14, 28–15, 28–16).

The impulse components are $I_x = -1832$ lbs·sec, $I_y = 183$, lb sec (Eqs. 28–12 and 28–13).

The truck velocity components after impact are $V_{12s} = 62.2$ ft/sec (Eq. 28–19) and $V_{12y} = 1.84$ ft/sec (Eq. 28–20). The resulting velocity of the truck is 62.3 ft/sec or 44 mph. The heading angle of the center of gravity is 1.7 deg.

The transverse distance of 5 ft requires a total sliding distance of 168 ft under an angle of 1.7 deg. Upon assuming a wet friction coefficient of 0.3, Eq. 16–20 yields a total time of 3.84 sec required to slide 5 ft across. Consequently, the light truck required 3.84 sec to skid 168 ft (or 5 ft side displacement) from the time of impact. An accident avoidance analysis involving the oncoming vehicle (second collision) would answer whether or not 3.84 sec were sufficient for collision avoidance.

40-8. MULTIPLE VEHICLE COLLISION

The paragraphs that follow are a summary of information taken from the police report and witness statements.

On May 12, 1974, driver no. 1 was traveling south on I80 in Cassia County, Idaho. Vehicle no. 1 was a 1968 Pontiac Wagon. Passengers were a 10-year-old female and a 2-year-old male. Both passengers were located behind the front seat. The rear seats were folded down. Vehicle no. 2, a Winnebago (20 feet long, small motor home) was also traveling south bound. Driver no. 2 never saw vehicle no. 1. A severe dust and sand storm developed, blocking much of the view of the road way and vehicles ahead, as stated by driver no. 2. Vehicle no. 2 slowed down to "practically" nothing. Specifically, driver no. 2 states that his vehicle (Winnebago) was going between 1 and 2 mph and was 50 feet away from several cars that had crashed when vehicle no. 2 was impacted from the rear. Driver no. 2 was thrown backwards, his hands left the steering wheel, his feet left the foot controls. Vehicle no. 2 collided with a Toronado in front of it. The Winnebago impacted the Toronado in a straight rear end collision. The impact caused three people sitting in the front seat, including the driver, to be ejected from the Winnebago. Two ejected people fell on the roof of a Toronado, involved in a prior collision. One ejected passenger remained hanging down from the Winnebago. The occupants of the Winnebago were 36 m, 39 f, 18 f, 18 m, 8 f, 6 f. The Winnebago came to a sudden stop when impacting the cars ahead, as stated by driver no. 2.

Driver no. 1 states that she does not remember anything about the accident. The roadways were dry, no tire marks were found. The Pontiac came to rest approximately 4 ft beyond the apparent point of impact established by debris. The police states that the dust storm was so severe that they had to close off traffic in both directions for several hours. A total of 15 cars were involved in several collisions. The only fatality was the 2 year old male passenger in vehicle no. 1. He impacted the back of the front seat in a "secondary" collision, permanently deflecting the back rest of the front seat by approximately 1 ft. Driver no. 1 sustained minor injuries.

The speed of Vehicle no. 1 (Pontiac Station Wagon) immediately before impact must be determined.

The weights of the vehicles were Pontiac 4786 lb, Winnebago 10,800 lb.

Collision Calculation

The speed of the Winnebago (vehicle no. 2) must first be approximately determined from the data associated with the impact of vehicle no. 2 and the Toronado. The only information available indicates that the front seat passengers of vehicle no. 2 were ejected upon the roof of the Toronado. A minimum speed may therefore be obtained from the horizontal distance and vertical drop traveled by the ejected passenger. A passenger must exhibit this speed in order to be ejected onto the roof of the Toronado. Due to friction between passenger and seat and energy absorbed by breaking the front windshield, the actual speed is expected to be slightly higher.

The minimum horizontal speed V is

$$V = \frac{4\ell}{\sqrt{h}}, \text{ ft/sec} \qquad (40\text{–}9)$$

where

h = vertical distance fallen, ft

ℓ = horizontal distance traveled, ft

For $h = 2$ ft, $\ell = 7$ ft, Eq. 40–9 yields $V = 19.8$ ft/sec or 13.6 mph. The speed of the Winnebago after impact with the Pontiac may be determined by Eq. 16–19. The retardation is a function of engine drag and tire rolling resistance.

The engine drag may be determined by Eqs. 19–5 and 19–6. The engine drag may be ignored in this case due to the extremely low speed and the automatic transmission in vehicle no. 2, effectively disconnecting the engine from the drive wheels.

The rolling resistance is determined by Eq. 18–2 as

$$R_R = 0.017 \times 10800 = 183.6 \text{ lb}$$

The deceleration is determined by Eq. 17–4 as

$$a = \frac{(183.6)(32.2)}{10800} = 0.547 \text{ ft/sec}^2$$

Inspection of the results shows that the deceleration could have been obtained by $(0.017)(32.2) = 0.547$ ft/sec^2.

Substitution of the appropriate values into Eq. 16–19 yields the speed V_{22} of the Winnebago immediately after being impacted by vehicle no. 1, as

$$V_{22} = \sqrt{(19.8)^2 + (2)(0.547)(50)} = 21.1 \text{ ft/sec or } 14.4 \text{ mph}$$

The results indicate that the rolling resistance reduces the speed only from 14.4 mph to 13.6 mph.

The speed of the Pontiac after impact is assumed to be zero.

The speeds of the impacting vehicle may be determined by Eq. 28–4, solved for the velocity of vehicle no. 1 prior to impact V_{11}, yielding with $m = W/g$ and g cancelled

$$V_{11} = \frac{W_1 V_{12} + W_2 V_{22} - W_2 V_{21}}{W_1}$$

$$= \frac{(4786)(0) + (10800)(14.40) - (10800)(2)}{4786}$$

$$= 28 \text{ mph}$$

If the Winnebago is traveling 1 mph prior to being impacted (instead of 2 mph), the speed of vehicle no. 1 is 30.5 mph.

The results are shown graphically by the velocity-time diagram in Fig. 40–6.

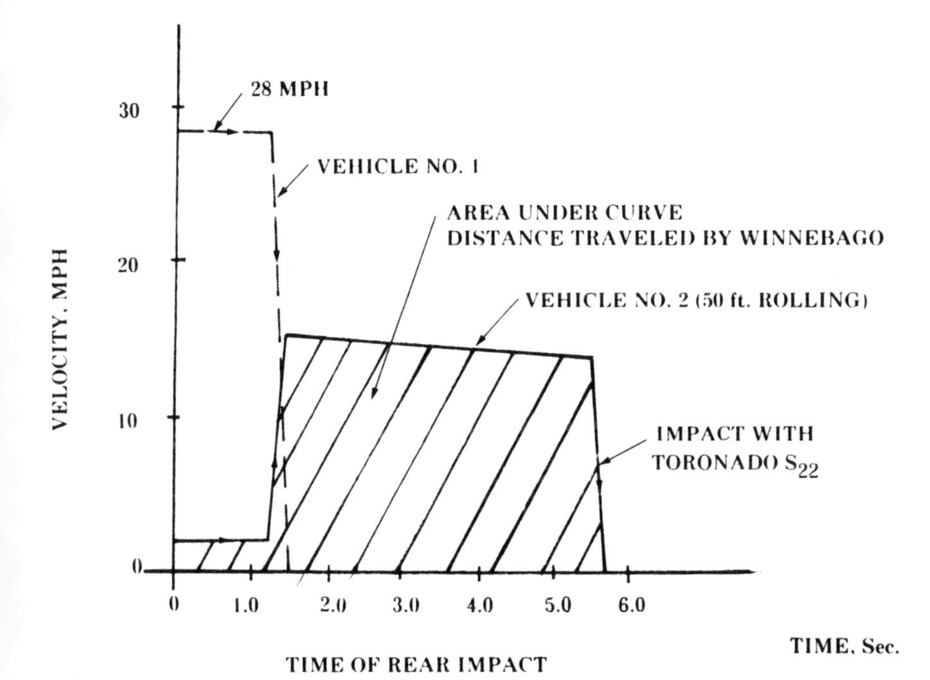

Figure 40–6. Multiple Rear End Collision Velocity-Time Diagram

PART 8

SPECIAL TOPICS

The objective of Part 8 is the brief review of accident investigation programs and presentation of important findings. If necessary, the appropriate publications containing detailed data must be reviewed.

Part 8 is concluded by a brief review of expert witness factors. Special accident and related studies are found in Refs. 31–48.

CHAPTER 41
MULTIDISCIPLINARY ACCIDENT INVESTIGATION PROGRAM (MDAI)

41-1. OBJECTIVE

The multidisciplinary accident investigation projects have been involved in motor vehicle accident investigation under the sponsorship of the U.S. Department of Transportation, the Motor Vehicle Manufacturers Association and the Canadian Department of Transportation. The MDAI teams are composed of professional personnel representing medicine, psychiatry, engineering, and accident investigation. The immediate purpose is the evaluation of the precrash, crash, and postcrash collision events which are considered to be significant in accident causation or injury production. The accident data are collected in a case report and stored in a computer bank at the University of Michigan for the National Highway Traffic Safety Administration (NHTSA). The data are available to the public.

41-2. MDAI DATA COLLECTION

Approximately 10,000 accidents have been investigated until 1977. The data available are mostly related to crash events and injury production. Data relative to vehicle handling are limited.

The data recorded have been divided into general, vehicle, occupant, and injury. During the investigation program the data file has been supplemented to include such data as driver occupation, trip plan, and precrash vehicle motion. All data are recorded by the investigating team in the Collision Performance and Injury Report (Ref. 6).

The number of MDAI teams has varied. By 1974 the following accident investigation teams existed:

Ann Arbor, HSRI-III
Baylor College of Medicine
Boston University
Calspan-IIIA
Calspan-IIIB
Ministry of Transport, Ottawa, Canada

Georgia Institute of Technology
Highway Safety Res. Inst.
Indiana University
McGill Univ., Montreal
University of Miami
Maryland Medical/Legal Foundation
Univ. of Montreal, Ecole Polytechnique
Univ. of New Brunswick
Univ. of New Mexico
Oakland County, HSRI-III
Ohio State University
Research Triangle Inst.
University of Rochester
Univ. of S. California
Stanford Res. Inst. (2)
Stanford Res. Inst. (1)
Stanford University
Southwest Res. Institute
Trauma Res. Group, UCLA
Tulane University
Univ. of California (Siegel)
Univ. of Houston
Univ. of Kentucky
Univ. of Michigan (Huelke)
Univ. of Oklahoma
Univ. of Toronto
Univ. of Utah
Univ. of Alberta
Univ. of British Columbia
Univ. of Manitoba
Univ. of Saskatchewan

The emphasis of accident investigation during the last years (1976–77) has been changed to more specialized studies and a national accident sampling system (Section 41–3).

41–2.1. General Data. Included in the general data collected by MDAI teams are accident location, road type, road surface, traffic controls, collision mode, accident avoidance maneuver, and driver errors.

41–2.2. Vehicle Data. Included are vehicle identification, loading, optional equipment, overall damage index, damage to individual parts and components, tire type and condition, steering column crush performance, windshield performance, seat performance, and complete occupant compartment crush dimensions.

41–2.3. Occupant and Injury Data. Included are seating location, posture, age, weight, height, sex, use of seat belt, ejection (degree and area), severity of injury, injury details, occupant contact with vehicle, driver occupation, driver psychological and physiological factors.

A typical computer data output may reveal data on injuries for, e.g., the right front passenger not wearing seatbelts in an intersection collision, or simple multipurpose vehicle rollover. Another example might be the determination of accidents caused by a vehicle defect such as a tire failure, or a steering or brake system defect.

41–3. NATIONAL ACCIDENT SAMPLING SYSTEM (NASS)

Accident statistics using police report data or data collected by regional disciplinary accident investigation teams lack a national probability sampling plan, i.e., the reliability of such national accident statistics is unknown. The NASS is expected to provide basic national accident statistics on a continuous basis and to provide a nationally representative network of locations at which teams are available to perform a number of short-term special traffic safety studies without delays. The new program was initiated in 1976.

CHAPTER 42
SPECIAL ACCIDENT STUDIES

42-1. BRAKING ACCIDENT CAUSATION

A review of all MDAI cases shows that in approximately two percent of these accidents the investigator noted brake malfunctions as contributing to the accident cause. In several cases, the investigating officer noted "loss of brake pedal" and no detailed followup investigation was carried out. Nearly all cases that showed brake malfunctioning as contributing to the accident involved faulty brake maintenance or driver attitude as direct cause of the brake problem. As the detailed review of individual cases revealed, in approximately 89% of the braking accidents a brake system failure was noted as the primary cause of the accident. In approximately 25% of these cases information concerning brake failure was based on driver or police statements and no indepth vehicle examination was carried out to verify the accident cause. Vehicle instability during braking due to wheel lockup was noted in 11 percent of the cases as primary accident cause. The important finding, however, is that of the 64% of the cases that were verified as brake system failures, all were due to faulty brake system maintenance or driver attitudes toward proper vehicle inspection. The highest failure rate was associated with wheel cylinder leakage (28%), followed by master cylinder leakage (10%), loose vacuum hoses (7%), broken brake lines (7%), and others such as wet brakes, excessive drum wear and improper adjustment. In 24% of all braking accident cases worn brake linings or drums were noted as either primary or secondary brake failure.

Based on these findings, two areas of braking accident causation are identifiable. The most significant accident cause is directly related to improper maintenance, consisting of 78% of all cases that were determined as brake failure by the investigating officer or accident investigation team. An additional 11% were noted on the police report as brake failure without verification. The second most important braking accident cause relates to vehicle instability during braking, most often caused by premature rear wheel lockup or improper brake force distribution. This category comprised 11 percent of all braking accident cases.

Based on the U.S. Department of Transportation accident statistics available, one must conclude that involvement of brakes in accident causation is small with less than 2% and that braking requirements forcing higher levels of performance onto the brake system and the vehicle may not result in the expected benefit payoff because most brake failures are either maintenance related or due to driver and owner attitudes. Although high braking performance may be designed into a motor vehicle, in-use and service factors generally affect the available performance to a degree beyond the control of the manufacturers.

42-2. STEERING AND BRAKING ACCIDENT AVOIDANCE

The accident avoidance analysis was applied to approximately 1000 MDAI cases. Since the data required for the avoidance analysis are not stored in the computer files, each report was reviewed and relevant data retrieved.

The driver responses to the accident threat are shown in Table 42-1, indicating that approximately 19% of the drivers involved in a collision attempted to brake, 9% to steer and nearly 6% to steer and brake. This finding is slightly different when compared to earlier results obtained from a MDAI file computer printout, where, depending on factors such as speed and road surface conditions, approximately 20% of the drivers attempted to brake, 8% attempted to steer, and 15% attempted to steer and brake. All percentage figures tend to decrease as vehicle speed goes up. It was also found that in the case of a straight road for the drivers that provided a control input nearly 80% of the drivers attempted to brake, as compared to only 12% when traveling on a curved road.

Table 42-1. Driver Accident Avoidance Actions

Braking	19.48%
Steering	9.00%
Combined Braking and Steering	5.82%
No Action	65.70%

Table 42-2 presents the distribution of accident types by accident avoidance maneuver. Inspection of Table 42-2 indicates that, e.g., theoretically 19.40% of the intersection collisions could have been avoided by the accident avoidance maneuvers indicated. The entries in the column designated by "Locked Wheel" represent those collisions that could have been avoided through locked wheel, i.e., increased pedal forces or braking effectiveness. In the process of actual accident investigations on the spot calculations are carried out to determine the approximate contribution of vehicle, driver or environment to accident causation. Detailed followup investigations concentrate on areas that have a high probability of providing the necessary data for an accurate accident causation assessment. For the cases collected under the "Locked Wheel" column, reviews of the specific cases or improved vehicle examinations and driver interviews generally produce the information necessary to determine whether the brake torque production was degraded or the brake system was improperly designed. The column designated by "Lane Change" represents those accidents that can be avoided through a lane change maneuver, the column designated by "Lane Change/Antiskid" those that can be avoided by lane changing and antiskid braking. The column designated by "Turning/Antiskid" those that can be avoided by turning and antiskid braking, and the column designated by "Radar" those collisions that can be avoided by automatic brake application. The Lane Change/Antiskid and Turning/Antiskid columns contain accidents that can be avoided by either normal or limit lateral acceleration lane change or turning maneuvers. The braking inputs are assumed to be sufficiently severe to require antiskid hardware. The data presented in Table 42–2 do not indicate whether drivers can or do utilize the accident avoidance potential available. The data presented show to what extent improvements in braking hardware combined with increased driver skills to fully utilize the steering and braking capability of the automobile will result in the increased accident avoidance indicated. In the accident data analysis a perfect antiskid system having a braking efficiency of unity was assumed. Rear-wheel-only antiskid systems and other less complex systems could be included in a more detailed analysis. However, as an inspection of the data in Table 42–2 indicates, the retention of steering capability during a lane change or turning maneuver is of significance. Table 42–2 shows that more than half of the drivers could have avoided the collision with standard or advanced brake system hardware. For the accident type designated by Intersection, e.g., a total of 19.4% of the vehicles could have avoided the collision by means of various avoidance maneuvers and hardware. The largest contribution is associated with a combined steering and antiskid braking maneuver, yielding approximately 14.3 percent. Approximately 3.9% of all vehicles involved in collisions could have avoided the accident by improved braking effectiveness, most generally indicating those conditions in which the driver attempted to brake but did not produce a pedal force sufficiently large to develop a deceleration that the road surface was capable of providing.

Table No. 42–2. Distribution of Accident Type by Accident Avoidance Maneuver

Accident Type	Avoidance Maneuver and Hardware (Percent)					
	Locked Wheel	Lane Change	Lane Change/ Antiskid	Turning/ Antiskid	Radar	Total
Intersection	1.52	0.084	7.26	7.08	3.46	19.40
Head On	1.41	0	2.70	5.56	0.844	10.51
Rear End	0.42	0	1.77	3.54	0	5.73
Road Run Off-Straight	0.25	1.18	2.06	1.806	0.39	5.69
Road Run Off-Curve	0	0.76	1.45	3.29	0.09	5.59
Fixed Object	0.09	0.25	1.86	1.35	0	3.55
Auto-Pedestrian	0.19	0	1.01	1.60	0.25	3.05
Road Run Off-Roll	0	0.25	0.84	0.76	0	1.85
Others	0	0	1.05	0.33	0.28	1.66
Total	3.88	2.52	20.00	25.31	5.31	57.03

Inspection of Table 42–2 indicates that approximately 5.3% of the vehicles could avoid a collision by means of automatic brake application. A review of the 1971 NHTSA Accident Summary files indicates that approximately 8% of the vehicles are involved in rear end collisions. Since not all rear end collisions are avoidable, the findings reported in Table 42–2 appear to be in general agreement with other accident facts.

42-3. ACCIDENTS WITH FIRES

Collision induced fires in the United States occur in approximately one-tenth of a percent of all accidents. German accident statistics show fires in 0.24% of all accidents. The reason for the higher frequency may be due to larger number of smaller cars not providing equal protection to gas tank rupture. The involvement of fatal injuries is approximately ten times of that associated with other collision modes. The threat of increased injuries due to a vehicle fire is larger when an evacuation-extrication difficulty exists. The cause of the fire cannot always be determined accurately. The main reasons are fuel leakage, in combination with electrical or metal to pavement sparks. See Section 32–4 for additional details.

42-4. REDUCTION OF INJURY BY SAFETY BELTS AND HEAD RESTRAINTS

The effectiveness of seat belts in reducing fatalities and injuries has been established by many studies. The injury reduction is greater for the driver than for the front seat passenger. The probability of fatal or severe injuries is reduced by approximately 30 to 50% for driver and front seat passenger of full size automobiles when restraint systems are used.

The use of seat belts also reduces the frequency of injuries to different body areas.

Head rests or restraints reduce the frequency and severity of neck injuries in rear end collisions. In vehicles equipped with head restraints the proportion of cervical spine injuries is almost 13% lower than in similar cases without head restraints.

42-5. SINGLE VEHICLE ACCIDENTS

Single vehicle accidents are not uniformly distributed over a day. Approximately one-third of all accidents occur at night and are mostly caused by road runoff due to alcohol, speeding, driver inattentiveness, and improper passing. States such as Utah or Nevada show a higher percentage of single vehicle accidents than states with larger population.

42-6. VEHICLE ROLLOVER

Rollover occurs in approximately 1 out of 20 accidents. Nearly 85% of the rollovers occurred during a collision with another vehicle or obstacle. The risk of fatal injury is approximately four times greater in a rollover accident than in accidents without rollover. When occupants are ejected during rollover, fatal injuries increase by a factor of 11 when compared to the average risk of injury.

42-7. INJURY TO CHILDREN

The risk of injury to children seated in the front is significantly higher than that of children seated in the rear. Even moderately severe crashes exhibit twice as many serious injuries to children on the front seats than on the back seats. Children seated on the lap of the front seat passenger run a high risk of severe, dangerous and fatal injuries. In terms of injury severity of adults and children, in approximately 70% of the accidents involving children and adults, children sustained more severe injuries than adults, in 20% children and adults suffered injuries of the same severity, and only in 10% are the injuries to adults more severe. Children sustain head injuries approximately twice as often as adults. Effective safety measures for children are special child restraint systems and to some extent travel on the back seat.

42-8. VEHICLE CHARACTERISTICS AND ACCIDENTS

The results of a doctoral dissertation on accidents in England were used to determine the contribution of different vehicle design parameters and service factors on accident involvement (Refs. 1 and 2). A statistical manipulation of the raw data is used to determine possible accident potentials. For example, accident rates are shown for such factors as degree of understeer, tire inflation pressure imbalance, roll stiffness imbalance, and braking instability. The raw data alone without "statistical treatment" in many cases do not show such a pronounced trend as determined by the statistical analysis.

42-9. ACCIDENT COST

An accurate assessment of the cost of motor vehicle crashes to society is difficult to obtain. The Office of Program Analysis of the National Highway Traffic Safety Administration has studied the basic losses to society from 1975 motor vehicle accidents. The average cost of a fatality should not be interpreted as the total cost or the value placed on a life. Not included in the cost analysis are such factors as pain, suffering, affection or grief.

The 1975 data are: 46,800 fatalities at $287,175.00 per fatality, 4000 injuries at severity AIS 5 at $192,240.00 per injury, 20,000 injuries at severity AIS 4 at $86,955.00 per injury, 80,000 injuries at severity AIS 3 at $8,085.00 per injury, 492,000 injuries severity AIS 2 at $4,350 per injury, 3,400,000 injuries at severity AIS 1 at $2,190.00 per injury and 21,900,000 property damages at $520.00 per property damage.

The total estimated cost to society from motor vehicle crashes is $37.5 billion.

42-10. SMALL CAR VS. BIG CAR SAFETY

Detailed analysis of accident statistics collected in the State of New York show an overinvolvement of large passenger cars in accidents (Ref. 3). For example, the accident rate of full size passenger cars such as Buick or Chrysler is approximately 1.5 times as high as that associated with VW passenger cars. The injuries sustained by the occupants of smaller vehicles are approximately 3 times as severe as those associated with the occupants of heavy passenger cars. The data show that large passenger cars are more dangerous to the road users, since they are involved in more accidents and produce more injuries to the small car occupant. The belted driver of a small car is likely to suffer fatal or serious injuries approximately twice as much as the belted driver of full size passenger cars. For the unbelted driver the corresponding ratio is approximately 2.7 to 1.

CHAPTER 43
EXPERT WITNESS

43-1. DEFINITION OF EXPERT WITNESS

An expert witness is a person allowed to testify in court and whose opinions are considered evidence. An expert formulates his opinion from facts supplied to him or developed during his investigation, analysis, and reconstruction of the accident. To be able to do this, the expert must be skilled in his profession, have experience related to the subject area under consideration, and must be educated sufficiently to be able to correlate facts. A significant measure of expertise is that the expert exhibits knowledge far above that of the layman. This measure may be established by education such as a bachelor's, master's or doctoral degree in mechanical engineering, experience in industry or research, relevant publications by the expert, and particular tests and analyses conducted in connection with the accident under consideration.

Whenever a court feels that conclusions and opinions are needed which are not within the ability of the jury, and which demand special knowledge and expertise, an expert witness may give his opinion and conclusion after proper foundations have been established for such. Rule 702 of the Proposed Rules of Evidence for United States Courts and Magistrates provides the following definition of an expert testimony:

If scientific, technical, or other specialized knowledge will assist the trier of fact to understand the evidence or to determine a fact in issue, a witness qualified as an expert by knowledge, skill, experience, training, or education, may testify thereto in the form of an opinion or otherwise.

The expert's qualifications must be sufficient to convince the trial judge that he has the necessary expertise in the area under consideration to the case.

In one case the court stated that in "view of the importance of the function entrusted to the expert witness, it is of great importance that the court carefully scrutinize his qualifications to guard against being led astray by the pseudo learned or charlatan who may purvey erroneous or too positive opinions without necessary foundation."

43-2. PREPARATION

The preparation, i.e., all work done by the expert prior to trial, is of considerable importance. Although it is true that juries are not predictable, a court case is won through good preparation.

The preparation begins with obtaining all information and facts that may be evidence in court. This is particularly true for depositions of potential courtroom witnesses. If the formulation of the accident i.e., the accurate assembly of facts, reveals that a particular witness is misstating the facts, the expert must through specific testing, literature survey, analysis, or any other appropriate means prepare to counter the expected testimony.

The expert must at all times communicate in all openness with the attorney he is assisting in the case. Frequently, experts and more so non-experts hide certain facts relating to their background, opinions about the accident causation, ability to testify about a particular phase of the accident, or other information from the attorney prior to trial, only to experience embarrassment and poor performance in court.

The expert may or may not want to prepare a formal report of his investigation. Telephone communications may be used to transmit all important findings without being discoverable. When a written report is prepared, it must be factual, state findings and reasons for the expert's opinion. The report should contain recommendations for the next necessary steps required to strengthen the findings. These steps may include purchase of a damaged vehicle for further testing or detailed examination, securing of tires of the accident vehicle for traction testing at the accident site, or hiring of a specialist.

An ongoing preparation of an expert not necessarily related to any particular case involves the reading and review of all pertinent publications, including magazines, books, and research reports.

43-3. COURTROOM APPEARANCE

The purpose of an expert testimony in court is to present and correlate facts so that the members of the jury not skilled in the particular field are able to determine the true facts of the accident. The expert is expected to give an unbiased testimony. He should not volunteer information. He should answer questions in precise and clear terms easily understood by the jury and the judge.

When the expert is testifying in court, the opposing attorney will attempt to prevent the expert from testifying based on lack of qualifications or related factors. The attorney will try to discredit the expert's testimony in the minds of the members of the jury during cross examination by having the expert answer questions that lessen or change the expert's opinion on certain aspects of the case. The jury is not obligated to accept the opinion of an expert, and consequently, anything an expert says or conveys when on the witness stand should influence the jury such that true facts are established. To accomplish this the expert must be dressed such that nothing in his appearance (suit, hair, jewelry) influences the jury in the "wrong" direction. If the jury wastes much of its intellectual energy on studying the expert's appearance, not much is left for understanding the problems involved in the case.

The language of an expert on the witness stand must be precise, simple, slow and directed towards the members of the jury. Short answers are more easily understood and put a better control into the hands of the attorney. During cross examination the opposing attorney may within limits try to attack the expert's integrity. A good expert knows after a few questions by the opposing attorney what questions will follow in a particular subject area. Even if the attorney exhibits hostility, the expert must remain calm, precise, and answer questions so that the jury is positively impressed by his performance. A good expert witness has no reason to be afraid of a cross examination, and in fact, must utilize this phase of his testimony to improve upon his performance. Any questions asked by the opposing attorney, and in particular those for which he does not know the approximate answers in advance, are potentially dangerous since the expert may strengthen his position. If the expert did not clearly hear the question by an attorney, and this may frequently be the case since some attorneys wander over the courtroom without facing the expert witness while asking questions, the expert must request a repeat of the question by the attorney or the court reporter. If the expert does not understand a question, he must indicate so and request a rephrasing of the question. If the expert unintentionally gives a wrong answer, he must request of the judge to make the correction before leaving the witness stand.

Frequently, the expert will use displays during his testimony to better demonstrate his findings to the jury. These displays include films, slides, photographs, manuals, books, models, or pieces of hardware. Important considerations in the preparation of courtroom demonstrations are that the opposing attorney may object to their use in court if they contain information not yet established as evidence. Examples are accident diagrams showing point of impact, or photographs of the accident site taken a long time after the date of the accident. While displays may be used to demonstrate a particular viewpoint, the opposing attorney will try to utilize it to his advantage. In a particular accident involving an intersection collision in open country, a light truck ran a stop sign and impacted a passenger car on the right side. The defense used the fact that the driver of the passenger car saw the light truck, however, never attempted to execute an avoidance maneuver. A movie was made using model cars 1/40 scale simulating the precrash phase 900 ft prior to the point of impact, the impact phase, and the vehicle motions after impact until the vehicle comes to a rest. The film demonstrated that the driver of the passenger car had a clear view of the approaching truck. The collision phase revealed the violent nature of the impact and may influence the jury towards a greater measure of sympathy toward the victims of the collision if it were shown in court. Consequently, after a detailed review of the film it was decided not to use it in court. The defense was accomplished by using calculations relating to the passenger car accident avoidance maneuver. The results showed how many seconds before the impact the passenger car driver could have avoided the collision through braking.

Another important factor to be considered in preparing court room displays relates to the jury's use of the displays or exhibits. The jury has all exhibits available during the elaboration in the jury chambers. A photograph may be reviewed and used during the discussions, a slide requiring a slide projector may not. Similarly, a working model requiring complicated instructions for its operation may be useful when the expert explains it, but may be useless in the chambers.

Experience has shown that a good expert witness has the following qualities.

1. Seeks the truth and tells the truth
2. Is flexible to adjust to changing situations particularly in court
3. Assists "his" attorney in all phases of the investigation and during trial relating to his area of expertise
4. Remains objective and does not become an advocate
5. Is so well prepared and capable in court, that anything he does or says assists the jury to determine the truth
6. Exhibits jury and judge appeal

APPENDIX

DEFINITIONS OF SELECTED TERMS AND A BRIEF REVIEW OF THE USE OF MATHEMATICAL EQUATIONS

DEFINITIONS

Acceleration: increase of velocity per unit time; ft/sec^2, g-units; Eq. 16–2.

Angular velocity: circumferential velocity divided by radius; rad/sec; Eq. 16–24.

Brake effectiveness: the braking force produced by the brake system; also expressed by the deceleration achieved by brake system; Eq. 20–5a.

Braking efficiency: indicates to what extent the vehicle-brake system utilizes available road friction; d'less; Eqs. 20–11 and 20–12.

Brake factor: gain of wheel brake, expressed as ratio of drum or rotor drag divided by application force in wheel cylinder; d'less; Eq. 20–3.

Brake fade: indicates a decrease of the effectiveness of the wheel brakes due to excessive brake temperature; also due to excessive speed, or lining contamination.

Brake system response time: time delay between the instant the brake pedal displacement begins and the instant vehicle deceleration begins; sec; Eqs. 20–9 and 20–10.

Coefficient of friction: the drag force divided by the normal force; d'less; Eq. 18–2.

Coefficient of restitution: indicates the relationship between plastic and elastic deformation in a crash; d'less; Eqs. 28–8 and 28–9.

Cornering stiffness: the side force produced by a tire divided by the associated slip angle; lb/rad or lb/deg; Eq. 22–36.

Critical speed: maximum allowable forward speed of a vehicle or vehicle-trailer combination; ft/sec/ Eqs. 22–40 and 22–54.

Deceleration: decrease of velocity per unit time; ft/sec^2, g-units; Eqs. 16–2 and 20–5a.

Drag: a force acting on the vehicle (excluding inertia); lb; Eq. 19–1.

Force: a force exists when a body changes its form or motion; lb; Eq. 17–1.

Gravitational constant: indicates the acceleration of free-falling body; ft/sec^2 or g-units; Eq. 17–2.

Impulse: the product of force and time; acting between two colliding bodies; lb · sec; Eqs. 28–2, 28–12, and 28–13.

Lateral acceleration: sideways acceleration produced during a turning maneuver; the associated force (centrifugal) tends to push the body to the outside of the turn; ft/sec^2 or g-units; Eq. 22–1.

Limit speed: level of speed at which a vehicle can negotiate a turn without exceeding maximum tire traction available, ft/sec; Eqs. 22–10 and 22–16.

Mass: a physical measure indicating make up of a body (number of molecules); it can be considered a measure of a body's inertia or resistance to change of motion; lb · sec^2/ft; Eq. 17–2.

Momentum: product of velocity and mass; lb · sec; Eq. 28–2.

Normal force: vertical force between two bodies; frequently applied to tires; lb; Eqs. 22–17 to 22–20.

Radius of gyration: measure of mass distribution in rotation; in.; Eq. 31–3.

Side sliding velocity: velocity required to trip vehicle into rollover; ft/sec; Eq. 22–33.

Slip angle: angle between direction in which tire is moving and direction in which tire longitudinal axis is pointing; rad or deg; Eq. 18–8.

Speed: velocity without concern for direction; ft/sec or mph.

Super-elevation: lateral road slope to increase safe turning speed; Eq. 22–35.

Tire slip: difference between circumferential velocity of tire and vehicle, divided by vehicle speed; d'less or %; Eq. 18–3.

Velocity: change of position per unit time and direction of travel; ft/sec or mph.

REVIEW OF MATHEMATICS

The proper use of mathematical equations is important for the lawyer for the following reasons:

1. The lawyer may want to carry out simple calculations himself.

2. He may want to probe the opposing expert's knowledge of the subject matter by asking penetrating questions relating to the physical process described by the equation.

3. He may want to determine the relationship of various parameters in the equation by solving for certain factors in the equation.

An equation is a convenient form of expressing relationships among several parameters. In general, an equation contains letters, numbers, and mathematical symbols.

Numbers or letters are used to indicate addition, subtraction, multiplication, and/or division. For example, consider Eq. 17–8. The term on the left side of the equation, ΔE_k represents the change or difference (indicated by the "Δ," the Greek letter delta) of the kinetic (indicated by the subscript "k") energy (indicated by the capital "E"). The right-hand side consists of two brackets. In the first one "W" is divided by the number 2 and by g (gravitational constant). The second bracket is the difference of the square of the velocities (indicated by the exponent 2) before (indicated by the subscript 1) and after (indicated by the subscript 2) impact. Any number, letters, or words can be used to define a particular parameter. For example, the subscripts "1" and "2" are used in Eq. 16–2, "zero" in Eq. 16–7, "t" in Eq. 16–19, "c" in Eq. 16–26, "crit" in Eq. 18–9, and "limit" in Eq. 22–10. All subscripts define a particular meaning of velocity.

Dimensions of different components may be defined by subscripts. Consider Eq. 20–5a. The pedal force is designated by F_p, where "F" designates force, the "p" pedal. Similarly, the master cylinder area is designated by A_{MC}, where "A" stands for area, and subscript "MC" for master cylinder. In the case of the brake factor two letters are used, designated as "BF" and no subscript is used.

In addition to numbers and common letters, Greek letters are used to designate a particular parameter. For example, the friction coefficient is designated by the Greek letter μ (pronounced mu). Subscripts may also be used to define different coefficients of friction.

A listing of the Greek symbols used in this book is given below.

α (alpha) – angle
γ (gamma) – angle
δ (delta) – angle
Δ (capital delta) – difference
ϵ (epsilon) – angular acceleration
η (eta) – efficiency
θ (theta) – angle
μ (mu) – friction coefficient
π (pi) – 3.14
ρ (rho) – density; ratio
φ (phi) – angle
Φ (capital phi) – brake force distribution
χ (chi) – relative center of gravity height
ψ (psi) – relative rear axle load
ω (omega) – angular velocity

Consider Eq. 17–1. This equation relates three parameters, namely the resultant force F_{res}, the mass m, and the acceleration a, caused by the resultant force. If one wants to solve for the acceleration a, the following rules apply: letters or numbers multiplied on the left side, go to the right side as dividers, and visa versa. Consequently,

$$F_{res} = ma$$

or,

$$ma = F_{res}$$

or,

$$a = \frac{F_{res}}{m} \text{ (divided by } m\text{)}.$$

For subtraction or addition a similar rule applies. Letters or numbers added, i.e., having a plus-sign on the left side of the equation, are subtracted or get a minus-sign on the right side of the equation, and vise versa.

For example, solve for velocity V in Eq. 18–4. Eq. 18–4 is

$$\mu = \mu_0 - kV$$

The minus kV-term is brought to the left side as a plus-kV term, i.e.,

$$\mu + kV = \mu_0$$

The μ-term on the left side is brought to the right side as a minus μ-term, i.e.,

$$kV = \mu_0 - \mu$$

The k-term multiplied on the left side is divided on the right side, i.e.,

$$V = \frac{\mu_0 - \mu}{k}$$

Another mathematical rule requires that the computations inside a parenthesis are carried out first. Consider Eq. 19–15. First the square bracket term must be computed, i.e.,

$$\left[\frac{h}{1} + \left(\frac{R}{1}\right)(k-1)\right];$$

then it is multiplied by a, and the result subtracted from (32.2) $\left(\frac{\ell_R}{\ell}\right)$, and this result divided into a.

The evaluation of a lengthy, but algebraically straight forward equation is explained next.

Consider the numerical evaluation of Eq. 20–5a. The smallest brackets must be computed first. Eq. 20–5a may be simplified for the reader unskilled in mathematics. One can substitute simple looking letters for a combination of letters in Eq. 20–5a, as long as the nature of the equation is not changed. For example,

$$a = (A - p_0)[B_F + B_R]\ C$$

where the meaning of the new letters is:

$$A = \frac{F_p \ell_p \eta_p}{A_{MC}}$$

$$B_F = (A_{WC}\ BFr)_F$$

$$B_R = (A_{WC}\ BFr)_R$$

$$C = \frac{32.2}{WR}$$

The "new" equation may still be simplified to read

$$a = D \times E \times C$$

where

$$D = A - p_0$$

$$E = B_F + B_R$$

The computation of the deceleration a is as follows:

1st compute A
2nd compute B_F
3rd compute B_R
4th compute C
5th compute D
6th compute E
7th $a = D \times E \times C$, the desired result.

Consider Eq. 16–15. The velocity V_t after sliding over a distance S must be computed. Consequently, the term $2a$ (divided) on the right side is multiplied on the left side, i.e.,

$$2aS = V_0^2 - V_t^2 \quad \text{(multiply left side by } 2a\text{)}$$

or,

$$V_t^2 + 2aS = V_0^2 \quad \text{(add } V_t^2 \text{ on the left side)}$$

or,

$$V_t^2 = V_0^2 - 2aS \quad \text{(subtract } 2aS \text{ on right side)}$$

or

$$V_t = \sqrt{V_0^2 - 2aS},$$

meaning the square-root of $V_0^2 - 2aS$. The square-root is evaluated by first computing the difference $V_0^2 - 2aS$, and then taking the square-root.

Several equations use the term sin α or cos α (e.g., Eq. 19–7). The mathematical term sin α (pronounced sign) or cos α (co-sign) are fixed numbers for a given angle α. The fixed numbers are collected in tables or given automatically by an electronic computer, when the angle is put in. In addition to the "sin α" and "cos α" the tangent (tan) cotangent (cot α) are used (Eq. 22–35).

LIST OF REFERENCES

1. Ian S. Jones, *The Effect of Vehicle Characteristics on Road Accidents,* Pergamon Press, 1976.
2. Ian S. Jones, *The Role of Vehicle Handling in Accident Causation,* SAE Paper No. 750115.
3. Stanley Hart, *Big Cars—Safer For Whom?,* Third International Congress on Automotive Safety, Vol. II, July 1974, San Francisco, California.
4. R. Limpert and F. E. Gamero, *The Accident Avoidance Potential of the Motor Vehicle: Accident Data, Vehicle Handling and Safety Standards,* Third International Congress on Automotive Safety, Vol. II, July 1974, San Francisco, California.
5. *Minicars Research Safety Vehicle (RSV),* US Department of Transportation Contract No. DOT-HS-5-10215, December 1976.
6. *Collision Performance and Injury Report,* National Highway Traffic Safety Administration (DOT), Office of Accident Investigation, 1972.
7. *Auto-Motor and Sport,* No. 5, 28 February 1976 (German).
8. *Tire and Rim Association Yearbook 1976,* 3200 West Market, Akron, Ohio, 44313.
9. K. C. Ludema and B. Gujrati, *An Analysis of the Literature on Tire-Road Skid Resistance,* Mech. Eng. Department, The University of Michigan, Ann Arbor, Michigan, 1971.
10. William H. Crouse, *Automotive Chassis and Body,* 4th Edition, McGraw-Hill Book Company.
11. R. Limpert, *Engineering Design Handbook, Analysis and Design of Automotive Brake Systems,* US-Army Material Development and Readiness Command, DARCOM-P-706-358, December 1976.
12. William H. Crouse, *Automotive Emission Control,* McGraw-Hill Book Company, 1971.
13. M. Mitschke, *Motor Vehicle Dynamics,* Springer Publisher, 1972 (German).
14. R. E. Wild, *Wet Traction Test Program,* US Department of Transportation, Publication No. DOT-HS-800917, August 1973.

15. R. Murphy, R. Limpert, and L. Segel, *Bus, Truck, Tractor-Trailer Braking System Performance,* Vol. 1 and 2, US Department of Transportation, Contract No. FH-11-7290, March 1972.

16. R. Murphy, et al., *A Computer Based Mathematical Method for Predicting the Braking Performance of Trucks and Tractor-Trailers,* Highway Safety Research Institute, The University of Michigan, September 15, 1972.

17. J. E. Bernard, et al., *A Computer Based Mathematical Method for Predicting the Directional Response of Trucks and Tractor-Trailers,* Highway Safety Research Institute, The University of Michigan, June 1, 1973.

18. T. W. Keranen, et al., *Component Degradation Brake System Performance,* Vol. 1 and 2, US Department of Transportation, Publication DOT-HS-800751, May 1972.

19. MVSS105A—*Hydraulic Brake Systems Vehicle Test Program,* US Department of Transportation Publication DOT-HS-800978, November 1973.

20. I. R. Ellis, *Vehicle Dynamics,* London, England, Business Books Ltd., 1969.

21. *Mechanics of Pneumatic Tires,* US Department of Commerce, National Bureau of Standards, NBS Monograph 122, 1971.

22. Buschmann and Koessler, *Motor Vehicle Handbook,* Vol. 1 and 2, Wilhelm Heyne Publisher, Munich, Germany, 1976 (German).

23. R. D. Ervin, et al., *Vehicle Handling Performance,* Vol. 1 and 2, US Department of Transportation, Contract No. DOT-HS-031-1-159.

24. H. Dugoff, et al., *Vehicle Handling Test Procedure,* US Department of Transportation Contract No. FH-11-7297, November 1970.

25. H. Isermann, *Overturning Limits of Articulated Vehicles with Solid and Liquid Cargo,* Deutsche Kraftfahrtforschung No. 200, 1970. (German).

26. D. T. McRuer and R. H. Klein, *Automobile Controllability—Driver/Vehicle Response to Steering Control,* Vol. 1 and 2, US Department of Transportation No. DOT-HS-801407, February 1975.

27. P. F. Bohn and R. J. Keenan, *Hybrid Computer Vehicle Handling Program,* US Department of Transportation Contract No. DOT-H-213-3-695, July 1974.

28. J. R. Hartz, *Computer Simulation of Vehicle Handling,* US Depart-

ment of Transportation Contract No. FH-11-7563, September 1972.

29. *Ford Motor Company Engineering Technical Education Course Notes,* David Cole, *Vehicle Dynamics;* Leonard Segel, *Advanced Vehicle Dynamics.*

30. D. J. Eaton, *Man-Machine Dynamics in the Stabilization of Single-Track Vehicles,* Ph.D. dissertation, The University of Michigan, Ann Arbor, Michigan, 1973.

31. K. J. Tharp, *Multidisciplinary Accident Investigation-Pedestrian Involvement,* US Department of Transportation NTIS No. DOT-HS-801165, June 1974.

32. *Interior Safety of Automobiles, Road Traffic Accidents and their Consequences,* German Association of Third-Party Liability, Accident and Motor Insurers, Hamburg, Germany, 1975 (English).

33. *The 1970 International Automobile Safety Conference Compendium,* Detroit, Michigan, May 1970, Society of Automotive Engineer, Inc., 400 Commonwealth Drive, Warrendale, Pa. 15096.

34. *The 1970 International Automobile Safety Bibliography, Literature through January 1970,* Society of Automotive Engineer, Inc., 400 Commonwealth Drive, Warrendale, Pa. 15096.

35. B. F. Pierce, et al., *Human Force Considerations in the Failure of Power Assisted Devices,* US Department of Transportation No. DOT-HS-800889, July 1973.

36. G. L. Mol, et al., *Truck and Bus Driver Task Analyses,* US Department of Transportation No. DOT-HS-800835, May 1973.

37. J. O'Day and R. E. Scott, *An Analysis of Truck Accident Involvement,* HIT Lab. Report, April 1974, Vol. 4, No. 8, The University of Michigan, Highway Safety Research Institute.

38. G. R. Hatterik and J. R. Bathurst, *Accident Avoidance Skill Training and Performance Testing,* US Department of Transportation No. DOT-HS-800852, March 1976.

39. A. F. Brayman, *Impact Intrusion Characteristics of Fuel Systems,* US Department of Transportation No. DOT-HS-800296, April 1970.

40. *Investigation of Motor Vehicle Performance Standards for Fuel Tank Protection,* US Department of Transportation, NTIS No. PB 177690, September 1967.

41. *Fuel Tank Protection,* US Department of Transportation, NTIS No. PB 191148, June 1969.

42. N. B. Johnson, *An Assessment of Automotive Fuel System Fire Hazards,* US Department of Transportation, NTIS No. PB 208241, December 1971.

43. A Goldsmith, *Flammability Characteristics of Vehicle Interior Materials,* US Department of Transportation, NTIS No. PB 189653, May 1969.

44. C. I. Gatlin, et. al., *Prevention of Electrical Systems Ignition of Automotive Crash Fire,* US Department of Transportation, NTIS No. 197616, March 1970.

45. C. M. Sliepcevich, et. al., *Escape Worthiness of Vehicle and Occupant Survival,* Part 1, 2, and 3, US Department of Transportation, NTIS No. PB-198772, December 1970.

46. O. M. Severy, *Headlight-Taillight Analyses from Collision Research,* Reprinted from SAE Transactions, Vol. 75, 1967.

47. J. R. Treat and K. B. Joscelyn, *A Study of Determining the Relationships between Vehicle Defects and Crashes,* US Department of Transportation No. DOT-HS-800661, November 1971.

48. D. H. Weir, et. al., *An Experimental and Analytical Investigation of the Effect of Truck-Induced Aerodynamic Disturbances on Passenger Car Control and Performance,* US Department of Transportation Contract No. FH-11-7570, October 1971.

Index

A

B

O

P

84 09